HARRIMAN'S
New Book
—— OF ——
Investing
Rules

Every owner of a physical copy of this edition of

HARRIMAN'S
New Book
— OF —
Investing
Rules

can download the eBook for free direct from us at
Harriman House, in a DRM-free format that can be read on any eReader,
tablet or smartphone.

Simply head to:

ebooks.harriman-house.com/newbookofinvestingrules

to get your copy now.

HARRIMAN'S
New Book
— OF —
Investing
Rules

THE DO'S & DON'TS OF THE WORLD'S
BEST INVESTORS

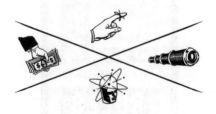

Edited by CHRISTOPHER PARKER

Foreword by JONATHAN DAVIS

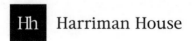
Harriman House

HARRIMAN HOUSE LTD
18 College Street
Petersfield
Hampshire
GU31 4AD
GREAT BRITAIN
Tel: +44 (0)1730 233870

Email: enquiries@harriman-house.com
Website: www.harriman-house.com

First published in Great Britain in 2017.
Copyright © Harriman House Ltd.
Original chapter text and photographs remain copyright © of individual authors or firms.

Hardcover ISBN: 978-0-85719-684-2
eBook ISBN: 978-0-85719-685-9

British Library Cataloguing in Publication Data
A CIP catalogue record for this book can be obtained from the British Library.

Hh Harriman House

Contents

CONTENTS

Editor's Note

THIS IS AN argumentative book.

What matters is the price you paid, argues Michael van Biema. Forget the price you paid, says Anthony Bolton. Avoid experts and fund managers, argues Anthony Garner. Pick the right fund managers, says Sandy Cross. Investing is an art, argues Richard Buxton. Investing must be approached as a science, says Ken Fisher. Passive index investing offers the safest route to riches, argues Tim Hale. But a chapter later Ian Helsop posits that the market-cap-weighted nature of the S&P 500 and FTSE 100 means that passive investing has created a feedback loop of ever increased flows into the largest companies – a recipe for real danger.

Passive vs active, fund managers vs private investors, trend following vs stock picking – there is no lack of opposites in this book. (At one point, Jacob Rees-Mogg even quotes Mao.)

None of this was designed. I simply sought, in the great *Harriman Book of Investing Rules* tradition begun by Stephen Eckett and Philip Jenks in 2001, to bring together a fresh selection of the most interesting and eloquent exponents of as wide a range of investing approaches as possible. And of course no contributor saw any other chapter before writing their own.

The arguments happened of their own accord.

In this entirely accidental way I hope the book captures something of the open-minded world of investing – a marketplace of ideas as much as shares in companies, where every trade is a kind of argument.

Such collision of ideas is hopefully not only enjoyable because of the sheer variety but illuminating too. As the late Christopher Hitchens said, the phrase 'more heat than light', intended to disdain arguments as a furious waste of energy, is based on a faulty premise: after all, we get light from heat.

I therefore hope – whether enjoying the arguments or taking up your own with any of the chapters here – that this book is never less than light reading in at least two senses of the term, even if it is over 500 pages.

CHRISTOPHER PARKER
Petersfield, 2017

Acknowledgements

Though this book is full of disagreements, none of its many contributors were disagreeable to work with. All were extremely generous with their time and words, and unfailingly patient as the book worked its way towards print. I owe all of them my sincere thanks.

I would also like to thank Will Gold, James Whiteman and Chris Cudmore for their vital help with several chapters, as well as Jonathan Davis for contributing a wonderful foreword and for his advice while editing the book.

Some chapters in this book are reprinted or adapted from authors' longer (or unpublished) works with the permission of the author and publisher, and three make a return from previous *Rules* books. I would like to thank the authors and publishers for their generosity in allowing this. I hope it is not begrudged by the reader too much, despite the 'New' in this volume's title – in some cases it brings long-lost material back into print, in others it condenses insights otherwise only available at great cost and many hours of reading (of course, I encourage readers to seek out the complete works to get the full experience). And there remains over 100,000 words of new content here.

Foreword by
Jonathan Davis

"*PER VARIOS CASUS, per tot discrimina rerum tendimus.*" This elegant Latin phrase, which I am sure classical scholars amongst you will recognise as coming from Virgil's *Aeneid*, is how Ben Graham introduced *The Intelligent Investor*, his classic book on investment, still as wise and readable today as it was when it was first published nearly 50 years ago. He translated it as meaning "through chances various, through all vicissitudes we make our way".

Navigating through a constantly changing world is a concept with which investors are all too familiar. It is their task after all to try and make money in markets which are constantly buffeted by the unexpected – be that a political event, an economic surprise, a central bank policy announcement or just a disappointing company earnings report. Nothing stands still for long in investment because the world of human endeavour it reflects is always in a state of flux.

The way to survive and prosper as an investor therefore depends on combining an understanding of how markets behave, resilience in the face of the unexpected and – not least – a deep pool of experience on which to draw. Whether you prefer to call it brilliance, intuition or skill, the reality is that it is experience – not just your own, but also that of all those who have gone before you – that counts for most over time. And the simplest way to capture the essence of experience is by making and absorbing a set of rules.

Now it is easy to think that a list of dos and don'ts might be rather a simplistic way to enhance your understanding of what will and will not work in such a specialised field as investment. Don't be so hasty. The behavioural psychologist Daniel Kahneman, winner of a Nobel Prize in 2002 for his work on decision-making and uncertainty, has built his career and reputation by demonstrating how simple precepts – what we call rules of thumb, but more formally known as heuristics – can be powerful and effective tools for capturing generations of human experience. What we call expert intuition is mostly accumulated wisdom in disguise.

It goes without saying, however, that the intuition you want to tap into is not that of every man, but that of the best in the business, for Prof Kahnemann also tells us that human beings are prone to any number of biases which, unchecked, can and do lead us astray. This book, a successor volume to several popular versions published over the past 15 years, counters this by bringing together in a readable and meaningful format some of the most important lessons acquired by top investors over the course of their careers. All but two of the many contributors to this version are new – it is a big and bold book, covering a broad spectrum of markets and topics.

Of course, there are many different styles of investing, and many different asset classes in which to invest, so you will need to pick and choose which of the authorities assembled here best matches your own temperament and interests. What works in the bond or property markets may be violently or subtly different from what works in stock markets. Investors in funds need to focus on different things from stock pickers. As the editor drily notes, some contributors are significantly at odds with others. Such conflict also enlightens.

What makes a good investment rule? For me it needs to be clearly articulated, straightforward to understand and yet capture a certain fundamental truth about investment, one that has stood the test of time. One favourite of mine was coined by the wise and well-read American investment consultant, Charles D. Ellis. His classic book, *Winning the Loser's Game*, contains the definitive rule on market timing ("Don't do it. It is a sin").

Another personal favourite was part of a list devised by Nigel Lawson, the former Chancellor of the Exchequer, during his earlier time as City Editor of the *Sunday Telegraph*. It reads: "Bad figures always take longer to add up than good ones". By this he meant beware of companies whose results come out later than normal. It usually means there is something fishy or unpleasant they didn't want to tell you about.

Of course the pedantic will always says that there are exceptions to every rule, as indeed there are. Warren Buffett, as in so many things, has laid down a marker for investment rule-making with his simple two-part exhortation: "Rule Number One: don't lose money. Rule Number Two: don't forget Rule Number One." He is entitled to make things sound that easy, as he has the wealth accumulated over more than 60 years to prove it.

The rest of us, whether we agree with all of them or not, can only benefit from reflecting on the heady mixture of insights, truisms and challenges to conventional thinking that make up the content of this title.

JONATHAN DAVIS
Oxford, 2017

JONATHAN DAVIS *is one of the UK's leading writers on investment. A professionally qualified investor, he is the author of three books about investment, has written regular columns for the* Financial Times *and* The Spectator, *podcasts regularly for the* Money Makers *website (*www.money-makers.co*) and is an advisor to investment companies. His website is at* www.independent-investor.com.

Frank Armstrong

FRANK ARMSTRONG, III, *is the founder and president of Investor Solutions, Inc., an SEC-Registered Investment Advisor in Miami, Florida. Frank is a former US Air Force pilot with 250 combat missions in Vietnam, followed by 19 years with Eastern Airlines. A financial industry veteran of over 40 years, he is the author of four books on investment theory and retirement planning.*

"THE WORLD ISN'T GOING TO END. THIS BABY ISN'T GOING DOWN, AND THIS SHIP ISN'T COMING APART. YOU MUST BE ON BOARD IN ORDER TO REACH YOUR DESTINATION."

Investing from the Cockpit

I N A PREVIOUS life, I was an Air Force pilot and then an airline pilot. Rules I learned then are directly applicable to my life as an investment advisor.

I began my career as an investment advisor 43 years ago when after Vietnam I was furloughed from Eastern Airlines. Landing as gracefully as I could, I used my college degree in economics and business to transition to a job designing pension plans for small business owners. That in turn led to full service financial planning and eventually opening my own Registered Investment Advisor. Today that firm, Investor Solutions, Inc. (investorsolutions.com), manages over $750 million for several hundred clients in 39 states and five foreign countries.

Here are some cockpit rules that you can apply directly to your investment portfolio:

1. PLAN AHEAD.

Strategic Air Command Aircrews used to joke that the SAC motto, "Peace is our Profession", should have continued "But, flight planning is our obsession." Four of us on a Tanker crew spent a full day planning and filling out the paperwork for a six-hour mission. More time planning than flying! But, when we got to the aircraft, we knew *exactly* where we were going and what we were going to do. As little as possible was left to chance. Whatever our mission was, we couldn't just take off and fly around aimlessly.

Similarly, you are highly unlikely to get a decent outcome for your investment plan without some detailed planning.

Industry professionals joke that while a family may spend weeks researching a flat-screen TV, they don't spend ten minutes planning their retirement. It sounds funny, but you know it's true.

There are many parts to an investment plan. For instance:

- How much capital will you need to maintain your lifestyle?
- How many years until you retire?
- What's an appropriate withdrawal strategy?
- How can you maximize your tax advantages?
- How much risk should you take?
- What is the range of returns you should reasonably expect?
- What asset allocation is appropriate for each stage of the trip?
- What funds will best execute the asset allocation strategy?
- How much will Social Security (or the equivalent for readers outside the US) contribute?

Each of those are important variables that will dramatically impact the outcome for better or worse. Screw up just one part and you are likely to have a disaster.

You only get one shot at retirement accumulation. You can't learn this game as you go along. You can't hit rewind in real life. Early mistakes may never be made up. Spend some time planning your financial future.

It's painless to get started. There are a huge number of free resources available on the internet that can help. For instance, my company has over 100 financial calculators that will help you do everything from mortgage illustrations to a retirement plan calculation that is integrated with Social Security:

- investorsolutions.com/media/calculator

(Other resources are of course available – head to Google and you'll be sure to find alternatives.)

Speaking of calculators, the Social Security Administration calculator is already preloaded with your earnings history, age and other information so they can turn out a personalized Social Security projection at various ages:

- www.ssa.gov/retire/estimator.html

Now would be a perfect time to begin to plan for your family's future. If you can't do it yourself, or don't want to do it, engage a competent financial professional. One way or another, plan ahead.

2. FIND THE HIGH-PROBABILITY SHOT.

When two enemy fighter pilots approach each other they start maneuvering for a position behind the other. The contest usually ends when one finds himself at the enemy's six o'clock position. That's the high-probability shot. While very occasionally a pilot might succeed in a head-on shot, that's the hard way to do it, and it leaves him open to additional risk. After they pass each other, the enemy pilot might very well end up on his six. Game over! So fighter pilots study tactics which, combined, result in strategy with the highest possibility of success.

Whatever you are doing, whether it's basketball, chess, medicine, law, or home construction there is an elegant solution, a low-risk approach, and an easy way.

For investors, the high-probability shot is the strategy that maximizes the return per unit of risk the investor is willing to accept. There are a few tactics that individually advance you toward that goal, but used together they are truly powerful:

- Don't take more risk than you need to and can tolerate.

- Divide your portfolio into risky and riskless parts. The mixture of the two should reflect your risk tolerance, liquidity needs, goals and objectives.

- Diversify both portfolios widely to avoid unpleasant surprises while obtaining market rates of return. The gold standard is global diversification.

- Use low-cost collective investments like index funds and ETFs. They deliver market returns at the lowest cost, risk, and tax costs possible.

- Utilize tax-free or tax-deferred accounts wherever possible.

- Start early because time is the most valuable commodity for investors wishing to accumulate assets.

- Accept market returns. Don't try to time markets or identify mispriced securities. It's a loser's game. The evidence against active management is clear beyond a reasonable doubt.

- Consider overweighting your portfolios to favor small companies, cheap stocks (value), and more profitable companies. Those tilts have been shown to reliably enhance returns over reasonable periods of time.

- Stay the course. Don't react to headlines, herd mentality, market predictions, fear or greed.

3. YOU NEED COMMITMENT.

Flying an underpowered aircraft at close to its maximum gross weight on a runway just barely long enough was a normal day at the office for tanker crews. But if you are going to soar with eagles, first you need to get it off the ground.

As the aircraft slowly accelerated, we spent a long time on the runway. It wasn't unusual to break ground a second or two before the end of the runway.

So, takeoffs had our full and undivided attention. Flight planning for takeoff was a serious matter that generated a dozen numbers, the most important of which was Critical Engine Failure Speed or S1, our go/no-go point. If one of our four engines fell right off the wing after S1 it was far better to take off than try to stop on the remaining runway. We were committed! Short of catastrophic failure we were going flying!

If, after planning, you have a well-designed global asset allocation plan that meets your unique needs, once you put your money down, you are committed. If the planning was right in the first place, changing your mind every few minutes is not a viable option. Things will happen, but if you are prepared, staying the course is almost always the right thing to do. Jumping in and out is highly unlikely to enhance your portfolio.

The other part of commitment for investors is that they must actually contribute some capital. America has a huge savings problem which is reflected in a woeful preparation for retirement. The days of the guaranteed pension are gone, not likely to ever come back. If you don't make an early commitment to savings, not even the best investment advisor or asset-allocation strategy is going to help you. You will never be able to retire comfortably. In other words, planning *and* execution are necessary for a successful mission.

4. EXPECT TURBULENCE.

Back in another life I flew Airbus 300s for the departed Eastern Airlines. While they may appear to be arrogant and cocky, professional pilots have a great deal of concern about their passengers. They would willingly die to protect them. Keeping them safe, comfortable, happy and stress-free is mission one!

Turbulence is a fact of life. It makes passengers cranky. So, we spent a fair amount of time avoiding it. But sometimes it must be simply endured. All we could do, short of staying home, was reassure passengers. No airline could ever guarantee you that you won't have an occasional bump in your journey. Few trips would ever be completed if the pilot turned around at the first bump. If we waited for a guarantee of smooth air we would never leave the terminal.

Pilots expect occasional turbulence. After a few thousand hours in the air, they know it goes with the territory. Occasionally the air is bumpy. What's the big deal? The airplane is inherently stable. When bumped it tends to return to its former attitude. The airplane is so strong that several commercial airliners have withstood five to seven times the G forces that they were designed for.

So, when the plane is bumping along, the pilot's primary concern is usually trying not to spill his coffee. He doesn't enjoy the turbulence, but besides a concern for his passenger comfort, he isn't worried.

But on the other side of the cockpit door things may be different. Most of the experienced passengers will sleep right through it – but a few passengers see a different world. There they are, trapped in a big aluminum tube, hurtling along at about 500 miles an hour seven miles above the ground! At the first sign of turbulence, anxious glances are quickly followed by wide eyes and white knuckles. This thing is out of control! It's going down! The pilot must be insane! Why doesn't he get us on the ground? Oh, how I wish I had never seen an airplane!

That experience was good training to be an investment advisor. Just substitute investment advisor for pilot, investor for passenger, and market decline for turbulence.

As an investment advisor, I expect an occasional market downturn. It's built right into the system. I don't like it. I do every thing I can to avoid it. I try to make it as small as possible. But sometimes I just have to live with it. Market downturns are not the fun part, but they are business as usual in the financial arena.

We endured the Crash of '87, the Crash of '89, the Tech Wreck of 2000, and the near disaster of 2008. Markets endured, recovered, and went on to new highs.

Our economy is incredibly strong, stable and resilient. But markets must go down occasionally in order to function. There is no way to anticipate when that might happen. We must accept a measured amount of risk (the market fluctuations) in order to earn the extra returns necessary to accomplish our life goals.

Many investors are not comfortable with market volatility. They feel out of control, and imagine all the worst possible outcomes. Their version of safety is to chuck it all and seek refuge in cash. Of course, that's the classic 'buy high, sell low, and wonder why we don't make money in the stock market' behavior. Investors that panic and follow the herd are unlikely to succeed. It's a recipe for failure.

The world isn't going to end. This baby isn't going down, and this ship isn't coming apart. You must be on board in order to reach your destination.

5. UNDERTAKE CONTINUOUS MAINTENANCE.

Airplanes don't fly around long without maintenance. That varies from a quick inspection every night to completely stripping the aircraft to the bones, inspecting and rebuilding. Keeping several million moving parts perfectly airworthy for a projected useful life of 50 years takes a little TLC. Parts wear out and must be replaced. Other parts need to be upgraded to take advantage of improved design and efficiency.

By the way, aircraft mechanics are professionals certified by the FAA. You expect before you put your family on an airplane that the person signing it off as airworthy has the training, testing, certifications and experience to care for your precious cargo.

Your investment portfolio needs continuous maintenance, too. Clearly you would like to avoid catastrophic failures. But avoiding crashes is only part of the problem. Keeping it running at optimum efficiency will greatly enhance your future security. This involves:

- **Rebalancing to keep the original risk profile.** Left to its own devices a very well-designed portfolio will morph over time as asset classes diverge to grow or fall at different rates. It's counterintuitive to sell assets that have appreciated in value in order to buy underperforming asset classes. But, rebalancing enforces a discipline of buying low and selling high at the margin that adds considerable value over time.

- **Addition of new desirable asset classes.** Thousands of new investment products are introduced each year. Most are clones of existing products, or a bad idea recycled under a new brand name. However, a very few offer valuable diversification benefits that over time will enhance performance while reducing risk. We prefer to incorporate new products after they have stood the test of time. I'd much rather be late adopting a new asset class than jump on to something that I didn't fully understand and have it bite my clients.

- **Substitution of cheaper funds.** The market has vastly improved pricing for exposure to asset classes through the mutual funds and ETFs that offer them. The internal expenses and trading costs today are a very small fraction of what they were when I entered the security business. If there are no tax consequences and low trading costs it's always better to own a low-cost portfolio than an expensive one. Costs matter and small incremental cost reductions add up to large differences in performance over the long haul.

- **Dividend avoidance.** ETFs and mutual funds announce their estimated dividends in advance. Those dividends will come with a tax cost. If selling the fund in a taxable portfolio just before the dividend is declared has a smaller cost than recognizing the dividend, that will clearly save capital that can live to grow for you. It takes a few calculations to net out the costs and benefits, but because taxes are the greatest expense investors face, it's well worth the effort. Keeping dollars in play that would otherwise get taxed away pays huge dividends.

- **Tax-loss harvesting.** Occasionally investments go down in value. It's annoying when that happens. But it gives the investor an opportunity to recognize a taxable loss that she can deduct against gains otherwise in her portfolio. If she doesn't have gains, she can store them against future gains. Again, it takes a few calculations to sort out long-term gains and short-term gains, but it's a very positive thing for long-term performance. Think of it as turning lemons into lemonade.

- **Conversion of short-term gains to long-term gains.** Whenever you must sell a security you should look at the tax implications. If that security has a short-term gain, the tax will be approximately twice as high as if you waited to sell it when it qualified for long-term gain. Perhaps you should sell another security at less tax cost, or simply wait until it qualifies for the lower taxation.

Tax-aware investing is complicated and tedious unless you have sophisticated software to track your portfolio on a daily basis. But every dollar that marches away to the tax man is never coming back. It can't be reinvested or spent. So your yardstick for measuring performance must be after tax returns.

There is nothing magic about portfolio maintenance. It's just the basic TLC that keeps a portfolio tuned up and performing optimally for the long haul.

Every decision to buy or sell a security involves multiple trade-offs. Many investors can't or won't take the time and effort to incorporate it into their long-term strategy. If so, they might be well advised to hire a professional to do it for them. Protecting that precious cargo must be mission number one. After all, your investments are your future.

6. HAVE A GOOD TRIP.

When aircrews meet each other anyplace in the world, they often end their conversations with: "Have a good trip". It's a metaphor for life. If you plan, follow a few basic rules, exercise judgment and discipline, your life and investment experience can be a good trip.

So, let me say to you all: Have a good trip!

Glen Arnold

GLEN ARNOLD, *PhD, used to be a professor of investing but concluded that academic life was not nearly as much fun, nor as intellectually stimulating, as making money in the markets. As a wealthy investor he now spends most of his time running his equity portfolio from an office in the heart of rural Leicestershire, far from the noise of the City of London.*

His main research focus explores the question 'What works in investment?', drawing on the ideas of the great investors, academic discoveries and corporate strategic analysis — see **www.glen-arnold-investments.co.uk**. *While he used to teach on this subject in the City, he would now rather concentrate on actual investment analysis, but does explain his investment choices and discusses investment ideas at* **newsletters.advfn.com/ deepvalueshares**.

He is the author of many investment books, including the UK's bestseller. His most recent title is The Deals of Warren Buffett – Volume 1 *(Harriman House, 2017).*

"ACCEPTING THE MARKET'S 'VALUE' PLACED ON A SHARE IS TO ABDICATE RESPONSIBILITY FOR THINKING."

Investing Tenets of the Private Investor Who Trained the Professionals

1. UNDERSTAND BEFORE YOU BUY.

I F YOU DON'T understand it, don't buy it. View shares as part ownership of a business, not as gambling counters in a game of chance, where you barely understand the rules. Be a business analyst rather than a share analyst.

A virus often sweeps across share-buying communities inducing many to place money in things they do not understand. Not having a clue about the underlying business of, say, fintech or bio-pharmaceuticals, investors bet enormous sums on hope of a good outcome.

Consider the 2017 IPO of Snap Inc. Its returns to shareholders are deeply buried for a long time. Annual revenue was $405m and *losses* over $500m. And yet its shares sold for 18 times revenues, a market capitalisation of $30bn, ahead of Kellogg's. Do Snap shareholders understand the competitive forces facing their company over the next decade?

While the virus-infected are getting all worked up about what might be – if only their company becomes *the* dominant network or *the* blockbuster drug supplier – they overlook the simple-to-understand mundane company that churns out profits. OK, it might have a proven record, observable historic earnings, but it is a bit boring; nothing like as exciting as the dream of making it big by holding shares in a company with no profit record, burning up millions, which *might* just be the next Microsoft.

Most such companies, of course, will never be the 'one' – they will be also-rans.

The 1920s had its own version of this pandemic, when new technology included the magic of electricity, wireless, movies and the telephone. Punters didn't need to understand business models or competitive environments; didn't need to know whether a company had a strong economic franchise with pricing power. Nor to judge the quality of these factors against the price being asked for a share. No! All they needed to know was there would be growth in sales – profits would follow, automatically, right?

You need to analyse a business before buying its shares. What is its value? You need facts – not to try to value expectation and hope. Relevant facts include earnings generated in years gone by, because these facts are likely to cast light on what is to come. The balance sheet is also important, e.g. do net assets amount to more than the market capitalisation? Is the company over-burdened with debt? These are the quantitative facts. But even more important are the qualitative facts, e.g. does the firm's market position allow it to charge high prices relative to costs because it offers something special, as with say Burberry or Disney? Are the managers competent, skilled at generating wealth? Are they people of high integrity, treating all shareholders fairly? Is the company in a stable position regarding industry dynamics, competitive advantages (if any) and the financial structure? The quantitative and the qualitative elements go into the mix to be weighed. The investor differentiates between noise and key value factors.

More important than the will to win is the will to prepare; investors prepare by understanding businesses. The task is difficult. This is the reason why so many of the great investors declare they do not have the facts nor the intellectual wherewithal to evaluate many or most companies. Warren Buffett advises us to stay within our circle of competence. "Your goal as an investor should simply be to purchase, at a rational price, a part interest in an easily-understandable business whose earnings are virtually certain to be materially higher five, ten or 20 years from now." (1996 Letter.)

2. SMALL INVESTORS CAN OUTPERFORM THE PROFESSIONALS.

The thoughtful, dedicated private investor can outperform the professional fund manager due to her many advantages, including the ability to concentrate a portfolio; to take the risk of being different from the herd; to avoid institutional constraints; and to find good companies from everyday experiences.

Small investors should not feel intimidated by the professional. Fund managers are subject to so many constraints, and susceptible to errors in logic and flaws of character, that the well-equipped private investor, following sound principles, can outperform them. I've helped in the training of many fund managers. While very capable at quantitative analysis – they have CFA qualifications, after all – when it comes to the more important qualitative, and the following of simple and sound investment principles (rather than speculative principles), well, let's just say, many drift a little.

Very high IQ is not a requirement. Peter Lynch, a great fund manager, apart from saying that all the math you need in the stock market you get in the fourth grade, declared: "The true geniuses, it seems to me, get too enamoured of the theoretical cogitations and are forever betrayed by the actual behaviour of stocks, which is more simple-minded than they can imagine. It's also important to be able to make decisions without complete or perfect information." A mass of data can cause some to make elaborate scrutiny and synthesis of non-essentials. Share investing is an art that blends knowledge of history, psychology, sociology, business strategy analysis, economics and political science as well as data 'facts' from the past. Quantification alone will not do.

Disadvantages of the professional in more detail

(i) They move a long way down the diminishing marginal attractiveness curve

Imagine each investor put shares in order of attractiveness. The first on the list is a terrific bargain, at a low price relative to estimated future cash generated for shareholders. The second is a very good buy, but is slightly less good than number one. And so on, down to, say, share 35 which is a lot less interesting than the first few. Professional investors are instructed, nay drilled, that they must diversify to a much greater extent than 35. Some of these portfolios have 100 shares – they have moved so far down the curve that the marginal share is really not that attractive.

(ii) Professionals are more sheep-like than they let on

Bargains are found where companies and sectors are not yet talked about by the large fund managers. Once one or two get wind of a good prospect, word travels fast in the close fund manager community. The herd moves in the same direction. Hot shares are bid up and no longer bargains. Private investors can stand aside from the popular themes of the day and look in areas professionals are ignoring.

(iii) Small companies cannot be bought

I think I'm right in saying that, when I taught at Schroders, the smallest company in which managers invested client funds had a market capitalisation of at least £200m. Similar rules apply at other large fund houses. But more than half of UK-quoted companies are under £200m, which means that small companies are often neglected by the professionals, leading to potential under-pricing.

(iv) Their knowledge is spread too thinly

Imagine running a fund with 100 shares in 30 industries, from oil through retail to media. How do you become expert on all these industries? Of course, you can't. The keen small investor who devotes himself to the study of an industry or a handful of industries he knows something about can achieve much better results than most jack-of-all-trade professionals.

Also, the professional stuck in an office limits serendipity intervening. Small investors come across wonderful opportunities in everyday living, from finding a young restaurant chain in a few northern towns but poised for worldwide greatness, to discovering an excellent ethos and talent at a small medical company.

(v) Admin and rules get in the way

Fund managers devote considerable time to writing reports to justify their fees, as well as marketing. They usually invest the money handed to them at all times, even if they think shares are overvalued; whereas the small investor can hold cash at such times – masterly inactivity. Professionals risk careers if they allocate money too far away from benchmark allocations, and are forbidden to heavily overweight those shares for which they hold most conviction.

3. THE MARKET IS THERE TO SERVE YOU, NOT TO GUIDE YOU.

Many people treat market prices as a guide to the value of a share. The market, in its manic-depressive fashion, often sets prices that are far from the true value of a business. Be independent, do your own valuations and exploit prices rather than being led by them.

Given the market doesn't always price shares correctly, accepting the market's 'value' placed on a share is to abdicate responsibility for thinking. Instead of evaluating the fundamentals of a business, you accept what the average opinion of share buyers and sellers deems an appropriate price. Price is not the same as value; make sure you underpay for value.

Prices don't respond simply to what is happening to a company, but move in response to the consensus view of what might happen to the company, its industry or the economy. But this consensus may be wide of the mark.

Great investors are so disciplined they insist on treating the market as though it is not there, except in one important respect: they check to see if the market is doing anything foolish. Sometimes it's depressed about a company or about shares generally, making mountains out of molehills, exaggerating the ordinary downs of business life, thinking they are major traumas. Then the market may be willing to sell you shares at a price way below true value – take advantage and buy.

At other times the market is euphoric, pricing above any reasonable assessment of value. Many punters feel compelled to join in a market moving skyward. They like to buy when prices are rising, taking comfort from the company of other excited people (social confirmation is always comforting). Again, true investors take advantage, selling shares to others willing to pay above the odds.

4. REMEMBER THE DIFFERENCE BETWEEN INVESTING AND SPECULATION.

The distinction between investing and speculation is not determined by the type of security you buy, nor by the length of time you hold, but by the attitude of mind when you buy. An investor conducts thorough analysis to understand the underlying business, only buys when reassured as to the safety of the principal committed and aims merely for a satisfactory rate of return rather than stretching the boundaries in targeting extraordinary returns. Operations not meeting these requirements are speculative. Speculators tend to be more interested in guessing price moves over relatively short periods.

Many people who claim to be investors are, in fact, speculators. This is not because they buy what are commonly thought of as speculative-type instruments – say, derivatives. Nor is it because they only buy and hold securities for short periods of time in rapid succession. They count as speculators because they do not do the three things that investors do:

1. conduct thorough analysis

2. build in a margin of safety when buying

3. aim only for a satisfactory rate of return.

My first investing rule covered thorough analysis, so I'll look at the other two now, but only after a great quote from Benjamin Graham, who originally defined investment as the three factors listed above:

> "The speculative public is incorrigible. In financial terms it cannot count beyond 3. It will buy anything, at any price, if there seems some 'action' in progress. It will fall for any company identified with 'franchising', computers, electronics, science, technology or what have you, when the particular fashion is raging." (*The Intelligent Investor*)

How modern this quote seems, and yet it was written in 1973.

Building in a margin of safety is something all bridge engineers do. They don't design a bridge that only just withstands adverse circumstances in terms of wind or loads – they make sure there is plenty of extra strength. Likewise, when valuing shares: first, expect to arrive at a range of reasonable intrinsic values rather than a single point, but second protect yourself with a margin of safety so even if the analysis contained errors or the vicissitudes of the market cause a drop you are reasonably well protected. For example, if that range is £2 to £3, do not buy if the price is £1.95 – the margin of safety is not large enough.

Margin of safety concerns downside risk. Risk is properly defined as the threat to the preservation of capital and to a modest rate of return on that capital over the long run (not beta and sigma). The threat level depends on trouble affecting the business fundamentals and spending power taken away by tax and inflation.

Don't expect to get rich quickly from the stock market. With such an imperative you do risky things, imperilling capital, e.g. borrowing or buying hot areas. OK, so you might be lucky once or twice, but ultimately you will be headed for a loss. Have reasonable expectations of the returns you will receive from the stock market.

Timing the market – trying to predicting short-term movements and buying before a rise, or selling before a fall – is speculative. Long-term observers are convinced that such activity is futile.

5. DO NOT PAY HIGH FEES.

When managing your portfolio, do not let money slip away in trading costs, taxes and fees. When paying someone else to manage your money make sure the fees do not take away the bulk of the investment gain.

One way for investors to underperform is to overtrade. Constantly buying and selling is not required to build up a great portfolio. Simplicity brings low costs. Investing only after a period of thorough analysis and reflection means instructions to brokers will be few and far between, saving fees, and ensuring you only invest when convinced on margin of safety. Also, the tax system gives a boost if you are not regularly realising profits but allowing compounding to work its magic without interruption and without the taxman taking a regular slice.

When placing money in a fund, vigilance over costs needs to be even greater. The typical manager turns over fund contents every 18 months. Taking into account brokerage and tax on trading, clients could easily pay 0.8% pa in transaction costs. Let's be generous and say much of this trading is necessary due to share buybacks, dividend reinvestment, etc. so that the 'excess trading' costs falls to only 0.4% pa. Doesn't sound much?

But, let's do some simple maths:

If a £100,000 fund grows at the return on the underlying investments, say, 7% per year, after 20 years there will be £386,968.

If the same fund grows at 7% minus 0.4% cost of normal transactions: £359,041.

With 0.8% costs – bumped-up by an element of excess trading – there will be £333,035 after 20 years. Holders of the fund are £26,006 worse off simply because of overtrading. And this is before we take into account (a) tax on gains or (b) fund manager's fees, which are often much more important than overtrading.

Some managers charge 1.5% pa to manage a fund. After 20 years, combining this cost with a 0.4% transaction element results in only £270,430 – the gain on the fund compared with the underlying shares is 41% lower (declining from £286,968 to £170,430).

It can get a lot worse: some pensioners place money with a wealth manager charging 1% on top of the fund charge. With 1% for the wealth managers, 1.5% for the fund managers, plus 0.4% for trading, the £100,000 grows to only £223,365.

6. DIVERSIFY, BUT NOT TO MEDIOCRITY.

You are vulnerable if you invest in only one or two shares, so diversify. Beyond ten securities, however, the benefits of further diversification become small – your knowledge is going to become more thinly spread. Better to concentrate on shares within your circle of competence, where you have an analytical edge, than diversify into areas you don't understand.

All investors make mistakes, even the great ones. Investors should be diversified so that any one mistake will not cripple them. But beyond that point, as Philip Fisher said, "take extreme care to own not the most, but the best... a little bit of a great many can never be more than a poor substitute for a few of the outstanding." Over-diversification means that you:

(a) run out of attractive places to put money

(b) can't watch all your companies, checking to see if the fundamentals have altered.

7. STUDY STOCK MARKET MISPRICING.

Make yourself aware of the remarkable findings in academic papers examining whether the market can be beaten. Generally, they conclude that it is very difficult to outsmart the markets (doing better than just buying a broad spread of investments and going to sleep for a decade or two). However, there are some nuggets of gold hidden in the academic jargon and maze of statistics. The findings provide rigorously derived corroborative evidence of what many great investors have been telling us for decades, and, in some cases take things a little further.

Studies of share returns using millions of pieces of data have shown what academics call 'anomalies' – patterns of returns not fitting the paradigm of pricing efficiency. I call the most convincing of these anomalies 'stock market inefficiencies'. They present opportunities to follow rules to shortlist companies that may set you on the road to outperformance – if the historical inefficiency continues. In many cases the pattern seen in the data does disappear and so it's a fool's errand to continue investing that way. In other cases, systematic mispricing is caused by decision-making flaws deep in the human psyche difficult to escape. When these psychological issues are widespread we have more reason to believe that the anomaly will persist. Of course, any company on the shortlist is then subject to crucial qualitative examination, including tests of business prospects, managerial competence and integrity, and stability.

8. READ THE PHILOSOPHIES OF THE GREAT INVESTORS.

There is a lot to learn from the best investors. You can learn from their mistakes – you can't live long enough to make them all yourself. You can learn from their hard-earned experience what works and what does not.

The great investors follow the principles of bottom-up analysis in an independently minded fashion. Wonderfully inquisitive about profit, balance sheet, cash flow, business strategy and people, they learn and continuously improve by devoting more time to reading and thinking rather than doing. They are always trying to widen their circle of competence – while not stepping outside it.

Within the realm of investing, there are plenty of alternative approaches. Examples include:

- **Low share price relative to past earnings,** whether that be recent earnings or those averaged over many years.

- **Growth at a value price.** Philip Fisher conducted such a thorough analysis that he was able to successfully anticipate rapid advances in earnings.

- **Low price relative to combinations of value metrics.** Benjamin Graham was an expert here.

- **Net current asset value.** E.g. Graham, Buffett and Walter Schloss.

- **Niche investing.** Strong competitive position and financial strength of fast-growing small and medium-sized firms operating in a niche with high potential (e.g. Peter Lynch).

- **Economic franchise investing.** Buffett and Munger excel at finding businesses with strong business moats subduing competition, promoting pricing power and high rates of return.

- **Global value approach.** John Templeton searched the world for bargains (low PERs) which required particular awareness of social, political and economic forces.

9. KEEP YOUR EMOTIONS IN CHECK.

The investor's worst enemy is likely to be himself – his feelings and compulsions, his decision-making flaws. A sound investment strategy can be scuppered when the crunch time comes because excitement, fear, impatience, greed and other emotions get in the way. Being temperamentally well-suited for investment is far more important than IQ or knowledge of accounting, economics or stock markets.

Guard against:

1. **Getting caught up in minutiae** and forgetting that the process must be kept as simple as possible – doing the ordinary extraordinarily well.

2. **Becoming rigid in method and thought.** Charles Darwin pointed out it was neither the strongest nor the most intelligent that survives, but the most adaptable to change. Continually challenge and amend your best ideas. Identify and reconcile disconfirming evidence.

3. **Over-optimism.** Optimism can lead to big bets on hope rather than evidence.

4. **Greed and impatience.** Feeling you should be making double-digit returns every year pushes boundaries of prudence by, say, borrowing, punting on risky areas, hyperactively rushing to the latest

hot theme, or selling for a quick profit. Patience is needed when you sit with a lot of cash, waiting for excellent investment opportunities rather than mediocre ones. Patience is also needed if the market does not yet realise the value you have spotted.

5. **Panicking when shares fall.** Falling markets present the best opportunities, especially when shares are being sold indiscriminately due to macroeconomic shock. As Buffett says: "Fear is the foe of the faddist, but the friend of the fundamentalist."

6. **Fear of failure.** Investors experience much failure, but some people cannot accept these regular ego knocks and give up trying.

10. ENJOY THE JOURNEY.

Enjoy the journey as well as the rewards, because the journey is where you live. If you don't enjoy investing then hire someone else to do it for you (someone trustworthy and not pricey for mundane performance – excellent performance can be rewarded, though).

Investing can be time-consuming and, at times, emotionally draining, and, given that there are many ways of joyfully spending time with family and friends, and with purposeful and fulfilling work, perhaps, for many, investing is not the right path.

Martin Bamford

MARTIN BAMFORD *is a Chartered Financial Planner, Chartered Wealth Manager and CFP professional. As managing director of Informed Choice, an award-winning firm of Chartered Financial Planners in Surrey, he is responsible for managing £250m of client investment assets. He is the author of several bestselling personal finance books, including* Brilliant Investing: What the Best Investors Know, Do and Say *(Prentice Hall, 2007).*

"YOU SHOULD VIEW RISK CAPACITY AS A SAFETY VALVE ON YOUR INVESTMENT DECISIONS."

Britain's Bestselling Financial Planner on Dealing with Risk and Reward

W HEN WE TALK to clients about investing money, risk is a big part of that conversation.

The link between risk and reward is well-documented; you don't get one without the other, regardless of how desirable that might be. If you want the potential for higher returns, you have to accept higher risk to your capital.

Every investor is familiar with the adage that the value of their investments might go down as well as up. In a sense, that's what investing is all about – the ability to profit from higher returns by exposing your money to greater levels of risk. Investors should get a 'risk premium' in return for their willingness to invest in assets riskier than cash.

Since the early 1950s, investors have been able to refer to the model put forward by Nobel Prize winner Harry Markowitz. His work helps in the selection of investments in the most efficient way by analysing various possible portfolio combinations.

It's thanks to Markowitz that we have the 'efficient frontier' concept, demonstrating that each portfolio has a boundary for a given level of risk and potential reward. Portfolios which are constructed in an efficient manner sit right up against this boundary. Inefficient portfolios fall below the boundary line, suggesting that the same return could be had for less risk, or risk levels maintained for the prospect of higher returns.

Decisions about investment risk have evolved a great deal since the models put forward by Markowitz. When we speak to clients today, we are always discussing three distinct aspects of investment risk: attitude, capacity and goals. The following three rules cover how investors should, in my experience, approach them.

1. FIND YOUR COMFORT LEVEL.

Your *attitude* towards investment risk is the aspect of investment risk which dictates how well you can sleep at night. Assessment of risk attitudes has evolved a great deal, moving from pigeon-holing investors into a 'cautious, balanced or aggressive' profile to the use of research-backed psychometric tools to really understand attitudes.

Psychometric profiling is valuable at this stage in the investing journey because it effectively identifies characteristics like tolerance for ambiguity, desire for profit and investment experience.

All of these factors will influence a risk level at which you feel comfortable as an investor. It's important you find that level before you do anything else.

But you can't stop there.

2. MAKE SURE YOU CAN STILL AFFORD TO FEED THE CATS.

Decisions around investment risk should not end with your attitude. From assessing risk attitudes we move to understanding *capacity* for risk. This is all about the impact any investment losses might have on your wider financial position. If your portfolio fell by 20%, could you still afford to feed the cats?

To understand risk capacity, it's important to think about the timescale of your investment, how much you can afford to lose, and how quickly you would need to get your hands on the money in the event of an emergency.

Investors who are prepared to invest for a long time, or who can afford to lose a big chunk of their portfolio without it dramatically changing their lifestyle (or who have other capital available to access in the event of a financial emergency), are thought to have a high capacity for risk.

If an investor has a shorter time horizon in mind, cannot afford to lose much of his capital or has no other financial resources on which to call, then capacity for risk is generally much lower and could represent a constraint on risk levels.

While risk capacity does not change your attitude towards investment risk, it might restrict it. You could find yourself with an aggressive risk profile but a limited capacity to take risk with your money.

As a result, you should view risk capacity as a safety valve on your investment decisions, holding you back from taking the risks your identified attitude meant you originally wanted to take.

3. LINK YOUR PORTFOLIO TO GOALS.

The third part of risk is too often overlooked by investors: linking your portfolio to your goals.

After all, what is the purpose of investing your money? Investing for the sake of investing is rarely a good idea. Instead, you should invest to meet specific goals.

Those goals need to be detailed and go beyond the traditional approach of investing for capital growth, income or both.

You may not even need to invest – it's possible! One of the most satisfying moments in my work as a financial planner is meeting with a client, analysing her situation and concluding she needs to take no investment risk to meet her goals. In other words, she already has all of the wealth she needs to achieve her goals in life and runs a very low risk of running out of money in her lifetime.

The best way to determine your goals is by using lifetime cash flow forecasting. By factoring in your assets, liabilities, income and expenditure – both now and what you expect to happen in the future – it's possible to build a robust model for the rest of your life.

Applied to this model are a set of realistic assumptions about the future, including price inflation, investment returns and longevity. These assumptions need to be kept under regular review and adjusted to keep them on track as conditions materialise.

When using lifetime cash flow forecasting, there is no guarantee that the trajectory of your life will remain the same or that unexpected expenditure or capital losses will not materialise. Alongside the projection, it pays to consider a range of 'disaster scenarios' and the impact these would have on achieving your goals. The standard set of scenarios includes death, disability and market crashes.

Linking your portfolio construction to your financial goals in life could result in needing to take less risk with your money. In some circumstances, it could mean you need to take on greater risk in order to stand a realistic chance of achieving those same goals.

Where a higher level of risk is needed to increase the likelihood of achieving your goals, there are tough decisions to be made. Do you exceed the level of risk deemed appropriate by your attitude to and capacity for risk, or instead consider revising your goals to something more achievable?

Moving away from the relatively simplistic question of risk attitude, and including factors such as capacity for loss and goal setting, offers investors the opportunity to make more appropriate investment decisions which are driven by need and any relevant constraints, rather than comfort level alone.

John Baron

JOHN BARON *is one of the UK's leading experts on investment trusts, a regular columnist and speaker at investment seminars, and author of* The Financial Times Guide to Investment Trusts.

He is a director of Equi Ltd which owns the investment trust website **www.johnbaronportfolios.co.uk.** *The website reports on the progress of seven real investment trust portfolios, including same-day details of trades, new portfolio weightings and yields. The portfolios pursue a range of strategies and income objectives, and enjoy an enviable track record relative to their benchmarks.*

Since 2009, John has also reported on two of these portfolios in his popular monthly column in the Investors Chronicle *– fees are donated to charity.*

John has used investment trusts in a private and professional capacity for over 35 years. After university and the Army, he ran a broad range of investment portfolios as a director of both Henderson Private Clients and then Rothschild Asset Management. Since leaving the City, he has also helped charities monitor their fund managers.

"A SUCCESSFUL INVESTOR MUST BE PREPARED TO BE A CONTRARIAN. A BENCHMARK CAN ONLY BE BEATEN WHEN DEVIATING FROM IT."

Insights of an Investment Trust Expert

Recognising when sentiment and fundamentals diverge is the essence of a good investment decision. This is no easy task but it can be doubly rewarding when it comes to investment trusts. Their particular characteristics, including their closed-ended structure, ability to gear and lower cost – all of which help to account for their superior performance over unit trusts – present a wealth of opportunities to informed investors.

* * *

However, the prerequisite for any successful investment journey is clarity regarding financial goals and risk tolerances.

1. DETERMINE YOUR GOALS.

Equities produce better returns than bonds and cash over the long term. But the path is rarely a smooth one. Market corrections are part of the investment cycle, which is one reason it is important to adopt a long-term investment approach.

It is also why it is important, at the outset, to ensure that portfolio construction truly reflects investment objectives, risk tolerances and time horizons. Other factors to consider can include currency exposure and income requirements.

Choosing the appropriate benchmark and timescale to monitor a portfolio's performance can also help in attaining financial goals. However, never let benchmarks dictate how a portfolio is constructed – they cannot be beaten if they are simply copied.

Furthermore, in pursuing a long-term approach, it should be remembered any meaningful performance comparisons therefore require a minimum five-year period. At best, over the short term, benchmarks should be seen as a reference point for monitoring a portfolio's progress.

* * *

Clarity about investment objectives, risk tolerances and required timescales can then be complemented by the application of tried-and-tested investment principles.

2. TIME IN THE MARKET IS BETTER THAN MARKET TIMING.

Once invested, it is important to remain so provided such an approach continues to reflect investment objectives and risk profiles. Many investors try to time the markets, and a few are successful. But for most long-term investors it is better to remain invested.

The evidence certainly suggests that the longer one is invested, the more likely a positive return will result. Recent research from Fidelity has shown that over the period 1980–2012, investing in global equities for 12 years or more produced no negative returns. By comparison, five-year periods produced a 16% chance of a negative return.

Furthermore, a few years ago Fidelity also showed that missing out on just the ten best trading days of the MSCI World Index over a ten-year period from 31 December 2002 would have resulted in negative returns of -4.6%. Had an investor missed the best 20 days then the negative return would have extended to -32.1%.

Bad luck aside, evidence further suggests some investors have a tendency to buy after markets have risen, and to sell when they have fallen – and then to remain in cash for too long, and so exacerbate the original mistake at additional cost. This is easy to criticise with the benefit of hindsight, but difficult to counter at the time.

Yet it is precisely at such times that markets tend to bounce – when the bad news is in the price. The single best trading day during the past 10–15 years was on 24 November 2008 when, in the middle of the financial fallout from a ballooning credit crisis, the UK equity market rose 9.2%.

Barclays has also highlighted that investors who tried to time the market from 1992 to 2009 were down 20% compared to those who had simply stuck with it. So ignore the noise and chatter. The evidence suggests that time in the market is better than market timing.

3. DO NOT SPEND YOUR DIVIDENDS UNLESS YOU HAVE TO.

There is another reason to stay invested – to enable the full harvesting of dividends, which account for the vast majority of market returns over time. Legendary investor Jeremy Siegel calculated in 2005 that, over the previous 130 years, 97% of the total return from stocks came from re-invested dividends. $1,000 invested in 1871 would have been worth $243,386 by 2003. Had dividends been reinvested, the figure rises to $7,947,930!

The message is clear: do not spend your dividends unless you have to. Re-investing dividends is the best way of growing wealth over time – and to fully access these dividends, investors must stay invested.

However, there is a downside to this rule: the longer in the market, the greater the chance of a market setback. This can be particularly galling if one is about to realise financial objectives – especially after a long investment journey. A couple of strategies, pursued together, can help to mitigate the effect of such an event: diversification and regular rebalancing.

4. DIVERSIFY TO REDUCE PORTFOLIO RISK.

The aim of diversification is to reduce portfolio risk by investing in 'uncorrelated' assets – asset classes that tend not to move in the same direction over the same period.

Equities, bonds, commercial property, renewable energy, commodities, infrastructure, 'real assets' (such as gold, vintage cars, rare stamps or fine wine) and cash are, to varying degrees, examples. Whilst few investments will escape a major market correction unscathed, adequate diversification away from equities will help to reduce losses.

This important investment discipline is often overlooked – especially in rising markets. There are no fixed rules as to the pace and extent of diversification. An investor's risk profile, time horizon, income requirement and investment objectives are key factors. But there are some general principles which can be helpful.

The four 'seasonal' portfolios (Spring, Summer, Autumn and Winter) covered on the investment trust website **www.johnbaronportfolios.co.uk** reflect an investment journey over time and, as such, best illustrate how we gradually increase diversification as time unfolds.

When starting, it makes sense to focus on equities because of their history of superior returns – so the Spring portfolio consists only of equity holdings, as longer time horizons usually allow greater tolerance when it comes to volatility. However, as time passes, the portfolios become increasingly diversified.

One of the key asset classes employed is bonds – mostly corporate, as the portfolios are wary of government debt. Bonds usually act as a good counterweight to equities. Each is driven by different economic forces – as such, when one rises in price, the other usually falls. The weightings in the Summer, Autumn and Winter portfolios gradually build in ranges of 5–10%, 15–20% and 25–30% respectively.

Other less-correlated assets also become increasingly evident as the journey unfolds including commercial property, renewable energy, infrastructure and commodities. The website's Rationale and Diversification pages have more details.

How many asset classes should one employ? The answer, as with investment generally, is to keep it simple – four or five asset classes usually suffice. As Warren Buffett once said: "Wide diversification is only used when investors do not understand what they are doing." Too much diversification also increases costs.

Meanwhile, in addition to greater diversification, a further objective as time passes is for the website's portfolios to produce a higher and, importantly, still growing income. Commercial property, infrastructure, renewable energy, together with a greater focus on higher-yielding equities within the portfolios' declining equity weightings, all help to achieve this goal.

Accordingly, the Autumn and Winter portfolios currently yield 4.4% and 5.9% respectively. Such asset classes also help the Dividend portfolio achieve a yield of 4.9%. It should, of course, be remembered that whilst income levels should rise with time, yields are also a function of portfolio value and so can vary as portfolio values change.

5. REBALANCE – BUT NOT TOO FREQUENTLY.

Rebalancing is one of the first principles of investing, and yet it is often overlooked. The concept is simple. A 60/40 equity/bond split may, because equities perform well, turn into a 70/30 split. Evidence suggests it pays to rebalance provided one's risk profile and investment objectives remain in sync.

Forbes has shown that $10,000 invested by way of a 60/40 split in the US in 1985, and rebalanced annually, would have been worth $97,000 in 2010 – whereas an unbalanced portfolio would have been worth $89,000. However, again, do not rebalance too frequently. Keep it simple and dealing costs low – for most investors, an annual rebalance is usually sufficient depending on how markets have performed.

Furthermore, it is sometimes forgotten that as much attention should be given to the process of liquidation, as investment timelines approach, as to the running of the portfolio. A gradual and balanced liquidation as the finishing line approaches is one method. There are others. Peace of mind should never be underestimated, particularly at the end of a long investment journey!

* * *

In addition to tried-and-tested investment principles, insights borne of experience often assist when managing a portfolio.

6. BE PREPARED TO BE A CONTRARIAN.

Sir John Templeton once said: "It is impossible to produce superior performance unless you do something different from the majority." As touched on previously, a successful investor must be prepared to be a contrarian. A benchmark can only be beaten when deviating from it – and it should be remembered this may involve periods of underperformance.

However, it should also be remembered that remaining committed to an over-arching strategy over time can be rewarding. Whilst acknowledging that a portfolio can contain a blend of strategies and preferences at any point in time, the overall objective of the portfolios run by the website www.johnbaronportfolios.co.uk is to search for and hold companies which are adding value and creating wealth – often by solving problems.

This company-specific approach has more than outpaced the general advance of markets over time. And by remaining focused on such an approach, investors can better see volatility as an opportunity – and capitalise from it.

7. SEIZE THE ADVANTAGE!

Some have suggested it can be difficult for private investors to compete with the professional fund managers – the pension funds, banks, investment houses and wealth managers. Yet the private investor has many advantages – the most important being time.

Many professional fund managers are trapped into a three-monthly cycle of trustee or actuary meetings, which encourages the shadowing of benchmarks. Private investors are free of this restraint. They can afford to take a longer-term view, and therefore stand a better chance of recognising mispricing and being able to capitalise from it.

To benefit from this natural advantage, patience is a virtue. Unloved assets can take time to come right, but then more than make up for lost time when they do. Warren Buffett once said: "The stock market is a device for transferring money from the impatient to the patient."

8. KEEP IT SIMPLE.

Meanwhile, it is important investors remember that investment is best kept simple to succeed. Complexity usually adds cost, risks confusion and hinders performance. When diversifying a portfolio, do not use too many different asset classes – the simpler, the better. But perhaps more importantly, investors should avoid overly complicated investments – especially if they are difficult to understand.

Accordingly, the website portfolios avoid hedge funds, absolute return funds, structured products, multi-manager funds and any other investment vehicle or approach which have high costs and poor transparency. Many tend not to live up to expectations.

In keeping investment simple, investors are also keeping costs down. Picking complicated or expensive products can easily cost a further 1.5% a year in fees – this may not sound a lot, but it can materially affect the final sum achieved. A £100-a-month investment producing a 5% annual return will be worth £150,000 after 40 years. But if a further 1.5% in annual costs is deducted, the final portfolio value will fall to just £105,000. This is a significant difference.

9. BE SCEPTICAL OF 'EXPERT' FORECASTS.

At the very least, question consensus forecasts. The renowned economist J. K. Galbraith once said: "Pundits forecast not because they know, but because they are asked." Successful investors tend to be sceptical – after all, one of the prerequisites of being a contrarian is to question the consensus.

In doing so, such investors are asking what could go wrong – their default position is not to own a stock. This contrasts with those fund managers who are more focused on short-term relative performance for fear of being left behind by their peers – scepticism takes a back seat as non-ownership is less of a possibility.

10. HARNESS EINSTEIN'S EIGHTH WONDER.

One should never ignore the magic of compounding – allegedly described by Einstein as the eighth wonder of the world. Compounding is the regular reinvesting of interest or dividends to the original sum invested, with the effect of creating higher total returns (capital plus income) over time. Time and a decent rate of return allow the concept to fully bloom.

£100 a month invested over 20 years and producing a 3% annual total return (the dividends/interest are not withdrawn) will produce a final portfolio value of £32,912. If the rate increases to 7.5% (the average long-term return for US equities) then the final figure rises to £135,587. The challenge is to achieve the higher rate of return. Again, the message is clear – start early, be patient and try not to interrupt the magic of compounding.

* * *

Having acknowledged the importance of investment principles and insights, most portfolios would benefit from using investment trusts when seeking stock market gains.

11. HARNESS THE POTENTIAL OF INVESTMENT TRUSTS.

Investment trusts are ideally suited to help the private investor. Despite being less well known, investment trusts have a superior performance record when compared to their better-known cousins – unit trusts and OEICs. They have on average beaten most of the global investment benchmarks whether delineated by region or country – unlike unit trusts and OEICs. Part of the reason is they have charged lower fees.

Another reason is because of their structure. Investment trusts are 'closed-ended', in that they have a fixed number of shares like other public companies such as M&S or BP. But instead of specialising in the management of clothes or oil, they specialise in the management of financial assets – usually other public companies. And as with other public companies, the share price does not always reflect the value of the assets – and usually stands at a discount.

This allows investors to take advantage of movements in the discount, which is often influenced by swings in sentiment towards the investment and/or underlying portfolio. Indeed, the market will usually present opportunities and risks that are often exaggerated by the fluctuation of discounts. Therein lies the investor's opportunity.

As a first step for those new to investment trusts, the ideal purchase is when a trust, run by a fund manager with a good long-term track record, stands at a wider-than-average discount – possibly because of a market wobble or the sector and/or manager is out of favour. It is usually wise to ignore the short-term noise and focus on the long term. Should sentiment improve, the investor benefits from both the underlying assets rising in price and the discount narrowing.

The ideal sale is when the discount has narrowed considerably from its average and factors may suggest caution, such as a change in manager or outlook for the underlying markets. Should a portfolio's assets fall in price, investors can further suffer from a widening of the discount. Needless to say, there are many nuances to such trades.

A further consequence of the closed-ended structure is that, like other closed-ended companies, investment trusts can borrow to buy more assets. Historically, this has benefitted share prices because markets have tended to rise and such gearing has also enhanced the returns from good fund management. But gearing can make for a volatile share price which is another reason to monitor the discount, as well as the level, cost and duration of the debt, and to see investment trusts as a long-term endeavour.

Other factors to take into account when judging the value of an investment trust include the reputation of the manager and the investment house, the underlying strategy, the outlook for the sector or region, the valuation of both the trust relative to its peer group and the portfolio relative to its universe, the level of management and any performance fees, and whether the portfolio's income is covering the trust's dividend and the extent of its revenue reserves (particularly if investing for income).

Changes regarding most of these factors can, to varying degrees, influence swings in sentiment. Capitalising on such swings can be profitable in the short term. However, it should be remembered that such an approach is best employed when initiating a long-term holding. Choosing and sticking with a trust which has a good track record often results in better long-term performance than constantly dealing in an attempt to capture short-term price movements.

Website portfolios

Words and theories can only be tested when put into action. The website www.johnbaronportfolios.co.uk reports on the progress of seven real and benchmarked investment trust portfolios, including same-day details of trades, new portfolio weightings and yields. Members are informed by email whenever the website is updated. The portfolios pursue a range of strategies and income profiles, whilst adhering to the investment principles and insights touched upon previously.

Four of the portfolios reflect an investment journey over time and so are named after the seasons. Spring's objective is capital growth courtesy of a portfolio comprised entirely of equities. Over time, the bond and 'other' less correlated elements increase to both generate a higher income and to help diversify holdings and so protect past gains. The Winter portfolio finishes with a yield of 5.9% at time of writing.

The three remaining equity portfolios pursue distinct objectives. The LISA portfolio helps smaller portfolios capitalise on the Government's Lifetime ISA (LISA) proposals – and therefore could be seen as a precursor to the four 'seasonal' portfolios. The Thematic portfolio focuses exclusively on special situations. Meanwhile, the Dividend portfolio seeks a high and rising income and yields 4.9%.

Whilst never complacent, the portfolios are performing well relative to their respective benchmarks – the website's Performance page has more details. Meanwhile, both the Rationale and Diversification pages have a statistic summary of the portfolios and overview of the other portfolio pages, whilst the Subscription page gives details of the seven-day trial allowing free access to the website's closed pages.

Andy Bell

ANDY BELL *is chief executive and co-founder of AJ Bell (ajbell.co.uk), one of the UK's largest providers of online investment platforms and stockbroker services. Graduating from Nottingham University in 1987 with a first-class degree in Mathematics, he qualified as a Fellow of the Institute of Actuaries in 1993 and started AJ Bell two years later alongside Nicholas Littlefair.*

Andy is the principal driving force behind the business, and his focus is increasingly on future strategy and growth opportunities. He is also a published author with the bestselling guide to do-it-yourself investing called The DIY Investor *(Harriman House, 2017).*

"PICKING FUNDS IS EASIER THAN YOU MIGHT THINK."

How to Be a Successful DIY Investor

H UNDREDS OF THOUSANDS of individuals in the UK face the same predicament, namely where to invest their hard-earned money in order to generate adequate returns to hit their financial goals.

This applies to individuals who are just getting into a savings habit and people who have already amassed a sizeable fortune.

I don't need to tell you the importance of saving for the future. There are plenty of articles in the media about the dangers of not having enough money in retirement. Instead, my mission is to ensure people have the easiest journey possible to find suitable products and make investments relevant to their personal goals.

Finding suitable investments involves a process but it isn't that complicated to follow. Many people simply need a helping hand on their journey and they'll soon find out that investing can be relatively straightforward.

The internet has fuelled the age of the DIY investor and, in turn, that's led to a wealth of information relating to why, how and in what to invest.

The call for assistance isn't only coming from people still in the early stages of saving for the future. You'd be amazed at how many individuals who already have some money under their belt still don't know where to put their cash in order to generate a return better than inflation.

The advent of pension freedoms in recent years has changed the landscape completely. Not being forced to buy an annuity when you retire has led to a proliferation of people becoming interested in investing.

On a smaller scale, some individuals may have been offered a generous cash sum to transfer out of a defined benefit pension scheme, and even they need help understanding where best to park that money.

For the most, being in control of savings including your pension is liberating but it is also nerve-racking. It doesn't have to be.

Taking the funds route

Anyone inexperienced with investing or lacking confidence should start with investment funds rather than individual stocks, in my opinion.

You benefit from diverse exposure to lots of assets, meaning there are plenty of things in your underlying portfolio to cushion any problems experienced by a single asset. If you owned individual shares then you would directly feel the pain if one of them fell by a large amount on bad news, for example.

There are various different types of funds on the market which either passively track an index or are actively managed by an individual or a team within an asset management business.

For this chapter of the book I'll focus on actively managed funds, principally unit trusts and OEICs (open-ended investment companies). Most of the same principles I'll shortly discuss apply to investment trusts as well.

Active management means someone else is making the investment decisions on a day-to-day basis, namely a fund manager. Your job is to find an investment fund whose strategy suits your investment goal, time horizon and risk appetite. That's not a straightforward task. There are thousands of funds on the market and varying levels of fund manager quality. I'll explain how to filter the pack in a second.

Competition between fund managers to deliver the best performance is fierce. The more successful the fund, the more money the manager makes, which means their interests and yours are very much aligned.

If you do not see yourself having the time, energy or inclination to trade individual company shares, investing through funds can be an efficient way to get exposure to all sorts of markets across the globe – including equities (another word for stocks and shares), bonds, commercial property and many other asset classes.

Even sophisticated DIY investors will often use funds in their portfolio, if only to access sectors or geographical regions as an easier way to get exposure than through individual company shares. If you want exposure to a fast-growing emerging market, for example, then a fund is one of the best ways to do this.

I will now run you through five important steps for how to choose the best funds for your needs.

1. ASK YOURSELF: WHAT DO YOU WANT TO ACHIEVE?

Picking funds is easier than you might think. It requires a systematic approach and a short amount of time for in-depth research once you've built a short list of products that meet your needs.

You should always start by writing down your investment goal and time horizon for achieving that goal; i.e. why you want to invest, how much you want to make and when you will need to access that money.

For example, let's say you are a 40-year-old who wants to build up an investment portfolio that will pay for your child's university education in ten years' time; alternatively you might be a 50-year-old who wants to have a decent sized ISA in 15 years' time to bolster a workplace pension.

You then need to establish your appetite for risk. For example, it's no good buying a fund with high-risk assets like biotech firms or miners if you have to rely on that money in five years' time to pay certain bills. Those types of businesses can generate high returns – but they can also experience large losses if drug trials fail or commodity prices are weak, for example.

In contrast, buying a very low-risk fund may not be appropriate if you need to make 12%+ annual returns in order to hit your investment goal. You need to find a balance between taking on enough risk to generate the desired returns and not being too bold so as to risk losing a large chunk of your money.

Importantly, you may need to rethink your time horizon if your financial goal requires you to take excessive risks. It is better to be invested for a bit longer than to go in all guns blazing with high-risk investments and hope nothing goes wrong.

Income, growth or both?

Investors fall into different camps. Some want to generate a regular income from their investments, particularly people in retirement. Others don't need income at present and simply want to grow the value of their investments over time. And there are people who want a bit of both.

It is fairly easy to see which funds offer income, growth or both as they will either have the styles in their product title or it will be clearly explained on their website. Many investment platforms will also have fund screening systems to help you filter the funds universe.

2. DON'T LIMIT YOURSELF TO ONLY BUYING FUNDS THAT HAVE DONE WELL IN THE PAST.

There will be a temptation at this point to pick the funds which have the best past performance data. Many people assume a fund that has done well in the past will continue to thrive in the future. They may also ignore funds that haven't done well, presuming they are inferior products.

Don't make this mistake. You need to understand the bigger picture, namely how the broader markets were performing and whether a fund should have unperformed or outperformed due to the style of their investment strategy either being out of, or in, favour.

I would look at discrete annual performance data over at least five years; a ten-year period is even better. That will show you if a fund has been fairly consistent with its returns or whether it simply had one or two good years over a decade which made its headline data (also known as cumulative data) look attractive.

For example, let's say a fund has gone up 80% over ten years. It may have seen eight years with negative or flat performance but had two amazing years (perhaps because the overall market was soaring) with which to achieve that large overall performance when looking at a ten-year view.

It is important to recognise that not all managers who are performing poorly are doing a bad job. It may well be that their investment style is out of favour.

They might be value investors who only buy stocks when they are really cheap in the belief that the market has priced them incorrectly. They may struggle when the market is chasing growth stocks, even ones that are trading on high valuations.

The fund will stand a chance of having a stronger period of performance when its style comes back into favour.

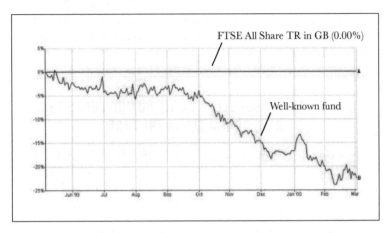

The chart above illustrates how a well-known fund underperformed the broader stock market by more than 22% in less than a year. Would you buy that fund if it appeared on your list when filtering the market? Many people would probably say no. That would have been the wrong decision, as the next chart illustrates:

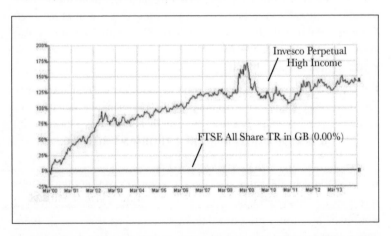

The fund in question is Invesco Perpetual High Income, which went on to outperform the market by 143% over the subsequent ten years.

The fund manager during that period was Neil Woodford who now runs a selection of well-known funds including Woodford Equity Income Fund.

3. UNDERSTAND EACH FUND'S INVESTMENT PROCESS.

This is where you will have to do a bit of legwork. It is paramount to understand how a fund manager will use your money. You must understand their investment process, namely what they want to achieve and how they will do so.

I would steer clear of funds that fail to properly explain their process. You need to have utmost faith and trust in a fund manager; so why would you hand over money not knowing how they will use it?

Examples of processes include:

- Backing young companies which have the potential to be much bigger in the future and which could disrupt traditional markets.

- Finding companies which generate high returns on the money they invest in their business.

- Building a portfolio of companies tied into thematic investment topics such as profiting from an ageing population.

I have great respect for fund managers who are disciplined and have a clear plan for what they want in an investment.

For example, asset manager Liontrust prides itself on having detailed investment processes published on its website, saying this helps investors to understand how its teams manage money and the fact that the process is "predictable and repeatable".

It is helpful to understand a fund's process before you invest. Good fund managers are hard to find and you should only invest when you believe they can outperform, otherwise use a passive solution such as an ETF.

4. KNOW WHICH ARE THE IMPORTANT BITS ON FACTSHEETS.

Regulation has led to the introduction of a two-page factsheet called KIID, which is better known as a *key investor information document*. It aims to provide investors with a transparent and succinct overview of funds in a common format.

Its aim is to help clarify the facts and help you find out more about whether a fund could meet your investment goals.

It details what the fund is trying to achieve and how it is going about it, although you may find this information to be very basic compared with the way some asset managers discuss their process on their website.

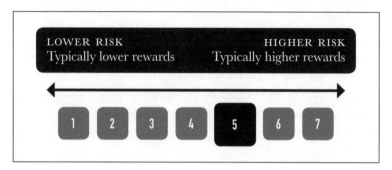

The KIID will show the annual charge for the fund and it gives a risk profile, scoring from 1 (lowest risk) to 7 (highest risk). It will also show some past performance data.

Admittedly the KIID looks like very dry reading, particularly as it is a text-heavy, visually unappealing document. However, I would urge you to read all the information as it does provide valuable insight into how a fund works and what it will cost you to own.

You may find references to factsheets which will either be longer documents produced by the fund manager including commentary on how the fund is performing and a list of the largest holdings; or they will be a link to various data points on the fund's performance, history and charts, such as those offered by Morningstar.

You may also see reference to something called the *Sharpe ratio*. This is a quick way of thinking about whether you are being adequately rewarded for the risks you are taking.

If a fund takes a lot of risk and you are getting a good return, it is likely to have a good Sharpe ratio. If the fund takes a lot of risk and you aren't getting a good return, the Sharpe ratio will be much less.

As a rule of thumb, a fund with a ratio above 1.0 is said to be doing well. A ratio above 2.0 is considered to be excellent.

5. LOOK AT THE RANGE OF 'FAVOURITE FUNDS' LISTS.

Researching funds isn't as hard as you might think. However, I appreciate many people just want to be presented with a ready-made short list of good funds.

Fortunately there are many places which provide such a helping hand. Firstly, take a look at the wide range of 'top fund' lists produced by various financial services providers.

For example, AJ Bell Youinvest has a 'favourite funds' list which includes 50 actively managed funds selected for being low-cost, great value for money, having a proven track record and a high-quality fund management team.

A lot of work goes into creating these types of lists. Criteria used by the bigger financial services companies flagging their preferred funds will range from mathematical analysis and interviews with fund managers to votes by a judging panel of investment experts.

You may also wish to look at ratings given to funds by the likes of Morningstar and Lipper. Finally, read the personal finance sections of newspapers and specialist magazines/websites such as *Shares* (www.sharesmagazine.co.uk) and *Money Observer* (www.moneyobserver.com).

Alistair Blair

Following a degree in PPE at Oxford, ALISTAIR BLAIR *set up a fish business which failed after three years. He rehabilitated his employment credentials via an MBA at Manchester Business School, which led to ten years in the City – in corporate finance for Hill Samuel, and a stint at Fidelity Investments doing work of a corporate finance nature on holdings in its funds.*

After a disagreement with the boss he turned to journalism, working as a freelance writer for the Investors Chronicle, *the* Financial Times *and many other publications. He wrote a popular book about share price charting, won a Business Writer of the Year award and founded the 'No Free Lunch' column at the* Investors Chronicle, *which he wrote weekly for 15 years until 2012.*

During this time he also launched a new fish business, which eventually grew to require his full commitment. He continues to run this business, whilst keeping an eye on his SIPP.

"IN MY YOUTH
I TRIED MARKET
TIMING AND
DISCOVERED I WAS
NOT VERY GOOD
AT IT."

Eleven Quick Tips for Time-Limited Private Investors

THE ONLY INVESTMENT fund I run is my own SIPP. I set this up about ten years ago and the results have been quite satisfactory. I work full time in my own company and aim to spend only a few hours per month on the SIPP.

1. THE LONGER YOU HOLD IT, THE BETTER YOU KNOW IT.

I invest for the long term. I wouldn't buy a share which I didn't hope to hold for at least several years. This reduces the time required to monitor the portfolio – a significant advantage for a time-limited investor. The longer you hold it, the better you know it. This stance also makes one very choosy.

2. BE CLEAR ON SELLING.

Nevertheless, you need to be clear on selling. A share that triples inside a year is likely to be poised for regret. Mistakes are fuzzier, but I also try to be realistic about shares which lose value because my initial analysis of the prospects appears within a few months to have been fundamentally erroneous.

3. A PORTFOLIO OF 15–25 SHARES IS ENOUGH.

I own 15 to 25 shares. If I am at the top end of this range and find a new attractive share, I sell a holding in order to buy the new share. I aim to review my holdings when their annual results are announced; 25 holdings (or two reviews a month) takes up all the time I have available. At the other end of the scale, a portfolio of under 15 shares would be too prone to shock.

4. DON'T LET SINGLE HOLDINGS EXCEED 15% OF YOUR PORTFOLIO.

Successful selections which approach 15% of the portfolio value can also cause shock and are trimmed to that level.

5. DON'T TIME MARKETS – JUST HOLD GOOD COMPANIES FOR DECADES.

I am fully invested at all times. In my youth I tried market timing and discovered I was not very good at it. My investing horizon is decades away and I am optimistic that soundly managed companies selling good products or services will prosper in the long term.

6. DON'T PANIC, RE-EVALUATE.

Do not sell in a panic after sudden price collapses based on normal commercial disappointments. Re-evaluate against the original investment proposition, which is always based on the long term. If the long-term case still holds, the eventual rehabilitation would present an opportunity to increase the holding. Remember that the longer you hold it, the better you know it... warts and all.

7. FORGET FALLING SHARES.

Never buy a falling share. It's like trying to catch a knife. But (as with rule 6) do review shares whose charts form a nicely shaped, months-long bottom including at least several weeks of sustained recent upside.

8. SAY NO TO IPOS.

Never buy an initial public offering (IPO). The information available is too likely to have been edited by the sellers.

9. BEWARE BAD BALANCE SHEETS.

Never buy a share with a lousy balance sheet. That's not an investment – it's a speculation.

10. MANAGEMENT MATTERS.

Evaluate the management separately from the company's commercial proposition. Look at their histories and how long they have worked together. In general, avoid new top teams. And even with established teams, if you're not convinced they take outside shareholders' interests seriously, do not be spellbound by sheer commercial appeal.

11. DON'T RUSH TO BUY.

Found an exciting new share? It still looks great after your initial review? It's very energising, isn't it? Resist immediate action. If you're planning to hold it for years, you don't need to rush to buy it. Have another look next week.

Good luck.

Michael van Biema

MICHAEL VAN BIEMA *is the founder of the van Biema Value Partners, LLC. Mr van Biema was on the faculty of Columbia Business School from 1992 to 2004, where he taught general corporate finance, capital markets, securities analysis, value investing and entrepreneurial finance in both the regular and executive MBA programs. He has also served as director of a multi-year, multimillion-dollar research project into productivity in the service sector funded by the Alfred P. Sloan Foundation.*

He received his BA from Princeton University in Electrical Engineering and his PhD from Columbia University. Before joining the faculty of Columbia Business School he was involved in several start-up ventures.

Mr van Biema is the author of numerous publications, including an article in the Harvard Business Review *entitled 'Managing Productivity in the Service Sector' (summer 1998), and co-author of the books* Value Investing: From Graham to Buffett and Beyond *(Wiley, 2001), and* Concentrated Investing *(Wiley, 2016). He has lectured internationally on value investing.*

"IN GENERAL, TIME IS THE ENEMY OF THE INVESTOR. BUT THERE IS A WAY TO MAKE TIME YOUR FRIEND."

Concentrated Value Investing in Six Simple Steps

1. WHAT MATTERS MOST IS THE PRICE PAID FOR THE VALUE RECEIVED.

A BASIC PREMISE of modern investing is that risk controls return, and the higher the risk the higher the expected return. This seems quite reasonable: if I place a wager, the lower my odds of winning (the higher my risk), the higher my return should be (the better the payout I should be given).

This thinking, however, has been translated to the investment field with the idea that the higher an investment's volatility (range of outcomes), the higher the expected return (payout) should be.

This would also be sensible – except for a couple of things.

The first and most important is *time*. When one places a bet, that bet is good for a single instant in time and that instant is determined by the game one is playing (the coin is flipped, the dice are rolled, the wheel is spun). In investing, one places one's bet in a single instant in time but the game is only over when you, the investor, decide to sell.

In addition, your 'chip' – your investment's actual value – is perhaps less than you thought when you purchased it, *but also perhaps more*. The problem is that you usually do not know exactly what the value to you is until the game is over.

So equating an investment's volatility to its risk is perhaps a useful concept for the short-term investor or for an investor who may be a forced seller. But for an investor who has a long-term time horizon and the necessary capital backing not to be forced into selling, the concept of volatility as risk is flawed. For a long-term investor, risk is more correctly defined as the probability of the permanent loss of invested capital. This is why most long-term investors stress the concept of the *margin of safety* as part of their investment approaches.

The margin of safety of an investment can be defined as the amount of money that can be reasonably estimated to be returned to an investor if things go wrong. My favorite example of this is that of a jewelry company that makes simple gold bracelets, the stock of which one can buy for $10 a share. If one took that company's inventory and melted it down and sold it purely for the value of the gold, and if that gold was worth $9 a share, the margin of safety of the company would be 90%. The risk in purchasing the shares of this company therefore depends not on the volatility of the share price, but rather on the difference between the per-share purchase price and the value per share of the company's inventory. In fact, if this company's stock became more volatile and one were now able to buy the shares at $8 per share, the investment would not become more risky but rather far less risky.

In other words, what really matters in investing is the price paid.

2. MAKE TIME YOUR FRIEND.

In general, time is the enemy of the investor. The longer it takes for an idea to work out, the lower the return realized. So many investors limit themselves to ideas with hard catalysts that should in theory at least define the time period for an investment. But there is a way to make time your friend. You can find investments that pay you to wait.

Even if there is no hard catalyst for the realization of value, certain investments produce an attractive cash return so that one can wait for mean reversion to take its course. Typically, this cash flow comes in the form of dividends, but in certain situations it may come in other forms as well, such as buy backs and liquidation payouts. Another important factor in making time your friend is to focus your energies on companies that have pristine balance sheets. A company that is highly leveraged can force your hand in difficult environments and this is something that you, as a long-term investor, want to try to avoid.

3. YOU NEED A CONCENTRATED PORTFOLIO IF YOU DON'T WANT INDEX-LIKE RETURNS.

Portfolio management is another dimension of risk that must be managed. The two ways of thinking about managing portfolio risk are through diversification or concentration. Managing portfolio risk through diversification is simple and works. It has only one significant drawback: it has a strong tendency to generate index-like returns. With a 15-stock portfolio you have a 1:4 chance of outperforming the market, with a 250-stock portfolio your chances drop to 1:50. A concentrated portfolio is more difficult to manage successfully and will be significantly more volatile, but for the long-term investor it will not have the same tendency to generate index-like returns.

4. THERE ARE LOTS OF PRETTY GOOD INVESTMENT IDEAS AND RELATIVELY FEW GREAT ONES.

To misquote Mark Twain: "I wrote something long, because I did not have time to write something short." Investing is above all else a field that requires great personal discipline. In terms of portfolio management this means that less is frequently more. While I have co-authored an entire book on the topic of portfolio concentration,* perhaps the most important message it brings is that most managers are not selective enough in forming their portfolios and that higher levels of performance are often achieved with higher levels of concentration.

Typically, one invests a large amount of time and effort in analyzing a company. After that investment of time and effort has been made, it is human nature to want to include that company in one's portfolio and realize a return. It is much more difficult to discard that effort and move on. But it appears that this willingness or discipline to move on can have a significant impact on a manager's long-term returns.

5. TIMING IS SOMEWHERE BETWEEN VERY HARD AND IMPOSSIBLE.

Timing things correctly is inherently somewhere between very hard and impossible. So if an investment's success depends on timing, beware.

* *Concentrated Investing: Strategies of the World's Greatest Concentrated Value Investors* (Wiley, 2016).

Many investors seem to make implicit assumptions about timing; this can be very dangerous.

6. ASK YOURSELF THREE QUESTIONS FOR EVERY SHARE.

Finally, for every position in your portfolio ask yourself the following three questions:*

1. What do I think it is worth?
2. Why doesn't the rest of the world understand what it is worth?
3. What is going to make it become what it is worth?

Not having good answers to these questions can be hazardous to the health of your portfolio.

---

* I am greatly indebted to Alan Kahn for coming up with these questions in the context of interviewing our managers.

John C. Bogle

JOHN C. BOGLE *is Founder of The Vanguard Group, Inc., and President of the Bogle Financial Markets Research Center.*

The Vanguard Group is the world's largest mutual fund organization, and comprises more than 370 mutual funds with current assets totaling more than $4 trillion. Vanguard 500 Index Fund, the world's first index fund, was founded by Mr Bogle in 1975. For his "exemplary achievement, excellence of practice, and true leadership," Mr Bogle holds the AIMR Award for Professional Excellence, and is also a member of the Hall of Fame of the Fixed Income Analysts Society, Inc.

In 1999, he was named by Fortune *magazine as one of the investment industry's four 'Giants of the 20th Century.' He was named one of the world's 100 most powerful and influential people by* TIME *magazine in 2004.*

"IN THE FIELD
OF INVESTMENT
MANAGEMENT,
FOXES COME
AND GO, BUT
HEDGEHOGS ARE
FOREVER."

Investing Insights of the $4 Trillion Man

1. THERE'S NO ESCAPING RISK.

ONCE YOU DECIDE to put your money to work to build long-term wealth, you have to decide, not whether to take risk, but what kind of risk you wish to take. "Do what you will, capital is at hazard," just as the Prudent Man Rule assures us.

Yes, money in a savings account is dollar-safe, but those safe dollars are apt to be substantially eroded by inflation, a risk that almost guarantees you will fail to reach your capital accumulation goals.

And yes, money in the stock market is very risky over the short term, but, if well-diversified, should provide remarkable growth with a high degree of consistency over the long term.

2. BUY RIGHT AND HOLD TIGHT.

The most critical decision you face is getting the proper allocation of assets in your investment portfolio – stocks for growth of capital and growth of income, bonds for conservation of capital and current income. Once you get your balance right, then just hold tight, no matter how high a greedy stock market flies, nor how low a frightened market plunges. Change the allocation only as your investment profile changes. Begin by considering a 50/50 stock/bond balance, then raise the stock allocation if:

1. You have many years remaining to accumulate wealth.
2. The amount of capital you have at stake is modest (i.e. your first investment in a corporate savings plan).
3. You have little need for current income.
4. You have the courage to ride out the booms and busts with reasonable equanimity.

As these factors are reversed, reduce your stock allocation accordingly.

3. TIME IS YOUR FRIEND, IMPULSE YOUR ENEMY.

Think long term, and don't allow transitory changes in stock prices to alter your investment program. There is a lot of noise in the daily volatility of the stock market, which too often is a tale "told by an idiot, full of sound and fury, signifying nothing".

Stocks may remain overvalued, or undervalued, for years. Realize that one of the greatest sins of investing is to be captured by the siren song of the market, luring you into buying stocks when they are soaring and selling when they are plunging. Impulse is your enemy. Why? Because market timing is impossible. Even if you turn out to be right when you sold stocks just before a decline (a rare occurrence!), where on earth would you ever get the insight that tells you the right time to get back in? One correct decision is tough enough. Two correct decisions are nigh on impossible.

Time is your friend. If, over the next 25 years, stocks produce a 7.5% return and a savings account produces a paltry 1% return, $10,000 would grow by $51,000 in stocks vs less than $3,000 in savings. (After 2.5% inflation, $24,000 vs a loss of $3,000). Give yourself all the time you can.

4. REALISTIC EXPECTATIONS: THE BAGEL AND THE DOUGHNUT.

These two different kinds of baked goods symbolize the two distinctively different elements of stock market returns. It is hardly farfetched to consider that investment return – dividend yields and earnings growth – is the bagel of the stock market, for the investment return on stocks reflects their underlying character: nutritious, crusty, and hard-boiled.

By the same token, speculative return – wrought by any change in the price that investors are willing to pay for each dollar of earnings – is the spongy doughnut of the market, reflecting changing public opinion about stock valuations, from the soft sweetness of optimism to the acid sourness of pessimism.

The substantive bagel-like economics of investing are almost inevitably productive, but the flaky, doughnut-like emotions of investors are anything but steady – sometimes productive, sometimes counterproductive.

In the long run, it is investment return that rules the day. Since the beginning of the 20th century, the annual investment return was 9%, almost precisely equal to the stock market's return of 9.5%. In the 1970s and 2000s, investors soured on the economy's prospects, and tumbling price-earnings ratios provided a negative annual speculative return averaging -5.3%, reducing a solid annual investment return of 7.6% to a market return of just 2.3%. In the 1980s and 1990s, on the other hand, the outlook sweetened, and a soaring P/E ratio produced a sugary 7.4% annual speculative boost to an investment return of 10.1%. Result: an unprecedented total return on stocks averaging 17.5% per year during two consecutive decades.

The lesson: Enjoy the bagel's healthy nutrients, and don't count on the doughnut's sweetness to enhance them.

Conclusion: Realistic expectations for the coming decade suggest returns well below the market's long-term average.

5. WHY LOOK FOR THE NEEDLE IN THE HAYSTACK? BUY THE HAYSTACK!

It was Cervantes who warned us, "Look not for a needle in a haystack". While that phrase has become deeply imbedded in our language, it has yet to gain acceptance from most mutual fund investors. Too many of us spend countless hours poring over fund records, getting information from news articles and television interviews and friends, and from hyperbolic fund advertisements and well-intentioned fund-rating services. We devote all this time and effort in an attempt to buy the right stocks, bet on the right investment styles, and pick the right money managers – in each case, in advance.

When we do so, we rely largely on past performance, ignoring the fact that what worked yesterday seldom works tomorrow – the past is rarely prologue. Investing in equities entails four risks: stock risk, style risk, manager risk, and market risk. The first three of these risks can easily be eliminated, simply by owning the entire stock market – owning the haystack, as it were – and holding it forever.

Yes, stock market risk remains, and it is quite large enough, thank you. So why pile those other three risks on top of it? If you're not certain you're right (and who can be?), diversify.

Owning the entire stock market is the ultimate diversifier. If you can't find the needle, buy the haystack.

6. MINIMIZE THE CROUPIERS' TAKE.

The resemblance of the stock market to the casino is not far-fetched. Yes, the stock market is a positive-sum game and the gambling casino is a zero-sum game... but only before the costs of playing each game are deducted. After the heavy costs of financial intermediaries (commissions, management fees, taxes, etc.) are deducted, beating the stock market is inevitably a loser's game. Just as, after the croupiers' wide rake descends, beating the casino is inevitably a loser's game. All investors as a group must earn the market's return before costs, and lose to the market after costs, and by the exact amount of those costs.

Your greatest chance of earning the market's return, therefore, is to reduce the croupiers' take to the bare-bones minimum. When you read about stock market returns, realize that the financial markets are not for sale, except at a high price. The difference is crucial. If the market's return is 7.5% before costs, and intermediation costs are approximately 2%, then investors earn 5.5%. Compounded over 50 years, 5.5% takes $10,000 to $145,000. But at 7.5%, the final value leaps to $372,000 – more than two and a half times as much – just by eliminating the croupier's take.

7. BEWARE OF FIGHTING THE LAST WAR.

Too many investors – individuals and institutions alike – are constantly making investment decisions based on the lessons of the recent, or even the extended, past. They seek technology stocks after they have emerged victorious from the last war; they worry about inflation after it becomes the accepted bogeyman, they buy bonds after the stock market has plunged.

You should not ignore the past, but neither should you assume that a particular cyclical trend will last forever. None does. Just because some investors insist on fighting the last war, you don't need to do so yourself. It doesn't work for very long.

8. SIR ISAAC NEWTON'S REVENGE ON WALL STREET – REVERSION TO THE MEAN.

Through all history, investments have been subject to a sort of Law of Gravity: what goes up must go down, and, oddly enough, what goes down must go up. Not always, of course (companies that die rarely live again), and not necessarily in the absolute sense, but relative to the overall market norm.

For example, stock market returns that substantially exceed the investment returns generated by earnings and dividends during one period tend to revert and fall well short of that norm during the next period. Like a pendulum, stock prices swing far above their underlying values, only to swing back to fair value and then far below it.

Another example: From the start of 1997 through March 2000, NASDAQ stocks (+230%) soared past NYSE-listed stocks (+20%), only to come to a screeching halt. During the subsequent year, NASDAQ stocks lost 67% of their value, while NYSE stocks lost just 7%, reverting to the original market value relationship (about one to five) between the so-called 'New Economy' and the 'Old Economy.'

Reversion to the mean is found everywhere in the financial jungle, for the mean is a powerful magnet that, in the long run, finally draws everything back to it.

9. THE HEDGEHOG BESTS THE FOX.

The Greek poet Archilochus tells us, "the fox knows many things, but the hedgehog knows one great thing." The fox – artful, sly, and astute – represents the financial institution that knows many things about complex markets and sophisticated marketing. The hedgehog – whose sharp spines give it almost impregnable armor when it curls into a ball – is the financial institution that knows only one great thing: long-term investment success is based on simplicity.

The wily foxes of the financial world justify their existence by propagating the notion that an investor can survive only with the benefit of their artful knowledge and expertise. Such assistance, alas, does not come cheap, and the costs it entails tend to consume more value-added performance than even the most cunning of foxes can provide. Result: the annual returns earned for investors by financial intermediaries such as mutual funds have averaged less than 80% of the stock market's annual return.

The hedgehog, on the other hand, knows that the truly great investment strategy succeeds, not because of its complexity or cleverness, but because of its simplicity and low cost. The hedgehog diversifies broadly, buys and holds, and keeps expenses to the bare-bones minimum. The ultimate hedgehog – the all-market index fund – operated at minimal cost and with minimal portfolio turnover, virtually guarantees nearly 100% of the market's return to the investor.

In the field of investment management, foxes come and go, but hedgehogs are forever.

10. STAY THE COURSE: THE SECRET OF INVESTING IS THAT THERE IS NO SECRET.

When you consider these previous nine rules, realize that they are about neither magic and *legerdemain*, nor about forecasting the unforecastable, nor about betting at long and ultimately insurmountable odds, nor about learning some great secret of successful investing. For there is no great secret, only the majesty of simplicity. These rules are about elementary arithmetic, about fundamental and unarguable principles, and about that most uncommon of all attributes, common sense.

Owning the entire stock market through an index fund – all the while balancing your portfolio with an appropriate allocation to an all-bond market index fund – with its cost-efficiency, its tax-efficiency, and its assurance of earning for you the market's return, is by definition a winning strategy. But if you only follow one final rule for successful investing, perhaps the most important principle of all investment wisdom is: stay the course!

Anthony Bolton

ANTHONY BOLTON, *a graduate of Trinity College, Cambridge, worked in investment management for over 40 years, most of this time in the City of London. He is considered one of the UK's most successful fund managers.*

His first job was with a small merchant bank, Keyser Ullman, from where he went on to join a South Africa-owned investment firm, Schlesingers. In 1979 he joined Fidelity International – part of the Boston-based Fidelity Group. He started at the time they were launching their first four funds specifically for UK investors and he ran one of these, the Fidelity Special Situations Fund, for 28 years. During that time it averaged a return of just under 20% pa and became one of the largest funds for UK investors with over a quarter of a million investors. In 2010 he moved to Hong Kong for four years to run Fidelity China Special Situations PLC. He retired in 2014 but remains a director and advisor at Fidelity. He has also written a book about investment called Investing Against the Tide *(FT Prentice Hall, 2009).*

Anthony, who is 67 years old, lives in West Sussex and is married to Sarah. They have three children, Emma, 36, Olly, 33, and Ben, 29, and four grandchildren. Anthony loves listening to music, particularly opera, and his hobby is composing music.

"I WOULD RATHER
HAVE A GREAT
BUSINESS RUN
BY AVERAGE
MANAGEMENT
THAN A POOR
BUSINESS
RUN BY STARS."

Long-Term Lessons from a Legendary Run

INVESTMENT IS NOT an exact science, and I know of no successful professional investor who has not had to learn from experience the many pitfalls that lie in wait. Over the course of my 28 years managing the Fidelity Special Situations Fund, I had plenty of time to reflect on the factors that matter in becoming a successful stock picker. These are some of the lessons that I took from the experience:

1. UNDERSTAND THE BUSINESS FRANCHISE AND ITS QUALITY.

Businesses vary greatly in their quality and sustainability. It is essential to understand the business, how it makes money and its competitive position. Like Warren Buffett, my ideal was to find businesses with a valuable franchise which could sustain the business over many years. A simple question I asked was: How likely was the business to be here in ten years' time – and how likely was it to be more valuable than today?

2. UNDERSTAND THE KEY VARIABLES THAT DRIVE THE BUSINESS.

Identifying the key variables that affect a company's performance, and in particular those that it cannot control, such as currencies, interest rates and tax changes, is essential to understanding a share's dynamics. To my mind an ideal business is one that is largely in control of its own destiny. I remember the opposite of this, a UK chemical company I met many years ago. At one exchange rate it had a prosperous business: but at a higher value of sterling it was totally uncompetitive and possibly had no business at all.

3. FAVOUR SIMPLE OVER COMPLEX BUSINESSES.

If a business is very complex, it will be difficult to work out if it has a sustainable franchise. It may need experts to spot a flaw. The ability to generate cash is a very attractive attribute: in fact, the most favourable of all attributes. All else being equal, companies that need a lot of capital expenditure to keep going are less attractive than those that don't. A private equity specialist once told me the stock market overvalues growth and undervalues cash generation. Private equity investors do the opposite. On this measure I'm on the side of the private equity investors.

4. HEAR DIRECTLY FROM THE MANAGEMENT.

Candidness and lack of hyperbole are the key management attributes to look for. In my experience, second-hand information is always inferior to first-hand information. Having met hundreds of companies in many different industries over the years, the thing I valued most was hearing a candid, balanced view of a business. That means the minuses as well as the pluses (all businesses have both). I liked managers who did not overpromise but then consistently delivered a bit more than they indicated. Be most wary of those who promise the sky; they are unlikely to deliver. That said, I am in the Warren Buffett camp in that I would rather have a great business run by average management than a poor business run by stars.

5. AVOID 'DODGY' MANAGEMENTS AT ALL COSTS.

I used to think the dynamics of a strong-looking business would make up even for 'dodgy' management. Having invested in a few companies that have subsequently 'blown up', managements that are either unethical or that sail close to the wind became complete no-go areas for me. I learnt that, even with corporate governance checks and outside accountants, there are too many ways that senior people can pull the wool over an investor's eyes. Many years ago an Italian contact told me, helpfully, not to touch Parmalat for this reason. It turned out to be an excellent piece of advice. As Warren Buffett says, the CEO who misleads others in public may eventually mislead himself in private (as you are by now well aware I am, like many others, a great Buffett fan. The Berkshire Hathaway annual reports are a treasure trove of investment advice and financial wisdom).

6. TRY AND THINK TWO MOVES AHEAD OF THE CROWD.

Try to identify what is being ignored today which could re-excite interest in the future. The stock market doesn't look very far ahead and therefore, somewhat like chess, looking a bit further out than others often can pay dividends. I think I'm good at knowing the types of situation that will excite investors, where there can be 'blue sky' in the future. I would try to find companies where this was currently being ignored but would impact investor psychology again in the future.

7. UNDERSTAND THE BALANCE SHEET RISK.

If the stock picker has to learn only one lesson, this has to be near the top of the list. If investment is about limiting the downside and avoiding disaster, then taking on balance sheet risk should only be done with one's eyes open. Balance sheet risk has been the most common factor behind my worst investments. In my experience, most analysts are poor at assessing this risk and many do not analyse balance sheets at all. As well as debt in its various forms, one needs to be able to analyse pension fund deficits and value redeemable convertible preference shares where there is little likelihood of conversion. Both of these have a number of characteristics in common with conventional debt.

8. SEEK IDEAS FROM A WIDE RANGE OF SOURCES.

I liked lots of ideas from sources I believed to be well informed about particular companies or industries. The more there are to pick from, the more chances you have of finding a winner. The most obvious sources are not always the best. I particularly liked sources not widely used by most institutions. On the other hand I was not proud and pinching an idea from a competitor whom I rated was just as acceptable to me as from a stockbroker!

9. WATCH CLOSELY THE DEALING BY COMPANY INSIDERS.

No indicator is infallible, but dealings by directors of companies are a valuable confirming or non-confirming tool. Particularly look for multiple transactions. Buys are generally more important than sells and some directors have better records than others.

10. RE-EXAMINE YOUR INVESTMENT THESIS AT REGULAR INTERVALS.

Investment management is all about building conviction for an investment opportunity and then re-examining this conviction over time, particularly when new information arises. Conviction or strength of feeling is important and should be backed. However, conviction must not develop into pig-headedness. If the evidence changes, so should one's views. At any point you should be able to summarise the reasons you own a company's shares in just a few sentences.

11. FORGET THE PRICE YOU PAID FOR SHARES.

The price you paid is totally irrelevant; it is only psychologically important. Have no hesitation in cutting losses if the situation changes. A classic example of this was Deutsche Babcock, a German engineering conglomerate that was involved in a number of areas, including shipbuilding. Our analyst who covered the stock came into my office one morning in a very excited state. The chief executive, whom we admired and who had a good record, was leaving the company. He was also planning a management buyout of its best division, shipbuilding, which was the prime reason we owned the shares. I immediately told our trading desk to sell the whole position, aggressively if need be. Although I took a big loss on the position, a few months later the receivers were called in.

12. PAST PERFORMANCE ATTRIBUTION IS GENERALLY A WASTE OF TIME.

If life is about making mistakes and learning from them, so too is the stock market. However, performance attribution – the business of analysing in detail which stock or industry 'bets' a manager has made relative to an index or benchmark – has become very fashionable. However, as it mainly involves looking in the rear-view mirror, it tells you nothing about the future.

I recognise that, with balanced mandates, some attribution is necessary and customers such as pension fund trustees require it. Too often, however, the tendency is to believe the immediate past is going to be repeated in the future. When one is not doing well, to be constantly reminded of the fact by consultants is rarely a help, and in fact may well be counterproductive! Temperament is important. If you are a manic depressive, don't think of becoming an investor. It is important to treat success and failure with equanimity. On the other hand, analysing your mistakes ('Why was I wrong and were there ways of predicting this?') is different and very worthwhile.

13. PAY ATTENTION TO ABSOLUTE VALUATIONS.

Investors need some sort of reality check to avoid their being sucked into a stock at times of great exuberance. Looking at absolute valuations at times like this will help. I liked to buy stocks which within the next two years you could see would be on a single-figure price-earnings multiple, or have a free cash flow yield well above prevailing interest rates. If you only look at relative valuations, how stocks compare to each other, you can go seriously astray.

14. USE TECHNICAL ANALYSIS AS AN EXTRA INDICATOR.

Technical analysis excites widely different views amongst investment professionals. Some are passionate exponents, while others see it as nothing more than hocus-pocus. I viewed it as a framework for help in decision-making. It is one of the factors which helped me decide the size of bet I took. I used it as a confirming or denying factor. So if the technical analysis supported the fundamental analysis, I would be prepared to take a bigger position. If it didn't, I would take a smaller position. I would also re-examine my fundamental views to check we were not missing something if the technical situation deteriorated. I found it more useful the bigger the market capitalisation of a company.

15. AVOID MARKET TIMING AND MAJOR MACRO BETS.

I wanted to place my bets where I believed I had a competitive advantage. Many commentators have written over the years of the difficulty of timing the market consistently. I only had a strong view about the level or direction of the market perhaps five or six times in the 28 years managing the Special Situations Fund. The occasions when I had such strong views (bullish in March 2003, bearish in March 2006) did seem to be coming more frequently towards the end of my time managing the fund – maybe it's to do with getting old! Even then, I certainly wouldn't bet my whole fund on such a view. A time I might add a macro input was when I was trying to decide between two shares in an industry, where

I thought both were fundamentally attractive, but I only wanted to buy one. A macro view may then be the deciding factor in which to buy (say one benefited from a strong dollar and one did not).

16. BE A CONTRARIAN!

If an investment feels very 'comfortable' you are probably late. Try to invest against the crowd. Avoid getting more bullish as the share price rises. When nearly everyone is cautious about the outlook, they are probably wrong and things are going to get better. Equally, when very few are worried, *that* is the time to be most wary. I found the times I could be the most help to some of my less-experienced colleagues was when there was great optimism or pessimism. This was when I reminded them that the stock market was an excellent discounting mechanism. By the time everyone is worried about something it is normally largely in the price. Investors need to be constantly reminded that this is how markets work.

Jeroen Bos

Dutch investor **JEROEN BOS** *has lived in England since 1978. He has a diploma in Economics from the University of Sussex and has worked his entire career in the financial services industry, mainly in the City of London. He worked for many years at Panmure Gordon & Co, the stockbroker, and it was here that his interest in value investing developed. This process accelerated after the October 1987 stock market crash, during which time he took inspiration from* The Intelligent Investor *by Benjamin Graham.*

At the end of 2003 Jeroen joined Church House Investment Management to manage CH Deep Value (Bahamas), which in March 2012 became the CH Deep Value Investments Fund. He is the author of Deep Value Investing *(Harriman House, 2013 and 2018).*

He lives in Sussex, is married and has three sons.

"I AM A DUTCHMAN AND WE ARE KNOWN AROUND THE WORLD FOR BEING CAREFUL HOW WE SPEND OUR MONEY. VALUE INVESTING MADE IMMEDIATE SENSE TO ME."

How to Go Deep Value Diving for Bargain Shares

1. CHEAPNESS IS NOT ENOUGH.

I WAS FIRST introduced to the term 'value investing' shortly after I began my career in the City at the stockbrokers Panmure Gordon & Co in the early 1980s. I am a Dutchman and we are known around the world for being careful how we spend our money. Value investing made immediate sense to me, and the idea of getting something worth more than what I had paid for it was extremely appealing.

I soon came across lots of small metal bashers and textile companies trading at deep discounts to their net asset valuations. At that time there were many such stocks available in the market and I bought them eagerly. Unfortunately, they often proved to be dreadful investments. They would be trading at big discounts to net asset value (NAV) and had usually been loss-making for extended periods, with working capital positions that became increasingly constrained. They looked very cheap – and, unfortunately, remained that way.

Or got cheaper.

I continued to buy such stocks, attracted by their seeming cheapness, but my investment performance remained lacklustre at best. Undeterred, I kept looking for new value investing opportunities wherever I could find them. From this process I at least learned to read a balance sheet very quickly – something that has proved useful ever since. However, my investments all followed, more or less, the same story: they appeared to be trading at huge discounts, and carried on doing so quite happily after I bought them.

I was missing something – cheapness was not enough.

2. READ BENJAMIN GRAHAM.

So, as well as studying balance sheet after balance sheet, I read every article I could lay my hands on that dealt with value investing. My 'Eureka' moment came in 1987 when the equity markets around the world collapsed and a client of mine said to me: "This is the ideal time to read *The Intelligent Investor* again."

If there is one thing that you take away from this chapter it has to be to read Benjamin Graham's fantastic book. It will make you a better investor without you really having to try.

Back in 1987, I immediately went out and bought the book and read it cover to cover. I have reread it many times since. It helps the value investor to build a proper framework for investing and covers a huge number of issues to consider when thinking about investing. But one page from the book, in particular, had a big impact on me. (I still quote the last sentence in client presentations.)

Graham brings up an old example of a value investment, the Great Atlantic & Pacific Tea Co, "which dates back many years but which has a certain fascination for us because it combines so many aspects of corporate and investment experience." As Graham says, "here is the story":

> "A. & P. shares were introduced to trading on the 'Curb' market, now the American Stock Exchange, in 1929 and sold as high as 494. By 1932 they had declined to 104, although the company's earnings were nearly as large in that generally catastrophic year as previously. In 1936 the range was between 111 and 131. Then in the business recession and bear market of 1938 the shares fell to a new low of 36.

> "That price was extraordinary. It meant that the preferred and common were together selling for $126 million, although the company had just reported that it held $85 million in cash alone and a working capital (or net current assets) of $134 million. A. & P. was the largest retail enterprise in America, if not in the world, with a continuous and impressive record of large earnings for many years. Yet in 1938 this outstanding business was considered on Wall Street to be worth less than its current assets alone – which means less as a going concern than if it were liquidated."

The last sentence essentially set me on my investment career. A company trading at a discount to its net working capital position is priced as if it is worth "less as a going concern than if it were liquidated". This is a *much* more promising prospect for investment than cheap stocks trading at big discounts to NAV.

3. WORKING CAPITAL IS KING.

There is nothing really wrong with looking for stocks trading at big discounts to NAV: but a discount to NAV only tells only a very small part of the investment story. What Graham highlights here is the importance of **working capital**.

This essentially means the difference between current assets (i.e. cash, debtors, inventories, etc.) and current liabilities (trade payables, tax, provisions, etc.). Current assets should be very liquid and fairly easy to value, and the higher the amount of current assets in proportion to the total assets of a company, the better.

It is all very well to have an asset value but if the vast majority is made up of *fixed* assets (property, land and machinery, etc.), by their very nature these assets are mostly illiquid and the ascribed carried value can be very different from what they are worth in reality. (Land may actually be worth a lot *more*, but it depends on the circumstances.)

Companies need to be analysed closely and individually, and this one measurement won't be enough to pick winning value stocks. But let's say we're considering two potential old-fashioned metal bashers: one is very heavy on fixed assets and the other has a very high working capital position. Both have the same NAV and share price and both are loss-making. My inclination would always be to look at the potential investment with the higher working capital position – that balance sheet should have a lot more liquidity. It's a much more attractive starting point, and a far better indication that you might have found a genuine value investment.

There is something even better than finding companies trading at a discount to working capital. In rare cases we can find companies that are not only trading at a discount to their working capital position, but (as Graham highlights in the example of A. & P.) are actually *trading at a discount to their liquidation value*.

This is where current assets minus current liabilities and non-current liabilities results in a figure higher than the market capitalisation of the company. In theory we can buy all the outstanding shares of such a company and put it into liquidation, paying off all of its debts, and end up with a profit from the liquidation process. The investment process has paid for itself. I haven't even mentioned fixed assets in such cases – we essentially get them for free. They're the icing on the cake. And they can be substantial.

Shares trading at a discount to their liquidation value are called 'bargain issues' or 'net-nets', because their stock market value is less than their value net of current liabilities and net of non-current liabilities. They only appear at certain times, when the markets are exceedingly pessimistic or a particular stock has been hit by a perfect storm.

They're rare. But they're out there.

4. LOOK FOR NEW 52-WEEK LOWS, DOWNWARD CHARTS AND THEN STUDY THE BALANCE SHEET.

So how do you go about finding bargain issues or net-nets? How do you analyse potential investments when you've found them? Every potential investment comes with its own problems, and all the issues with a company need to be considered individually, but the following are the key practical starting points I use in my investing:

- I look for stocks that have hit new 52-week lows.

- I want to see a price chart that represents a prolonged and steep downward trajectory. Sideways share price movements are not of interest.

- I then have a look at the balance sheet and ask a number of important questions. Is the company a net-net? Is it, at least, reasonably liquid and at a good discount to NAV? Has it been profitable in the past? (If not it becomes difficult to get excited.) Has it generated cash flow? What is the debt position? (Is it manageable? Long-dated or short-term?) Are there institutional shareholders on the shareholder list? (This can be very important should things start to go wrong and shareholders need to call management to account.) Are the auditors well known (and not, for instance, the ones that looked after Madoff)?

I'm looking for companies with liquid assets trading at a discount to NAV with prospects of generating profits and cash flow in future and with manageable debt burdens – ideally with some institutional shareholders, but always with reputable auditors. And if I can find a net-net, all the better. After that, I dig into the company and its market and competitors in greater depth in order to evaluate its chances of turning around at some point and surprising the market. And then I decide whether or not to buy.

Deep value investing in action

A real-life worked example is probably the best way to show all this.

At the beginning of this chapter I mentioned that I started my career at Panmure Gordon, the London-based stockbroker, in the 1980s. When I joined it was still a partnership, but the landscape was changing very fast in the 1980s, especially with Big Bang in 1987. The partnership was first sold to a regional bank from North America before being sold to German firm Landesbank, which subsequently sold it again. This unhappy process continued till the company got listed on the London Stock Exchange in April 2005.

When I spotted the company as a potential investment in late 2015, the price chart showed that it had traded as high as 225p in 2013 and had since then more or less been on a downward trend. When I came across it it was trading at 100p or so.

Looking at the then-latest set of results published on 29 September 2015 for the half-yearly report, the balance sheet showed a net-net figure of £16,471,000 as at 30 June 2015. The number of shares outstanding at the time was 15,545,473, giving a net-net value per share of 105p. So it was trading on the right side of the net-net valuation: that was a good start. We had found a bargain issue.

The company had produced a marginal loss. That was not a real problem – and it had been consistently profitable for a number of years before that. It had a number of institutional shareholders, another good sign. Cash flow had been all over the place – not unusual for these businesses – but still remained positive, and it was debt-free.

So it ticked most of the boxes mentioned above. Stockbroking is a volatile business at the best of times, but we should remember that this company had been around for some 140 years, which should mean something. But there was something else, something that did not immediately show and only came out on further investigation: it boasted a corporate client list of 140 clients. This was one of the reasons the firm was so well known in the market. More importantly, I thought it could be a huge earnings driver for the company under the right market conditions.

Compared to other quoted London brokers, Panmure Gordon was one of only two that were trading at a big discount, but the other quoted one lacked the substantial number of corporate clients, limiting its earnings capability in good times (once they arrived again). Other brokers traded on far higher levels and were for that reason of no interest to us.

We decided to buy the shares and ended up with a 3% position in the company, which was duly announced under market rules. We paid an average price of 64.5p for this holding. The stock was lacklustre for quite a while after we bought it, touching a low of 45.5p in 2016. This is certainly not unusual – when we buy a company it is hardly ever profitable at that point in time (or it wouldn't be cheap and despaired of by sellers willing to let it go for less than it is worth). It is no surprise for things to take some time to work out in deep value investments. And, of course, there is no guarantee that they will. But that's why buying shares trading at a discount to working capital is important: you can be a happy holder as long as your margin of safety of the difference between what you have paid and the underlying value of the company remains.

Fast forward to September 2016, the company released interim results that showed a return to profit and that its corporate clients had been quite active, with 29 transactions in the period under review. We continued to be happy holders. Management initiatives and a cyclical upswing was helping Panmure Gordon move in the right direction.

Our investment in the company was really pushed along when the company announced on 17 March 2017 that a recommended acquisition had been made at 100p per share – a 55% profit on our original investment.

Jonathan Boyar

After graduating from Cornell University with a B.S. in Applied Economics and Business Management, JONATHAN BOYAR *started his investment career at GAMCO Investors. He then joined Boyar where he established Boyar's Alternative Viewpoint which was a research product specifically designed for the $1.4 billion Global Analyst Research Settlement. This award winning research product was purchased by major banks such as Deutsche Bank, Bear Stearns, Credit Suisse, Lehman Brothers, Morgan Stanley and Merrill Lynch.*

In 2004 Jonathan received a Dean's Merit Scholarship from Cardozo School of Law. Upon Graduation he worked as a litigator at the nationally recognized medical malpractice defense law firm Martin Clearwater & Bell.

In 2008 he rejoined Boyar and is currently President of Boyar's Intrinsic Value Research and a Principal of Boyar Asset Management. Jonathan has been interviewed by Barron's, Welling on Wall Street *and* GuruFocus. *He has also been a presenter at both the London Value Investor Conference as well as the GuruFocus Value Conference.*

"INVESTORS WHO JUDGE YOU ON YOUR SHORT-TERM PERFORMANCE RESULTS ARE ACTUALLY A HINDRANCE TO YOU AND YOUR OTHER INVESTORS."

Patience Makes Perfect

THE BOYAR VALUE Group has been providing independent stock market research and money management services since 1975. Because we publish our research for some of the world's leading investors, we get to listen to their feedback on our investment ideas. Continually providing research for such a sophisticated group (who are not shy in telling us when they think we are wrong and the reasons why) enables us to constantly improve our craft.

1. BE PATIENT.

By being patient and looking for opportunities that are either underfollowed (i.e. spinouts or post-bankruptcy reorganizations) or out of favor (due to circumstances that you believe to be temporary), it is possible for individuals to outperform the pros, as many professionals are hamstrung with clients who will fire them if they underperform in the short term. This is a significant competitive advantage for the regular investor – the only 'client' you need to answer to is yourself. If you adopt the mindset of treating each stock as something you intend to hold on to for many years, and pay no heed to the day-to-day stock price fluctuations, you will put the odds of investment success in your favor.

Being a value investor oftentimes entails taking a contrarian position. This is psychologically difficult to do as it can be quite lonely going against the prevailing 'wisdom' of the crowd. Value investors are often early to the party but if you conduct proper research and determine that a given company is selling at a significant discount to intrinsic value, it can be quite rewarding *provided that you are patient*. As legendary investor Jesse Livermore once said, "throughout all my years of investing I've found that the big money was never made in the buying or the selling. The big money was made in the waiting."

2. MAKE SURE YOU HAVE THE RIGHT CLIENTS.

For a professional investor, a corollary of this is having the 'right' clients. Investors who judge you on your short-term performance results are actually a hindrance to you and your other investors. You need to find clients who are true partners that believe in your strategy and will allow you to make investments that are measured in years and not months.

During the dotcom bubble when our firm did not purchase a single internet stock we were called dinosaurs. We were told that traditional valuation metrics like price-to-earnings and book value no longer mattered and had been replaced by such reliable indicators as 'eyeballs'.

It was frustrating watching companies with no earnings and questionable future prospects become market darlings, while companies with solid balance sheets and good long-term growth prospects were left for dead. However, we stood by our investment philosophy and while we did not participate in the upside, we more than made up for any underperformance when the dotcom bubble burst and our style of investing became in vogue again.

Today we are beginning to experience that same lonely feeling as stocks like Tesla and Netflix have become the market leaders and our style of investing has underperformed. Our bet is that history will once again repeat itself and purchasing companies for less than they are worth will prove to be the best way to invest over the long term.

Patience in practice

The benefits of patience – and having the right clients – were brought home to me in a particularly memorable meeting shortly after the global financial crisis. I was visiting the office of a successful hedge fund manager client who wanted to know our two highest conviction stock ideas.

"Two of our favorite ideas right now are Home Depot and Madison Square Garden," I told him. I then went through our investment case for both companies, and the multiple catalysts we had identified for each.

I discussed how MSG had recently been spun out of Cablevision and one of the reasons we believed it to be undervalued was that it received very little sell-side coverage. According to our calculations, if you took the value of its 'trophy' assets – which included the Knicks, the Rangers, and the Garden itself – they were worth significantly more than the current enterprise value of the company.

For Home Depot, we believed that poor industry fundamentals were masking the operational progress made under CEO Frank Blake. In addition, you had a margin of safety because we estimated that the company's owned real estate accounted for a significant percentage of its current market capitalization.

The manager was intrigued. He asked, "What are the catalysts?"

I explained how Home Depot could profit from an eventual housing recovery, as this would cause both new houses to be built and current home owners to embrace major home improvement projects. Either of these would translate to significantly improved sales and margins.

MSG, I explained, was in the middle of a costly renovation that we believed was masking the firm's true cash-flow-generating ability, as capital expenditures were temporarily elevated. Also, the new arena would help the Knicks and Rangers command higher ticket prices, and create opportunities for high-margin sponsorship revenue. There could also be additional spinouts on the horizon and we believed that the end game for James Dolan, the owner, was to go private.

"So what's the time frame?" was the hedge fund manager's next question.

I told him it was impossible to provide a cast-iron time frame. All of it would take time – but meanwhile he'd be owning great assets at a significant discount to intrinsic value. Value gets recognized: it's just a matter of how long it takes.

He had to pass on both ideas.

"If I underperform for a year or two, my investors will disappear," he said. "These are perfect investments to buy – for my kids."

MSG increased its value by ~400% in the ensuing years. Home Depot increased in value by ~350%.

Patience pays off.

Ashton Bradbury

ASHTON BRADBURY *started his career with the Liverpool office of Charterhouse Tilney stockbrokers in 1988 before moving to London in 1991 to join Hill Samuel Investment Management and specialise in small company investment. After periods with Hill Samuel and HSBC Asset Management, Ashton joined Old Mutual Asset Management UK Ltd (now Old Mutual Global Investors) in 2000 and set up the Old Mutual UK Small and Mid-Cap team, subsequently becoming Head of Equities.*

Industry awards won by Ashton over his career included the Coopers & Lybrand best performing small company fund in 1997, fund manager of the year awards from each of Investment Advisor *magazine (1998),* Citywire *(2002) and* Investment Week *(for UK Mid-Cap in 2007) and the* Investment Week *Outstanding Achievement Award in 2009.*

Ashton retired in December 2014.

"IT'S RARE FOR A TRADING STATEMENT TO SAY: 'THE BUSINESS IS PERFORMING BADLY, TRADING CONDITIONS ARE TOUGH AND THERE IS NO LIKELIHOOD OF IMPROVEMENT', EVEN THOUGH IT'S OFTEN TRUE."

Go Top-Down and Bottom-Up for Better Investing Outcomes

THE JOB OF a fund manager should be an easy one. All you have to do is buy shares that are going to go up in price and sell shares that are going to fall in price, and then keep doing it for a long time. Of course, the tricky part is working out which is which.

If I learnt one thing over my career it is that there is no single way of doing this job, no perfect style or golden rule. One size doesn't fit all and each situation is different. What is important, however, is to find an approach that suits you as an individual. If you are by nature impatient for quick rewards then don't buy deep value shares where that value may only be recognised over the long term. If you know that you have a tendency to panic when an investment starts to go wrong, then panic early – not after the third or fourth profit warning!

So before I embark on explaining some of the pointers that worked for me, and some that did not, I should give you a précis of my character so you can put my approach into context.

I am fiercely competitive and struggle to accept second best. I am generally impatient and, whilst calm under pressure, have a tendency to worry and typically look for what could go wrong before considering what might go right. I like to have all available information but am then quick to make decisions and I am not afraid to change my mind. Oh, and finally I am slightly obsessive and find it difficult to switch off.

Many of these personality traits mean that I should probably have pursued any number of careers rather than become a fund manager.

1. COMBINE TOP-DOWN AND BOTTOM-UP INVESTING FOR THE BEST POSSIBLE OUTCOME.

There is always a debate in the investment community about the merits of a top-down investment style relative to a bottom-up approach.

Those favouring top-down investing focus on global economic or thematic trends and seek to invest in businesses that will benefit from them. Bottom-up investors focus on the merits of the individual company, which they expect to win out over time because of a unique product or exceptional market position. They claim to pay little attention to the wider economic background.

I thought the best approach was to combine the two but to recognise that at different points in the economic and market cycle more weight should be given to one or the other. After all, in an ideal world we would all create portfolios full of companies benefitting from favourable economic conditions that also have a strong market position and unique products!

I always had a view – not always the correct one – about prevailing and likely future economic conditions and I wanted to make sure that the overall positioning of my funds was consistent with that view. So if I thought the UK consumer was going to enjoy a period of strong income growth, and so was likely to increase spending, I would want to have good exposure to retailers and pub companies and housebuilders, for example. It's not rocket science. I would then try and identify the companies from within those groups that would give me the best possible returns based upon the individual merits of the companies; a combination of top-down and bottom-up.

At most points in the cycle if I found a truly exceptional business operating in an industry that I did not particularly favour I would still be prepared to invest, taking the view that the exceptional qualities of the business would outweigh some marginal macro or economic headwinds.

So for me investing was about combining these two distinct approaches to get the best possible outcome. There is one caveat to this, which is that if you genuinely feel that we are at a major turning point in the economic cycle the top-down should dominate your thinking. As an example: if we are heading for recession, even the weakest utility company is likely to do better than the very best housebuilder, simply because it is more protected from the economic background.

In these instances, getting the top-down call right can massively outweigh the impact of bottom-up-driven stock selection. Fortunately these dramatic turning points do not happen very often but anyone in the market in 1999–2000 or 2002–2003 or 2007–2009 (to name just a few such moments) will vouch for the importance of calling these turning points correctly.

2. THERE IS NO REASON YOU CAN'T BE BOTH A VALUE AND A GROWTH INVESTOR.

I must have been asked innumerable times over my career: 'Are you a value or growth investor?' To which the answer is: 'Why can't I be both?'

I have never understood why so many people view these as mutually exclusive investment styles. Surely if I am able to identify a business with good long-term growth prospects (a growth stock) I can also identify a company which, notwithstanding potential short-term problems, is fundamentally undervalued (a value stock). After all, a prerequisite before making any type of investment is to relate the value placed on the business by the market to the company's long-term prospects. If it is not, then that is akin to saying that the valuation of a company should play no part in the investment decision, which is clearly ridiculous. So, for example, a company trading on an apparently expensive 25× future earnings could actually represent compelling value if you genuinely feel it is likely to produce compound earnings growth of, say, 15–20% over the long term. Is that a growth company, a value stock, or, more reasonably, a fast-growing business that represents good value?

Keeping an open mind about the type of company you are prepared to invest in broadens the range of investment opportunities and gives the investment professional the opportunity to tailor the balance of the portfolio in anticipation of changing market conditions. If you think the market is going to focus on high-growth stocks, then make sure these are well-represented in the fund; conversely, at the early stages of the economic cycle, 'value' stocks typically come into their own, and you need a good exposure to that sort of business for the fund to perform well. A fund manager who decides for philosophical reasons only to invest in one or other of these types of businesses is simply restricting his ability to perform well through an economic and market cycle. Why would you want to do that?

I had periods when I underperformed because I got it wrong, but I have never viewed as acceptable the statement often seen in investment circles along the lines of: 'I am a growth investor and so I underperformed because the market favoured value stocks which I don't invest in'. I have never understood why so many clients and advisors seem to accept this. Surely the job of a fund manager is to perform well through a range of conditions not just when everything is in their favour.

All that said, as a private investor you are not subject to the demands of trying to beat the market and competition year in year out, so if your personal disposition favours growth companies or depressed and out-of-favour stocks (value plays) then go with what you know best.

3. ONLY BUY (OR HOLD) IF YOU CAN IDENTIFY A SOURCE OF OUTPERFORMANCE.

If you are investing in a company expecting it to outperform the market (as a professional investor would), that outperformance can only come from a handful of sources:

- Is the company going to grow profits faster than the market for a long period of time?
- Is the company going to be positively re-rated by the market?
- Is the company going to deliver a positive surprise such as higher profits than the market expects?

It might be a household name with great brands, a fantastic market position and global reach, but if it cannot do at least one of the three things mentioned above then don't invest in it. You would be better off buying an index tracker.

In an ideal world you find a business that is going to do all three of these things and then real money can be made. However, they are few and far between.

If you understand why you bought the shares in the first place you can also then make a sensible judgement about when to sell them. Ask yourself: why did I buy that anyway? If you were clever enough to identify an undervalued cheap business and the shares have re-rated to, say, the market average, what is there to go for from that point? Has it done what you bought it for? Don't fall into the trap of assuming that a recovered undervalued situation has miraculously been transformed into the next great growth stock. The chances are it is just a recovered recovery stock. Sell it and do something better with the money.

4. COMPANIES DON'T WIN BY ACCIDENT – OR FOREVER.

My preference was generally to run winners and cut losers and there is good reason for that. Companies don't win by accident: there is always a reason. It could be a great product, a high-quality management team, a favourable economic tailwind, structural change working in their favour or some combination of all these. That's why companies that are doing well can often do well for long periods of time, until something changes.

Of course, the opposite is also true: if a business is poorly run, faces a challenging economic background, has a weak market position, or is in a declining industry, it won't magically start to perform better without some fundamental change, a topic I shall return to later.

However, never forget that even winning companies typically don't win forever – so don't become complacent about long-held and much-loved (usually because they have gone up in price) investments. Never mind when or at what price you bought it, the correct question to ask (as per rule 3) is: 'From today's price, in today's conditions, where am I going to get my return from?'

5. ON MOST OCCASIONS, THE ECONOMY WINS.

Never forget that most businesses are affected at least to some degree by the general economic conditions in which they are operating; even an ordinary business can be made to look like a great one if it is operating with a favourable tailwind, until of course that changes.

If you sense that trading conditions in the industry or sector in which the company operates are likely to become more difficult, be aware that it takes a truly exceptional business to buck that trend. The impact of a weaker background often takes time to filter down to an individual company but it almost always gets there in the end. So beware statements along the lines of: 'Despite more challenging conditions in our industry, our business is resilient and continues to perform well.' That may well be true for now – but in the end, on most occasions, the economy wins out. The stock market likes to move quickly but the real world takes rather longer!

6. WATCH OUT FOR THE TELLTALE SIGNS IT'S TIME TO SELL.

To sell well you need to spot issues that might affect a company in the future before they become obvious to everyone else, even if it is just identifying that the company's valuation has become too high notwithstanding the business's good prospects.

Stating the obvious, this is not easy. However, there can often be some telltale signs if you are prepared to look:

- For those with an accounting bent, look for signs that all might not be as well as the profits growth suggests: weakening cash flow or increased use of provisions are classic early-warning signs.

- Analyse the language used in the company statements. When all is going well, in my experience, statements are clear and concise. In contrast, when there is some concern, statements become longer, less specific and more ambiguous – almost as if the impact of every word has been weighed, checked and reconsidered before it has been committed to paper. Chief executives do not make statements by accident.

- Look out for seemingly odd decisions that don't seem to fit with the business strategy. If a company that has a long history of strong organic growth suddenly starts making acquisitions, ask yourself why. It may be for valid strategic reasons, but equally it may be because the underlying growth in the business is soon to slow. There is always a reason.

- Consider why a highly regarded chief executive in a successful business has decided to step down. It might absolutely be part of a long-term retirement plan or for the opportunity to move on to a larger business. However, ask yourself this: if you were that chief executive and you thought your business had exceptional prospects over the next couple of years, which were likely to lead to a sharp rise in the share price, would you step down? Chief executives are often good judges of when to move away from – or into – a business, so take note.

- I've already touched on the macro but if you start to see statements from companies operating in a similar business to your own investment that are increasingly cautious do not ignore them. Even if your company says things are still fine, it may only be a matter of time before the downturn reaches them. The weakest see it first – but generally a downturn in an industry will catch everyone in the end.

7. NEVER, NEVER, NEVER WORRY ABOUT THE BOUNCE.

Never decide to hang on to a troubled share simply because you are worried that it might bounce after you have sold it. Once you have sold the share, you no longer have any economic interest in it so what happens to it has become irrelevant. What matters is what you do with the money. If you sell something and it subsequently doubles but you have reinvested in something that has trebled, you have made the right decision. Concentrate on what lies ahead not what has gone before.

8. WHAT'S WRONG WITH MOMENTUM ANYWAY?

Not long after joining Old Mutual, I remember being questioned on my investment style by one of the company's quantitative fund managers (with a brain the size of a small planet). Having given what must have been a woefully inadequate description of my approach, he commented: "Well, aren't you just a momentum manager then," and walked away.

Having dusted myself down I thought for a moment: 'Well, no, I'm really not "just" a momentum manager – but even if I am, and it works, so what?'

It's important to define what could be meant by momentum, for there are two very different types.

The first is a view that shares with positive price momentum (going up) tend to keep doing well and so the rising share price is itself a good buying signal. Conversely, a share with poor momentum (falling in price) should be avoided. The thought behind this runs along the lines that the City is full of very bright and well-informed people, so if they are prepared to buy a share at ever higher prices, thus creating positive share price momentum, it must be a sign that the business is doing well. Conversely, if these same bright people are prepared to sell a share at lower and lower prices it must be a sign that there is trouble ahead.

There is no question that buying a share which has a nice rising left-to-right share price chart can give you a warm feeling, but remember that these chart or momentum patterns have a horrible habit of breaking down when you least expect it. If you are going to make a decision based on share price momentum alone, at least try to understand what might be causing the momentum so you have a chance of working out when it might have run its course.

The more valuable form of momentum, which often gets caught up in the same conversation, is profits momentum. This is the view that if a company reports higher profits than the market is expecting (and so everything else being equal the share price goes up) it is quite likely to do it on a number of occasions over a period of time. Again, the opposite is also true; one negative profits warning often leads to another.

In part this reflects human nature: if a business has strong trading momentum, natural conservatism suggests that it will not be fully reflected in profits forecasts straight away. The converse is also true: if a business is performing badly, there will be a natural tendency to want to believe things will improve even if there is not necessarily a clear reason why they should. That can lead to profit expectations being based on too optimistic a premise, with the inevitable consequence that more than one downgrade is required before profit forecasts find their base level. It is very rare to read a company trading statement along the lines of: 'The business is performing badly, trading conditions are very tough and there is no likelihood of improvement in the foreseeable future', even though in many instances that would be a realistic appraisal of prospects.

On a longer-term view, market analysts will tend to assume mean-reversion; a rapidly growing stock will slow and an underperforming business will recover. Of course, if those trends are structural in nature, mean reversion may not happen for many years – hence one profits upgrade leads to another and a weak business can experience a whole series of downgrades with commensurate impacts on the share price.

Identifying profits momentum can be a useful tool to add to your armoury. If you are going to use this technique, try to spot the trend early, as the power of upgrades tends to diminish over time as the market begins to expect, and so has priced in, the next upgrade from companies where the trend is well established. That is not to say, of course, that such a company cannot still be a successful investment – it is just that you need a different reason to continue holding it.

9. MANAGEMENT REALLY MATTERS.

Corporate change can often provide the best investment opportunities. I am not talking about changes to the economic environment – though they are always important – but change within a company itself.

A change to the chief executive at an underperforming business can often be the first step on the road to recovery. Look at the record of the incoming CEO. Does she have a successful record of building or improving the performance of a business? If so there is every chance that she might do so again. Timing is everything, not just from an investment perspective, but also from the point of view of a new CEO. Perhaps they have identified the key issues at the business and are confident they can fix them; perhaps their knowledge of the industry suggests that an upturn in conditions is just around the corner. It is no coincidence that management change often occurs at around the bottom of the cycle.

A change in CEO at an underperforming business does not guarantee success but it should certainly arouse the interest of investors. The rewards can be significant. As the recovery unfolds, profit expectations rise and the rating of the company improves as investors' confidence in its prospects starts to grow. This combination can lead to a tremendous recovery in the share price.

Always be alert to the opportunities provided by change. Ask yourself whether the underlying problems of the company are self-inflicted and so can be fixed, and if so does the incoming management have the record to suggest that they will be able to make the required changes?

10. UNDERSTAND YOURSELF.

I always felt it was important for a fund manager to understand his own strengths, weaknesses and patterns of behaviour; particularly his weaknesses. If you know what you are good and bad at you can hopefully play to your strengths and avoid making the same mistakes time after time.

For example, I know that I was always impatient for performance and so had to try and resist the temptation to change my portfolios too often. I was good at spotting potential trouble before it became obvious but had to try and avoid jumping at shadows.

Stay humble and avoid hubris. When the job is going well it can be the best job in the world – your fund is performing well, confidence is high, what could possibly go wrong? Well, pretty much everything: no one gets it right all the time and the next problem is almost certainly just around the corner. If you can remain level-headed when all is going well (or badly), you have a much better chance of making the correct investment decisions.

Conclusion

When I first moved to London to become a professional fund manager my then-boss said to me: "Ashton, you need to understand that in this job when you are bottom of the league tables you will worry about being fired and when you are top of the league tables you will worry about being bottom." Having retired after nearly 25 years in the industry I can safely say that he was right.

At least as a private investor you will not have that constant sense of pressure brought about by the need to perform. That gives you the luxury to invest on a time frame and in a manner to suit yourself. Whilst I hope that one or two of the things that worked for me might be helpful to you, there really is no right or wrong way to invest. Find a style that works for you, stick with it – and enjoy investing in the stock market.

Kathleen Brooks

KATHLEEN BROOKS *is Research Director for City Index. She specialises in the FX market and uses both fundamental and technical analysis methods for her research. She is the author of* Kathleen Brooks on Forex *(Harriman House, 2013) and* Currency Trading for Dummies *(Wiley, 2015), and regularly features on global media. She has more than ten years' retail trading experience.*

"DATA IS ONLY USEFUL IF IT CAN BE USED TO GIVE US MORE INFORMATION ABOUT HOW A MARKET WORKS OR HOW AN ASSET PRICE MOVES."

Five FX Fixes to Trade Like the Best

---

1. LOOK AFTER YOUR DEVICE.

THIS MAY SOUND like an odd rule to open with, but with the explosion of trading on mobile and tablet devices you need to make sure that your device is in tip-top shape before you embark on trading the FX market. Imagine you are holding an open position in cable that is currently going your way and you are sitting on a nice $1,000 profit. You decide to close that position to lock in the profit, however, at the very moment you try to close the trade your system crashes or you lose power. This is extremely frustrating and can be very costly, especially if some breaking news changes the direction of the market rendering your trade a failure. This actually happens, and to good traders.

If trading is your hobby, and you are doing it in-between your 'real' life – working, commuting, picking up the kids from school – then always:

- make sure that your phone or tablet is fully charged if you plan on using it for trading that day
- have a back-up charger that can be used if you get caught short and your device needs some juice urgently
- ensure that your phone has enough storage space for the size of the app or program that you are running (beware that running large charting programs with live prices can eat up a lot of space and suck energy from your device pretty quickly)
- use stop-losses, especially if you use a mobile or a tablet to trade on, to ensure that a lack of power doesn't wipe out your account.

2. BE THE PHILOSOPHER TRADER.

Sometimes it's not the latest economics books or MBA case studies that we need to read, sometimes it's something that is seemingly unrelated to financial markets. For example, I find that some of the Eastern philosophers have given me my most meaningful 'ah-ha' moments about trading the FX market, and I've written two books on FX! Confucius's teachings essentially say that the world is constantly in flux, that the universe is random and too hard to control, and that human beings are works in continual progress. I apply these ideas to the FX market:

1. The $5-trillion-a-day FX market is in constant flux and is not always going to go the way of my carefully structured trading plan. That is why I only risk a small percentage of my account on any one trade and put a lot of emphasis on a trading plan.

2. Because the market is large, capricious and unforgiving, I don't beat myself up if I fail to get in on a winning trade. A good strategy is to wait for a pullback to then go long on a currency, so you are entering the trade at an attractive price. By rigidly sticking to this, I have missed some opportunities to make money in the FX market. However, if I always traded based on the mood of the markets I know that I would have lost more money than I would have made by now. Also, by always deciding when I am going to enter a trade it is a tiny modicum of control that I can have on the unwieldy FX market.

3. Confucius would argue that it is futile to try and pigeonhole yourself by saying you are a compulsive person, or a jealous person, or a compassionate person. We are all of these things at different times and plenty more besides. This is why I never commit to being one type of trader, even though that is what convention says we should do. We are either a technical trader, a fundamental trader or a data analyst. I am all three, and sometimes I am none of these things. I find that over time I need to adjust my trading style. Sometimes, especially when markets are quiet or range trading, I decide to use a technical strategy; sometimes when a big geopolitical event is coming up like a US presidential election I choose to trade on fundamentals. Sometimes I use interest rates, sometimes I use my forecasting models, and sometimes I use all of these methods together. This works for me, and I will stick with it.

3. USE DATA WISELY.

The impact of technology on trading can't be underestimated. It is why retail trading in the FX market can take place. Technology has also made a vast amount of data available to traders, both large and small. When we are confronted by a sea of data, be that historical prices going back years, correlations between FX pairs or of asset classes, or regression models with multiple inputs, always ask yourself: What am I trying to understand?

Data is only useful if it can be used to give us more information about how a market works or how an asset price moves. One of the smartest FX traders I have come across was a statistical wizard with advanced maths and science degrees. However, his best piece of advice to me was to always chart the data first. If you want to see whether the Norwegian krone has a relationship with the oil price, first of all chart it. By doing this you can visually tell if there is a relationship. You can then see the relationship on various timescales, and decide if it is worth further analysis.

Also, for those of you who may be scared off by reams of statistical analysis, don't fear. A chart can often tell you what you want to know. For example, after the UK voted to leave the European Union in June 2016, GBP/USD and the FTSE 100 had a strong inverse correlation that was evident on a chart. Smart traders would sell the pound every time the FTSE 100 looked like it was making another significant high. Although this relationship didn't last forever, it was alive for a few months and didn't require traders spending precious time on complex regression analysis to make a decision. While sometimes sophisticated data modelling is necessary, it is possible to use data to determine simple relationships and trade on the back of your findings.

4. EXPERIMENT WITH MODELS, BUT ALWAYS KNOW YOUR LIMITS.

Maths was not my strong point at school, but I soon realised I had to brush up my skills to really understand the FX market. Not only is the FX market huge, fast-moving and liquid, but I found that those who had the edge tended to do detailed data analytics, which I was desperate to learn. So, I read up on how to build statistical models, I found out what regression analysis was and got going. The first model I made looked at how changes in interest rate differentials between countries could impact an FX pair. This was a simple regression model that included this one input to try and determine in which direction a currency would go next.

I worked really hard on the model and was so pleased when it started spewing out figures. I would write notes on where the said currency was expected to go (it was USD/CAD), but invariably I always seemed to be wrong. I was disappointed, but I wasn't willing to give up on statistical analysis quite yet. I decided to put together a more complex model, this time trying to determine the monthly US Non-Farm Payroll report. I used four inputs this time to create my own prediction for the NFP figure. My thinking was that if I could predict the NFP number, then I could compare it to the economist estimates. If I predicted a bigger number then I would be dollar bullish, if I predicted a smaller number then I would be bearish on the buck. The first month I tried this my model missed completely. However, virtually no economist predicted it correctly either as it was a freakishly low NFP reading. The next month I was right! I predicted that the number would be bigger than expected and the dollar rallied. However, it didn't stay strong for long, and before the day was out my trade was flat.

What had gone wrong? I had put too much trust in my model. Just as currencies don't rally on interest rate differentials alone, neither does the NFP data always trigger a long-term response in the greenback. The lessons learned included:

- Currency markets are too vast to have just one driver.
- Models are very useful but they shouldn't be used in isolation.
- Make sure you trade in context.
- In the same way that you shouldn't only use your gut when you trade, don't only use your model.

Most models that traders build for themselves tend to have a narrow focus. I am not talking about the complex algorithms used by multi-billion dollar hedge funds here. When you trade a market as deep and liquid as the FX market, you can't have a narrow focus. You need to remember that currencies have multiple drivers, including economic data, geopolitical factors, central banks, as well as pure supply-and-demand drivers. Unless your model has all of these factors included, treat models as part of the picture, but not all of the picture, and don't be afraid to ditch the model if it isn't working for you.

5. IS FX TRADING RIGHT FOR YOU?

This is relevant for traders new to FX and for those who have been trading for some time, and requires you to be honest with yourself. The factors that make FX trading so unique, exciting and at times profitable, can also make traders nervous wrecks, confused and ultimately lose money.

The FX market is unique in that you can go both long and short of a currency, you can trade on leverage, you can margin trade and you can ultimately magnify both your profits and your losses. For some traders (usually those with a strict risk-management plan in place) this can be exciting stuff, and they would never trade any other market. For some people, they just aren't suited to it, so they would be better to call it quits. The second set of people should find the market that suits them best, rather than stick to one that they don't enjoy trading.

There is no shame in trying something and then finding out that it isn't for you. This is why I tell beginners to the FX world to start small and I advocate getting off your demo account after a few tries and risking your own money to get a real taste of what it is like. Once you have progressed to a live account, make sure that you only deposit a small amount, make sure you can afford to lose the money, only use 10% of your available capital for each trade, and try not to have more than two trades on at any one time. This way you can test the market, try various strategies. And if it's for you, you can ramp up your trade sizes. And if it's not, you can walk away without too much damage to your bottom line.

If you have been trading FX for some time and are going through a particularly tough losing streak, then take a break. It doesn't mean that you'll never trade FX again, but a break from the market could give you time to remember how currencies have multiple drivers and you may have just missed something by focusing too intently on one currency pair or one strategy. When you are ready to go back, you may find that you have dispensed with your blinkers and can see the markets a lot more clearly. This can be a very useful exercise even for the seasoned trader.

Mike Brooks

MIKE BROOKS *is Head of Diversified Multi Asset at Aberdeen Standard Investments. Mike joined Aberdeen in 2015 from Baillie Gifford where he was an Investment Manager in the Diversified Growth team. He co-founded the Diversified Growth strategy at Baillie Gifford in 2008, playing a leading role in the development of the philosophy and process, in the ongoing management of the fund and in the successful expansion of the client base. Mike joined Baillie Gifford in 2000 as Head of Investment Risk. Prior to this he was Head of Quantitative Research at Aegon Asset Management. Mike is a qualified actuary.*

"NOT EVERYTHING THAT CAN BE MEASURED IS IMPORTANT AND NOT EVERYTHING THAT IS IMPORTANT CAN BE MEASURED."

How to Be Genuinely Diversified

1. HARNESS THE BENEFITS OF DIVERSIFICATION.

D IVERSIFICATION HAS BEEN described as the one free lunch in investment. Most investors could dramatically improve their long-run returns and/or reduce risk by having a more diversified portfolio. This is particularly important in the challenging investment environment that we are currently in and are likely to be in for years to come. The bond bull market that has supported returns from traditional balanced portfolios over the past 30 years is potentially over, and this tailwind is likely to become a distinct headwind in the next few years.

The good news is that a far broader range of investments is now more readily accessible to investors. This includes asset classes such as emerging market bonds, infrastructure, property, high-yield bonds, loans, asset-backed securities, insurance-linked securities, marketplace lending and aircraft leasing. Diversifying not only helps you sleep easier at night, but can also improve returns and lead to more rational thinking in times of market panic.

2. HAVE A LONG-TERM PERSPECTIVE.

Investing for the long term sounds like an obvious strategy, but it is surprising how few investors actually adopt it. We live in a world of information overload with constant ticker-tape 'news' on short-term macroeconomic or earnings data. The belief that this short-term information is important, and that we can successfully trade on it, is a siren call that is difficult to resist.

In reality, this short-term news is typically more harmful than helpful in the pursuit of good long-term returns. Ignoring it to focus on fundamental return drivers over medium-to-long-term horizons leads to better investment decisions and better long-term returns.

3. IGNORE BENCHMARKS AND THE HERD.

Over my investment career, there has been an increasing focus on risk relative to benchmarks and comparison with peer groups, typically over periods of less than three years. This is a natural consequence of investment managers being judged against index benchmarks. The managers want to manage their risk of being fired, and the committee that appointed the managers wants to manage the risk that its decision looks stupid in hindsight.

Crucially, however, this has resulted in many investors taking their eye off the key goal of producing good long-term returns while managing the risk of capital loss.

4. TAKE A PRAGMATIC APPROACH TO RISK.

As computational power and statistical analytics have become readily available over the past 30 years, the investment industry has increasingly used risk models. This has led to many investors relying on backward-looking models that focus on the short term and treat investment risk as something that can be measured statistically with precision. However, when it comes to risk in investment markets, I am strongly of the view that not everything that can be measured is important and not everything that is important can be measured.

Investment markets are driven by human responses to events and the behaviour of other investors. Markets can move from relative calm to chaos in a short space of time. It is therefore more important to have a forward-looking perspective on risk. Be clear on how much money you are prepared to lose and over what time frame. Think about prospective risks and how much of a return you are receiving to take these risks.

5. TAKE ADVANTAGE OF IRRATIONAL BEHAVIOUR.

The behavioural biases that permeate investors' decision-making can often give rise to some of the most attractive investment opportunities. The ability to take advantage of these opportunities will depend on having a flexible investment approach and the fortitude to take a contrarian position. A diversified approach can help by ensuring that you haven't suffered the pain of most investors in the initial market fall and are therefore psychologically more prepared to add on weakness. It also means you have a broader range of opportunities to exploit.

6. BE OPEN TO NEW IDEAS... BUT TREAT THEM WITH HEALTHY SCEPTICISM.

Some investors are set in their ways and closed to new ideas. Others, meanwhile, may jump on the latest bandwagon. The trick is finding the sensible middle ground between these extremes. The investment world is constantly evolving, and some of the most fruitful investments are those that are unconventional and take time for others to get comfortable with. Many investors are heavily rooted in conventional investments that do not pose a risk to their career, following the mantra of 'Nobody ever got fired for buying IBM'.

But it is also crucial not just to buy into the latest investment story. The tech bubble was a classic example of investors believing 'it's different this time' and suspending normal valuation metrics and investment disciplines. The key to a successful investment is doing thorough research and ensuring that the fundamentals of the investment case stack up.

7. IGNORE SHORT-TERM PERFORMANCE.

Many investors will judge a manager based on their recent performance. In practice, however, short-term performance is more about luck than skill. To get a view on skill, performance should be evaluated over periods of five years or longer.

Academic studies have shown that a focus on short-term performance can lead to investors firing managers with poor recent performance and hiring those with good recent performance. The net effect of this has been that investors incur significant transaction costs but no improvement in subsequent performance. The evidence is clear: focusing on short-term performance is bad for your wealth!

8. UNDERTAKE THOROUGH RESEARCH.

Investing is easy. Understanding what you're investing in is a completely different matter. It is important to invest with managers who have the breadth and depth of research capabilities to make sound investment decisions.

9. BE SENSIBLE WHEN THINKING ABOUT FEES.

Fees charged by asset managers have come under pressure in recent years, and rightly so in many cases. Too many managers have charged high fees without adding value, and the rise of index-trackers is a natural response to this.

However, there is a danger of the baby being thrown out with the bath water. An excessive focus on low fees constrains the investment universe to equities and government (or investment-grade) bonds at a time when the long-term prospects for these asset classes do not look good. There tends to be a cost to accessing diversifying asset classes; generally, this cost is amply rewarded in improved return prospects. Hence the focus should be on value for money rather than purely on low costs.

10. BE AWARE OF YOUR OWN BEHAVIOURAL BIASES.

In investment, we are often our own biggest enemies. We are all prone to various behavioural biases that can result in poor investment decisions. As Warren Buffett said, "Investing is simple, but it is not easy". The best we can do is to try and be aware of these biases and employ disciplines to mitigate them.

Personally I find a diversified approach helps keeps most of my biases at bay. It helps me avoid excessive bets in my favoured investments, with the subsequent regret when things go wrong. It also gives me a greater ability to think clearly and pick up bargains in times of market stress.

David Buik

DAVID BUIK *is 73 years of age. He is the son of impecunious Canadian parentage, who denied themselves all the luxuries of life to send their only son to Harrow. He abused that privilege by failing to trouble the examiners three times at 'A' level in any of the subjects he studied. Such was the exasperation of his father, who was managing director of Canadian Pacific Steamships, that he was quickly forced to make arrangements to become a management trainee at the distinguished merchant bank, which was also one of the leading issuing houses of the day – Philip Hill, Higginson Erlangers. In a period of five years he probably learnt more about the machinations of the City of London there than he did during the other 50 years he has been in financial markets.*

After five years at PHHE/Hill Samuel he was earning the princely sum of £950 a year, which was hardly enough to keep a man about town in the style that he wished to be accustomed to. At the time he was obsessed with the idea of becoming an actor's agent. After six months of fruitless negotiations with London Artists, owned by the Grade Organisation, he hastily accepted a job over an alcohol-fuelled luncheon with the money broker of the day – RP Martin & Co – at the princely sum of £1,500 a year plus bonus. The day after he had agreed in principle to join RP Martin, Robin Fox, CEO of London Artists and father of actors James and Edward, offered him a job at £2,000 a year! Upon telling his father that he had found the job of his dreams and that he would not be going to RP Martin, his father told him that if he was a man of his word he would go to RP Martin for a year and if not would he please leave the house. He was crestfallen, and hardly spoke a word to his father for six months. The rest is history.

David Buik spent the lion's share of his career involved in broking UK domestic products and their derivatives. Much of his career was spent setting up small boutique operations – Kirkland-Whittaker, London Deposit Agencies, eventually sold to Godsell & Co (EXCO) and Money Market Agencies, which became the cornerstone of Prebon Yamane's global operation. These companies benefitted from the fruits of the Eurodollar market in the 70s, which was responsible for 300 trading banks setting their stalls down in London, the abolition of exchange controls in 1980 and Big Bang in 1986.

His mainstream career ended in Tokyo in 1998 and he has spent the last 19 years reinventing himself as market commentator for City Index, Cantor Index, BGC Partners and finally with the aspiring investment banking operation for SMEs, Panmure Gordon & Co.

"EQUITY WAS A WORD I COULD JUST ABOUT SPELL; BUT KNOWLEDGE OF? WHAT I KNEW COULD BE WRITTEN ON ONE THUMBNAIL!"

Reflections on a Life in the City

I SINCERELY HOPE that this chapter is at the end of this publication. I must confess I am not known as the fountain of all knowledge in the world of equity trading/research, nor am I the doyen of investment strategy. I have no investing rules, per se, to share – but perhaps by looking back over a long life working in and around finance, and focusing on some particularly important moments, some small lessons will emerge of their own accord.

Having failed to attain any academic achievement at school I was banished to seek my fortune at one of the City's leading acceptance houses of the day, Philip Hill, Higginson Erlangers, whose prowess was very much in the world of news issues and M&A activity. I spent five thoroughly enjoyable years learning all aspects of the business, until I could not afford to stay there any longer. I was lured in to the spider's web of intrigue surrounding the relatively unknown world of money broking. The advent of the Eurodollar market – which saw 300 banks open offices in the 70s – the abolition of exchange control in 1980 and then Big Bang saw me build small operations in this sector. I was involved on the peripheries of Exco International, which took its IPO bow in 1980. I was eventually embroiled in the development of Prebon Yamane, culminating with a final throw of the dice working in Tokyo. I had spent 38 years plying my trade – with huge enjoyment and limited success!

I made the transformation from a serious manager of a domestic fixed interest inter-broker-dealer operation encompassing its underlying derivative products back in 1999 into a market commentator/historian out of a combination of a character shortfall on my part, when working in Japan, coupled with a life-changing tragedy and a smidgen of good luck – by being in the right place at the right time.

When working in Japan for Prebon Yamane, I disregarded Japanese management protocol after a period of protracted frustration. Never tell Japanese management the blunt facts of business life, always respectfully advise them! I forgot the eleventh commandment in a moment of madness and was repatriated to London post-haste with zero job prospects. It was an acute requirement that my unfortunate position of being in the ranks of the unemployed needed to be rectified without delay. Money brokers greeted my application for a job, despite nearly 40 years of experience, with total derision.

I took counsel from a venerable 'out-placement' advisor, who told me that he might be able to find me some sort of job within nine months. My riposte was terse – "You have nine days!" I must confess that I was rather underwhelmed at an offer made to me by ICAP CEO Michael Spencer and his CEO at City Index to undertake their marketing and public relations at a derisory salary. First and foremost I was not sure that financial spread betting was quite my metier. However, beggars cannot be choosers. Thus started my attempts to reinvent myself in an area of finance with which I had no previous experience. Equity was a word I could just about spell; but knowledge of? What I knew could be written on one thumbnail!

I joined City Index in 1998 at the same time that Michael Spencer and Martin Belsham appointed a chief dealer, Lewis Findlay – a former successful bond trader at Sanwa Bank. He was a very imaginative and innovative thinker and within a short period of time he had turned a very average spread betting function into a seriously competitive spread betting bookmaker, by breaking ground in quoting prices in single shares on US stocks without foreign exchange exposure. City Index also added to its variety of products by quoting fixed odds on financial products.

My sojourn at City Index did not last long. An opportunity to expand a more visionary stance to the world of spread betting – which had come under a wet sail courtesy of the 'TMT' explosion at this time – manifested itself at Cantor Fitzgerald. Lee Amaitis, Cantor Fitzgerald's London CEO, always had a passion for spread betting. He was also prepared to back his judgement with money in promoting the business, especially with the development of online trading. Cantor Index was the first in that sector to set its stall down.

I was never quite sure what role I was going to play at City Index, in terms of promotion and PR. However, it struck me early on that the flows in spread betting were considerable and maybe TV, radio and the newspapers would enjoy some insight. In 1999, City Index's contacts with financial luminaries, including brokers and banks, was fairly limited. Nonetheless the IPO market was on fire with one after another hitting the market. Companies like Freeserve, Logica, ARM Holdings, Durlacher, Autonomy and many others came to the market and provided heaven-sent opportunities to make 'grey markets' in these companies before they were quoted unconditionally on the London Stock Exchange. The learning curve was vertical and often the level of business was exaggerated but spread betting at the time provided an excellent barometer as to how investors would receive these flotations. The media responded fairly positively as there were not too many people attempting to promote the idea of market flows and activity.

Lewis Findlay, Ian Jenkins, Rachel Woodford and I joined Cantor Index from City Index in December 1998. It is interesting to recall that our move coincided with equity trading ebbing and flowing with considerable volatility between 1998 and 2001. During this period fortunes were made and lost, mainly in the tech stocks as well as media stocks such as Sky, Pearson and Vivendi plus telecoms such as Vodafone, BT, Deutsche Telecom and O2. I know of at least a dozen millionaires created in this period. Most of them gave it back. Many will recall there was a massive sell-off between 2000 and 2003 – up until the time of the second Gulf war.

Not only was the development of Cantor Index one of the most exciting periods of my professional career, it was also one of the most informative. Though the Chinese walls between Cantor Fitzgerald and Cantor Index were very clearly defined, I learnt more about equities from the hard-nosed and streetwise professionals of Cantor Fitzgerald in a year than I had learned since my management trainee days at Philip Hill, Higginson Erlangers, where I inhaled more knowledge over a three-year period than I gleaned from the rest of my 55-year career. I like to think I put the invaluable knowledge I gleaned to good use in attempting to paint an exciting story as vividly as I could in one of the most electrifying and demanding periods in the evolution of financial markets since Big Bang in 1986. I shall always be eternally grateful to the BBC, ITV, Sky, LBC, Bloomberg, CNN, CNBC, ABC, Channels 4 and 5 and Reuters for their patronage over many years. Without their support I would have been thrown on the scrapheap of financial ignominy many a moon ago!

Though not a household name in the UK in 1998 – apart from its prowess in the international bond and US Treasury market – Cantor Fitzgerald was a hugely effective agency broker in London, with access to Wall Street flows and activity. Cantor Fitzgerald was worth its weight in gold to me. There were so many very experienced professionals who had great contacts – David Smith, Bill Millar, Peter Agnelli, Dan Davies,

Paul Hutchings and Johnny Halliday immediately coming to mind. At the time the London Stock Exchange had acquired the services of Clara Furse as CEO. Even she could not be bothered to touch base with the management, such was her ambivalence to those brokers not in the top tier. She and her management team totally underestimated the level of business CF executed. I shall always be eternally grateful to them for their wisdom, advice and knowledge. Their contribution went a long way to providing Cantor Index with the momentum it required to compete with the likes of IG Group, City Index and CMC Markets.

Having dealt with my 'character defects', I must now deal with the tragic aspects of my extraordinary journey of change. I, of course, refer to 11 September 2001 – venue, the Connaught Hotel – time, 12.30 pm. My colleague at Cantor Fitzgerald (now BGC) Graham Cowdrey and I arrived at the Connaught to have lunch with Clerk of the Course at Ascot, Nick Cheyne, and Mike Dillon, the effervescent 'king of PR' at Ladbrokes. We were there to discuss the forthcoming Christmas meeting which Cantor had sponsored for a few years, with Ladbrokes spicing up the day's revelry with their renowned hurdle race. The occasion was obviously convivial. Graham Cowdrey left the table sharp at 2.00 pm for a meeting.

For some reason I had not turned my mobile off. The phone rang at 2.05 pm. Rather embarrassingly I took the call. It was Graham to tell me that a jumbo plane had ploughed into the North Tower of the World Trade Center (approx. 1.46 pm BST). I wasn't certain if he was being serious but the tone of his voice and his insistence that I return to the office without delay was grave enough for me to race back to America Square in the City with indecent haste.

I passed a Dixons shop on the way back to witness the constant replay of this atrocity on television. I just couldn't get a grip on what was happening. I knew it was going to be personal for me and hundreds of people who worked with me in London, as Cantor Fitzgerald's offices in the North Tower of the WTC were on floors 101–105 and the plane had gone in below that level. Six hundred and fifty-eight employees, colleagues and friends perished. Cantor's affiliate company, Eurobrokers, was on the 84th floor and 64 poor souls died in the wreckage. The money markets are very eclectic, with significant mobility, despite tight contracts. Cross-company relationships had been built up over many years. Consequently, from a human perspective, the damage would be lasting, if not irreparable.

I finally arrived back at the office at about 3.00 pm to see everyone leaving the building at the double in floods of tears – some uncontrollably weeping, full of anguish and pain. The building was emptied due to possible threats to New York-based companies in London. Desperate conversations of intense fear and emotion had taken place just over an hour before, between linkmen on our dollar and derivative desks and their counterparts in the World Trade Center. Forlorn message were shouted down the link lines from the burning inferno. Our mates knew there was no hope for them. All they could do was pass on messages of love to their families, who would grieve for years. The levels of distress that afternoon were so intense for all to see. In those circumstances human beings are very frail.

I doubt a single employee slept a wink that night. We were turning over in our minds the ramifications of what had happened. The next morning everyone turned up for work full of awe and trepidation. What sort of state would equity and bond markets find themselves in? As it happens, the New York Stock Exchange closed with a view of restoring some order, but more about that later. As you can imagine, television cameras and snappers appeared in their droves outside the building. The level of distress over the loss of staff – all known to the management – coupled with their responsibility for putting contingency plans in place for the rejuvenation of the business, was such that the lot to speak to the media fell on me.

In hindsight I fear my performances in front of over a dozen TV and radio channels were pitiful. I found it almost impossible not to cry, despite very sensitive treatment by my inquisitors. As the morning went by I realised a sense of anger and resentment had galvanised all of us. We were *never* going to give in to terrorism. Let them be damned! The tears were very prevalent for days but the memories of our friends returned very vividly. The camaraderie was at its zenith.

At the time of this tragedy our very energetic and innovative chief executive Howard Lutnick had taken the day off to take his son to school for the first time. By the grace of God he survived. Howard's input in rebuilding Cantor Fitzgerald was priceless. It was also fortunate that there had been a recession on Wall Street, so good people were available to rebuild the company.

Accountancy procedures and technology had sensibly been duplicated in London and it was here that Lee Amaitis's and Shaun Lynn's leadership provided vital impetus in putting this inter-broker dealer back on its feet. I have never been prouder of working with such a magnificent bunch of colleagues who put their shoulder to the wheel for not only the renaissance of the business but also for the benefit of the families of those who were barbarically slaughtered by mindless terrorists. Those who have remained at Cantor/BGC since that dark day still shed a tear or two, but this tragedy has triggered unimaginative resolve.

The market that most observers watched then was equities. The FTSE 100 closed at 5033 on 10 September and on '9/11' it fell to 4750, but it recovered to 4550 by 19 September 2001. The NYSE closed shortly after the World Trade Center collapsed in a heap of rubble. The day before the DOW finished the session at 9605. Exchanges reopened on 17 September. The DOW had fallen to 8920 – that was a significant movement in those days. I recall Boeing's share price falling by 30%! Within a month the DOW had recovered to 9400.

And finally to the little piece of luck that befell me. My career as a spokesman and market commentator for Cantor Index changed by way of culture in 2007, at the start of the banking crisis. The resulting recession, coupled with a severe credit crisis, was the worst experienced globally since 1929. It was triggered by incompetent governments, inadequate regulation, greed and avarice of the few (but the very influential) in the banking ranks and profligacy by the consumer. This toxic combination brought the world's economy to its knees. There were very few people with experience and knowledge who were prepared to comment. I was amongst a few who had not been directly involved, but who had more than a handle on what was going on and what the ramifications might be. Consequently, I was in demand by the media.

After five years the level of hysteria started to die down, though not the anger and resentment. My race was run in terms of the frenetic activity, which was starting to be unsuited to someone as stooped in age as I was. As I entered the twilight zone, I moved to a part-time market commentator's role at Panmure Gordon, which I have relished and enjoyed. It has given me particular pleasure to see Patric Johnson put this highly respected investment banking advisor to SMEs back on the road before he hands over to Ian Axe as CEO. He is the representative choice of both Qatar and Bob Diamond, who have pumped fresh capital into the business. These are very exciting times for a company like Panmure Gordon, which has very go-ahead and innovative ideas.

As you can see, my career has been very much a rollercoaster, but hugely enjoyable. I may not be the richest man in the world, but probably the most contented.

Robbie Burns

ROBBIE BURNS *has been a full-time trader since 2001 when he quit his day job for sitting in his pants in his living room with a laptop. He wrote the* Sunday Times *'My DIY Pension' column and now writes monthly columns for* **ADVFN.com** *and* Master Investor. *He also writes a diary and lists all his new trades at his website:* **www.nakedtrader.co.uk**

Robbie has written four editions of his bestseller, The Naked Trader, *two editions of* The Naked Trader's Guide to Spread Betting *and has a debut novel on the way.*

Robbie works properly for six days a year when he hosts seminars for traders and investors, teaching his methods live from the markets. He refuses to take part in investor days, speeches, talks, etc. as he would miss Cash in the Attic.

Robbie is married, with one son aged 12. He enjoys terrible dance music, awful TV, and eats too many Twix bars and too much toast and jam. (His dentist drives a Maserati.)

"TOPSLICING –
IT'S LIKE HAVING
YOUR CAKE AND
EATING IT, ALL THE
WHILE SOMEONE IS
STILL BAKING NEW
LAYERS FOR THE
CAKE."

The Naked Trader
Laid Bare

A rebel's rules

A s a rule I don't like rules. I guess I like to be a bit of a rebel. It's one of the reasons I became a trader and investor, after all. I remember the day I made the decision. It was almost 20 years ago in 1998. I was sitting in an office with the glamorous view of a carpet warehouse and the A4 road and I asked myself: "Is this how I want to spend the rest of my life?"

(Answer: "Nope!")

So I took steps. I built up my cash through a number of small businesses on the side, including a remarkably profitable *Buffy the Vampire Slayer* telephone information line (what can I say? It was the 90s). I worked for BSkyB at the time and after office hours I used the shiny Reuters machine on my desk to learn all I could about the markets. Then in 2001 I quit to trade full time.

I haven't looked back since (though I did end up shorting the company that owned that carpet warehouse). Between 2002 and 2005, I wrote a column for the *Sunday Times*, 'My DIY Pension', in which I managed to double the money from £40,000 to £80,000. And indeed over the 15+ years that followed quitting my job I have traded my way to more than £2m in my ISA and spread betting accounts. (With only small annual cash contributions ever added to the pot.) That £40,000 DIY Pension has also been turned into almost £500,000.

I enjoyed not having to follow anyone else's rules so much that I wrote my first book, *The Naked Trader*, to try and help others enjoy the same freedom I had. It was designed to put people on the first rung of the escape ladder. The book has gone through four bestselling editions in the 12 years since its first release – along with *The Naked Trader's Guide to Spread*

Betting and my book on trading psychology, *Trade Like a Shark*. Clearly I am not the only one who looks to trading and investing for freedom.

However, while trading or investing for a living *does* bring freedom, and I *really* don't like rules... the fact is, you can't trade or invest at random. Well, you can – but not for long, and not without looking like a total plonker. And, of course, not without ending up a hell of a lot less free than you were before you donated your life savings to Mr Market.

Trading naked

I am not here to preach the Gospel of the Naked Trader. There are lots of ways to make a living from investing.* I've just found a way that works for me. It's not based on any magical new theories. It doesn't involve any whizzy technical packages or more glowing screens than the Starship Enterprise. I do not sit at my desk all day buying and selling shares on my computer. (Sitting on my sofa all day watching *Better Call Saul* is another question.)

I guess, if you were to sum up my approach, you'd call it medium to long-term growth investing, with a focus on small and medium-sized companies. But I have to admit I almost died of boredom writing such a sentence and only a stiff mug of Yorkshire Tea could revive me. What it all comes down to is this:

- I like companies with room to grow. (To get technical, this means firms in the £50m to £950m range as they have more room for growth than FTSE 100 stocks. But I buy FTSE 100 shares on occasion.)

- I don't like companies with a lot of debt. (Again, to be a technical bore, I never buy anything with a net debt greater than 3× the full-year pre-tax profit or what the likely pre-tax profit might be next year.)

- I like rising dividends, profits and turnover.

- I like a positive-looking chart in an upward trend.

- I like companies that do things that make sense and can actually be understood – and demand for whose products is likely to grow.

- I like shares that can be bought and sold easily (i.e. with good liquidity).

*   And yes, I know I'm called the Naked Trader not the Naked Investor... but while I do trade, I really am much more of an investor than a trader.

- I like a share that isn't too expensive. (To be a bit technical again… I like a share's market cap, or total value, not to be any greater than 15 times its profits. I want my money back – and then some more on top. And anything more expensive than 15× market cap, in my experience, makes that too difficult.) I do sometimes add 'disruptor' companies that haven't made much profit yet but look likely to make big profits in the future.

- There cannot be any question marks about the stock. If there are any doubts, I'm not interested.

- I like companies that respond quickly to customers (and shareholders!).

- I'm also not too fussed about directors' dealings (and in fact they should probably be ignored completely as irrelevant or misleading), though if a director is buying a lot of shares in proportion to the amount he or she already owns that can at least be worth noting.

(I make exceptions to some of the above for property, oil and energy stocks as these have to be approached differently for a number of reasons, but there's no time to go into that here.)

Basically, I look for shares that have everything going for them, with no question marks, and I want to get at least 30% profit from each trade or investment. I am also quite happy to hold forever – though I'll skim profits off the top along the way while I do. I use dividends to cover the transaction costs of my trading and investing.

As Bob Dinda said, you should "select stocks the way porcupines make love – very carefully". I try to trade and invest by those words.

So that's got all my cards on the table and puts my rules below in context. They're from a private investor – and *for* private investors. But, all that said, I believe my rules can be useful for almost any approach to the markets, except for the ridiculous ones.

Here they are, in no particular order:

1. NEVER TRADE OR INVEST WITH MONEY YOU CAN'T AFFORD TO LOSE.

It makes you a lousy investor – nerve-wracked going into a purchase, for instance, and reluctant to accept losses when it's time to come out (or over-eager to snatch at profits by selling too soon). And the risk involved is ridiculous. This isn't something I've ever personally done, but having written several bestselling investing books a ton of people have written to me after losing their homes and destroying their marriages and doing all sorts of other terrible things all because they traded with money they couldn't afford to lose. (Somehow they never once purchased and read a copy of any of my books – available in all good etc., etc. – before they hit rock bottom.)

2. GET TO KNOW A COMPANY BEFORE YOU PURCHASE ITS SHARES.

Find out all there is to find out about it. What's it been up to? Who's it been seen with? What does it do at the weekends? What's it got to say for itself? You want to be all over it like Hercule Poirot with a laptop and a fibre optic connection.

3. DON'T BE TOO HASTY TO BUY A SHARE.

And never run after a share that seems to have got away. Like buses, another one will be along soon – chasing after the previous one is merely a good way to get run over.

4. THE OLD STOCK MARKET SAYINGS HAVE SURVIVED FOR A REASON.

It's a good idea to cut your losses and run your winners. And the only thing that comes from trying to catch a falling knife is finding it difficult to clap or tie your shoelaces for the rest of your life. (Not that there'll be anything worth applauding in your portfolio if you try it.)

5. BE CAREFUL OF OTHERS' ADVICE.

(Finally, a rule for rebels! To the barricades, brothers!) Buying (or selling) shares on others' say-so is not a good idea. Do your own research. Make your own decisions. People have their own agendas, after all. And it's *difficult* picking winning shares – as fund manager and author Lee Freeman-Shor found in his awesome book *The Art of Execution*, even the very best on Wall Street and in the City fail more than 50% of the time. There's no reason to think others are better than you. And at least if you have built your own case for getting in, you'll know what to expect – and when things have gone against expectations and it's time to get out.

6. PAY ATTENTION TO LIQUIDITY.

And if you are snapping up more than £3,000 in a small share, look up its exchange market size (since you're now operating like Hercule Poirot with a laptop, this shouldn't be difficult). If the EMS is below £1,000 of shares, it could be hard to flog them later. Be warned.

7. IF EVERYTHING'S DIVING, PUT ON YOUR SHORTS.

When the general market is diving – think the Global Financial Crisis, or pronounced hiccups like August 2011 – a FTSE short in a spread betting account can be a handy way of covering the losses in your portfolio without having to sell up just because everyone's running around the place with their hair on fire. (I never run around with my hair on fire, of course – it's just one of many reasons why bald traders make the best traders on earth.)

8. NEVER BUY A COMPANY THAT IS MAKING A LOSS.

I mean, why would you? Oh yeah, right, because it could be coming back – profits are just around the corner... and it's true, sometimes they are... but sometimes, in fact most of the time, they're not... and sometimes total bankruptcy is.

9. TRADE AND INVEST LIKE A SHARK, NOT A MINNOW.

I don't like to make investing out to be some ridiculously macho, testosterone-fuelled, gladiatorial combat – personally, the only thing I wrestle with when investing is the wrapper of a KitKat Chunky – but it is worth remembering that there is something of a battle to the stock market. Investing is a zero-sum game. If you win, someone else has to lose. And believe me, there are a hell of a lot of people out there eager to make sure you are on the losing side – and stay there. You've got to trade or invest with that in mind. Don't be a sucker. *Do* be suspicious. Be the shark not the minnow. (On a related note, only suckers rely on excess leverage, get-rich-quick trading systems, bulletin board recommendations, tipsters, etc.)

10. WATCH FOR CONFIRMATION BIAS.

Confirmation bias is when you think a share is just great and no one is going to convince you otherwise. You love it and are blind to any negatives. Always check before you buy: are there negatives I am ignoring? Go back one last time. What could cause the share to fall suddenly?

11. HAVE A PLAN FOR EVERY SHARE YOU BUY.

I now get out quick if something starts to fall. A 5% fall? I am probably gone. And use stop-losses as a back-up to that, placed well away from the current price.

12. EXERCISE CAUTION WITH MINING AND OIL EXPLORATION FIRMS.

A single negative report can make these shares go tumbling down the mineshaft/drill pipe. There's gold in them there hills – until it turns out, er, there isn't. Whoops! I would completely avoid them.

13. ALWAYS REMEMBER THE WORDS OF THE GREAT 20TH CENTURY ENGLISH PHILOSOPHER, CORPORAL JONES.

"DON'T PANIC!"

14. IT'S NICE TO SLICE.

Topslicing is taking some of your profits by selling part of your stake and leaving the rest to keep (hopefully) going up. It's like having your cake and eating it all the while someone is *still* baking new layers for the cake to keep it the same size or perhaps even bigger in time. (It also means, should the cake fall off the table, that at least you won't have gone hungry.)

* * *

Right, that's enough talk about cake. I'm off to enjoy one of the main perks of investing for a living. And that is, of course, eating a massive plate of cake whenever I want. The kettle is on – thank God I don't have to answer to a boss any more. (Please don't let Mrs Naked Trader see this paragraph.)

Richard Buxton

RICHARD BUXTON *joined Old Mutual Global Investors as head of UK equities in June 2013, and was appointed as chief executive in August 2015. He was previously at Schroders, where he managed the Schroder UK Alpha Plus Fund for over ten years. Prior to Schroders he spent more than a decade at Baring Asset Management, having commenced his investment career in 1985 at Brown Shipley Asset Management. Richard was awarded the Outstanding Contribution to the Industry honour at the Morningstar OBSR Awards in 2012 and has a degree in English language and literature from the University of Oxford.*

"THOSE WHOM THE GODS WISH TO DESTROY, THEY FIRST RAISE UP. THE MORE YOU DO THIS JOB, THE MORE YOU REALISE HOW LITTLE YOU KNOW."

The Hard But Rewarding Art of Investing

In 2012 I was astonished to be awarded the Morningstar OBSR Outstanding Contribution to the Industry Award at a black-tie awards dinner in the Grosvenor House Hotel. The following year, I was invited back to say a few words before dinner on things I had learnt from my investment career. I spoke from some scribbled notes, but here I have tried to flesh out what I attempted to convey briefly then to a wider audience.

1. INVESTING IS NOT A SCIENCE – IT IS AN ART.

One of the things I love about the job of being a fund manager is that the work exemplifies two true statements, which happen to appear contradictory. On the one hand, 'every day is different' – but on the other 'there is nothing new under the sun'.

Every day is different. You will be confronted every day with new combinations of macroeconomic data, corporate results, deals and news flow, together with ever-changing share prices, bond yields, currency values and that elusive but crucial chimera, investor sentiment. By definition, no two days are the same and you must absorb new information, analyse, ponder, discuss with colleagues and adjust incrementally your investment view.

Even the type of data which the market scrutinises can change radically over time. Early in my career, bond markets rose and fell on the regular publication of money supply numbers. Whether the data is even calculated these days is questionable, but it certainly doesn't move markets any more. Today's obsessively-watched figures tend to be US employment numbers, together with excruciatingly detailed analysis and exegesis of every last nuanced expression from key central bankers. No doubt this too will change in time.

But at the same time, there is nothing new under the sun. Not, to be clear, that there are not new inventions, new technologies, new companies, new competitors, disruptive business models and new opportunities to make or lose money. One of the challenges of investing is that there is so much new information, so much additional stuff you could learn about the companies and industries in which you invest – and how much they are changing – that there is a very real danger of spooking yourself out of deciding to do anything. Information overload can lead to investment paralysis.

One of the hurdles you must help the young graduate trainee analyst overcome is the continuous expansion of their first initiation note on a company or industry. They feel, quite correctly, that they don't know enough yet – that there is so much more history and information to understand and incorporate into their note, without which they cannot possibly reach an investment conclusion or recommendation. At some point you must take them gently to one side, point out that there will always be much more information out there which they will never know, but, sotto voce, as if disclosing a trade secret, *that it doesn't matter* – which invariably they refuse to accept in their early months. They will learn.

It is not that there isn't always vast amounts more new stuff to discover. Rather that in the relatively limited history of stock markets – slightly longer in terms of banking – there is nothing new in terms of basic drivers of markets.

Greed and fear is the usual shorthand, and it serves very well to encapsulate so much that is integral to the rhythm of markets. Bull markets and bear markets, the movement round the wheel of sentiment from euphoria to despair and back again are widely chronicled – and rightly so. There is an entire industry devoted to trying to combine indicators of investor sentiment, or risk appetite, with measures of valuation, funds flow, retail investor participation, M&A or IPO activity alongside real economy data for GDP growth, corporate profits and margins to try to establish exactly where we are in the economic and stock market cycle.

The historic data is frightening in demonstrating how an ill-timed entry to the market at a peak – or sale at a low – can wipe out the investor for a generation. But the reverse also applies, and timing entry to a market or a stock at a low can indeed bring staggeringly good returns. So no wonder so much attention is focused on trying to gauge the 'mood of the market', where we are on the spectrum between greed and fear.

This is at the heart of the dichotomy between the daily plethora of new information to absorb ('every day is different') and adjudging where today sits in the broader cyclical rhythm of activity ('there is nothing new under the sun'). What makes the job so fascinating – and difficult – is that the very nature of the daily process of reaction to new information renders it challenging to maintain the necessary distance and perspective to call whether absolute valuations still make sense. On a long-term view, is this investment still attractive?

This requirement for the successful investor to be able to observe the day-to-day on the ground but simultaneously from a 30,000-foot, bird's-eye view is one of the key challenges. It is why, for example, amidst lots of company-specific research reports, I enjoy also reading thematic or strategic pieces. The longer term the perspective, the better. Histories of stock market returns, classic volumes on previous economic and market cycles, are all essential reading to pull you away from the enormous gravity of the here and now, of today's share price.

Early in my career a stockbroking chum cited a wise fund manager client who allegedly stacked up all the brokers' research reports he received (printed and hand-delivered in those days, of course) – and read them three months later. Much short-term commentary could be discarded immediately. More importantly, so many recommendations were already rendered unworthy of time spent on them, having been overtaken by events, that this filtering process enabled him to focus on those genuinely sensible ideas. If the buy case still stacked up three months later, this was worth investigating further. This probably apocryphal tale was at its simplest a means to introduce the necessary distance between the daily noise and the longer term.

In my amateur philosophy, I think of this tension as akin to the fact that as humans we invent quickly but evolve slowly. The pace of invention and technological innovation is incredible, but the drivers of human behaviour hardly change. Shakespeare was born in 1564, whilst I was born in 1964. Roughly 13 generations separate us. If he were allowed a ghostly visit to today's world, he would no doubt be bewildered by the 21st century world. But he would completely recognise human behaviour, emotion and motivation – which is why, of course, we still flock to his plays 400 years later.

For me, key to maintaining a balance between the short- and long-term perspectives is to always keep in mind human behaviour. It is, after all, humans who will be drawn to successful products or services, driving successful businesses. It is humans, with all their foibles, follies and failings who will be managing the companies in which you invest. And it is humans – even if increasingly through the use of humanly-created technology – who will be driving stock markets. The psychology of the crowd, the judgement of risk and reward, the drivers of greed and fear – the more you can understand the human behaviour behind the markets, the better an investor you will be.

In the words of fund management giant Fidelity's founder, Edward Johnson II: "I know this business is no science. It is an art."

2. DON'T RELY TOO HEAVILY ON MODELS.

My favourite investment book of all time is *The Money Game*, published in the 1960s under the pseudonym 'Adam Smith'. I have lost count of the number of copies I have given to younger colleagues at the start of their investment careers. I urge you to read it, if you have not done so already, for its many wonderful insights wittingly expressed. At one point it states: "the study of numbers is rational, a search for the truth and the truth is called value... but value is only part of the game – and the game is irrational... we play it better when we understand that."

The development of computing and its use in investment was in its infancy when *The Money Game* was written, but the spreadsheet has a lot to answer for. There are, obviously, a lot of numbers in investment. We pore over our models, striving to understand operational and financial leverage, playing with revenue or margin assumptions to lead to good or bad outcomes for profits. It's such fun.

But essential though the models are, it is nigh-impossible to model human behaviour. The danger with even a simple company forecast model is that it is likely your sales assumptions will be too modest or smooth. If something takes off, it does not do so in single digits. Worse still, if consumers have a shock, they can rein in spending by degrees far sharper than most econometric models would predict. Some innate instinct, exacerbated by the herd instinct not to be an outlier, drives us all to be incremental in our forecasting, either positively or negatively. Yet the scale of improvement or deterioration in a company's fortunes, especially at turning points for it or the economy, is invariably far greater than people can ever bring themselves to put in the spreadsheet cell.

Modelling is at the heart of the modern economy. It drives companies' spending, investment and hiring plans. It powers the Treasury's perspective on economic growth and taxation policies, or the Bank of England's econometric models which feed its decisions on interest rates. Central banks and regulators model to determine bank capital rules, overseeing banks' and insurers' internal models for loan loss or mortality rates.

Whilst the creators of these models do learn over time from experience and seek to incorporate these insights into their modelling, the danger of all models of future outcomes is that 'stuff happens'. Macmillan's famous "Events, dear boy, events" should ring in every spreadsheet compiler's ears. Human behaviour is irrational. It is impossible to model accurately how humans are likely to behave in future, or in response to a changed set of circumstances.

So my second observation, linked to the first, is to be healthily wary of over-reliance on models – be they of a company or an economy's fortunes. Avoid the risk of being precisely wrong rather than roughly right, which the spurious accuracy of the model outcome can induce. Stand back from the model to ensure outcomes are plausible or make sense. Equally, be bold and put seemingly outsize changes into your models – and imagine that such ludicrous outcomes could happen. They may well.

For all the wise modelling undertaken in financial markets, Her Majesty the Queen was still able to ask after the Great Financial Crisis of 2008: "Why did no one see it coming?"

Fair question, Ma'am.

3. NEVER LET THE FACTS GET IN THE WAY OF A GOOD STORY.

From childhood onwards, we all love stories. Even if in adult life you never read a novel, it is likely you will enjoy television drama, detective series or the soaps, action movies or rom-coms. I would go so far as to say we all need stories, small fictitious journeys outside of our daily lives, with endings, be they good or bad. As time out from 'reality', as confirmation of the existence of a narrative – a journey with a beginning and an end – they help reassure us that our lives, too, progress. That we are not random beings, buffeted from pillar to post like the chrome ball in a pinball machine, directionless and possibly purposeless in a God-less world.

We define ourselves in a linear narrative. Born here to these parents, brought up here, educated there, worked at this, met my partner then, and so on. We strive to make our history logical and sequential, not random consequences of happenstance. The possibility it is otherwise is too frightening to contemplate. Memory being unreliable, we re-write our histories, turning the twists, turns and dislocations into a smooth journey of 'how I got where I am today… and where I'm heading'. We have to feel we are in full control.

The stock market loves a good story. The management turnaround story. The new product innovation story. The store or restaurant roll-out story. The acquisition machine story. The overseas expansion story. The installed base servicing recurring revenue story. The secular growth story. The new paradigm story. The China story. The India story. The shrink to grow story. The consolidation story.

As an investor it is important to know which story you are buying, so you know which narrative the market will latch onto and re-rate accordingly. You have to be alert to when the story from management changes. If the market decides the story it has been happily following is no longer the case, watch out. It treats shares harshly if the plot unravels. Conversely, though, you can make a lot of money out of the building momentum of a really good story. So identify what the story is, recognise it is a story, cross-reference it with the facts from time to time, but – my third observation – never let the facts get in the way of a good story.

4. THE STOCK MARKET IS A MECHANISM FOR INDUCING HUMILITY.

If you ever think you've cracked this investment game, that your numbers are fantastic, that the positive press comments about you are spot on, and, gosh, you really are quite good at this – *thwack*. The market will come up and hit you.

Your companies will have profit warnings. Stocks you don't own will get bid for. Companies you sold as expensive will re-rate and re-rate to your astonishment. Your cheap turnaround stocks will show absolutely no sign of turning around. Why can't the market see the value in this or understand the ludicrous quantities of good news priced into that?

It is the market doing what it does best – making fools of us all, at times. But most particularly if we are stupid enough to think we are on top of it.

I have cringed at press coverage – the 'star fund manager' label, or, even worse 'rock star manager'. Please. Those whom the gods wish to destroy, they first raise up. The more you do this job, the more you realise how little you know.

Humility is endless – and vital.

5. DON'T OVER-DIVERSIFY.

Be honest enough to recognise you probably don't have that many good ideas. Or if you are lucky enough to do so, focus on the ideas of highest conviction. I build a portfolio of around 35 shares, but even that might be described as slightly flabby – academic research suggests much more than 20 and you lose any additional benefit in terms of diversification. But I sleep easier having slightly more stocks in the portfolio. It still feels like putting all your eggs in one basket – and watching the basket very carefully.

Early in my career, I was – looking back – far too active. The very fact of coming to the office every day makes you feel as though you should transact, to demonstrate that you are doing something. Not to mention the siren voices of all those stockbrokers' calls urging you to buy this or sell that. Now I relish doing nothing. Let me put that slightly differently. Of course you are meeting your companies, reading results statements, discussing research reports and monitoring share prices. But you need not necessarily deal or change your portfolio.

Yes, of course share prices ping around all over the place and there may well be opportunities for the nimble screen-watcher to sell a few here and buy them back a bit lower down in a couple of weeks' time. But if you fundamentally like a company, the risk with this sort of fiddling about is that you aren't at your desk the moment when you should be buying them back. And there is no worse feeling than seeing a stock you really want to own going to the moon without you. I can still, after all these years, be 'penny wise and pound foolish' – trying to fine-tune an entry point to a share for a few pence and missing out on a spectacular bull run through such niggardly attempts to finesse one's buying price.

Be long-term, patient, low turnover and resist the temptation to fiddle with your portfolio. I rejoice when a month has gone by and I have not dealt at all – though it does present a few challenges for the monthly client conference call! Don't 'water the weeds and pull up the flowers': if a share you own keeps falling, don't rush to buy more until you have really re-examined the buy and sell case, to reinforce your conviction in the stock. If the market is against it, there may be no rush to buy more. Even more importantly, don't keep taking profits in your winners – great businesses can keep delivering. I'm delighted to have companies I've held for over a dozen years.

At one stage in my early career I watched colleagues build a significant position in clothing retailer Next when it teetered on the brink of collapse at 13p a share. They felt like heroes selling it at 60p some while later. It went on to £80.

Run your winners...

6. IF YOU FIND GOOD PEOPLE YOU WORK WELL WITH, STICK WITH THEM.

Fund management is lonely, but crowded.

There is just you, pitting your wits and judgement against the collective wisdom of everyone else in the market, which runs into the views of thousands. It is enormously exciting and a privilege to be allowed the opportunity to back your views with the savings of others.

It is fair to say that fund management attracts more than its fair share of loners, introverts, odd-balls and fruit-cakes – and I happily include myself in that statement. Maybe it has to – everyone has to be sufficiently confident to think that their view is right, their portfolio perfect and everyone else is wrong, day after day after day.

But at the same time, you need colleagues to bounce ideas off, to share reactions to a piece of news or a meeting with company management. I have been blessed with working with some exceptional people. Great colleagues and a good atmosphere at work, through the highs and lows of the market cycles, the bids and the profit warnings, are invaluable. Collectively, you will be wiser than you can ever be on your own.

7. KNOW YOURSELF AS A PERSON – NOT JUST AS AN INVESTOR.

Finally, it is too simplistic to say that 'experience counts', although it is indeed the case that you become a better investor the more you do it. It is not just that you have 'seen it all before' in terms of cycles, of the markets latching onto different stories it loves to narrate, that 'there is nothing new under the sun'.

To be a successful investor, you have to know yourself. Certainly know yourself as an investor – your strengths and weaknesses, your susceptibilities for certain types of story, or of management. But know yourself as a person, too – and this takes time...

If you don't know who you are and what makes you tick...

If you don't know what you value, and what you don't...

If you don't know what you respect and admire, and what you don't...

If you don't know what you want from life...

And what you want to give...

...then the stock market will be a very expensive place to find out, and you are unlikely to be a successful investor.

* * *

In the four years since I spoke at that Grosvenor House dinner, I have managed to lose both my parents – about which I'm sure Lady Bracknell would have something to say. I would like to dedicate these remarks to them, with love and gratitude. Without them...

Tobias
Carlisle

TOBIAS CARLISLE *is the founder and managing director of Carbon Beach Asset Management, LLC. He serves as co-portfolio manager of Carbon Beach's managed accounts and funds.*

He is the author of the bestselling book Deep Value: Why Activists Investors and Other Contrarians Battle for Control of Losing Corporations *(Wiley Finance, 2014). He is a co-author of* Concentrated Investing: Strategies of the World's Greatest Concentrated Value Investors *(Wiley Finance, 2016), and* Quantitative Value: A Practitioner's Guide to Automating Intelligent Investment and Eliminating Behavioral Errors *(Wiley Finance, 2012). His books have been translated into five languages. Tobias also runs the websites* AcquirersMultiple.com *– home of* The Acquirer's Multiple® *stock screeners – and* Greenbackd.com. *His Twitter handle is @greenbackd.*

He has broad experience in investment management, business valuation, corporate governance, and corporate law. Before founding the precursor to Carbon Beach in 2010, Tobias was an analyst at an activist hedge fund, general counsel of a company listed on the Australian Stock Exchange, and a corporate advisory lawyer. As a lawyer specializing in mergers and acquisitions he has advised on deals across a range of industries in the United States, the United Kingdom, China, Australia, Singapore, Bermuda, Papua New Guinea, New Zealand, and Guam.

He is a graduate of the University of Queensland in Australia with degrees in Law (2001) and Business (Management) (1999).

His new book, The Acquirer's Multiple: How the Billionaire Contrarians of Deep Value Beat the Market, *is due in late 2017.*

"SKEPTICISM, HUMILITY AND LOW COSTS MAXIMIZE OUR CHANCE OF SURVIVING. WITH LUCK AND TIME, WE CAN BEAT THE MARKET."

Zig When the Investing Crowd Zags

1. ZIG WHEN THE CROWD ZAGS.

For any potential investment we compare the crowd's view – the consensus – with our own. How do we find the consensus? It's revealed in the difference between the price of a stock and its value. We do our own research to work out the value. We look for stocks where our estimate diverges from the crowd's. In other words, we try to zig when the crowd zags.

Here's why: The only way to get a good price is to buy what the crowd wants to sell, and sell what the crowd wants to buy.

A 'good' price implies a lopsided bet: A small downside and a big upside. The downside is small because the price already assumes the worst-case scenario. That creates a margin for error. If we're wrong, we won't lose much. If we're right, we'll make a lot. An upside bigger than the downside means we break even though we err more often than we succeed. If we manage to succeed as often as, or more often than we err, we'll do well.

Undervalued and out-of-favor companies offer lots of chances to zig – make contrarian bets. When a company owns a scary, bad, or boring business, the crowd overreacts or grows impatient and sells. That's how the stock becomes undervalued. Given time, many businesses turn out to be less scary, bad, or boring than they seem at first. The reason is mean reversion.

2. BUY UNDERVALUED COMPANIES.

The bigger the discount to value, the better the return. This is true in the US, UK, Europe, Africa, Asia, Australia and New Zealand. It's true in developing and emerging markets. It's true globally. Deep discounts and good returns go together.

For most industrial companies, the Acquirer's Multiple is the best single measure of undervaluation. The Acquirer's Multiple is a company's enterprise value compared to its operating earnings. It is the metric private equity firms use when buying companies whole, and activist investors use when seeking hidden value.

The enterprise value is the 'true' price we must pay for a company. It includes the market cap. Market cap is the share price multiplied by the number of shares on issue. The market cap alone can mislead because it ignores other costs borne by the owner. The enterprise value also examines the balance sheet and off-balance sheet items. It rewards companies for cash. And it penalizes companies for debt, preferred stock, minority interests and off-balance sheet debts. These are all real costs paid by the owner.

Operating earnings are the income flowing from a business's operations. It excludes one-off items like sales of assets and legal settlements. We adjust operating earnings for interest and tax payments because they are affected by the capital structure: the mix of debt or equity. The adjustment makes possible an apples-to-apples comparison between two companies with different mixes of debt and equity.

For non-industrial businesses like financials – banks and insurers – book value is the better single measure. Whatever the proxy, the goal is deep undervaluation.

3. SEEK A MARGIN OF SAFETY.

This is a threefold test of the discount to the valuation, the balance sheet and the business.

First, the greater the company's discount to its value, the safer the purchase. A wide discount allows for errors and any decay in value. This is the corollary to the last rule, that the biggest returns flow from the biggest discounts. It breaks the received wisdom of the market and academia that higher returns mean more risk. Here, the greater the margin of safety, the higher the returns and lower the risk.

Second, on the balance sheet we favor cash and other liquid securities over debt. We watch for off-balance debts like leases and underfunded pensions. We look for credit issues and signs of financial distress. No company ever 'won' with too much cash, but many have sunk with too much debt.

Finally, the company should own a *real* business. The business should have strong operating earnings with matching cash flow. Matching cash flows ensures the accounting earnings are real, and not merely the figment of a clever embezzler's mind. We look for signs of earnings manipulation. Companies that own science experiments, or toys in search of a business model, are for speculators. But weak current profits in a stock with a good past record offers a good chance for mean reversion in those profits.

4. TREAT A SHARE AS AN OWNERSHIP INTEREST, NOT A MERE TICKER SYMBOL.

A share is an ownership interest in a company. This has two implications:

- First, a shareholder has rights as an owner of a company. Shareholders exercise those rights by voting at meetings.
- Second, shareholders should pay attention to everything a company owns. That includes its business and its assets, chiefly its cash.

We look at both the business and the balance sheet to find financial robustness. A business can be worth a great deal, worthless, or worth less than nothing (if it's a regular money loser).

In the same way, a balance sheet can hold great value, or have a negative net worth if the debt outweighs the assets.

Many investors follow profits – the fruits of the business – but ignore assets on the balance sheet. They ignore cash. A seemingly poor business with a strong balance sheet could represent hidden value. The asset value offers a free call option on any recovery in the business.

5. BE WARY OF HIGH EARNINGS GROWTH AND PROFITS.

Mean reversion is a powerful force. It pushes down on fast growth rates and high profits. And it pushes up on low growth and losses.

Fast growth and good profits attract competition. And competition eats away at the growth and profit. Investors following Warren Buffett's example seek highly profitable businesses with a 'moat' – a competitive advantage. But moats are harder to find – and easier to cross – than most investors realize.

Researchers have studied how businesses sustain high profits. The data show most highly profitable companies' profits mean-revert down over time. A small subset of businesses do earn persistent, high profits. But we have not yet been able to identify the causal factors *ex ante* – before the fact. In other words, we don't know beyond broad observations what factors predict steady growth and profits.

The evidence shows the odds of finding the next high-growth or high-profit stock are about the same as flipping a coin. Buffett's genius has been to identify these businesses. Mere mortals are better served buying at a steep discount to value.

The best place to find future growth and profit is in businesses enduring hard times. These businesses are also likely to trade at a wide discount to value. Buyers of these businesses can enjoy both an improvement in the business and a narrowing of the market price discount.

6. USE SIMPLE, CONCRETE RULES TO AVOID MAKING ERRORS.

Cognitive errors happen when we make odds-based decisions about uncertain future outcomes. Investing in the stock market presents exactly this type of problem.

The secret to avoiding these errors is to use a set of simple, concrete rules. Ideally, we should write them down and strictly follow them.

Simple, concrete rules are testable. They should be back-tested and battle-tested. The back test makes sure the rules work over historical data sets, ideally in different countries and stock markets. The battle test makes sure the rules work in practice. No strategy has ever failed in theory. Almost all have failed in reality.

7. CONCENTRATE, BUT NOT TOO MUCH.

If you want to match the market, buy the market. If you want to beat the market, you must do something different. That means buying only the best ideas, or 'focusing'.

The trade-off for focus is twofold:

- First, concentrated portfolios tend to be more volatile than the broader stock market. This means they move around more, both up and down. Good years for the market can be great years for the portfolio. Bad years for the market can be terrible years for the portfolio.

- Second, concentrated portfolios don't closely follow the market. We call this 'tracking error'. It means concentrated portfolios can go down when the market goes up, and up when the market goes down. The second kind of tracking error – portfolio up, market down – is great to have. But you won't notice it. You'll only notice when your concentrated portfolio is down while the market is up. Academics have found high tracking error to be associated with good long-term performance. But the market can beat portfolios of undervalued stocks for a long time. Tracking error won't feel good then.

Don't become too concentrated. Assume your calculations and thinking are wrong. Remember, it's more likely you are wrong and the rest of the market is right.

8. AIM TO MAXIMIZE AFTER-TAX GAINS OVER THE LONG TERM.

Our aim is to maximize the real, after-tax return over the long term. This has three important implications:

- First, thinking long term – beyond the next few quarters or years – offers a huge advantage to investors. Companies often become mispriced because the next year or so looks tough. This creates a good spot for investors willing to lag over the short term. We call this 'time arbitrage'. It offers an enduring edge available to patient investors, no matter the size of their portfolio.

- Second, the effects of compounding take a long time to become observable. But interest-on-interest or gains-on-gains become significant over the long term.

- Third, taxes and fees are hidden enemies of long-term compounding. High-fee mutual funds and other flow-through vehicles will struggle to beat passive indexes. But low-fee, active ETFs are more tax-efficient and can do so over the long term.

9. HEDGE WHEN THE MARKET'S EXPENSIVE AND FALLING.

Investors earn the best long-term returns by holding undervalued stocks and ignoring the stock market's booms and busts. Even so, many investors struggle to stay invested when the stock market is down by 20%

or more. They'll sell at the worst possible moment – right before the rally. One solution is to hedge the portfolio.

The trade-off for hedging is a slightly reduced return. And, if you haven't met a trend-based hedge before it can seem like voodoo. The idea is simple: hedge when the market falls. Don't hedge when the market rises. But how do we work out the direction of the market?

There are several trend indicators that we can use to work out the market's direction. The easiest is the simple moving average. The most common is the 200-day moving average. We work it out by taking the S&P 500's average closing price of the last 200 trading days. We then compare today's close to that average. Where the market closes above the average, the trend is up. When the market closes below the average, the trend is down. Simple.

Why 200 days? It's an arbitrary choice. Billionaire investor Paul Tudor Jones's advocacy of it likely has something to do with its fame. He talks about it in this interview with Tony Robbins in *Money: Master the Game* (Simon & Schuster, 2014):

> "My metric for everything I look at is the 200-day moving average of closing prices. I've seen too many things go to zero, stocks and commodities. The whole trick in investing is: 'How do I keep from losing everything?' If you use the 200-day moving average rule, then you get out. You play defense and you get out."

When Paul Tudor Jones gets out, we hedge. The hedge doesn't impact our decision to buy stocks or not. Our decision to buy a stock is a function of its margin of safety. We take Buffett's advice to ignore the market when buying undervalued stocks. But we take Paul Tudor Jones' advice – which we have tested ourselves – to hedge when the market goes down.

A moving average isn't perfect. It produces many *whipsaws* or 'false positives'. A whipsaw occurs when the trend indicates the portfolio should be hedged and the market goes up instead.

It also produces false negatives: the hedge is late to the party, missing the first few days of a big decline. The whipsaws and the false negatives cost money. But that's the trade-off to protect against big crashes.

While the trend is very effective by itself, it's most potent when it's combined with value. Here is a simple table showing yearly returns for the S&P 500 from 1950 to 2017. There are four possible markets in our trend and value study shown in the four boxes below:

	UNDERVALUED	EXPENSIVE
UP	15.4%	8.6%
DOWN	6.0%	-0.6%

(We defined 'undervalued' here as a below-average *q ratio*. The q ratio is a stock market value tool that compares asset market prices to replacement costs. Other stock market value tools – Shiller's cyclically adjusted price-to-earnings ratio or Buffett's total market cap-to-gross national product – give identical results.)

The best returns happened in undervalued, rising markets (Up + Undervalued = 15.4%). You don't want to hedge in a surging market. The worst returns happened when in expensive, falling markets (Down + Expensive = -0.6%). On average, that's a good time to hedge.

But here's the kicker. The next table shows the worst crashes in our four possible markets:

	UNDERVALUED	EXPENSIVE
UP	-17.7%	-32.6%
DOWN	-45.6%	-56.4%

The deepest crash at -56.4% happened in an expensive, falling market. (It was the last one that ended in 2009 – the so-called 'Credit Crisis'.) The shallowest decline occurred in an undervalued, rising market. Expensive, falling markets are bad news. They mean low returns and the worst crashes.

Most of the time the stock market goes up. Since 1950, it's been up 70% of all months. Crashes are rare, but gut-wrenching. If you're willing to trade a little return to avoid a big crash, hedge in expensive, falling markets.

Value investing is a logical, time-tested investment method. The best value investors zig while others zag. They maximize their margin of safety and minimize their costs and taxes. They treat high growth and profits skeptically. And they assume their calculations and thinking are wrong. Skepticism, humility and low costs maximize our chance of surviving. With luck and time, we can beat the market.

Robert Carver

ROBERT CARVER *is an independent investor, trader and writer. He spent over a decade working in the City of London before retiring from the industry in 2013. Robert initially traded exotic derivative products for Barclays Investment Bank and then worked as a portfolio manager for AHL – one of the world's largest hedge funds – before, during and after the global financial meltdown of 2008. He was responsible for the creation of AHL's fundamental global macro strategy, and then managed the fund's multi-billion-dollar fixed income portfolio.*

Since retiring, Robert has written two books: Systematic Trading: A unique new method for designing trading and investing systems *(Harriman House, 2015) and* Smart Portfolios: A practical guide to building and maintaining intelligent investment portfolios *(Harriman House, 2017). He manages his own portfolio of equities, funds and futures using the methods you can find in his books. His website is at:* **www.systematicmoney.org**

"IT'S BETTER TO HAVE A PORTFOLIO WHICH ISN'T QUITE RIGHT THAN TO INCUR MASSIVE TRADING COSTS FROM FREQUENT LARGE ADJUSTMENTS."

How to Invest Systematically

1. UNLESS YOU ARE A GENIUS USE A SYSTEM.

"I<small>N EVERY CASE</small> the accuracy of experts was matched or exceeded by a simple algorithm..." – this quote is from the book *Thinking, Fast and Slow* (Penguin, 2012) by Nobel-prize-winning psychologist Daniel Kahneman, and applies to many different fields including finance.

It's true that a simple system can't hope to beat the very best investors like Warren Buffett. But ordinary mortals will almost certainly do better if we stick with simple rules. Bad news: unless you've already got a long and successful track record it's quite unlikely that you're an investing genius. Assuming that you're not Warren Buffett, it's better to build a portfolio *systematically* using simple rules and principles.

2. THE FUTURE IS UNPREDICTABLE...

Predicting next year's rise in the FTSE 100 or S&P 500 is extremely difficult. For investors with longer time horizons, the task of predicting their average return over the next 40 years is effectively impossible.

Why? Firstly, many factors affect market prices: future inflation, interest rates, economic growth, corporate profitability and investor sentiment, to name but a few. These are all equally difficult to forecast.

Secondly, even if you could forecast the future, you also need to accurately say how markets will react to each piece of news. This also isn't easy. How many times have you heard a media pundit predict chaos or euphoria if some particular event happens, only for the actual market reaction to be completely different?

Finally, predicting the future isn't enough: you need to predict it better than everyone else. Market prices represent the collective opinion of every investor on the planet, based on all publicly available information.

That is a pretty serious competitor that you're trying to beat if you think you can start forecasting market movements.

3. ... BUT SOME THINGS ARE LESS UNPREDICTABLE THAN OTHERS.

Although the future is uncertain there are some predictions which are more likely to come true.

For example: a short maturity bond issued by a stable government like Norway will almost certainly be safer than shares in a speculative internet start-up. Also returns in closely related firms like Google and Facebook will probably be relatively similar – more similar than the returns of Facebook and Norwegian government bonds. Finally, an expensive actively managed fund, which currently charges higher fees than a passive competitor, will continue to do so.

These predictable properties of different assets – **risk, similarity** and **costs** – are fairly stable over time, and should be used to select your investments. You should **invest less in riskier assets**, **diversify your portfolio** as much as possible, and **avoid paying high costs**.

4. DIVERSIFY, DIVERSIFY, DIVERSIFY.

"I only have one piece of advice. Diversify. And if I had to offer a second piece of advice, it would be: Remember that the future will not necessarily be like the past. Therefore we should diversify."

– HARRY MARKOWITZ, PIONEER OF PORTFOLIO THEORY

Diversification has a bad name in some circles. Legendary portfolio manager Peter Lynch describes it as di*worsi*fication in his book *One Up On Wall Street*. It's true that if you can accurately predict the future you'd be better off in a concentrated portfolio with just a few carefully selected stocks. But this decision will be disastrous if your forecasting ability isn't as good as you think, or you're just unlucky.

The gains from diversification come from investing in mixed portfolios of dissimilar assets. So if future average returns can't be forecasted – but similarity is relatively predictable – then diversification is indeed the only free lunch in finance. All investors should first spread their wealth between unrelated asset classes like stocks and bonds. If possible you should also invest in different geographical regions and countries, and across different industries.

5. THERE IS NO RIGHT ASSET ALLOCATION... BUT THERE ARE SOME WRONG ONES.

Eighty per cent in stocks? Fifty per cent in stocks? Thirty per cent in stocks? It doesn't matter which you choose – there is no perfect answer if we can't predict the future.

Of course, if you can cope with the swings, then a higher allocation to equities makes sense. Just make sure you know what the likely risks are, as once you've made your decision it's important you stick to it. Naturally, more nervous types should instead overweight the less volatile bond markets.

Although there is no correct allocation which will suit everyone, there are some common mistakes to avoid. Firstly, it doesn't make sense for extremely risk-averse investors to stick exclusively to safe assets like bonds. You can generate more return, at the same level of risk, with a mixed investment portfolio of which around a third should still be in stocks. If that portfolio is still too risky for your taste, then you should dilute it with cash until you are able to sleep at night. Just don't forget that even cash isn't risk-free: its value will change in the future depending on how inflation pans out.

At the other end of the scale, even the most gung-ho investor shouldn't put 100% of her wealth into risky assets like stocks. At least a fifth of your cash should be in bonds. Adding a modest quantity of bonds to diversify your stock investments will reduce your risk, but won't damage the expected future value of your portfolio. Also, don't forget that the naturally higher volatility of stocks means an 80% stock allocation actually means around 90% of the risk of your returns will be generated by the equity market.

6. DON'T BUY INDIVIDUAL STOCKS UNTIL IT MAKES SENSE.

Who is more diversified: someone with a portfolio of ten shares, or his friend with two shares? The answer may not be as obvious as you think. The first investor owns ten US-based technology companies. The second has bought shares in a globally diversified stock investment fund, and a global bond fund. She is in fact far more diversified than the tech-loving investor.

Correctly diversifying with individual stocks means buying at least one share in each industry and every country: a portfolio of hundreds or even thousands of firms. Unfortunately, this is impractical. Minimum brokerage commissions makes the purchase of large numbers of shares uneconomic unless you are relatively wealthy. Also, buying individual equities in some countries is difficult and can be expensive.

Instead, use cheap passive funds like ETFs to diversify your portfolio across asset classes and countries. Buy shares in selected countries only if you can do it properly – and you can afford it.

7. AVOID EXPENSIVE FUNDS.

Investing decisions often involve weighing up expensive but supposedly superior options against cheaper inferior alternatives. The skill of active fund managers doesn't come cheap; you'll pay far more than for a cheap passive index tracker. Fancy new fangled 'smart beta' funds attract a premium management fee compared to their duller vanilla cousins. As well as their higher sticker prices, expensive funds will usually have higher trading costs that may not be adequately disclosed.

The costs of relatively expensive funds are very predictable. But any benefit they offer in the form of higher returns is much harder to prove. Many years of returns data are required to show that there was a significant benefit in investing in a given fund which can be statistically verified.

Your first instinct should be to go for the cheapest option unless there is strong evidence that it's worth paying more. That means only investing in funds and managers with a lengthy track record of beating the benchmark by a substantial margin.

Of course, any apparent brilliance in the past could still have been dumb luck. It's also possible that any historic outperformance could evaporate in the future. But at least with a decent track record you perhaps have some hope of earning enough extra money to pay those higher fees.

8. CAREFULLY REBALANCE YOUR PORTFOLIO.

Rebalance regularly: Most investors trade too much. But some trading is necessary to keep your portfolio from becoming unbalanced as prices change. Review your portfolio regularly and in a disciplined way. When an extreme market move happens you'll have a solid and well-practised plan to fall back on.

Rebalance systematically: Try not to panic and sell assets which have fallen drastically in price. Don't get greedy and sell assets which have risen for small profits. If you think it is better to own recent winners, or stocks that are better value, then do so systematically. Use fixed rules which will vary your portfolio proportions according to measurable indicators, rather than raw emotion.

Rebalance gradually: Don't frequently buy and sell huge chunks of your investments. It's better to have a portfolio which isn't quite right than to incur massive trading costs from frequent large adjustments.

Rebalance conservatively: If your long-term target is a 50% allocation to stocks, then you should never go below 30% or above 70%. Going beyond this would only make sense if you have a very reliable crystal ball to predict the future – which you probably don't.

9. STICK TO YOUR GUNS – TRY NOT TO BE EMBARRASSED.

There is no point having a system unless you stick to it, through good times and bad. Don't be tempted to deviate when your portfolio starts underperforming the market. Make sure you can cope with the potential embarrassment of being 'wrong'. With hindsight your system is unlikely to be perfect – but dropping it at the first sign of trouble will be a big mistake.

10. BE SKEPTICAL.

Don't listen to the market guru making confident predictions of what will happen next year: he probably can't predict the future. Avoid being blinded with science peddled by advocates of smart beta, robo investing, cryptocurrencies, or whatever the latest market fad is. Beware the fund manager with high fees and a relatively short track record of apparent outperformance. Finally, use several pinches of salt when reading advice doled out by bestselling authors (this includes me).

Jonathan
Clements

JONATHAN CLEMENTS *is the founder and editor of* HumbleDollar.com. *Born in London and educated at Cambridge University, Jonathan spent almost 20 years at the* Wall Street Journal *in New York, where he was the newspaper's personal finance columnist. He's also the author of six personal finance books, including his latest,* How to Think About Money.

"DYING EARLY
IN RETIREMENT
SHOULDN'T BE A
CONCERN. THE BIG
RISK IS RUNNING
OUT OF MONEY
BEFORE YOU RUN
OUT OF BREATH."

Nine Ways to Think Differently About Money

FOR MORE THAN three decades, I have written and thought about money – and I like to believe I've been fairly consistent in my financial philosophy. Today, I still live by the same principles I championed starting in 1994, when I became the *Wall Street Journal*'s personal finance columnist. I remain almost entirely invested in index funds, my portfolio is heavily tilted toward stocks, I'm a big believer in global diversification and I continue to argue that the key to financial success is great savings habits.

Yet, today, certain ideas loom much larger in my thinking, in part because of upheaval in the financial markets and changes in the economy. Here are nine financial notions that strike me as especially important for today's investor:

1. DEMOGRAPHICS ARE DESTINY.

Over the past 50 years, the US economy has grown roughly three percentage points a year faster than inflation, with half that growth coming from an expanding workforce and half from rising productivity. But with the workforce projected to grow at just 0.5% a year, well below the 1.5% historical average, economic growth will almost inevitably be slower – and that'll also mean more modest corporate earnings growth.

This is a problem not just in the US, but across the developed world. Result: stocks probably won't match their strong historical performance, though they will likely still outpace bonds and cash investments. Not all is grim, however: emerging market stocks don't face the same demographic headwinds – and have the potential to deliver strong long-run returns.

2. START WITH EVERYTHING.

When thinking about my portfolio, I used to begin with my home country's stock market – in my case, the US – and then consider which investments I should add to diversify that core holding. Today, my thinking begins with the so-called global market portfolio – the investable universe of stocks, bonds and other investments owned collectively by all investors – and then I decide what I want to subtract. I end up in roughly the same place, though this second approach has made me even more willing to invest abroad.

3. PONDER YOUR PAYCHECK.

For most folks in the workforce, their most valuable asset is their so-called human capital – their income-earning ability. I have come to believe that we should design our financial lives around that paycheck, or the lack thereof.

For instance, those who are employed may need disability and life insurance, in case they can't provide for themselves or their family. But they also have the freedom to invest heavily in stocks, because they don't need income from their portfolio. By contrast, those who are retired don't need to protect their human capital with disability and life insurance, but they probably ought to hold more bonds now that they no longer have a paycheck.

4. STAY GROUNDED.

In late 2008 and early 2009, many investors inflicted huge financial damage on themselves, by bailing out of stocks at deeply depressed prices. How can we avoid that mistake in future? We need a sense of the stock market's value that's distinct from current prices.

To that end, consider this approach: Imagine a line climbing steadily at 6% every year. That's my forecast for long-run nominal global stock returns, based on current dividend yields and likely growth in corporate earnings per share. I'm also assuming 2% annual inflation, leaving us with 4% real returns.

In the short run, however, stock performance will be all over the map. If nominal returns are above the 6%-a-year growth path, we should smile at our good fortune, but realize we'll likely pay a price later, in the form of lower returns. When performance is below 6% a year, we may not smile as much, but we should take comfort in the notion that – at some point – stock performance will likely play catch-up.

5. CONSIDER THE CONSEQUENCES.

We should think less about the odds of some risk becoming reality and more about the possible consequences. For instance, it's unlikely that other major stock markets will suffer the same fate as Japanese shares, which today languish at half their year-end 1989 price. But if the improbable came to pass, it would be devastating for anyone invested exclusively in that country's shares – which is why we should probably keep a significant portion of our stock portfolios invested abroad.

6. FIX YOUR FUTURE.

Over the past three decades, we've seen a collapse in the US savings rate. I think many Americans would like to save more, but simply can't – because they have boxed themselves in with high fixed living costs. At issue here are items like mortgage or rent, car payments, phone plans, student loan payments, cable bills and more.

My advice: we should aim to keep fixed living costs to 50% or less of our pretax income. That way, we'll suffer less financial stress, have a greater ability to save and have more money for discretionary 'fun' spending. An added bonus: these low fixed costs will give us extra financial breathing room should we lose our job or if we're retired and our portfolio takes a battering from rough financial markets.

7. DON'T EVER RETIRE.

As the developed world's population ages, the typical retirement age needs to rise, or we won't have enough folks producing the goods and services that society needs. This should not be a cause for despair. I'd like to see the distinction between work and retirement disappear, not just for the good of the economy – but for the good of our collective happiness.

The fact is, many folks get a lot of satisfaction from work. I have come to believe that retirement should be viewed not as a chance to relax after four exhausting decades, but as an opportunity to take on new challenges, both paid and unpaid. And if those opportunities are paid, all the better. Working part time can greatly ease the financial strain of retirement and, I believe, will become increasingly common.

8. DYING ISN'T THE PROBLEM.

Most of us tend to be overly optimistic – except, it seems, when it comes to our own life expectancy. For proof, look not only at the pitifully low US sales of immediate fixed annuities that pay lifetime income, but also at the many retirees who claim their government Social Security benefit at age 62, the earliest possible age. Both strategies make sense if you think you'll die relatively young.

Yet, for retirees, their biggest financial concern shouldn't be dying early in retirement. At that point, all their financial problems are over. Instead, the big risk is living longer than they ever imagined – and running out of money before they run out of breath. If that's the big risk, we should delay Social Security until age 66 and perhaps age 70, and also consider using part of our bond-market money to buy lifetime income annuities.

9. AIM FOR ENOUGH.

The goal of managing money isn't to outperform our neighbors, prove how clever we are or become the richest family in town. Rather, the goal is to have enough to lead the life we want.

If that's the overriding objective, it becomes far clearer how we should manage our money. We want to avoid unnecessary risks and pursue strategies that have a high likelihood of success. That means buying insurance against major financial risks and diversifying our portfolios as broadly as possible. It also means eschewing efforts to beat the market and instead buying low-cost index funds that simply replicate the performance of the market averages.

Michael Covel

MICHAEL COVEL *teaches beginners to seasoned pros how to generate profits with straightforward and repeatable rules. He is best known for popularizing the counterintuitive and controversial trading strategy, trend following.*

An avowed entrepreneur, Michael is the author of five books including the international bestseller, Trend Following, *and his investigative narrative,* TurtleTrader. *Fascinated by secretive traders that have quietly generated spectacular returns for seven decades, those going against the investment orthodoxy of buy and hope, he has uncovered astonishing insights about the right way to think, develop, and execute trend following systems.*

Michael's perspectives have garnered international acclaim and have earned him invitations with a host of organizations: China Asset Management, GIC Private Limited (a Singapore sovereign wealth fund), BM&F Bovespa, the Managed Funds Association, Bank of China Investment Management, the Market Technicians Association, and multiple hedge funds and mutual funds. He also has the distinction of having interviewed five Nobel Prize winners in economics, including Daniel Kahneman and Harry Markowitz, and he has been featured in major media outlets, including the Wall Street Journal, *Bloomberg, CCTV,* The Straits Times, *and* Fox Business.

Michael posts on Twitter, publishes a blog, and records his podcast weekly. His consulting clients are across hedge funds, sovereign wealth funds, institutional investors, and individual traders in more than 70 countries. He splits his time between the United States and Asia.

"THE TRUTH OF TREND FOLLOWING IS ITS PHILOSOPHICAL UNDERPINNINGS ARE RELEVANT NOT ONLY TO TRADING, BUT TO LIFE IN GENERAL."

Ten Tenets of a Trend Follower

1. PRICE IS THE PARAMOUNT TRADING SIGNAL.

IN AN INCREASINGLY uncertain and downright unfriendly world, it is extremely efficient and effective to base decision-making on the single, simple, reliable truth of price. The 24/7 never-ending fundamental data barrage, such as price-earnings ratios, crop reports, and economic studies, plays right into the tendency to make trading more complicated than it need be. Yet by factoring in every possible fundamental piece of data, which is impossible, you still would not know how much and when to buy, or how much and when to sell. The truth of price always wins if the debate is grounded in reason. Price is the only fact.

Market prices, traded prices, are the unequivocal objective data reflecting the sum total of all views. Accepting that truth allows you to compare and study prices, measuring their movements, even if you don't know a damn thing about fundamentals. You could absolutely look at individual price histories or charts, without knowing which market is which, and trade them successfully. That is not what they teach at Harvard or Wharton, but it is the foundation of making millions as a trend following trader.

The concept of price as the paramount trading signal is too simple for Wall Street to accept. This confusion or misinformation is seen across the mainstream press where they always emphasize the wrong numbers.

2. EMBRACE SPECULATION.

Speculation is unavoidable. It is all there is for making choices about market prices. Learning how best to speculate using prices is not only a worthy endeavor – it is a survival-of-the-fittest concept that traces back to the earliest literature of Wall Street.

You have to want to get ahead and be rich – the critics' condemnation, the player hating, the rank jealousy be damned. Speculation is not only honorable – it is life. Profit-seeking speculation is the absolute driving force of markets and without it there is only disintegration.

3. KEEP DOWN YOUR LOSSES, LET YOUR PROFITS TAKE CARE OF THEMSELVES.

In *How to Win and How to Lose* (1883) we see arguably the first trend-based market player arrive:

> "The shrewdest operator ever known on the London Stock Board was David Ricardo (1772–1823) who amassed an enormous fortune. In advice to a friend he sums up as the true secret of his success, the rule, every word of which is golden. 'Keep down your losses – never let them get away from you. Let your profits take care of themselves.'"

That precept is huge. Timeless. It does not come naturally. Intense study, practice, is the rock solid foundation.

If cutting losses and letting profits run is the trend following mantra, it is because harsh reality dictates you can't play the game if you run out of money. No money, no honey!

A good example of not letting profits run can be seen in trading strategies that take profits off the table before the trend is over. For example, one broker told me one of his strategies was to ride a stock up for a 30% gain and then exit. That was his strategy. Let it go up 30% and get out. Sounds reasonable. However, a strategy that uses profit targets is problematic at a root level. It goes square against the math of getting rich, which is always without question to let your profits run. If you can't predict the end or top of a trend, don't get out early and risk leaving profits on the table – you will need the biggest winners after all to pay for the smaller losers.

4. BUY HIGHER HIGHS AND SELL SHORT LOWER LOWS.

Understanding how a trend follower implements their philosophy is well illustrated in Ed Seykota's sugar story.

He had been buying sugar – thousands of sugar futures contracts. And every day, the market was closing limit up. Every day, the market was going nonstop higher and higher. Seykota kept buying more and more sugar each day limit up.

An outside broker was watching all of Seykota's action. And one day the broker called him after the market close, and since he had extra contracts of sugar that were not balanced out, he said to Seykota, "I bet you want to buy these other 5,000 contracts of sugar."

Seykota replied, "Sold."

After the market closes limit up for days in a row, Seykota says, "Sure, I'll buy more sugar contracts at the absolute top of the market."

Everybody instinctively wants to buy sugar on the dip or on the retracement. Let it come down lower they pine. "I want a bargain" is their thinking – even if the bargain never appears. Trend following works by doing the opposite: It buys higher highs and sells short lower lows.

5. DO NOT PERSONALIZE YOUR TRADING DECISIONS.

By not personalizing your trading decisions, your emotional indecision has the chance to decrease.

Your approach becomes more objective, more rational. You have enough confidence in your own decision-making that you never seek out investment recommendations. You're content to wait patiently for the right opportunity. And you're never too proud to buy a stock making new highs, even all-time highs.

For you, investing opportunities are market breakouts. Conversely, when wrong, you exit immediately, no questions asked. You view loss as an opportunity to learn, move on, and save money to play another day. Obsessing on the past is pointless. You approach trading as a business, making note of what you buy or sell and why in the same matter-of-fact way you balance your checkbook.

6. DO NOT PREDICT – REACT.

Predictive technical analysis rightly deserves poignant criticism. Consider a recent Red Alert example from HSBC: "The Head & Shoulders Top with the neckline acting as resistance comes on top of a potentially bearish Elliot Wave irregular flat pattern and the fact that the index is now backing off from the old 2015 highs. A close below 17,992 would be very bearish. Pressure would ease above 18,449."

Good luck with that.

But there is a second type of technical analysis that neither predicts or forecasts. This type is based on reacting to price action, as trend trader Martin Estlander notes: "We identify market trends, we do not predict them. Our models are kept reactive at all times."

Instead of trying to predict market direction (an impossible chore), trend following reacts to movements whenever they occur. This enables a focus on the actual price risk, while avoiding becoming emotionally connected with direction, duration, and fundamental expectations.

This price analysis never allows entry at the exact bottom of a trend or an exit at the exact top. And you won't necessarily trade every day or week. Instead, trend following waits patiently for the right conditions. There is no forcing an opportunity not there.

Don't try to guess how far a trend will extend. You can't. You will never know how high or how low any market might go. Peter Borish, former second-in-command with Paul Tudor Jones, lays bare the trader's only concern: "Price makes news, not the other way around. A market is going to go where a market is going to go."

7. FORGET DISCRETION.

Successfully making fortunes isn't about excitement. It's about winning.

Decisions made at the discretion of the trader can be changed or second-guessed nonstop. These discretionary gut-trading decisions will be colored by personal bias. I have yet to see a multi-decade track record produced by gut trading. It's 100 per cent fantasy. Many imagine the process is like a fighter pilot strapped into the cockpit armed with an instinctive feel, or even an innate gift. It's not that.

Now, a trader's initial choice to launch a trading system is discretionary. You must make discretionary decisions such as choosing a system, selecting your portfolio, and determining a risk percentage (some would argue even these aspects can be made systematically too). However, after you've decided on the system-orientation basics, you can systematize these discretionary decisions and make them mechanical.

8. FORGET SEXY.

Since trend following has nothing to do with high-frequency trading, short-term trading, cutting-edge technologies or Wall Street hocus-pocus nonsense, its appeal is universally lost during extraordinary delusions unleashed inside the madness of crowds – that is, until bubbles pop. Trend following is not sexy until after the masses get poached and bleed out.

Nonetheless, if you look at how much money trend following has made before, during, and after assorted market bubbles, it becomes far more relevant to the bottom line of astute market players.

Markets of course are built by design to go up, down, and sideways. They trend or chop. They flow or don't. They are consistent, then they surprise. No one accurately can forecast a trend's beginning or end until it becomes a matter of record. However, if your trading strategy is designed to adapt, you can take advantage of changes.

9. CHANGE IS LIFE.

Like sunrise, sunset you can always expect a new trend following obituary, oblivious to the data, and rooted in purposeful ignorance, will be written every few years by an agenda-driven press, EMT defenders, and player haters despite the incredible amounts of money made by trend following practitioners.

Perplexed at Wall Street's lack of acceptance, one trend follower – John W. Henry – sees the danger in trying to be right:

> "How can someone buy high and short low and be successful for two decades unless the underlying nature of markets is to trend? On the other hand, I've seen year-after-year, brilliant men buying low and selling high for a while successfully and then going broke because they thought they understood why a certain investment instrument had to perform in accordance with their personal logic."

Trend following is much more than one trend following track record alone – this strategy has performed consistently for more than a century across an untold number of traders. And the reasons to explain why markets have tended to trend more often than not include investors' behavioral biases, market frictions, hedging demands, and never-ending market interventions launched by central banks and governments.

10. AS IN TRADING, SO IN LIFE.

The truth of trend following is its philosophical underpinnings are relevant not only to trading, but to life in general, from business to personal relationships. The old-pro trend followers were clear with me, in their words and actions: Trend following works best when pursued with the right mindset and unbridled passion.

Successful trend followers don't trade with grim resolve or with the intention to impress. They are playing a game to win and enjoying every moment of it. Like other high-level performers – think professional athletes and world-class musicians – they understand how critical it is to maintain a winning attitude for success.

Andrew Craig

ANDREW CRAIG *is the author of bestselling personal finance book* How to Own the World, *founder of personal finance website* www.plainenglishfinance.co.uk *and investment manager of the VT PEF Global Multi Asset Fund* (plainenglishfinance.co.uk/funds). How to Own the World *has been an Amazon bestseller and currently enjoys over 185 five-star reviews on Amazon.co.uk. At the time of writing, it is the second-highest-rated book about investing on Amazon. co.uk after Benjamin Graham's investment classic* The Intelligent Investor.

Andrew studied Economics and International Politics at the University of Birmingham, graduating in 1997. His first job took him to Washington DC to work as an intern for a US congressman on Capitol Hill. Here he was lucky enough to research various topical policy issues and write a number of speeches for the congressman.

On returning to the UK, Andrew began his career in finance on the Eurobond desk of SBC Warburg (now UBS) but moved to equities two years later to join the UBS smaller companies team. Andrew subsequently headed smaller company sales and sales trading at Williams de Broë and then held senior equity sales positions with Credit Agricole Cheuvreux and SEB in London and New York from 2007. Since

January 2015 he has been a partner at boutique specialist life sciences investment bank, WG Partners.

During his career in finance, he has met with the senior management teams of over 1,000 companies and with several hundred professional investors. Andrew has regularly been involved in high-profile stock market transactions. These have included the Kingdom of Sweden's sales of Nordea Bank AB in 2013 (totalling $7.6 billion) and the stock market flotation of several dozen companies including the likes of: easyJet, HMV, Burberry, Campari, Carluccio's, the Carbon Trust, lastminute.com and Arix Bioscience.

Since founding Plain English Finance, Andrew has appeared in numerous national and specialist financial publications including: the Mail on Sunday, the Mirror, CityAM, the Spectator, Shares and MoneyWeek magazines, YourMoney, This Is Money and Money Observer. He has been a regular commentator on Shares Radio and IG TV, was featured in Russell Brand and Michael Winterbottom's 2015 film The Emperor's New Clothes and interviewed by Eamon Holmes for the Channel 5 programme How the Other Half Lives.

Andrew does not claim to be any kind of financial 'guru' but he does have a sense of mission about spreading basic financial literacy. He believes that people owe it to themselves to learn enough about money and investment to get their financial house in order. The rewards of doing so are life-changing.

Andrew lives with his wife Rachel in south west London.

"OWNING THE WORLD IS IMPORTANT BECAUSE IT GRINDS OUT RETURNS."

How to Invest So That Crashes Don't Matter

I N O CTOBER OF 2016 I wrote a series of three articles. The first focused on a number of reasons a large stock market crash could very likely be imminent. The second set out counter arguments as to why this needn't be the case at all (these arguments have carried the day in the intervening few months as markets the world over have powered along between then and the time of writing, May 2017). Most importantly, however, rather than apologise for being yet another useless fence-sitting member of the financial commentariat, in the third article I pointed out that, to a great extent, it didn't matter whether there was a stock market crash or not. The reason for this, as I said at the time, is that:

> "I believe that I can arrange my financial affairs such that I am comfortable that whether there is a massive crash or whether stock markets power ahead, my ability to meet my longer-run financial goals will be largely unaffected. You should feel the same way too."

In my chapter of this *Rules* book I wanted to make that same argument again – that crashes needn't matter. How can this be possible? The answer comes in three parts:

1. OWN THE WORLD.

First, you need to ensure you own all or, at the very least, most major assets in most major regions of the world. This should include cash, bonds, property, equities, commodities (including precious metals) and a good split between the US, Asia and Europe (where I include Switzerland and the UK). I call this 'owning the world'.

It isn't that hard to evidence that the wealthiest and most financially literate people in the world have invested like this for centuries. In fact, I would go as far as to argue that investing this way is one of the reasons such people became disproportionately wealthy in the first place, especially when they did this over generations.

It might intuitively make sense to you why this approach works: in 2007–2009, for example, stock markets around the world more than halved but oil hit an all-time high in 2008 and gold went up nearly 20% in 2009. Sometimes Asia is on fire and Europe stagnates and sometimes America is the place to be. The easiest thing to do is just do your best to own all asset classes in all areas of the world as inexpensively and tax-efficiently as possible. You have a low probability of working out the next 'hot' area or what the top performing asset class is going to be in the next few years. More often than not, not even the experts get this right and I would argue that amateur investors who try to time markets this way significantly increase their probability of losing money. Far easier to just own it all.

You might think that this approach will mean you end up with indifferent performance but the evidence of history is that this is not the case. In the early 1980s, US investment writer, Harry Browne, said about this approach: "Over broad periods of time, the winning investments add more value to the portfolio than the losing investments take away."

Award-winning British investor, Tim Price, has called this kind of diversification "the only free lunch in investment", and Jack Meyer, who used to run the Harvard University endowment fund and achieved an average return of 15.9% a year under his tenure (910% compounded), has said:

> "The most powerful tool an investor has working for him or her is diversification. True diversification allows you to build portfolios with higher returns for the same risk. Most investors are far less diversified than they should be."

European aristocrats, Victorian industrialists or American 'robber barons' needed an army of bankers and lawyers to invest like this. The great news for you in 2017 is that it is far easier to invest like this today than it was for them. You can get started with very little money. You can invest using tax-sheltered accounts such as an ISA and this can all be done from the comfort of your own home using your computer or even your smartphone.

2. AUTOMATE.

Secondly, you should look to automate your investments by direct debit each month if at all possible. This achieves something that will be very good for your peace of mind over time: that something is called 'smoothing' or 'averaging in'. It also removes you from the equation – which, with very few exceptions, is also a very good idea.

To explain: the S&P 500 index in the US (a good proxy for 'the stock market') fell from around 1,500 in October 2007 down to the rather spooky and Biblical level of 666 in March 2009 (that is a 56% collapse. Ouch!). It then went from 666 all the way to north of 2,300 as I write (that is a 245% recovery. Nice!).

The problem is – human nature is such that if you had tried to time your investments to take advantage of these moves, you would almost certainly have got it wrong. In fact, the situation is actually worse than that: there is a high probability you would have sold low and bought high and timed your investments about as badly as it is possible to do.

Why is this? Because we are hard-wired psychologically to get this wrong. We humans are pack beasts. We pay a disproportionate amount of attention to what everyone else around us is doing. Much as we fight it, very few of us have the knowledge or self-confidence to be truly contrarian. When the market bottomed at 666 in March 2009, nearly everything you would have read or seen in the news would have gone on about how risky stock market investment is and how much money everyone had just lost. Every dinner party you had attended people would have been saying the same thing and bemoaning how much they had lost. Fear, woe, pessimism, anger, general wailing and gnashing of teeth. As a result, you would have been highly unlikely to have considered putting your hard-earned savings into the stock market. Everyone would tell you you'd be crazy to even consider it: "Brrr. Too risky! Look what just happened!"

Arguably even more insidious, however: as the market recovered from the bottom – 10% up, then 20%, 30%, 40% and all the way up to 245% (today) – it would have been perfectly natural for you to have said to yourself (pretty much every month): "Damn! I must have missed it now. I'm too late". You would then not have invested.

After a year or two of this, the next thought you might have would probably be something like: "Damn! I really must sort this investment thing out. Look! The market is up 245%. It just keeps going up. My mate has made a fortune. I've been avoiding it the whole time and missing out. Right. That's it. I'm in."

You know the rest. Just as you decide it is time to get back in, along comes the next dotcom or Lehman-style crash and you get absolutely flattened and spend the next decade licking your wounds. Especially if, as so many people do, you wade into a stock-market-only kind of investment rather than owning the world as described above. The cycle repeats. This really happens. Time and time again. It is human nature. We are hard-wired to do this.

The solution is to *take yourself out of the equation*. You really should ignore the news completely and automate your investments. Do not try to second guess what is going to happen. Do not try to time the market and start thinking 'I should buy this now or sell that now'. Do not ask supposed 'experts' what they think, either. Just invest what you can afford, every month, without fail, into something sensible (more on this shortly) until such time as you want to live on the proceeds (a time that will arrive sooner than most people dream is possible if you actually do this).

In our example of the S&P 500 above – had you been automating your payments monthly, you would have bought in at 1,500 just before the crash (ouch) but then every month after the crash too (at levels along the lines of 680, 750, 850, 930, 1,000 and so on – all the way up to 2,300! Lovely!).

The net result of this approach is that you grind out consistent and meaningful returns (far higher that interest rates) through the economic cycle, no matter what is happening. Thanks to Einstein's eighth wonder of the world – compound interest – the tortoise then thrashes the hare and you will end up with more money than you thought possible.

3. STICK TO YOUR GUNS.

Finally, you must have confidence in your game plan and stick to your guns (doing this is far easier once you understand a bit more about finance).

Professors Elroy Dimson and Paul Marsh of London Business School have shown that investing in UK smaller companies has achieved an annual return of no less than 15.4% going back as far as 1955!* You read that right. Fifteen point four per cent a year for 60 years!

Making that sort of return on the money you save and invest will make you wealthy really rather quickly – particularly if you're using an ISA account so that you don't even incur any tax liability. You can literally become an ISA millionaire in a few years.

There is a problem, however (although it is a problem with a solution as we shall see): although this performance track record over no less than 60 years is amazing (and almost entirely unknown by the vast majority of people other than a small minority of folks in the City), the 15.4% returns didn't come smoothly every year. Some years smaller companies powered ahead by 30% or even 40% or more. On several occasions between 1955 and the present day, however, they fell by more than 50%.

If you refer back to rule 2, above, you will understand that these falls will so often cause people holding UK small caps to give up in fear, crystallise their 50% loss and then never invest in the space again – a terrible result all round and nowhere near the 15.4% annual return they could be making. This is why having confidence in what you are doing and sticking to your game plan is so important.

When doing speaking events, I quite often say that investment success is truly 90% about admin and only 10% about what you invest in. If you have actually made the effort to set up an investment account with a good quality company, optimised your ISA and pension arrangements and set up the necessary regular direct debits, you will be 90% of the way to investment success. The final 10% is about choosing something sensible to make those payments into and sticking to your guns.

UK smaller companies have produced more than 15% pa for 60 years. Terry Smith's Fundsmith Fund has produced 19.8% annualised returns for the last six years (www.fundsmith.co.uk/fund-factsheet). Baillie Gifford's Scottish Mortgage Investment Trust has returned 300% over the last ten years (www.bailliegifford.com/individual-investors/funds/scottish-mortgage-investment-trust/performance). The list of these sorts of things is longer than you think.

By investing monthly in these sorts of assets and sticking to your guns, you can achieve really good investment returns. Most people have no

---

* www.london.edu/news-and-events/news/uk-small-and-mid-caps-outperform-in-2015#.WAem7_ArK_U

idea about any of this – which is a fundamental failure of our education system.

That said, all of the above ways of making these returns carry with them a good deal of volatility. I am delighted that one of my friends has made more than 50% in his pension fund from his holding in Fundsmith over the last two years, but I warn him every week that this holding will almost certainly fall a long way in the next crash. As long as he has the confidence to average down when this happens, he will be fine.

The problem is that it takes a great deal of mental fortitude to do this, even if you have prepared for it. This is why owning the world is so important – because it grinds out the returns without those 50% down years scaring you out of your position, making you give up on investment and turning a paper loss into a real one as a result.

It is also crucial as you get closer to retirement. Losing £5,000 from your £10,000 pot in your 20s is an entirely different problem to that of losing £500,000 from your £1,000,000 pot at 60.

In summary

If you own the world, automate your investments and stick to your guns, you should make high single-digit to low double-digit returns through the economic cycle no matter what the latest headlines are.

Even better, doing this removes a great deal of worry. Once you have done the admin needed to put this in place, you can sleep well at night and spend your precious time doing whatever it is that you love to do, rather than waste it on following financial markets and worrying about Trump, Clinton, Syria, Brexit, killer bees, immigrants, earthquakes, aliens or whatever else the papers are trilling about this week.

Sandy Cross

SANDY CROSS *is an investment manager and Director at Rossie House Investment Management, where he specialises in managing private client portfolios. Sandy has a particular expertise and interest in investment trusts. He previously worked at Standard Life Wealth, where he was a portfolio manager and Head of the Edinburgh office. Prior to this, Sandy worked in London at HSBC Investments. He started his financial services career in Hong Kong as a portfolio management trainee with NatWest Investment Management Asia.*

Sandy is a graduate of the University of Edinburgh and also has an MBA from Imperial College. He is a Chartered Fellow of the Securities Institute.

"IF YOUR MANAGER LOVES AN ACQUISITIVE COMPANY, ACQUIRE HOLDINGS IN SOMEONE ELSE'S FUND."

Six Tips for Talent-Spotting Active Fund Managers

I AM A great believer in active fund management. I see the attraction of passive funds: getting more or less average performance for a bargain basement price isn't a bad thing. However, my colleagues and I remain convinced that when it comes to investing, man (or woman) can do better than machine. We are sure that there are genuinely talented managers operating in the market and that we can use them to diversify our clients' holdings while also making them better returns than if we simply tracked the wider market indices. Below are a few thoughts on how we find the funds run by those talented managers.

1. LOOK FOR THE FUND MANAGERS WHO ENJOY MACRO STORIES BUT MOSTLY IGNORE THEM.

Everyone loves a story. And if that story manages to make something complicated and inherently unpredictable look like it might be both straightforward and pretty predictable, all the better. So children read fairy tales (from which they get the idea that morality somehow only comes in black and white) and investors devour market research (from which they get the idea that the complexity of markets can somehow be tidied up via a pertinent chart or too). But just as fairy tales are an unsatisfactory preparation for real life, so investment stories tend to turn out to be a dubious basis on which to invest. That's largely because most macro forecasts – on the direction of markets and of economies – are wrong. Consider the efforts of the US Federal Reserve. It is well-resourced and packed to the gunwales with very intelligent people. There have been eight recessions in the last 60 years. Those people have forecast none of them. It's just too hard. Far better, we find, to skip the fallacy of precise macroeconomic forecasting in favour of assuming that there is always a range of outcomes possible and looking to build portfolios that will be resilient to them.

2. REMEMBER THAT INVESTING IS ABOUT COMPANIES.

The bright side of forecasting failure is that it doesn't matter nearly as much as you think it does to long-term investors. Investing, whether you do it through funds as we do in our business, or you own individual equities directly, is about companies – their products, their cash flows, their profits, their management's expertise and their cultures. And while identifying the trends in these isn't easy it comes with many fewer variables than forecasting the direction of global interest rates. Better to focus on what is useful and possible than what is usually impossible and not necessarily useful (forecasting a macroeconomic trend correctly doesn't mean you will have any luck predicting its effect on the sales of the actual investment in question).

3. INVEST WITH MANAGERS WHO HAVE SOME SENSE OF STOCK MARKET HISTORY.

The past is easier to grasp than the future. It can also help us to minimise the mistakes of the future. I strongly recommend that new investors visit the Library of Mistakes in Edinburgh. There – as is the case in the libraries of many a business school – you can find shelves groaning with research that comes to one key conclusion: about three quarters of M&A is a complete failure for shareholders. I can therefore tell you with some certainty that shares in companies engaged in M&A (beyond small infill acquisitions) are less likely to be good investments than those that stick to organic growth. I can also tell you that any deal described as 'transformational' is to be avoided like the plague. If your manager loves an acquisitive company, acquire holdings in someone else's fund.

History teaches us similar lessons about leverage. We always want to be ready for a crisis (there is almost always one on the way). And we know that it is the companies with the most debt that come a cropper the fastest in a crisis. Having debt to pay back and banks to keep happy reduces their flexibility and their autonomy – both things managers really need when the chips are down. Long-term investors are far better off accepting lower annual returns in return for a greater degree of financial resilience – and a greater chance of long-term survival. So check your managers' top ten holdings list – if there are too many highly leveraged firms you may be better off avoiding the fund.

4. BE IN IT TOGETHER.

You want to see a manager investing in their own fund. If it isn't good enough for his money why should it be good enough for yours? Check their holdings before you give them yours. There are all sorts of definitions of risk around in the financial world. The only one that should matter to most investors is the risk of permanent loss of capital. If a manager isn't investing in his own fund you might wonder why he reckons his own capital isn't safe there.

5. MAKE SURE YOUR MANAGER ISN'T OVERWORKING HIMSELF: LESS TRADING IS GENERALLY BETTER.

A big difference between a successful asset manager and an unsuccessful asset manager is often turnover. Low turnover means lower costs (which are a helpful predictor of long-term performance). But it also suggests a higher level of conviction. You want a manager who has a clear strategy which brings him good ideas and who then gives those ideas time to play out. All too many managers get swayed by the short-term direction of the market: it takes only the smallest of worries that their own strategy might mean they underperform the market in the short term for them to adopt someone else's. We're looking for the small number of managers in the market with a bit more stamina than most. The ones who have a (good) plan and stick to it regardless of what everyone else is up to.

6. LISTED FUNDS – AN OLD BUT SUCCESSFUL IDEA.

If you want to invest for the long term you could well be best off in a listed fund (an investment trust in the UK). These are effectively companies, the purpose of which is to invest in other companies. But their key virtue is that their pool of capital is fixed. Investors can sell their shares, of course, but they can't actually pull capital from the fund. This means that the trusts can hold investments for the very long term and that they can invest in the kind of illiquid assets that other funds would see as too risky (on the basis that they couldn't be sold in a hurry rather than that they are inherently dangerous). So you can use an investment trust to buy into the kind of things you may want for diversification these days

– smaller companies or property, for example. And if it goes wrong you will find that unlike with most investment products there is someone obvious to complain to. As listed companies, trusts have independent boards. If you don't like the way they are investing your money just turn up to the AGM and tell them so.

Lawrence A. Cunningham

LAWRENCE A. CUNNINGHAM *has written a dozen books, including* The Essays of Warren Buffett: Lessons for Corporate America, *published in successive editions since 1996 in collaboration with the legendary Mr Buffett; the critically acclaimed* Berkshire Beyond Buffett: The Enduring Value of Values *(Columbia University Press 2014);* Contracts in the Real World: Stories of Popular Contracts and Why They Matter *(Cambridge University Press, 2012); and* Quality Investing: Owning the Best Companies for the Long Term *(Harriman House, 2016).*

Cunningham's op-eds have been published in many newspapers worldwide, including the Financial Times, New York Times, *and* Wall Street Journal, *and his research has appeared in top academic journals published by such universities as Columbia, Harvard, and Vanderbilt. A popular professor at George Washington University, Cunningham also lectures widely, delivering as many as 50 lectures annually to a wide variety of academic, business and investing groups.*

"AS THEY SAY IN POKER, 'IF YOU'VE BEEN IN THE GAME 30 MINUTES AND YOU DON'T KNOW WHO THE PATSY IS, YOU'RE THE PATSY'."

Warren Buffett's Investing Rules

1. DON'T BE THE PATSY.

IF YOU CANNOT invest intelligently, the best way to own common stocks is through an index fund that charges minimal fees. Those doing so will beat the net results (after fees and expenses) enjoyed by the great majority of investment professionals. As they say in poker, 'If you've been in the game 30 minutes and you don't know who the patsy is, you're the patsy'.

2. OPERATE AS A BUSINESS ANALYST.

Do not pay attention to market action, macroeconomic action, or even securities action. Concentrate on evaluating businesses.

3. LOOK FOR A BIG MOAT.

Look for businesses with favorable long-term prospects, whose earnings are virtually certain to be materially higher five, ten, twenty years from now.

4. EXPLOIT MR MARKET.

Market prices gyrate around business value, much as a manic depressive swings from euphoria to gloom when things are neither that good nor that bad. The market gives you a price, which is what you pay, while the business gives you value and that is what you own. Take advantage of these market mispricings, but don't let them take advantage of you.

5. INSIST ON A MARGIN OF SAFETY.

The difference between the price you pay and the value you get is the margin of safety. The thicker, the better. Berkshire's purchases of the Washington Post Company in 1973–74 offered a very thick margin of safety (price about 1/5 of value).

6. BUY AT A REASONABLE PRICE.

Bargain hunting can lead to purchases that don't give long-lasting value; buying at frenzied prices will lead to purchases that give very little value at all. It is better to buy a great business at fair price than a fair business at great price.

7. KNOW YOUR LIMITS.

Avoid investment targets that are outside your circle of competence. You don't have to be an expert on every company or even many – only those within your circle of competence. The size of the circle is not very important; knowing its boundaries, however, is vital.

8. INVEST WITH 'SONS-IN-LAW'.

Invest only with people you like, trust and admire – people you'd be happy to have your daughter marry.

9. ONLY A FEW WILL MEET THESE STANDARDS.

When you see one, buy a meaningful amount of its stock. Don't worry so much about whether you end up diversified or not. If you get the one big thing, that is better than a dozen mediocre things.

10. AVOID GIN RUMMY BEHAVIOR.

This is the opposite of possibly the most foolish of all Wall Street maxims: 'You can't go broke taking a profit'. Imagine as a stockholder that you own the business and hold it the way you would if you owned and ran the whole thing. If you aren't willing to own a stock for ten years, don't even think about owning it for ten minutes.

Job Curtis

JOB CURTIS *is a director of the Global Equity Income team at Henderson Global Investors. He has been the fund manager of The City of London Investment Trust since 1991 and co-manager of the Henderson Global Equity Income mutual fund (for US investors) since 2006.*

Job graduated in 1983 from Oxford University with a degree in philosophy, politics and economics. He has worked on stock market investing for 34 years, since 1992 with Henderson. Earlier in his career he worked for Grieveson Grant (stockbrokers) 1983-1985, Cornhill Insurance (investment department) 1985–1987 and Touche Remnant from 1987 until it was taken over by Henderson in 1992.

"IT IS ALWAYS
EASIER TO BE
PATIENT
IF YOU ARE
RECEIVING A
DECENT
DIVIDEND IN THE
MEANTIME."

Successful Equity
Income Investing

1. INVEST IN ABOVE-AVERAGE YIELD AND GROWTH.

I AIM TO invest in stocks which have an above-average yield relative
to the UK stock market's FTSE All-Share Index and can grow their
profits and dividends. This mixture of yield and growth is attractive
for many investors. A significant part of the long-term return from
equities comes from the dividends paid by companies. In the analysis
of companies that I do with colleagues in the Global Equity Income
team at Henderson Global Investors, we take care to look at how well a
company's dividend is covered by profits and cash so that it can make the
necessary capital expenditure for its future growth.

2. AVOID THE HIGHEST YIELDS.

Share prices with a dividend yield at the highest end of the market
range are riskier. The stock market is fairly efficient and a high yield may
indicate a lack of growth or even the possibility of a dividend cut. High
yield shares are sometimes called 'value traps'. There are exceptions that
prove the rule and Provident Financial, the non-standard-lender, is an
example of a stock in City of London's portfolio which was on a high
yield, performed very well for a number of years, but has recently given
up all its gains and stopped paying a dividend.

3. AVOID LOW OR ZERO YIELD.

Obviously, if you are looking for income, you will tend to avoid zero- or
very low-yielding shares. It is also worth noting that there are unrealistic
expectations for many low- or zero-yielding stocks. When such companies
disappoint, the adverse share-price reaction can be magnified, with shares
falling further than percentage decline in profits estimates as investors
derate the stock. The most extreme example of this in my career was
in 1998 and 1999 when technology shares soared upwards on excitement

about the internet. They then fell back dramatically from 2000 to 2003 as they failed to match the overhyped expectations of investors. Indeed, many companies had large market capitalisations despite not paying dividends or even making profits. Ironically, much of the vision of the transforming nature of the internet for the economy and society has proved to be correct over the next two decades. But the episode shows the danger of investing in overvalued stocks that fail to meet expectations.

4. DIVERSIFY YOUR PORTFOLIO.

When it comes to comes to constructing a portfolio, diversification is, in my opinion, an important part of successful equity income investing. However big a company is, the unexpected can happen. A good example was oil giant BP and the Macondo oil spill in the US Gulf of Mexico. BP had to suspend its dividend and suffered a severe share price fall. Another example was Royal Bank of Scotland, which was one of the largest stocks in the UK market and then lost most of its value in the global financial crisis of 2007–2009. I therefore firmly believe in having a spread of investments rather than having a small number of eggs in one basket. City of London's portfolio typically has between 100 and 120 investments. This also allows smaller investment in stocks where I may not have high conviction, possibly because they have some short-term problems, but where there is significant long-term upside. And it is always easier to be patient if you are receiving a decent dividend in the meantime.

I also believe in having exposure to a range of sectors, both cyclical and non-cyclical, so that the portfolio can perform under different economic conditions. UK equity income funds, such as City of London, can have up to 20% of their portfolio invested in overseas listed companies. By doing so, we have owned stocks, such as Microsoft, which has no equivalent in the UK and has been a good dividend grower.

5. AVOID LEVERAGE.

As an income investor, I am wary of companies with a high level of debt. This is particularly true of companies in cyclical industries. During an economic downturn, the profits of such companies will decline significantly and they will have to focus on paying the interest on their debts, leaving their dividends vulnerable to being cut if there is not enough left over to pay for them. Companies with very stable earnings, such as regulated utilities, are more suitable for taking on leverage. For example, customers of water companies continue to pay their bills during recessions.

6. EMBRACE INVESTMENT TRUST ADVANTAGES.

The closed-ended structure of investment trusts is a big advantage for achieving consistent dividend growth. The reason is that investment trusts are allowed to retain up to 15% of their investment income each year. They put this into a revenue reserve which will grow in the good years for dividends. During bear or falling markets, when there are dividend cuts, investment trusts can dip into their revenue reserves to continue growing their dividends even if they have not been covered by earnings in that particular year. In contrast, open ended funds (OEICs) have to distribute all of their investment income each year and have no revenue reserve to utilise when there are dividend cuts across the market. During the bear market of 2007–2009, some 25% of UK companies cut their dividends and it would have been hard for an OEIC to avoid doing the same. For seven of the 26 years of my management of City of London's portfolio, we have had to use the revenue reserves to grow the dividend. Without the revenue reserves, City of London could not have achieved its 51 years of annual dividend increases.

Mark Dampier

MARK DAMPIER *has been head of research at Hargreaves Lansdown, the UK's largest independent stockbroking firm, since 1998. He has been in the financial services industry for 32 years, initially working as an advisor helping individual clients to invest their money. He holds a BA Honours degree in Law. He has become one of the best-known and most widely quoted figures in the fund management industry. He wrote a regular column in the* Independent *on funds and markets for many years, and regularly comments in the national press and on broadcast media.*

Effective Investing *(Harriman House, 2015) was his first book (and, he swears, definitely his last!). In his spare time, depending on the season, you will find him shooting, skiing, sailing or fishing.*

"THE BEST REACTION IS INVARIABLY NO REACTION."

Investing, Warts and All

T HIS CHAPTER IS very much investment as I see it, warts and all. I often find that advisors, worried they may fall foul of regulatory rules, give academic exam-style answers to clients' queries rather than provide real-world guidance. If regulated by the FCA (as I am), one is not permitted to mention one's own investments to clients, as even this can apparently be interpreted as financial advice. However, journalism is outside the regulatory remit of the FCA, so I am free to discuss my own investments at length in a newspaper or book. Go figure.

I hope this chapter will provide some useful tips for successful investment, though there are exceptions for almost every rule – so none of these basic principles should be chiselled into stone!

1. GET ORGANISED.

Logistics is an obvious place to start. To manage your own investments you need to be organised. When I started out 32 years ago, computers for everyday use were in their infancy. Most investors had stockbrokers to manage their portfolio, and paid a small fortune for the privilege. In the 1980s the mainstream arrival of the unit trust revolutionised private investment. Exchange controls were abolished in 1979 and unit trusts then offered a way not only to invest in the UK, but in overseas markets too.

My first investment was a Japanese unit trust. Henderson Japan made 75% in the first six months of my investment and helped kick-start my investment career. I was not the only one to catch the bug and, while many investors still used advisors and stockbrokers, others began to see the benefits of self-management. It was unquestionably cheaper. However, the administration involved was vast, so it was only really an option for the time-rich. A spread of 15 unit trust holdings, not unreasonable for a £100,000 portfolio, meant 30 separate statements would hit the doormat over the course of a year. None of the valuations or statements were standardised across the different fund groups and to work out the aggregate value required a copy of the *FT* and a calculator.

The rise of technology and the investment platform revolutionised private investment once again. A valuation is now available 24 hours a day at the click of a mouse, investments are all held in one place, dealing is fast and efficient and a consolidated tax certificate every April makes tax returns a breeze. This all comes at a cost, of course, but this is small in comparison to the time and effort saved. Platforms also generally come with additional benefits: analytical tools, research, and performance data, for example. So, while you need to be organised to manage your own investments, time spent on selection of the right platform makes this easier and is time well-spent.

2. YOU HAVE TO BE PATIENT AND DISCIPLINED.

Patience and self-discipline are where many investors fall down. The average holding period for funds is now around three years – far short of the five-to-ten-year investment horizon recommended. Fault lies with the media and, ironically, platforms. The growth of the internet has been a blessing in most cases but investors have also been cursed with too much readily available information. Rather like the evolution of satellite TV, there may be more available but it is not necessarily all good quality content. The requirement to produce a constant stream of fresh content has, I believe, led to poorer quality financial journalism. Worse still, it has become highly emotional and this often drives investors to make rash investment decisions starved of fact. Coupled with the ease of dealing through a platform, portfolios are subjected to frequent and ill-advised trading.

Investments are not a 'get-rich-quick' scheme. Patience is required for a portfolio to grow. Anyone who professes otherwise is a gambler, not an investor, and their advice is likely to lead to disappointment and loss in very short order.

3. BE HAPPY DOING NOTHING.

A long-term view with as few investment decisions as possible is the secret sauce to a successful investment portfolio. Legendary investor Warren Buffett's "don't just do something, sit there" line encapsulates my own investment philosophy and is a view shared by some of the most successful fund managers of our generation. Nick Train, of Lindsell Train, has made very few investment decisions over the past five years, and Neil Woodford's funds have similarly low turnover. Their conviction is not swayed by short-term events. Indeed, they often welcome price falls as this provides the opportunity to top-up favoured positions at temporarily reduced prices.

With bad news or uncertainty comes the temptation to make investment decisions based on short-term factors. In 2016, in the months prior to the UK's referendum on EU membership, or Donald Trump's election as US president, many investors attempted to predict the result and position their investments accordingly. When stock markets fall, the temptation is to run for the hills, cash everything in and hide. This is not advisable, if for no other reason than the very tricky task of deciding when to buy back in.

Very few investors foresaw the financial crisis, but suppose you sold your entire portfolio just prior to the collapse of Northern Rock. Would you have bought back in at the bottom of the market in early 2009? Not many would, as there was little to suggest stock markets would rise and the media was still full of doom and gloom. Many might still be in cash to this day. Yes, the fall in 2008 was painful – but a good quality fund manager has more than made up for those losses since. So, while I do not wish to foster complacency, my advice is to ignore the noise. If a financial event appears on the ten o'clock news, don't get caught up in the emotion, particularly when you do not fully understand what is going on. The best reaction is invariably no reaction.

4. KEEP IT SIMPLE.

Unit trusts were originally designed to provide investors with diversified exposure to the stock market. However, it was not long before fund management marketing departments realised they could also sell funds with a devotion to niche areas, such as technology, oils, mining, healthcare, water, or more recently, robotics. While they have their uses, specialist funds are an area to avoid unless you have the stomach for a rollercoaster ride. No matter how skilled the fund manager, there is nowhere to hide when their particular area of focus falls out of favour. Investors typically buy specialist funds when the area is in vogue, and frequently touted in the media. In other words, they invest at precisely the wrong time. I refer to these funds as 'sex and violence' funds but I suspect the typical investor tends to get all the violence and none of the sex.

For those who cannot resist speculation on something sexy, the rules must change. These funds are generally not long-term investments. Buy when the area is downtrodden and unloved and sell when others begin to get excited. This might sound easy in theory, but it is remarkably difficult in practice.

5. FOLLOW THE MANAGER.

The performance of an actively managed fund is ultimately down to the decisions taken by the fund manager. An investor therefore takes on the risk that the manager may be no good or a good manager leaves the fund to go elsewhere. It is, therefore, important to check the manager's history and keep on top of any changes in personnel.

A number of successful and experienced fund managers have left established houses to set up on their own. I generally favour these investment boutiques, as they allow managers to cultivate a team and working environment to suit their approach. They also typically have a large stake in the business, which aligns their interests with those of their investors and makes it more likely they will stick around for the long term.

If this sounds too complicated, passive funds offer another option. They have no active fund manager risk and typically offer cheap fees but it is important to remember they never provide an index return – all passive funds underperform the index they track over the long term.

Whether you choose to invest in active or passive funds, investment trusts, shares or a mixture of them all, the important point is to be invested in the first place. Keep it simple, remove emotion, trade less, and the stock market can provide a wonderful way to grow your wealth over the long term. That said, it is important to remember the reason you invest in the first place. For most, it is to improve the quality of life. If an investment portfolio will give you sleepless nights or the emotion is likely to get the better of you, stick to cash – investment is not for you.

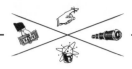

Elroy Dimson, Paul Marsh & Mike Staunton

ELROY DIMSON *is chairman of the Centre for Endowment Asset Management at Cambridge Judge Business School and Emeritus Professor of Finance at London Business School.* **PAUL MARSH** *is Emeritus Professor of Finance at London Business School.* **MIKE STAUNTON** *is director of the London Share Price Database at London Business School.*

They are the authors of the Credit Suisse Global Investment Returns Yearbook.

"OVER THE LONG TERM SIZE, VALUE, INCOME, MOMENTUM AND VOLATILITY HAVE A DECISIVE IMPACT ON PORTFOLIO PERFORMANCE."

Five Factors that Influence Investment Returns

SIZE, VALUE, INCOME, momentum and volatility have an important impact on portfolio returns. They should be monitored by all investors. While in the short term, there is often no strong pattern, over the long term these factors have had a decisive impact on portfolio performance.

1. SIZE: MICRO-CAPS ARE THE REAL STAR PERFORMERS.

It is now well established that returns from investing in small companies have, over several decades, brought higher returns than investing in large ones. In the UK, a £1 investment in large-capitalisation companies at the start of 1955 would be worth £1,087 today. An investment in medium-sized companies would have given a better result, and a better one still in smaller companies.

But the real star performers over this 61-year period were the so-called micro-caps – the bottom 1% by value of the UK equity market. A £1 investment in 1955 would have grown to no less than £27,256 by the end of last year.

2. VALUE: VALUE INVESTING WORKS.

There have been periods when value investing has yielded disappointing results. For example, in the 1990s, it was growth stocks that did well; value stocks trailed behind. (This pattern was reversed with the pricking of the dotcom bubble.) But again, over the very long term, there is a discernible pattern. Compare the performance of two groups of equities: those whose share price is low relative to the company's book value, versus those whose share price is high relative to book value.

In the UK, the group whose share prices are relatively low measured against book value saw an average annual return of 16% over the years 1955 to 2016. For shares with a high market price relative to their book value, the figure was 10.3%. Value investing worked.

3. INCOME: INVEST IN HIGH-YIELD STOCKS.

A separate measure of 'value' is the percentage dividend yield on a share. Here the *Credit Suisse Global Investment Returns Yearbook* has the advantage of a database that goes back to 1900.

In it are calculated the returns on a 'high-yield' portfolio versus those on a 'low-yield' one. The 100 largest UK stocks at the start of each calendar year are split into two groups – the 50 offering the highest yield and the 50 with the lowest. The returns of each group are calculated over the following 12 months and the process is repeated annually.

An investment of £1 in the low-yield group in 1900 would have grown to £6,810 by the end of 2016. But over the same period, £1 in the high-yield group would have swollen to £158,727 – more than 23 times greater.

4. MOMENTUM: BIG MO MAKES A DIFFERENCE.

Using the past momentum of share prices to predict future performance is counter-intuitive. If markets functioned with perfect efficiency, it should not be possible to secure above-average returns simply by buying past winners and selling losers.

Yet there are big returns from trading on momentum. There are many ways of putting this approach into practice. For example, when measuring past momentum it is possible to choose share price performance over three, six or 12 months when identifying winners and losers. Similarly, once bought, past winners could be held for one month or two, or longer.

Looking at the data since 1900, buying stocks that have outperformed over a prior period (winners) and selling those that have under-performed (losers) would have yielded substantial returns. In the *Credit Suisse Global Investment Returns Yearbook* this calculation is made by segregating stocks according to their previous 12-month performance. A one-month waiting period is then allowed before buying and holding for one month.

Using that formula, and looking only at the top 100 UK stocks, the winners would have returned an average 14.1% a year, while the losers would have returned only 3.6%. Of course, this approach involves a lot of buying and selling, so investors should take account of trading costs before embarking on a Big Mo investment strategy.

5. VOLATILITY: HIGH-RISK STOCKS FAIL TO DELIVER HIGH REWARDS.

Intuition suggests that investors should be rewarded for taking on higher risk: they will receive higher long-term returns from putting money into stocks whose prices are volatile, moving up or down more sharply than the market as a whole.

It's not that simple. Several studies have suggested that the opposite is true: investing in stocks that have been volatile in the recent past has delivered returns inferior to those from investing in shares whose prices are steadier. In other words, low volatility and high investment returns go hand-in-hand.

But these findings are generally based on short-term price movements – daily returns over three months. In the *Credit Suisse Global Investment Returns Yearbook* a longer-term measure of volatility is looked at, tracking share performance relative to the market over a 60-month period.

On that basis, there was little to choose between the returns from high-risk and low-risk shares in the years between 1960 and the turn of the millennium. Then came the bursting of the tech bubble in 2000. Prices of high-risk stock (for which read high volatility) collapsed. Since 2003, high-risk stocks have actually outperformed their low-risk rivals.

Certainly, over the full period from 1960 to 2016, high-risk stocks have underperformed. But that underperformance is attributable to their collapse when the tech bubble burst.

Stephen Eckett

STEPHEN ECKETT *started his career with Baring Securities and then later worked for Bankers Trust and S.G. Warburg, during which time he worked in London, Hong Kong and Tokyo. After settling in France he co-founded Harriman House which has become the leading independent publisher of financial books in the UK. He also writes books on finance including, most recently* Harriman's Stock Market Almanac.

"AS WARREN BUFFETT SAID, 'I'D BE A BUM ON THE STREET WITH A TIN CUP IF THE MARKETS WERE ALWAYS EFFICIENT'."

How to Profit from Stock Market Anomalies

1. CORRELATION IS NOT CAUSATION...

W E LIVE IN a digital age. A consequence of this is that we are swimming in data, and we can analyse this data easily with programs like Excel. Import a table of figures into a spreadsheet, click a button and we have a chart – it's amazing! Such power allows us to discover all sorts of patterns and associations in the data. But some of these patterns and associations – or correlations – are spurious. In other words, the mere existence of an association of events does not necessarily mean there is a causal link. This brings us to a phrase that is frequently heard today: 'correlation is not causation'.

This may sound like a modern phrase, but a search on Google Books finds variants of the phrase starting to appear in books from 1880. But, although the phrase may have been around for some time, its use has exploded in the last couple of decades with the growth of use of computers and the internet. Much weak research today can be dismissed briefly and effectively with the correlation is not causation critique.

A mini industry now seems to exist in identifying spurious correlations. For example, there is a correlation between annual per capita cheese consumption and the number of people who die annually by becoming tangled in their bedsheets (further spurious correlations can be found at www.tylervigen.com/spurious-correlations).

In the financial world, an example of spurious correlation would be the famous Super Bowl Indicator – which holds if the Super Bowl is won by a team from the old National Football League, the stock market will end the year higher than it began, and if a team from the old American Football League wins then the market will end lower.

But, while it is important to be sceptical of correlations, the possibility of a causal link should not be dismissed too quickly, however unlikely it may seem. As the statistician, Edward Tufte, says, "Correlation is not causation but it sure is a hint." In other words, strong correlations may highlight areas of interest for further investigation.

And if a correlation is identified it may still be possible to exploit it profitably without fully understanding any underlying causation – or, indeed, whether any such causal link actually exists.

2. CHOOSE CAREFULLY YOUR TIME PERIOD.

Since 1693 the average annual return for the UK equity market has been 2.7%. Since 1693! Impressed?

A price history of over 300 years is quite something. But we could question where this data came from, or what index is being used, or the consistency of the index calculation method over this period Or what the stock market comprised in 1693?

If we were looking to use this price history to make some forecasts of future price behaviour we might query whether data from 1693 or from 1993 was more relevant. It would seem likely that more recent data would be more useful as a basis of making those forecasts.

Just because you have data from, say, 1300 (as we do in the case of gold) does not mean you have to use it. Often more recent data will encapsulate better the current prevailing nature of price data than longer-term data.

But that's not necessarily always the case.

For example, by using regression analysis we can calculate a line of best fit for data series which enables us to make forecasts of fair value at future dates. If we do this for the FTSE All-Share Index from 1946, then regression analysis calculates a fair value of the index 51% over the actual value it is today. But if we do the same calculation on Index data from 1920 then we can derive a fair value just 1% over today's actual Index value. In this case, the longer-term data calculates a fair value closer to the actual value today.

The lesson is to be sensitive to the significant effect that your choice of time period can have on historic data analysis. So, choose your time period carefully, and carry out calculations for multiple time periods to understand the sensitivity of the results to time period.

3. BE WARY OF OVER-PRECISION.

Since 1980 the average return of the FTSE 100 Index in April has been 2.1745082433%. Do you find that too precise – would, say, 2.175% be better? And would 2.2% be too imprecise?

A great benefit of computers is that we can easily do calculations of great accuracy. And a great danger of computers is that we can easily do calculations of great accuracy. It is a danger because calculated numbers with great precision (e.g. a large number of decimal places) can give us false confidence in the calculation and its result. Great precision can help us lose sight of the rough assumptions that have been made for the calculation, the inherent estimations in the data and/or the use that the result will be used for.

In the case of the above calculation (the average return for the FTSE 100 Index in April), if we use the average with ten decimal places we can calculate that the average change in April since 1980 has been 162 index points (based on the current level of the index). How useful is this? Well, moderately useful; if the index moves over 162 points next April we can say that was above the average move for that month, and vice versa.

But if we now use the average return with only two decimal places (i.e. 2.18) we find the average move is still 162 points. If we use one decimal place (i.e. 2.2) the calculated average move becomes 163 points.

At which point we need to decide what level of precision we really need. Is two-decimal-place accuracy (with an average points move of 162) significantly better than just one-decimal-place accuracy (163 points)? And how are we going to use this calculated number? Is there a danger that if we used, say, the average return with four decimal places that this might confer a greater significance on the calculated average return than was warranted – especially given the large range of underlying data here?

If we use the average with zero decimal place accuracy (i.e. 2) we get an average move of 149 points. This is now a little far away from 163 points but, again, given the nature of the underlying data (i.e. a set of greatly dispersed monthly returns) the figure of 149 points may not be unrealistic to work with.

In the world of equity markets it is rare that calculations ever warrant precision of two decimal places or greater.

As John Maynard Keynes might have said (there is some debate), "It is better to be roughly right than precisely wrong."

4. SEE THE DATA VISUALLY.

Imagine analysing markets in the 1950s, or even the 1970s. When the only tools you had were a pencil and paper. Just to draw a simple chart could take hours of laborious work. Whereas today, with computers, we can do in seconds what might have taken days, or weeks back then. Not only do we have very powerful computers, we have simple programs, such as spreadsheets or charting software, that makes using the computers easy.

This can be a good and bad thing.

Because computer programs are so easy to use, they can make us lazy; they can channel our thinking into narrow fields, and they can lead us to analyse markets the same way as everyone else (because everyone is using the same programs). Further, when analysing markets quantitatively, one tends to find confirmation or rejection of conjectures that one is already looking for. Serendipity in quantitative analysis is difficult and rare.

But, while computers are powerful, we have an even more powerful tool at our disposal – the human brain.

The defining characteristic of the brain is pattern recognition – the brain is built around this function. One could argue that most of the unique features of the human brain – language, imagination, invention, and intelligence itself – derive from pattern recognition. We could define intelligence as merely a function of being able to store more patterns. And the human brain is unsurpassed in this; it is the world's most advanced pattern-recognition machine – computers don't even get close.

During human evolution, pattern-processing potential evolved as a result of enlargement of the cerebral cortex, particularly the prefrontal cortex and regions involved in processing of images. It is this that enables us to recognise visual organisation in complex data.

If we want to find more patterns in data, we need to go beyond mere quantitative analysis and unleash the full pattern-recognition power of the brain – a process that can allow better the possibility of chance discovery.

A simple way to start with this can be to introduce colour to the data. For example, use the conditional formatting functions in spreadsheets to assign colours to data values.

5. QUESTION THE PERSISTENCY OF ANOMALIES.

Having identified a market anomaly, we would like to know how persistent it is. In other words, an anomaly is not very useful if it only lasts a short time and its characteristics significantly change over time.

For example, there is a calendar anomaly that finds stock returns on certain days of the week abnormally strong relative to other days. A typical finding is that returns on Friday tend to be stronger than those on Monday. The problem is that these results do change a fair bit over time. For a certain period, say, Friday may see the strongest stock returns, but a few months later the strongest returns may occur on a Tuesday. If one is trading this anomaly, the situation needs to be monitored very closely for when the characteristics change.

By contrast, other anomalies can exhibit strong persistency over very long periods. A good example might be the Sell in May (or Halloween) effect – where stocks have greater returns in the six-month period November to April than May to October. Academic studies have shown that this effect can be seen to have existed from early in the 20th century; indeed, one academic paper recently claimed to have found evidence for the Sell in May effect from 1694.

Obviously, a trader can have far greater confidence that the Sell in May effect will persist than the day of the week effect.

6. FACTOR IN YOUR SPECIFIC TRANSACTION COSTS.

Coming across a market anomaly can be quite exciting with the prospect of low-risk profits. However, it is important to understand the difference between an anomaly being statistically significant and one that is economically significant.

An anomaly is a distortion in a financial market that would appear to contradict the Efficient Market Hypothesis. A statistically significant anomaly is one which has passed various statistical tests that indicate the results are probably not due to chance. And an economically significant anomaly is one that can be profitably exploited. In other words, just because an anomaly is statistically significant doesn't mean you can make money from it.

The issue here is transaction costs, which includes commission costs, the bid-offer spread, and market impact cost. The latter is particularly important in the case of anomalies. Strategies that seek to exploit anomalies usually need to be executed in a minimum size to be economically interesting, but sometimes the trade size can be large enough to move the market thereby reducing – and in some cases eliminating – the price anomaly.

So, a big question in this field is whether anomalies exist after taking into account transaction costs. And this question attracts fierce debate. A paper will be published with results that show almost no anomalies survive transaction costs (i.e. very few anomalies can be profitably exploited). In reply, papers will appear that criticise the first paper's assumptions and calculations, arguing that certain anomalies (e.g. that of momentum) easily survive transaction costs.

It is safe to say that there is no easy answer here. But it can be said that, to a certain extent, transaction costs differ between market participants, so each trader needs to carry out their own assessment of the impact of transaction costs.

7. FOLLOW THE LATEST RESEARCH IN ACADEMIA.

According to the Efficient Market Hypothesis (EMH), stock prices reflect all available information about companies and therefore investors can't beat the market by stock picking. Its assumption is that as soon as there is new information about a company, the share price reacts to assimilate the new knowledge.

Of course, we all know this is hokum. As Warren Buffett said, "I'd be a bum on the street with a tin cup if the markets were always efficient."

But, despite this, academics devote a lot of their time to disproving the EMH. One might think that is a little like shooting fish in a barrel, but if it keeps them happy... And investors can benefit from their industriousness.

In their quest to disprove the EMH, academics become hunters of market anomalies. If markets were efficient then anomalies would not exist – they would all be quickly arbitraged out of existence. So if an academic can show an anomaly exists they can publish a paper on it.

Investors can profit from this activity by monitoring new academic papers that are published in this field. Today this can be done easily online, for example at sites like SSRN (www.ssrn.com) or Google Scholar (scholar.google.com). Some useful phrases to search for include: "stock returns", "market efficiency", "momentum", "investor sentiment", and "calendar effect".

Unfortunately, it is nowadays quite rare to find genuinely new anomalies. So much current academic research is dedicated to re-visiting already known anomalies (to see how they are holding up in current markets), or investigating the existence of these anomalies in new markets (e.g. emerging markets). So, following this academic research does mean wading through a fair number of papers with titles like, 'Santa Claus rally and Nigerian stock market return', and 'Good Day Sunshine: Stock Returns and Weather, Evidence from Pakistan Stock Exchange'. But, overall, monitoring the publication of new research does not take long and can turn up some interesting results.

Alexander Elder

DR ALEXANDER ELDER *is a professional trader and a teacher of traders. He is the author of an international bestseller,* The New Trading for a Living *(Wiley, 2014), translated into 16 languages, and several other books. He is a popular speaker at trading conferences worldwide.*

Dr Elder is the founder of **SpikeTrade.com**, *a website that serves as a meeting place for serious traders. Members share ideas and participate in a weekly competition for the best stock picks. Dr Elder and his co-director Kerry Lovvorn contribute daily market reviews and post diaries of their own trades. They answer members' questions in the section called 'Q&A and Alex & Kerry'. This chapter is adapted from Dr Elder's answers to member questions, which have been assembled into an eBook,* The Trading Puzzle.

Readers of this chapter are invited to take a trial membership in SpikeTrade.

"THERE IS NOTHING WRONG WITH FUTURES; THERE IS EVERYTHING WRONG WITH PEOPLE WHO TRADE THEM."

Comments on Futures

1. THE DANGERS OF ETFS ON FUTURES.

I AM AN active futures trader with a strong dislike of ETFs. Let me clarify why I feel the way I do and suggest how to approach futures.

Some ETFs hold baskets of stocks, others hold physical commodities – or at least they say they hold them, which I am quite suspicious about. A friend who invests heavily in physical gold told me there was a scandal when one of the ETFs showed a commercial filmed inside a gold vault. Their pitchman was holding a bar of gold in front of the camera to show how solid their ETF was. Trouble is, gold bars have numbers, and when someone enlarged the picture it showed that the bar they were filming was not registered to them. An innocent mistake? I doubt it.

What if you buy a commodity ETF but hold that trade for only a few days? Now the risk of theft is lower, like running through a bad neighborhood rather than walking through it. Still, even short-term traders are stuck with another common ETF problem – most of them do not truly track underlying commodities. For example, I once bought crude oil futures and just out of curiosity glanced at two popular oil ETFs – USO and OIL.

Looking at these charts you notice immediately how differently they look. Wait, aren't ETFs supposed to track futures? Right, they are, in theory.

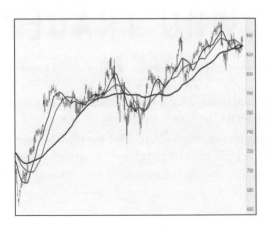

After looking at all three charts this weekend I drew a small spreadsheet. All three markets established a low during the previous week, then rallied, dropped to a new low on Thursday and then rallied again. I compared the depth of those Thursday penetrations: 0.35% in futures, but .96% in USO and a whopping 1.1% in OIL. Someone was really pushing ETFs down, shaking their stops. A multitude of such deviations is why I stay away from ETFs and trade futures which are much more honest.

2. GET MONEY MANAGEMENT DOWN COLD.

The lifetime of most futures traders is under three months. Futures can be deadly – but there is nothing wrong with futures; there is everything wrong with people who trade them. I find futures a lovely trading instrument, but any person who wants to trade them must have money management down cold. That's the main skill separating winners from losers in the futures game.

I call my approach to money management **the iron triangle of risk control**. Here are my basic suggestions for risk management in futures:

1. One side of the triangle is your maximum permitted risk, such as 2% of your account (expressed in dollars).

2. Another side is your risk per unit (per share or per contract) – the distance from your entry to your stop (also expressed in dollars).

3. Divide #1 by #2 to find the maximum number of units you may trade.

Let's apply this iron triangle to a market you might be interested in, e.g. S&P 500 e-minis:

1. Let's say your account is $40,000. Your maximum risk per trade is 2% of your account or $800. You may risk less but not more per trade.

2. Let's say you want to buy e-minis at 1,410 with a target of 1,430 and a stop at 1,404. This means you'll be risking six points per contract. One point in e-mini S&P futures is worth $50. This means your risk per contract will be $(1,410 - 1,404) \times \$50 = \$300$.

3. Dividing your maximum risk of $800 per trade by your risk of $300 per contract tells you that you may trade up to two contracts in your account.

I suggest printing out this explanation and taping it somewhere near where you make your trading decision. One of these days this iron triangle may save your futures account.

3. CONTROL FEAR WITH SMALLER TRADE SIZES.

Fear is a hugely subversive emotion; trying to trade while feeling afraid is like trying to ride a bicycle while terrified of falling.

The best method I know of fixing the fear problem is reducing your trade size. If you carry only ten or 20 shares, you feel no fear making those small trades. You trade with joy and clarity, and when the market throws a curve at you, you treat it as a puzzle to be solved, rather than with fear.

That's how I learned to trade size – starting with such a small size that all fear was removed, and gradually moving up to my present stance, where I routinely carry six-figure positions. Sharply cut down your trading size – make it a playful size. Set the parameters for increasing your size: after so many good trades go up a step in terms of size. This is the best psychological advice I can give on eliminating the sickness of fear from your trading life.

Suggested reading

To get started in futures, I recommend reading *Winning in the Futures Market* by George Angell – an excellent introduction, although I do not recommend that author's other books. The next book to buy is *The Futures Game* by Teweles and Jones. It is a big fat volume which you will not read from cover to cover, but only the chapters about those futures that interest you. There is also a chapter on futures in my *Come into My Trading Room*.

Scott Fearon

SCOTT FEARON *has spent over three decades in the financial services industry. Since 1991, he has managed a hedge fund in Northern California investing in fast-growing companies with little or no Wall Street coverage while shorting the stocks of distressed businesses in danger of filing for bankruptcy.*

He is the author of Dead Companies Walking: How a Hedge Fund Manager Finds Opportunity in Unexpected Places *(St. Martin's Press, 2015).*

"THE SAD FACT OF STOCK INVESTING IS THAT MOST INDIVIDUAL STOCKS SIMPLY AREN'T WORTH BUYING."

Stock Picking 101

1. MOST INDIVIDUAL STOCKS UNDERPERFORM THE INDEXES. INVEST ACCORDINGLY.

B ECAUSE NEARLY ALL indexes are market cap weighted, they have a natural upward bias. This positive slant gives many novice (and more than a few veteran) investors the impression that most individual stocks go up over time, too. The opposite is true. According to JP Morgan, two-thirds of stocks in the Russell 3000 underperformed the broader index between 1980 and 2014. The median stock lagged the index by a staggering 54% over that period and nearly half of all stocks declined 70% or more from their peak value and *never recovered.**

The sad fact of stock investing is that most individual stocks simply aren't worth buying. That means doing nothing is often more of a winning strategy than doing too much.

2. BUYING UNPROFITABLE COMPANIES IS USUALLY AN UNPROFITABLE CHOICE.

When we buy the stock of a company that is currently losing money, we are essentially playing the role of a venture capitalist. We're making an investment in the hope of receiving revenues and/or earnings sometime (probably deep) in the future. Unfortunately, we're not given the abilities venture capitalists who invest in these companies are given. We can't replace the CEO. We can't alter or amend the business's strategic direction. We are left on the outside looking in.

Beating the indexes is brutally hard (see rule 1). Beating the indexes with even a small percentage of your portfolio in speculative, money-losing businesses is virtually impossible. If a currently unprofitable company *does* buck the odds and grow into an index-beating investment, its stock

---

*   Cembalest, Michael. *The Agony and the Ecstasy: The Risks and Rewards of a Concentrated Stock Position.* New York: J.P. Morgan Asset Management. 2014.

will almost certainly be a better buy at $10 on its way to $20, or $50 on its way to $100, than it ever was at $7 or $5 or $2 a share.

3. SPEAKING OF LOW-PRICED STOCKS: DON'T BUY THEM!

There are many useful ways to evaluate a company. But the best valuation metric is often the simplest: share price. Every back test ever done shows that low-priced stocks underperform the indexes over lengthy periods of time. Sure, you might get lucky for a month or two and buy into a rally, but generally if you have a portfolio of sub-$10 stocks, you will almost certainly underperform, probably by a significant margin. Stock prices are signalling devices, and a stock selling in the single digits is signalling that something is rotten in Denmark. Either the company has a poor product, a poor balance sheet, a poor management team, or some combination of all three.

There's another reason to avoid single-digit stocks. The transaction fees you incur – the difference between the bid and the ask, on a percentage basis – are much greater in lower-priced stocks. If you buy a stock at $5 and you turn around and try to sell that same stock at that same moment, you're not going to get $5 for it. You're probably going to get closer to $4.95, meaning you've just lost 1% of your investment. That might not seem like much, but if you turn over a portfolio of $5 stocks twice a year, you're going to eat a full 4% of your annual returns just to play – and that's not even counting the commissions you have to pay your broker.

4. OVERTRADING IS DEADLY.

I have never met a filthy-rich day trader. I suspect they are a rare (or perhaps nonexistent) species. There is a good reason for this. Even if hyperactive investors manage to make consistently good decisions, they are moving in and out of positions so frequently that they are gifting huge portions of their returns to two very undeserving recipients: brokerage houses and the government. As John Bogle observed: "performance comes and goes but costs roll on forever."[*]

The best way to minimize our contributions to the sell side and the tax authorities is to invest with a minimum time horizon of two to four years. Of course, we won't hold every position in our portfolio that long. We're

---

[*]   Bogle, John C. 'In Investing, You Get What You Don't Pay For.' The World Money Show; February 2, 2005; Orlando, Florida.

bound to make mistakes that we will have to abandon along the way. (My personal mantra for losing stocks is '20% wrong and gone'.) But when we evaluate potential investments from a multi-year perspective, we not only inoculate ourselves from the temptation to buy into risky or speculative buys (see rule 2), we also keep more of our hard-earned returns.

5. THE ONLY FREE LUNCH IN INVESTING IS STATISTICAL DIVERSIFICATION.

The financial media is full of stories of bold fund managers staking large portions of their portfolio on their best ideas and reaping huge returns. This is a terrible idea, and a dangerous fantasy. The truth about long-term investing success, as unglamorous as it may be, is that it's more about consistently avoiding major drawdowns than winning one-time windfalls. Betting all your chips on a single play is probably a very exhilarating experience. Going broke? Not so much. Diversification minimizes volatility with no added cost.

6. GROWING ECONOMIES USUALLY PRODUCE GROWING STOCK RETURNS.

The benefits of statistical diversification apply to geography as well. Economies in the developed world just aren't growing very much anymore. Given our high debt loads and low birth rates, this sluggishness will likely continue. At any given time, however, other countries or regions *are* growing at a decent clip, and stocks in those areas are probably following suit. Investing a reasonable portion of your portfolio into reputable index funds from those faster-growing regions is almost certainly a good idea. Note: I do not recommend buying individual stocks in unfamiliar markets. Stock picking is hard enough in our own backyard (see rule 1).

7. REMEMBER THE THREE CS: CUSTOMERS, COMPETITORS, AND CAPITAL ALLOCATION.

When I visit a company's management team, the first thing I want to know is how they plan to expand the profitability of their business. What strategies do they intend to deploy in order to grow their margins? Next, I focus on what I think of as the three Cs: Customers, Competition, and Capital Allocation.

Customers: A company may be growing its revenues and earnings at the moment, but if its primary customers are in jeopardy, that growth is likely to decelerate in the future, quite possibly in an abrupt manner. You see this all the time in the energy sector. A company selling frac sand or downhole drilling services is doing great. Meanwhile, its biggest customer is one quarter away from filing for bankruptcy.

Competition: I don't know about you, but I'd rather invest in a company competing with troubled, crummy businesses on their way to oblivion than a company trying to square off against smart, ruthless, deep-pocketed killers like Amazon or Google.

Capital Allocation: If a company generates a lot of cash – and it better if I'm going to invest in it (see rule 2) – I want to know what its management plans to do with it. Will they invest in the business by making acquisitions? Will they spend it on capital expenditures? Or will they be willing to share some amount of that cash with shareholders like me by initiating or increasing dividend payouts?

8. SPEAKING OF DIVIDENDS: I PREFER THEM TO BUYBACKS.

Dividends accrue to shareholders and no one but shareholders. Buybacks, meanwhile, benefit option holders who have committed no cash of their own. And while buybacks boost earnings per share, by doing so they can mask problems like shrinking revenue growth (see rule 9).

A dividend isn't just a way to make a few extra dollars every quarter (though that is nice). A dividend also provides a level of security for shareholders. It shows us that we have bought into a company that is not just making enough cash that it can bear to share some of it with its investors, but that we have bought into a management team that is committed to doing so. Of course, there is a caveat to my love of dividends: high-yielding dividend stocks are usually terrible investments. Most back tests will show that stocks with dividend yields at or above 12% have traditionally underperformed, because a dividend cut – or outright elimination of the dividend – was imminent.

9. REVENUE GROWTH IS THE LIFEBLOOD OF SUCCESSFUL BUSINESSES – AND THE KISS OF DEATH FOR MANY SHORT POSITIONS.

Short selling is a gruesomely difficult way to make a living. I don't recommend it to anyone. You have to have an almost superhuman ability to manage risk and cope with disappointment – and one way to guarantee a disappointing (and likely brief) career as a short seller is to short 'expensive' stocks with rapidly growing top lines.

Almost all of the great stocks of the last few decades posted extremely rapid revenue growth. Most of them were quite pricey on a multiple of earnings and other valuation measures. Conversely, almost every successful short position I have ever entered suffered from shrinking revenues. Most, if not all, of them were 'cheap' by almost every valuation metric. As counterintuitive as it may seem, it's usually better to buy a stock at $100 than $10 and it's usually better to short a stock at $10 than $100. By the same token, the best place to find potential winners is often among stocks making 52-week highs, while the best place to scout potentially profitable shorts is almost always among stocks making 52-week lows.

10. DEBT MATTERS.

The other trait almost all of my profitable short positions have shared is growing debt loads and debt yields. An old adage on Wall Street is: 'debt prices predict, equity prices confirm'. Whenever the yield on a company's public debt is 15% higher or more than the yield on government bonds, bond investors are predicting that bankruptcy is highly likely. It's probably only a matter of time until the stock price of that company confirms their prediction (and loses all of its value). The people who invest in publicly traded debt are sophisticated folks who have 70 hours a week to analyze companies to death. If they don't think a company's bonds deserve a yield comparable to what they can get with other debt instruments, that means they are already carving up the reorganization in their minds.

A shocking number of investors simply don't understand how capital structures work. Bond holders don't just have first dibs on a company's assets, they also have first dibs on its operations. Most companies are reorganized in bankruptcy. They're not shut down. But the capital structure is always very different after a bankruptcy is over. The people who own the public debt get some percentage of the new company's stock. The people who owned the old company's stock lose everything.

Ken Fisher

KEN FISHER *is the founder, Executive Chairman and Co-Chief Investment Officer of Fisher Investments, an $85+ billion money management firm serving large institutions and high net worth individuals globally. With more than 2,200 employees, the firm has offices in Washington, California, Britain, Germany, Dubai, Australia, and Japan, with further global expansion under way.*

His Forbes *'Portfolio Strategy' column ran for 32 ½ years into 2017, making him the longest continuously running columnist in its history. Ken now writes weekly columns for* USA Today *and Germany's* Focus Money, *and a monthly column in the UK's* Financial Times. *Ken has authored 11 books, including four* New York Times *bestsellers, and has been published, interviewed and written about in publications globally. His books include* Beat the Crowd *(Wiley, 2015),* How to Smell a Rat *(Wiley, 2009),* The Only Three Questions That Count *(Wiley, 2006),* The Wall Street Waltz *(Wiley, 1987) and* Super Stocks *(McGraw-Hill, 1984).*

His 1970s theoretical work pioneered an investment tool called the Price-to-Sales Ratio, now a core element of modern financial curricula. A prize-winning researcher, his credits span a multitude of professional and scholarly journals in addition to his firm's output – both in traditional and behavioral finance. In 2010, Investment Advisor *recognized him on its 'Thirty for Thirty' list as among the industry's 30 most influential individuals of the last three decades. In 2017,* Investment News *named*

Ken to its inaugural list of 'Icons & Innovators' who have shaped and transformed the financial advice profession.

Ken is ranked #184 on the 2016 Forbes 400 list of richest Americans, where he has appeared since 2005. He and his wife Sherrilyn have three adult sons and four grandchildren. Ken's principal hobbies are lumbering history and western conifer tree science.

"TO THINK CLEARLY ABOUT MARKETS, YOU'LL NEED TO OUT-THINK YOUR BRAIN."

Invest By Knowing
What Others Don't

O VER MY CAREER I've learned a few guiding principles that have led my investment decisions. These principles helped me establish my investment process and build my firm. It all starts with acknowledging a simple fact: To be a successful investor, you must know something others don't.

Being smarter or better trained than other investors isn't enough. Typically, investors start with the false premise that investing is a craft, like carpentry or masonry. They believe investing is a skill they can learn with enough diligence and effort. They have their favorite information sources or set of absolutes they adhere to. However, there are no guarantees in investing. Those who aim to acquire the best technical skills believe they can – and will – beat the crowd. But they won't beat the market over the longer term if they treat investing like a craft. If investing were a craft, one method would have demonstrated superiority over time. Someone somewhere would have figured out the key to beat markets – a static, replicable formula everyone could follow to invest successfully. Investing would be learnable, like woodworking or medicine. But that's not how markets work.

Instead, investing should be treated more like a scientific inquiry than a craft. Investors should test hypotheses and evaluate methods, while investing with an open, inquisitive mind. The following principles will help you develop a process to test and retest your theories so you can ultimately learn what others don't. Investing is a difficult, lifetime pursuit. Just knowing these principles isn't enough. You must know what they really mean and how to use them. Then, you must apply them diligently, over and over again! If you can learn how to use these three principles, you can learn to start making better investing decisions. And that should give you an edge over your fellow investors. I hope they help you in your investment pursuits, as they have helped me in mine.

1. QUESTION WHAT YOU BELIEVE.

The starting point to knowing something others don't is to identify what you see wrongly. Ask yourself: What do I believe to be true that is actually false? As a society, we are encouraged to challenge someone else's views – especially politically. But we aren't trained to challenge ourselves or broadly accepted wisdom. There are many beliefs you likely share with your fellow investors. These beliefs have been built into decades of literature and are among the first things people learn when they start investing. However, many of these beliefs are nothing more than myths, sadly accepted as truths by the best and brightest minds and passed to the investing public through the media.

When reading or listening to media, it's intuitive to notice ideas you believe are false and run off to fact-check for yourself. But that's backwards. You should search the media for assertions you believe are true and then check to see if they aren't actually false. If you initially believe an assertion is true, then the overwhelming bulk of investors likely do too. But if you can prove yourself (and most other people) wrong, you may have some useful information.

Questioning what you believe allows you to know something others don't and identify where you otherwise would've been wrong (but thought you were right). This rule is all about reducing your own propensity to make mistakes.

2. FATHOM THE UNFATHOMABLE.

Once you question what you (and most others) believe to be true, the next step is to fathom what others think is unfathomable. I know – it sounds impossible. But it's easier than most assume. Simply question others' knowledge by contemplating what they assume simply can't be contemplated at all. This is the essence of out-of-the-box thinking. While the media and others fixate on the short and narrow, broaden your perspective. While they're clamoring about X causing Result Y, ask, 'What about Factor Q? Could Factor Q cause Result Y, instead of X?' It's in these moments – when you consider the unknown Factor Q – that you begin to challenge others' assumptions, test their methods and fathom the unfathomable.

Discovering something others don't already know isn't a eureka moment. It's not easy, either! You'll uncover Factor Q away from the incessant market and media noise. However, know that this process may lead you to plow through common media sources for clues – wasting time. Media is everywhere and constant. Your investment edge won't present itself in a front-page news story, publication, blog or doomsday email newsletter. No matter how buried a news story, it's already priced into the market. Instead, you must read, watch and listen to the media to know what everyone else is focused on, so you know exactly what you can look away from to find Factor Q.

Once you've found the Factor Q you believe actually causes Result Y and tested it, ask your friends and colleagues what they think. Are they aware Factor Q causes Result Y? As long as the response is a blank stare or a "You're crazy," you still have basis for an investment bet. Once people start accepting the same conclusions – or worse, you see it in the media – you've lost your edge. Winning at investing in the long-term requires constant innovation and testing. Keep questioning what you believe to be true and fathoming the unfathomable.

3. GET TO KNOW YOUR BRAIN BETTER.

The first two rules can help you find gameable bets, but your biggest investing problem is your brain. So, rule 3 asks you to think about the tricks your stone-aged brain might be playing on your investing decisions. Simply, human brains evolved as a result of our natural survival instincts in the face of starvation, treachery and woolly fanged beasts. This makes our brains especially ill-equipped to confront problems with investing. To think clearly about markets, you'll need to out-think your brain. Few investors have spent any material time trying to understand how their own brains work for – and against – themselves. This is the realm of behavioral finance.

If you understand your brain better, you'll recognize how to control yourself, so you can avoid many of the typical mistakes others make. And if you can understand why people behave as they do, you'll better understand how markets work, because investors aren't rational automatons. They're humans! Humans regularly behave in crazy ways when making financial decisions. However, many cognitive investing errors are avoidable. Once you recognize how your brain tricks you, you can elude these investing traps and focus on your investing goals.

Unfortunately, our cognitive biases don't work alone either. They work in concert. Your brain won't tell you when you're making a mistake because it doesn't recognize its cognitive errors – adding insult to injury. Take confirmation bias and hindsight bias. For example, maybe you 'just know' stock XYZ is going to go up, up, up. Its last four products have been wild sellers and the stock has done great. You do some more research on XYZ and seek out information confirming your bullish outlook. It's easy to believe further evidence – which agrees with you – is proof of your rightness! Ignoring contradictory arguments (and choosing to believe only the supportive info) is called confirmation bias. Likewise, hindsight bias preys on investors' memories. For example, maybe XYZ had a crummy Q3 and its stock suffered. Company XYZ's new product flopped! You, now reviewing your portfolio in Q4, say you knew the new product was going to be an obvious flunk. How could Company XYZ make such a mistake? Sorry! That failure couldn't have been reasonably predicted. Hindsight bias makes us perceive past results, which in the moment were unknown, as obvious outcomes.

Use rule 3 as a weapon. With every investment decision you make, ask, 'How is my Stone Age brain fooling me now?' Combined with rules 1 and 2, you now have a framework for knowing what others don't – the key to investing success: Question what you believe. Fathom the unfathomable. Get to know your brain better.

Anthony
Garner

ANTHONY GARNER *is a British national based in London. He left investment banking in 1992 and since then has been trading financial markets for his own account.*

He is the author of A Practical Guide to ETF Trading Systems *(Harriman House, 2009) and has also written articles on trading and investment for a number of publications, including* Investors Chronicle.

Anthony practised as a solicitor with London law firm Slaughter and May in the early 1980s, specialising in banking and commercial law. At Swiss Bank Corporation, he produced institutional research on South East Asian stock markets including Hong Kong, Singapore and Malaysia. He spent a year in Tokyo followed by postings to Hong Kong, Singapore and Zurich covering the Asian equity markets.

In recent years his sole focus has been on quantitative, rule-based investment and most recently his interests have centred on machine learning (a branch of artificial intelligence) as applied to financial markets.

"DON'T PICK STOCKS, DON'T BUY ACTIVELY MANAGED FUNDS AND DON'T TRADE. NOT IF YOU ARE A 'HOBBY' INVESTOR."

How to use ETF Trading Systems to Outperform the Experts

1. STUDY FINANCIAL MARKET HISTORY.

YOU NEED TO study history to achieve a sense of perspective, to understand what markets have achieved in the past and to divine where they might go in the future.

The following are excellent sources of deep historic data:

- www.bankofengland.co.uk/research/Pages/onebank/threecenturies.aspx
- www.econ.yale.edu/~shiller/data.htm
- www.nber.org/databases/macrohistory/contents
- fred.stlouisfed.org/categories/33060

Robert Shiller's dividend-adjusted data suggests that the compound annual growth rate (CAGR) of the US stock market since 1870 has been 8.98% and that of 10-year Treasuries 4.71%.

Short-term US Treasuries achieved a CAGR of 3.97% (from the Treasury yield culled from NBER and the Federal Reserve).

The UK stock market data from the Bank of England is not adjusted for dividends. The compound annual growth rate since 1709 is 2.55%.

The compound annual growth rate on UK bonds has been as follows:

- corporate bonds: 5.89% since 1854
- short-term prime paper: 4.17% since 1718
- long-term government bonds: 4.63% since 1753.

(I have not inflation-adjusted any of the data.)

Note for stocks the vast maximum peak to valley drawdown (80 to 90% in both the UK and US – the South Sea Bubble of 1721, the Wall Street Crash of 1929, the Nasdaq tech crash). Note the long flat periods where little growth was recorded.

As far as bonds are concerned, I was surprised by the lack of appreciable difference over the long term in short-term and long-term bond returns. Given that, I would prefer to stay at the less volatile short end of the curve.

As for where we are going, the Enlightenment, Industrial Revolution (and later the technological revolution) has driven stock prices since around 1760. There is no guarantee that growth will continue and prediction is futile. For hundreds of thousands of years, man lived as a beast and for all we know an unforeseen disaster could one day send us back to the Stone Age.

Hopefully we can expect similar growth in our investments in the future – but who can tell?

2. AVOID 'EXPERTS' AND FUND MANAGERS.

A friend asked my advice recently on a proposal he had received from a large and well-known UK wealth manager. It wanted to charge a 2% fee on his total investment simply to receive a transfer of his pension fund. Its annual management charges for choosing a bunch of funds run in any case by other firms amounted to 2.58% pa. Dwarfing the current return on bonds and for all we know on stocks as well for the next decade.

One of the world's largest banks quoted a friend of mine a 2% commission charge for dealing in US stocks when it can be done through a deep discount broker so cheap it is almost free.

As for investment advice – as Burton Malkiel argued, a monkey with a dartboard is a genius compared to most fund managers, and endless research over the past 60 years has demonstrated this amply. Don't pick stocks, don't buy actively managed funds and don't trade. Not if you are a 'hobby' investor.

Index-tracking funds are the way to go. Hats off to Vanguard and iShares and a small handful of others.

You can buy a single exchange-traded fund such as the iShares MSCI World ETF, and for annual management charges of a mere 0.5% you will be invested in almost every world stock market and thousands of shares. You will outperform the vast majority of active fund managers.

The hedge fund world is no better. Most of these Masters of the Universe eventually crash and burn, taking their clients' money with them.

The only people who make big money out of the fund management industry are the fund managers themselves. Same with the brokerage industry.

There are bright people in finance and a few have endured (skill or survivorship bias?) but eventually either their luck runs out or their returns deteriorate as the assets under management outgrow the capacity of their strategies.

There may be a case for real experts in some field who really understand a company's business to back their expertise and hold a few individual stocks. But don't bet the ranch.

3. CONDUCT RESEARCH AND BACK-TESTING.

As a stock analyst in the Far East I produced both fundamental research and technical analysis.

Looking back, it was very funny. We would stick our fingers in the air, project earnings and balance sheets a few years into the future and publish reports. We never told anyone to sell a stock – that would have been horribly bad for corporate business. Before publication, we would scurry round and look at what our competitors were saying and make sure we hadn't stuck our nose out too far.

As for technical analysis, we drew wonky lines all over the place, called them funny names and claimed they had some predictive ability.

None of us had heard of back-testing to see whether any of these ideas worked. And none of us thought of recording our advice to check whether any of it turned out to be correct. Or a load of useless garbage. I suspect it was the latter.

I produced worthy tomes on Asian-listed companies but I suspect most copies ended up in the waste bin.

You should back-test your ideas over past data.

I was recently approached by a newcomer to investment who told me he had devised a set of fundamental and technical rules.

I told him he had two choices:

- Invest in accordance with his rules and see what happens.
- Take his rules and see how their application over the past x years would have performed.

I prefer the latter approach.

Back-testing can be a very, very dangerous tool for two reasons. The first reason is that it is all too easy to keep on adding and adapting rules until it looks as if they would be hugely profitable. That may be the case – on past data. In all likelihood, such rules will be useless going forward since they have simply been fitted to the test data.

The second reason is that markets are largely unpredictable. Even more so with individual stocks. There are certain basic rules which seem to work. In technical analysis, momentum or trend following is one such approach. In terms of fundamental analysis, a stock won't increase in price over the long term unless its earnings grow and its balance sheet is sound. Tech companies have gone public over the past few decades with apparently unsustainable debts and no sign of any earnings; but they will not endure unless eventually these disadvantages are addressed.

I wouldn't do without back-testing but I expect my profits to be less and my drawdowns greater than my research suggests.

A spreadsheet is probably the best way to begin for the less technically inclined. For those with more ambition I strongly recommend learning a programming language. I am currently coding mostly in Python. Daily price data can be downloaded free from Quandl for many markets.

4. EXPECT SURPRISES.

Nothing ever turns out as expected in life or in the markets. Just because a system appears to have worked well over the past 100 years in back-testing does not necessarily mean it will work as well over the next 100. The maximum drawdown may well exceed anything seen in back-testing. The return will entirely depend on future economic conditions.

There is little further one can say. We have no idea whether we live in a random or deterministic, Newtonian universe. We have no way of predicting the future. We can only take a probabilistic approach and hope it works.

5. DIVERSIFY.

By using index-tracking ETFs you are already most of the way there: you will avoid stock-specific risk by investing in hundreds if not thousands of individual stocks.

You cannot avoid all risks: world stock markets rise and fall together in the global economy and even commodities have become alarmingly correlated during market crises. Nonetheless, wide diversification over economies, asset classes, currencies and instruments is the best protection you can hope for. And even then, it won't help much in a meteor strike.

Don't hold everything with one fund manager or broker or bank. Don't take any single bank credit risk if you can avoid it. Avoid exchange-traded notes and stick to funds which invest in the underlying assets themselves – be that gold, oil or stocks.

Here is the real test: think back in history and consider whether you would have been smart enough to avoid its many disasters. Recall the collapse of the Russian, Argentinian and German economies in the first half of the 20th century. Remember the prolonged downturn in the Japanese stock market following an unprecedented boom in the decades after the second world war. Recall the dramatic crash in tech stocks in the early 21st century. Think about the near bankruptcies in Iceland, Ireland, Greece and Italy. Ponder the severe and prolonged downturn in commodity markets after 2008.

Take exposure to short-term bonds, world equities, cash and commodities. As well as owning your own home. There isn't much more you can do to protect yourself and your investments.

6. DON'T BOTTLE OUT.

It's no good bottling out when the going gets tough. The fear element during a market crisis and a large drawdown is terrifying. But if you are well-diversified with index, bond and commodity trackers you should just sit tight, reckon you have done your best and expect that it will turn out right in the end. Bar revolution, war or meteor strike.

Stay within your comfort zone: know yourself. Trade small and stick to a low drawdown, low volatility approach with the bulk of your assets. If you bet the ranch, if you hold everything in one risky asset, if you overextend yourself with leverage – you will surely crash and burn eventually.

7. DON'T BET THE RANCH.

Most people should avoid any sort of trading. They should simply invest in a widely diversified and low-volatility portfolio and stick with it. Apply a few very simple rules such as re-balancing.

I have traded and I do trade. Sometimes with great success and sometimes with unpleasant losses. I try to stay within my comfort zone. Betting the ranch is never advisable.

I'm currently trading the S&P 500 volatility index but in small size relative to my net worth. I am working on all sorts of exotica and have become fascinated by the prospects for artificial intelligence and machine learning. I will continue to trade in all sorts of ways and on all sorts on instruments. But I will keep it in perspective and not be lured by greed to venture outside my capacity to weather losses.

8. DEVISE A FEW SIMPLE RULES.

Many advise against market timing or the application of any 'rules'. In doing so, they fail to acknowledge (or perhaps realise) that a stock index is a rule-based trading system.

The great majority of stocks have a terminal value of zero: businesses are born, they prosper (or not) and eventually fail. The stock index by contrast is a way to profit from general economic growth. As stocks prosper, they are included in an index; as they wilt and fail they are dropped.

Individual stocks are mean-reverting: they start with a value of zero and end with a value of zero. Dust to dust, ashes to ashes.

There are countless ways to follow market trends but they all apply the same principal: run your profits and cut your losses.

The first 'system' set out below is the stock index itself – the S&P 500 Index compiled by Robert Shiller.

The second 'system' is the standard 60/40 split rebalanced annually. 60% S&P 500, 40% US Treasuries.

Frankly, either of these first two systems is about as good as you will get. The 60/40 split is for those who cannot stomach the gut-wrenching drawdown and volatility of pure equity investment.

The other two systems add a gloss on each of these. 'Momentum' in these systems is the return of the S&P 500 over a one-month look-back period.

The momentum system rebalances each quarter. If the momentum is positive at the re-allocation date, invest 100% in the S&P 500, otherwise 100% in Treasuries. As you can see, in back-testing at least, the returns are similar to the S&P 500 but with greatly reduced drawdown and volatility.

The 60/40 momentum system also rebalances each quarter. If momentum is positive at the re-allocation date, invest 60% in the S&P 500 and 40% in Treasuries, if not then invest 100% in Treasuries. As can be seen, in back-testing this system achieves similar return to the 60/40 'system' but with greatly reduced drawdown and volatility.

The hope is that these systems are simple enough to prove robust and profitable in the future. But nothing in life is guaranteed.

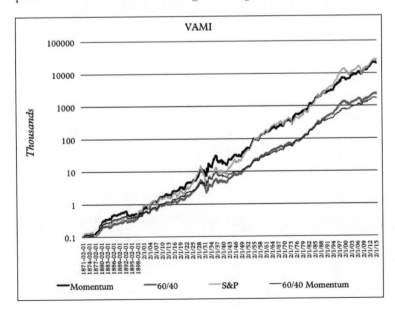

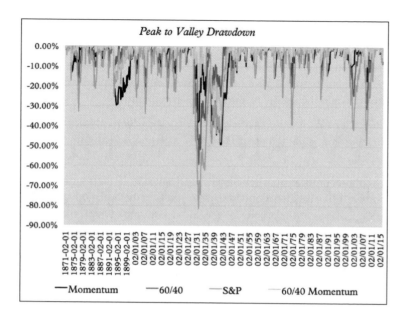

Peak to Valley Drawdown

—Momentum   —60/40   —S&P   60/40 Momentum

	Momentum	60/40	S&P	60/40 Momentum
Start	1871-02-01	1871-02-01	1871-02-01	1871-02-01
End	2016-06-01	2016-06-01	2016-06-01	2016-06-01
CAGR	8.77%	7.19%	8.98%	6.93%
Max Drawdown	-49.22%	-59.21%	-81.50%	-31.76%
1Y	-4.77%	1.00%	1.42%	-2.79%
3Y (ann.)	5.41%	6.76%	10.99%	3.30%
5Y (ann.)	8.34%	7.52%	12.36%	5.05%
10Y (ann.)	8.52%	5.30%	7.43%	5.57%
Since Incep. (ann.)	8.77%	7.19%	8.98%	6.93%
Best Day	51.07%	24.95%	50.97%	30.68%
Worst Day	-14.32%	-15.95%	-26.09%	-9.47%
Monthly Vol (ann.)	11.11%	8.28%	14.07%	6.69%
Best Month	51.07%	24.95%	50.97%	30.68%
Worst Month	-14.32%	-15.95%	-26.09%	-9.47%
Best Year	47.85%	32.30%	54.23%	28.77%
Worst Year	-26.52%	-24.06%	-41.51%	-15.24%
Avg. Drawdown	-4.64%	-3.68%	-6.43%	-2.52%
Avg. Drawdown Days	237.82	188.14	238.08	188.88
Avg. Up Month	1.85%	1.85%	3.00%	1.20%
Avg. Down Month	-2.35%	-1.68%	-2.84%	-1.43%
Win Year %	73.79%	78.62%	73.10%	82.07%
Win 12m %	76.30%	76.87%	71.80%	82.87%

Wesley Gray
& Jack Vogel

After serving as a Captain in the United States Marine Corps, WESLEY GRAY *earned a PhD, and worked as a finance professor at Drexel University. Dr Gray's interest in bridging the research gap between academia and industry led him to found Alpha Architect, an asset management firm that delivers affordable active exposures for tax-sensitive investors. He has published four books and a number of academic articles and is a regular contributor to multiple industry outlets, including the* Wall Street Journal, Forbes, ETF.com, *and the CFA Institute. Dr Gray earned an MBA and a PhD in finance from the University of Chicago and graduated magna cum laude with a BS from the Wharton School of the University of Pennsylvania.*

JACK VOGEL *conducts research in empirical asset pricing and behavioral finance. Dr Vogel is a co-author of* DIY Financial Advisor: A Simple Solution to Build and Protect Your Wealth *and* Quantitative Momentum: A Practitioner's Guide to Building a Momentum-Based Stock Selection System. *His academic background includes experience as an instructor and research assistant at Drexel University in both the Finance and Mathematics departments, as well as a Finance instructor at Villanova University He has a Ph.D. in Finance and an MS in Mathematics from Drexel University. Dr Vogel graduated summa cum laude with a BS in Mathematics and Education from the University of Scranton.*

"BEWARE OF GEEKS BEARING FORMULAS."

Axioms of the Alpha Architects

W E THINK A quote attributed to Warren Buffett says it all: "Investing is simple, but not easy."

On the one hand, investors simply need to identify an investment program that helps them achieve their financial goals and stick with that plan for the long term. Compound mathematics will take care of the rest. But, in practice, investing is a dynamic personal journey that forces investors to make decisions in an uncertain environment where misinformation is rampant, volatility is intense, and emotions are extremely high.

The rules outlined below may help investors make better decisions in the always complex, and always chaotic market environment. These rules serve as the core of our investment philosophy and build the foundation for many of our investing processes. Good luck.

1. UNDERSTAND YOUR EDGE AND WHY IT IS SUSTAINABLE.

We cannot overemphasize that identifying sustainable edge in the market is no cakewalk. More importantly, being smart, having superior stock-picking skills, or amassing an army of PhDs to crunch data is only half of the equation. Even with those tools, you are still only one shark in a tank filled with other sharks. All sharks are smart, all sharks have a MBA or PhD from a fancy school, and all the sharks know how to analyze a company. Maintaining an edge in these shark-infested waters is no small feat, and one that only a handful of investors has accomplished.

In order to achieve sustainable edge as an active investor, one needs not only skill, but also an understanding of human psychology, and an appreciation of market incentives (behavioral finance). One must always ask the following questions:

- Why are these securities mispriced?

- Why haven't other smart people already taken advantage of the mispricing?

If an investor can't reasonably address these two questions then it is likely the case that this investor is contributing to another investor's success. Always remember that for every buyer there must be a seller on the side of the trade.

2. ASK YOURSELF, "AM I TRYING TOO HARD?"

Everyone makes mistakes. It's part of what makes us human. Because humans understand their actions are sometimes flawed, it was perhaps inevitable that the field of psychology would develop a rich body of academic literature to analyze why it is that human beings often make poor decisions. Although insights from academia can be highly theoretical, our everyday life experiences corroborate many of these findings at a basic level: "I know I shouldn't eat the McDonald's Big Mac, but it tastes so good."

Because we recognize our frequent irrational urges, we often seek the judgment of experts to avoid becoming our own worst enemy. We assume that experts, with years of experience in their particular fields, are better equipped and incentivized to make unbiased decisions. But is this assumption valid? For more than 60 years a surprisingly robust but neglected branch of academic literature has studied the assumption that experts make unbiased decisions. The evidence tells a decidedly one-sided story: systematic decision-making, through the use of simple quantitative models with limited inputs, outperforms discretionary decisions made by experts.

Based on the evidence, investors should de-emphasize their reliance on discretionary experts and should instead approach investment decisions with systematic models. To quote Paul Meehl, an eminent scholar in the field, "There is no controversy in social science that shows such a large body of qualitatively diverse studies coming out so uniformly in the same direction as this one [models outperform experts]." In other words, pick a model, and stick to it.

3. BEWARE OF GEEKS BEARING FORMULAS.

Investors should always be skeptical of complexity and approaches that often seem too good to be true. Here are some basic questions to consider:

Why does this strategy need to be complex?

Is the complexity a front for the manager, or does the complexity of the strategy drive the alpha? There is seldom a connection between a strategy's complexity and its effectiveness. If you are having trouble understanding why the complexity exists, it may be intentional on the part of the manager. If the manager cannot justify the complexity relative to a simpler model than the complexity is not necessary.

How robust is the system?

Complexity is often correlated with data-fitting – for example, when managers identify a very specific allocation scheme that has worked in a small sample. If the complex system is slightly changed, do results completely dry up? If they do, then the system is not robust. Reversion to the mean and mediocre performance – or much worse – is in your future.

Can you explain the strategy to stakeholders?

Clarity and simplicity help facilitate communication and education, which breeds trust and confidence. Outsourcing investment activity to managers with highly complex, expensive and opaque investment strategies does not facilitate clear communication. And while it may not matter if the portfolio is making money, what happens when it starts losing? Suddenly, understanding becomes very important, as people start asking difficult questions. Defending a losing investment in a Vanguard index fund is easier than defending a loss in credit default swaps.

Risk management?

Any banker who lived through the 2008 financial crisis understands how complication can create risk-management problems. How does one risk manage a machine-learning algorithm trading leveraged exotic derivatives with a jump-diffusion model infused with a touch of fractal mathematics and string theory? Black boxes of this sort can be problematic for risk managers. In short, always ask yourself if the complexity of a strategy creates a risk management blind spot.

4. FOCUS ON VALUE AND MOMENTUM CHARACTERISTICS.

Never buy expensive stocks.

Benjamin Graham, who first established the idea of purchasing stocks at a discount to their intrinsic value more than 80 years ago, is known today as the father of value investing. Since Graham's time, academic research has shown that low-price-to-fundamentals stocks have historically outperformed the market. In the investing world, Graham's most famous student, Warren Buffett, has inspired legions of investors to adopt the value philosophy. Despite the widespread knowledge that value investing generates higher returns over the long haul, value-based strategies have continued to outperform the market. How is this possible? The answer relates to a fundamental truth: human beings behave irrationally. We all know what we should do over the long term, but we all live in the short term. And the harsh reality is that value investing strategies can require that an investor go through multi-year stretches of poor relative performance. Who wants to deal with that pain?

Ride winners and cut losers.

Eugene Fama, the 2013 co-recipient of the Nobel Prize in Economics and father of the efficient market hypothesis (also Wes's dissertation advisor), has summarized the academic research on momentum as follows: "The premier anomaly is momentum." When the father of efficient markets suggests momentum is the leading anomaly, we take note.

The empirical research on the momentum effect is compelling. For example, academic researchers have examined stock data going back over 200 years and identified a significant and robust historical performance record. As natural skeptics, we have independently verified many of the empirical results associated with momentum. Momentum is well grounded, historically. And while we never want to invest in a strategy simply because it has a great back-test, we believe that the momentum anomaly is a sustainable active investment strategy. We believe the strategy can persist because the returns are:

1. Driven by additional risk exposures that should earn higher expected returns.

2. Enhanced by mispricing that is difficult to exploit by short-term arbitrageurs.

5. INVEST WITH TRENDS.

Having your cake and eating it too is a great way to go. It's great to have the cake, and it's also great to eat the cake. But you can't have it both ways. Investors often demand the following: "Give me high, after-tax, net-of-fee returns, but with limited risk and volatility." Now, we certainly love high returns with low risk. We also love high reward with low effort and high calories with low weight gain.

Unfortunately, this brings us to our first problem: high returns and low risk don't really exist. Assets that earn high returns, such as equities (e.g. an S&P 500 index fund), come with a lot of risk (i.e. you can lose over half your wealth). One way to earn high returns but limit the risk is to develop a timing methodology that identifies how to sell the high-returning asset before it decides to jump off a fiscal cliff. But here is a problem: market-timing is extremely difficult.

Let's start this conversation with a concise summary of the academic analysis of a variety of systems that claim to have reliable market-timing ability: a waste of time.

There you go. You no longer need to read the classic academic papers on the subject. Our own research generally confirms this sad reality. We've reviewed hundreds of different concepts and the results are not promising. Most signals never survive intense empirical scrutiny.

But there is a glimmer of light at the end of this investing tunnel. Research indicates that trend-following systems, or systems that invest when past price patterns are strong, can capture most of the upside associated with asset classes, and yet sidestep the large drawdowns associated with these asset classes. Again, trend following is not a panacea because it requires some heroic investor behavior assumptions:

1. the ability to withstand short-term volatility
2. the courage to avoid short-run benchmark comparison
3. the conviction to stick to a model.

Tren Griffin

TREN GRIFFIN *works at Microsoft. He writes the* **www.25iq.com** *blog and is active on Twitter (@TrenGriffin). Tren was formerly a partner at Eagle River, a private equity firm controlled by Craig McCaw with investments in telecommunications and start-ups. He was the fourth employee of a start-up named Teledesic that at one point had a valuation of more than $3 billion. He previously worked as a consultant in Australia and Korea. He is the author of six books. including* Charlie Munger: The Complete Investor *(Columbia University Press, 2015).*

"IF A SECURITY IS NOT A PROPORTIONAL INTEREST IN A BUSINESS, WHAT EXACTLY IS IT?"

Charlie Munger's Investing Rules

---

1. YOU'RE BUYING A PROPORTION OF A BUSINESS. AND YOU NEED A MARGIN OF SAFETY.

"Ben Graham had this concept of value to a private owner – what the whole enterprise would sell for if it were available. And that was calculable in many cases. Then, if you could take the stock price and multiply it by the number of shares and get something that was one third or less of sellout value, he would say that you've got a lot of edge going for you. Even with an elderly alcoholic running a stodgy business, this significant excess of real value per share working for you means that all kinds of good things can happen to you. You had a huge margin of safety – as he put it – by having this big excess value going for you."

B EN GRAHAM'S INVESTING system involves four bedrock principles, two of which Charlie Munger introduces in the quote above:

1. a share of stock is a proportional ownership of a business

2. buy at a significant discount to intrinsic value to create a margin of safety.

If a security is not a proportional interest in a business, what exactly is it? It certainly isn't a piece of paper to be traded like a baseball card or a painting. With 'margin of safety', the fundamental idea is to buy an asset at a significant enough bargain price that the result will be good even if a mistake was made in evaluating the asset. Since risk is always relative to the price paid, buying with a margin of safety is a risk-averse approach. A range of future outcomes can still produce a satisfactory result if you buy an asset at a significant bargain.

2. TREAT THE MARKET AS YOUR SERVANT, NOT YOUR MASTER.

"Ben Graham [had] his concept of 'Mr Market'. Instead of thinking the market was efficient, he treated it as a manic-depressive who comes by every day. And some days he says, 'I'll sell you some of my interest for way less than you think it's worth.' And other days, 'Mr Market' comes by and says, 'I'll buy your interest at a price that's way higher than you think its worth.' And you get the option of deciding whether you want to buy more, sell part of what you already have or do nothing at all. To Graham, it was a blessing to be in business with a manic-depressive who gave you this series of options all the time. That was a very significant mental construct."

In this quote, Charlie Munger recalls Ben Graham's metaphor of Mr Market. Mr Market shows up every day, willing to quote you a price. Unfortunately, Mr Market is – in the words of Warren Buffett – "kind of a drunken psycho". For this reason and others, Mr Market should always be treated as your servant rather than your master. Why would anyone ever treat someone like this as wise?

Mr Market, in the short term, is a voting machine driven by highly volatile and fickle public opinion instead of a weighing machine measuring return on investment. When Mr Market offers you a price for an asset you have the option to do nothing. In other words, there are no 'called strikes' in investing. In investing there is no premium given for activity – in fact, there is a penalty, since it results in fees and taxes. For a value investor, it is Mr Market's irrationality that creates the opportunity. As Munger points out: "For a security to be mispriced, someone else must be a damn fool. It may be bad for the world, but not bad for Berkshire."

3. BE AS RATIONAL AS YOU CAN.

"The idea of a margin of safety, a Graham precept, will never be obsolete. The idea of making the market your servant will never be obsolete. The idea of being objective and dispassionate will never be obsolete. So Graham had a lot of wonderful ideas. Warren worshiped Graham. He got rich, starting essentially from zero, following in the footsteps of Graham."

Munger here introduces the final bedrock principle of value investing: be objective and dispassionate. In other words, be as rational as you can when making investing decisions. An investor will always make *some* emotional and psychological mistakes, but if you can do things like learn from your mistakes, use techniques like checklists, have the right emotional temperament, exhibit a strong work ethic and are a 'learning machine,' Munger believes some investors can outperform the market.

Only a very small number of 'know something' investors can do this. Munger believes that almost everyone is a 'know nothing' investor and should instead invest in a low-cost diversified portfolio of index funds and ETFs.

4. VALUE INVESTING WORKS BEST WHEN THE WORLD'S IN SHELL SHOCK — BUT CAN STILL FLOURISH WHEN IT ISN'T… IF YOU ADAPT.

"Ben Graham could run his Geiger counter over this detritus from the collapse of the 1930s and find things selling below their working capital per share and so on. But he was, by and large, operating when the world was in shell shock from the 1930s – which was the worst contraction in the English-speaking world in about 600 years. Wheat in Liverpool, I believe, got down to something like a 600-year low, adjusted for inflation. The classic Ben Graham concept is that gradually the world wised up and those real obvious bargains disappeared. You could run your Geiger counter over the rubble and it wouldn't click. Ben Graham followers responded by changing the calibration on their Geiger counters. In effect, they started defining a bargain in a different way. And they kept changing the definition so that they could keep doing what they'd always done. And it still worked pretty well."

The beauty of some systems is that they have the ability to evolve so as to adapt to new conditions. And that is precisely what happened in the case of value investing. After the Great Depression many people simply gave up on owning stocks. Loss-aversion was so strong among potential buyers that they were simply not rational when it came to the stock market. During this period it was possible for businesses to be bought at less than liquidation value. This was a boon for investors like Ben Graham. Unfortunately for them, that period of time only lasted for so long as memories faded and new investors entered the market. But the principles of value investing were still sound – if adjusted to the new market conditions.

5. BE HAPPY TO DO NOTHING — BUT PREPARED TO INVEST AGGRESSIVELY WHEN THE TIME IS RIGHT.

"I don't love Ben Graham and his ideas the way Warren does. You have to understand, to Warren – who discovered him at such a young age and then went to work for him – Ben Graham's insights changed his whole life, and he spent much of his early years worshiping the master at close range. But I have to say, Ben Graham had a lot to learn as an investor. His ideas of how to value companies were all shaped by how the Great Crash and the Depression almost destroyed him, and he was always a little afraid of what the market can do. It left him with an aftermath of fear for the rest of his life, and all his methods were designed to keep that at bay."

"I liked Graham, and he always interested and amused me. But I never had the worship for buying the stocks he did. So I don't have the worship for him that Warren does. I picked up the ideas, but discarded the practices that didn't suit me. I don't want to own bad businesses run by people I don't like and say, 'No matter how horrible this is to watch, it will bounce by 25%.' I'm not temperamentally attracted to it."

Charlie Munger is always looking for ways to evolve, adopt and even reverse his views. He is a learning machine. Munger is also excited by great managers running great businesses. And he gets positively ecstatic when every once in a while these managers are running businesses that are available for purchase in whole or in part at bargain prices. This does not happen very often so most of the time he patiently does nothing. But Munger is prepared to act very aggressively when the time is right.

6. THE MORE MONEY YOU HAVE, THE HARDER IT IS TO JUST INVEST IN OUT-OF-FAVOR COMPANIES.

"I think Ben Graham wasn't nearly as good an investor as Warren is or even as good as I am. Buying those cheap, cigar-butt stocks was a snare and a delusion, and it would never work with the kinds of sums of money we have. You can't do it with billions of dollars or even many millions of dollars. But he was a very good writer and a very good teacher and a brilliant man, one of the only intellectuals – probably the only intellectual – in the investing business at the time."

In this quote Charlie Munger discusses another reason why the value investing system had to evolve for Berkshire. The amount of money that Berkshire must put to work each year is way too big to hope that enough so-called 'cigar butt' businesses – ugly, unloved but with a few remaining puffs left in them before they are discarded – can be found to compose a full portfolio.

7. QUALITY MATTERS.

"Having started out as Grahamites – which, by the way, worked fine – we gradually got what I would call better insights. And we realized that some company that was selling at two or three times book value could still be a hell of a bargain because of momentum implicit in its position, sometimes combined with an unusual managerial skill plainly present in some individual or other, or some system or other. And once we'd gotten over the hurdle of recognizing that a thing could be a bargain based on quantitative measures that would have horrified Graham, we started thinking about better businesses. We've really made the money out of high-quality businesses. In some cases, we bought the whole business. And in some cases, we just bought a big block of stock. But when you analyze what happened, the big money's been made in the high-quality businesses. And most of the other people who've made a lot of money have done so in high-quality businesses."

Munger makes two key points here: 1) some bargains are only visible if you understand qualitative factors and 2) there are sometimes catalysts that can boost the value of the stock even further based on factors like scale advantages, favorable regulatory changes, improving secular phenomenon and better systems or business momentum.

8. A FEW GREAT DECISIONS CAN MAKE ALL THE DIFFERENCE.

"The great bulk of the money has come from the great businesses. And even some of the early money was made by being temporarily present in great businesses. Buffett Partnership, for example, owned American Express and Disney when they got pounded down. However, if we'd stayed with classic Graham the way Ben Graham did it, we would never have had the record we have."

"Iscar is not a Ben Graham stock – in fact, it would be the ultimate non-Ben Graham stock. It's located a few miles from the Lebanese border in Israel. It has a high ROE, doing business all over the earth, using a certain technology to produce carbide cutting tools. The reason I got so high on it so fast was that the people are so outstandingly talented."

Munger has made the point many times that only a few great decisions delivered most of Berkshire's financial returns. And (as per rule 5) Munger has also said repeatedly that a high-quality business selling a bargain price is not a common event and that if you are not prepared to act aggressively when that happens the opportunity will be lost.

9. DON'T OVERDO IT.

"Ben Graham said it's not the bad ideas that do you in. It's the good ideas that get you. You can't ignore it and it's easy to overdo it."

Almost everything can be taken to a point where what is wonderful eventually becomes toxic. The great humorist Mark Twain said once that: "Water, taken in moderation, cannot hurt anybody." Even water – in sufficient quantity – is not good for you. The same phenomenon applies to investing. What a wise person does at first, the fool does at the end.

10. KNOW YOUR LIMITS.

"Warren … was slower to come to the idea I learned that the best way to make money is to buy great businesses that earn high returns on capital over long periods of time. We're applying Graham's basic ideas, but now we're trying to find undervalued great companies. That concept was foreign to Ben Graham. Warren would have morphed into a great investor without Ben Graham. He is a greater investor than Graham was. Warren would have been great had he never met anyone else. He would have excelled at any field that required a high IQ, quantitative skills and risk taking. He wouldn't have done well at ballet, though."

The point about Warren Buffett being an unlikely ballet star is important, since it raises the idea of the 'circle of competence'. Risk comes from not knowing what you are doing, so it is wise to know what you are doing (i.e. stay within your circle of competence). The skill of every human being has limits. An important point in all of this is: you are not Charlie Munger and you are not going to be Charlie Munger. Having said that, you can learn from Munger and make better decisions than you would otherwise.

11. REVIEW PAST STUPIDITIES – BUT DON'T LET THEM MAKE YOU TIMID.

"It's important to review your past stupidities so you are less likely to repeat them, but I'm not gnashing my teeth over it or suffering or enduring it. I regard it as perfectly normal to fail and make bad decisions. I think the tragedy in life is to be so timid that you don't play hard enough so you have some reverses."

Of course, you can also learn from success, particularly if you remember that success can be a lousy teacher since what you may believe to be the outcome of skill may actually be the outcome of luck.

Charlie Munger freely admits he still makes mistakes, even after many decades as a business person and investor. Munger does advise people to strive to make new mistakes rather than repeat old mistakes. He has said that he made more mistakes earlier in life than he is making now. In other words, even though he continues to make mistakes like everyone else, he has marginally improved his ability to avoid mistakes over the years. Munger is fond of quoting Richard Feynman: "The first principle is that you must not fool yourself – and you are the easiest person to fool."

Robin Griffiths

ROBIN GRIFFITHS *is Head of Multi-Asset Research at ECU. He was previously Chief Technical Analyst at HSBC Investment Bank for 20 years before becoming Head of Global Asset Allocation at Rathbones, and then a director and technical strategist for Cazenove Capital Management.*

Robin was a Partner of WI Carr and Head of Technical Analysis at Grieveson Grant. Robin is a committee member and former chairman of the international Federation of Technical Analysts, and former chairman, now fellow, of the British Society of Technical Analysts. Robin has been a member of ECU's Global Macro Team for over 20 years.

"INVEST IN WHAT
IS HAPPENING AND
NOT WHAT YOU
THINK OUGHT TO BE
HAPPENING."

Rules Beat Judgement: Trend Following With Technical Analysis

1. IDENTIFY TRENDS AND BACK THEM.

EVERY THING IN life is programmed to a degree. Even when we think we are using our judgement we are simply following rules from our subconscious mind.

I got into the stock market in 1966 when I joined a firm noted for the quality of its fundamental analysis. I had a degree in economics and statistics and I had just read Ben Graham's book, *The Intelligent Investor* – the Bible of value investing. However, in practice, I learned that if a stock was extremely cheap it was cheap for a good reason. The companies that were growing fast were known by the market and this would be reflected in their rating.

I also learned that clients were only happy if the price of the share they had bought went up whilst they owned it, and contrary to what I had been taught these moves were not a Random Walk. On this planet, prices move in trends and these trends appear more frequently and persist for longer than the laws of chance allow. The game became one of identifying trends and backing them.

2. ONLY BET ON ONE VARIABLE AT A TIME.

The second thing I learned early on is that although we are expected to have an opinion on many things – like the share price, currency, the overall index, political risk etc. – we had almost no chance of being correct on all these issues simultaneously. Let's be generous and say you are able to be correct 80% of the time on any one variable. If there are more than three interrelated variables you can only expect to be right

80% of 80% of 80% of the time. Or 51% – in other words, back to a coin toss, no edge at all.

This is why you should only ever bet on one variable at a time.

3. THE STRATEGIC DECISION ABOUT WHICH MARKET OR CURRENCY TO BE IN SHOULD BE COMPLETELY SEPARATE FROM ONES TO DO WITH BUYING INDIVIDUAL STOCKS.

A British investor will decide up front to be in the pound sterling and to own UK stocks from the FTSE index and aim to beat that market and gain their own kind of money. An American citizen will decide up front that he only wants US dollars and to beat an index like the S&P 500. At present both UK and US investors will be thinking they have done well as their indices are at or near all-time highs. However, since the year 2000 the Briton is only up 10%, whilst the American is up 60%. If they had both been in the Indian market they would have been up 400%. And if instead they had been in China they would have been up almost 800%.

All this requires macro trades. We do them using funds or ETFs.

4. ONLY BUY WHEN THE TREND IS UP. ONLY SELL WHERE THE TREND IS DOWN.

Having picked our currency and market, we follow all the stocks in the relevant index. We measure their chart trends and rank them in order of strength. I do this by using regression analysis, but you could just as well use moving averages. The entire pack of charts can be divided into those going:

1. up
2. down
3. sideways.

We can now make the first cut of stocks that don't suit us, and eliminate all sideways trending stocks. We only ever want to buy a stock where the trend is already going up. And we only ever want sell where the trend is already going down.

5. AND ONLY BUY IN A BULL MARKET, AND ONLY SELL IN A BEAR.

We also only want to buy if we are in a bull market and we only want to sell if we are in a bear market. We use the 200-day moving average to decide this. If the index is above its 200-day line it is a bull. And if it is below the 200-day line it is a bear.

6. ELIMINATE WEAKER RISING STOCKS BY LOOKING AT THE RATE OF THE RISE.

Now we come to a further refinement. Many stocks that are in uptrends are not rising very fast, and they have quite a high probability of stopping and reversing just after you have backed them. We wished to eliminate these from our buying list.

By back-testing we discovered that it was the rate of rise that was critical. *The trend has to be rising at the rate of a half per cent per week or more.* If held for a year that would make 25% per year. If a company cannot do that, it is not worth backing – the risk of it reversing on us at the wrong moment is too great.

For this reason you should go on to divide the list into five categories not just the three mentioned above: you only want to buy those going up *fast*, and sell those going down *fast*.

7. DO NOT RANK TOO FREQUENTLY OR INFREQUENTLY.

Rank all the stocks once a month and – as per rule 5 – if the index itself is going up above its 200-day line, buy all of the top tenth. These are the cream of the crop.

Do not rank more frequently than monthly or less often than quarterly. We find from back-testing that monthly is a near optimum period.

Next month any stock that is no longer in the top tenth of the list is sold automatically and is replaced by the one that has moved above it. The rule changes to the portfolio are made monthly and not more frequently (which would lead to overtrading).

8. ONLY EVER PUT AN EQUAL AMOUNT OF MONEY INTO EACH STOCK.

This could be 30 holdings of 3% each. Following this principle, an index like the FTSE with only 100 stocks would result in a portfolio with only ten holdings. This would lead to too much stock-specific risk, so we prefer to use an index with more stocks in it so that we can hold more.

However, there is no need to go above 30. In the case of the S&P 500, we are only interested in the very strongest stocks well into the top 10%.

9. THE BEST MARKETS HAVE A STRONG TREND AND RELATIVELY SMALL VOLATILITY.

We find in practice that we hold stocks for between three and six months. The entire portfolio will turn over two to three times a year. We have tested this on 40 different world markets and have not found one where it does not work. However, it is better on some than others. The best markets have a strong trend and relatively small volatility.

If the index goes below the 200-day line, the portfolio is liquidated and – again, as per rule 5 – now we can sell short the bottom 10% of trends and have no longs at all.

It is important to note that we are not making any predictions when using this system: we are simply trend following. We are investing in what is happening and not what we think ought to be happening. To win we have to stick to the system even when it seems not to agree with our opinion. In the end, such rules are better as they are consistent – and have an edge.

Tim Hale

TIM HALE *graduated from the University of Oxford and holds an MBA from Cranfield School of Management. After a few years with Standard Chartered in Hong Kong working in corporate banking, he moved into the investment world, spending almost a decade at Chase Asset Management (now part of JP Morgan Asset Management) in London, Hong Kong and New York.*

Driven by his experience of the difficulties that many investors face trying to invest sensibly, he set up Albion Strategic Consulting in 2001. The firm has forged a unique niche working with around 50 of the UK's leading financial planning firms, helping them to establish systematic, risk-focused, low cost, passive portfolios for use with their high-net-worth clients, and working with them on the ongoing governance of this approach.

Tim's book, Smarter Investing: Simpler Decisions for Better Results *was first published in 2006 by FT Prentice Hall, and the third edition was published in early 2013.*

"A POLL OF OVER 1,000 PROFESSIONALS WORKING IN THE FUND MANAGEMENT INDUSTRY REVEALED THAT 2/3 OF THEM HAD SIZEABLE AMOUNTS INVESTED IN PASSIVE FUNDS. QED."

Four Simple Steps to Smarter Investing

Parsimony drives smarter investing

"The problem simply is that the great majority of managers who attempt to over-perform will fail. The probability is also very high that the person soliciting your funds will not be the exception who does well...

"...Further complicating the search for the rare high-fee manager who is worth his or her pay is the fact that some investment professionals, just as some amateurs, will be lucky over short periods. If 1,000 managers make a market prediction at the beginning of a year, it's very likely that the calls of at least one will be correct for nine consecutive years. Of course, 1,000 monkeys would be just as likely to produce a seemingly all-wise prophet. But there would remain a difference: The lucky monkey would not find people standing in line to invest with him."

WARREN BUFFETT, LETTER TO SHAREHOLDERS, BERKSHIRE HATHAWAY, 2017

T ODAY'S INVESTOR FACES a truly overwhelming choice of products, strategies and managers to choose from, with over 100,000 open-ended funds worldwide including around 10,000 in the US and some 2,500 in the UK (ICI, 2016). That is more than double the 45,000 companies listed on global stock markets! Combined with the easily made promises of market-beating skill sold by the active management industry (usually with a high price tag), many investors, perhaps not surprisingly, end up with investment portfolios built on sand.

Yet thanks to a 14th-century Franciscan friar called William of Ockham (a philosophical bedfellow of Jack Bogle), the astute investor can find a path through the investment industry's quicksand. Ockham's philosophy of being biased toward simplicity over complexity – known as Occam's razor (yes, it's spelt that way too), or the Law of Parsimony – leads investors to focus on the available (and growing) evidence, which guides them to do a few simple things exceptionally well. The outcome – as we will see – is a straightforward investment approach that is robust, simple to both implement and maintain, that will – in all probability – beat the majority of other approaches out there. Such smarter investing only requires three basic tools: simple mathematics, robust evidence, and a good dose of common sense. No need to worry about analysing balance sheets, picking stocks, or identifying a method for selecting market-beating fund managers. Leave that hard work to others.

Three key concepts to take on board

Unfortunately, it would appear that many investors fail to take note of the following:

CONCEPT 1: TRADING IN THE MARKETS REQUIRES WINNERS TO BE FUNDED BY LOSERS.

Investing over the long term is a positive-sum game, where equity and bond investors reap the long-term market rewards of ownership and lending respectively. However, attempting to beat the markets – as all 'active' fund managers aim to do – is a zero-sum game. In other words, every winning manager needs to be funded by a losing manager, given that investment professionals now represent the bulk of the players in the market.

Passive investors (a horribly negative-sounding description), who seek to capture the market return for a market risk taken on, largely sit on the sidelines. The average active investor will achieve a return below that of the market equal to the average fees and trading costs they incur. The average passive investor will, incontrovertibly, beat the majority of active managers because their fees and trading costs are, in general, far lower. That is just maths, not conjecture, as pointed out by Professor William Sharpe (Sharpe, 1991), who won the Nobel Prize for Economics. That's a good start for William of Ockham.

CONCEPT 2: INVESTORS OPERATE IN A VERY NOISY ENVIRONMENT.

Fund data revealing short-term, market-beating returns provide a very noisy signal, as active managers, by definition, do not own the market weight of stocks (or bonds). Most will do better or worse than the market simply by chance. Discerning true skill from luck requires over 20 years of data to be pretty certain that it is one and not the other. An ever-growing library of empirical evidence reveals that persistent, market-beating skill is exceptionally rare and hard to identify in advance (e.g. Blake et al. 2015). Active managers in response usually point to the seemingly great-looking track records of a handful of fund managers; but as the saying goes: 'the plural of anecdote, is not data'.

Other noise comes from the marketing activities of active fund management firms and financial journalism. Huge marketing budgets help push the short-term performance of a few 'star' funds, yet one rarely hears about the staggering 60% or so of funds that disappear altogether over a 15-year period (SPIVA, 2017). Apples-to-oranges comparisons against inappropriate market benchmarks, or fund sectors, combined with the potential conflicts of interest that financial journalists face when writing articles or creating 'best buy' lists – on account of the large advertising spend of sponsor firms – can cloud the picture still further.

The tyranny of function – in this case asset-gathering – is a rich and powerful beast at risk of acting contrary to the best interests of many investors, a view hinted at – somewhat unsubtly – by the UK's regulator, the FCA, in its recent report on the industry (FCA, 2016).

CONCEPT 3: THE RISK–AND–RETURN RELATIONSHIP IS RARELY BROKEN.

Investment nirvana is being able to capture high returns with low risk, so any manager or strategy that claims to be able to perform this alchemy tends to get the attention – even adulation – of investors. What they probably deserve is a good dose of skepticism. The risk-return relationship is almost impossible to break, although it can be improved through diversification. It is more likely that the investor does not know where the risks lie, from outright fraud (e.g. Bernie Madoff) to picking up pennies in front of a steam roller (i.e. strategies that deliver steady returns until a big loss occurs, such as high-yield credit or writing insurance of some kind). If it looks too good to be true, it probably is. If you want high returns, be prepared for material falls in the value of your portfolio from time to time.

Smarter investing in four simple steps

Bearing these three concepts in mind, there are four simple steps to building and maintaining a smarter portfolio.

STEP 1: BUILD A DEEPLY DIVERSIFIED PORTFOLIO TO WEATHER AN UNCERTAIN FUTURE.

Investing is a journey and the one thing we can be sure of is that markets will severely challenge us from time to time. History tells us that markets fail (e.g. Russia and China after the communists took over), suffer bouts of severe trauma (e.g. UK equities fell by 70% from 1972 to 1973 and by over 40% during both the 'tech wreck' and 'credit crisis' crashes of the 2000s). Even seemingly safe assets such as government bonds can suffer severe losses to purchasing power, as happened in the 1920s in Germany. Some assets may get expropriated (e.g. Argentina and Repsol in 2012). These are the real risks of investing, rather than short-term market volatility. Diversifying broadly across companies, sectors, geographies and asset classes is our major defensive weapon against the uncertainties of the future, whatever they may be.

The simple starting point for a portfolio is a balance between well-diversified, return-generating equity holdings and high-quality (e.g. AA) government and corporate bonds. For a UK investor that starting point might be a broad, global developed market index fund and a short-dated gilt index fund. Warren Buffett – revered by many as one of the greatest active investors of all time – suggested that on behalf of his wife, his estate's trustee should simply invest in a mix of an S&P 500 index fund and short-term US government bonds. All asset choices beyond this point become incremental refinements that seek to improve the relationship between return and risk in the portfolio. Even if you go no further, you will already own a portfolio that is better than most.

On the growth assets side (equities), the empirical evidence would suggest adding a moderate exposure to smaller companies, value (less healthy and thus relatively cheaper) stocks and emerging market equities to boost portfolio returns, and provide a little diversification. Equity market diversifiers such as global commercial property might be considered too.

On the defensive assets side (bonds), owning lower-quality bonds – particularly high-yield bonds – risks eroding the defensive qualities needed when equity markets fall, so stick with higher credit-quality bonds e.g. AA or A. Longer-dated bonds, which are more sensitive to movements in interest rates, add extra volatility with scant reward over time, so stick with shorter-dated bonds. Holding some inflation-linked bonds should provide protection against unanticipated inflation. If you own global bonds, picking a fund that hedges out non-base currency exposure (i.e. non-GBP currencies for a UK investor) makes sense. Never invest in a bond fund until you know its average credit quality and the average maturity of the bonds it owns.

There are no absolute right or wrong answers in this game, but certainly there are better and worse solutions. All things in moderation is a useful mantra. Each investor will be driven by his or her own preferences.

STEP 2: LET THE MARKETS DO THE HEAVY RETURN LIFTING.

Today, investors are very fortunate in that they can now own funds – passive funds – where returns come almost entirely from the markets, rather than manager skill. The broad efficiency of markets in pricing securities and the exceptionally high level of talent in the fund management industry competing against itself, make finding anomalously priced securities – the source of manager outperformance – rare, short-lived and hard to extract after costs.

The proof is in the data that tells us that around 80% to 90% of active fund managers fail to beat their market benchmark over a ten-year period (SPIVA, 2017). Of those that do, we still face the problem of discerning skill from luck. Studies on performance persistence invariably reveal that those that win in one period tend not to be the winners in the next period (Vanguard, 2017). It is estimated that around 3% of managers appear to be truly skilled but take most of the rewards for themselves in fees (Fama and French, 2009). Hats off to them, but don't underestimate the challenge of identifying who they are!

The realisation that portfolio returns come entirely from market rewards, in compensation for sensible risks taken in the portfolio, is liberating too. No more hiring and firing of managers. No more blaming yourself, or your advisor, for the funds that perform poorly. It is worth noting that a poll of over 1,000 professionals working in the fund management industry revealed that two-thirds of them had sizeable amounts invested in passive funds (Ignites, 2013). Quod erat demonstrandum.

STEP 3: CLING ONTO YOUR RETURNS FOR DEAR LIFE.

The financial and emotional costs of investing can devastate the growth of your wealth over your investment lifetime. Remember that costs are insidious. The simplest way to make the point is to calculate the difference between two strategies that deliver the same return before costs over 40 years (a pretty reasonable time frame for most investors). The low-cost strategy has costs of 0.15% pa and the high-cost strategy has costs of 1.5% pa. This is not an unrealistic picture of the difference between passively and actively managed funds. Using Professor William Sharpe's 'Terminal Wealth Ratio' calculation (Sharpe, 2013), an investor in the low-cost strategy would have an astounding 70% more wealth than someone investing in the high-cost strategy after 40 years.

Warren Buffett has recently estimated that around $100bn has been wasted over the past ten years by wealthy private and institutional investors wrongly assuming that sophisticated and expensive investment strategies represent good value. He also made a ten-year bet worth $500,000 for charity, nine years ago, that an S&P 500 index fund would beat five funds of hedge funds comprising over 100 individual hedge funds selected by the other side of the bet. It looks like he is going to win hands down, in part because he estimates that around 60% of all of returns of these funds have been pocketed by their managers, not their clients (Buffett, 2017). I rest my case.

The second cost danger comes from ourselves. As humans we suffer a range of illusions and behavioural biases that make us poor investors. Amongst many other traits, we tend to be overconfident, feel the pain of losses more than the pleasure of gains and make decisions using mental shortcuts that don't work too well. We are prone to chasing hot investments, getting in at the top and being shaken out at the bottom, which erodes wealth. This behaviour has been estimated to cost investors around 1% to 3% per year (Kinnel, 2015). Controlling ourselves becomes key to success.

STEP 4: UNDERTAKE SOME BASIC PORTFOLIO MAINTENANCE.

Rebalance your basket of assets back to their original mix, to ensure that it maintains a suitable level of risk and remains well-diversified. Once a year is fine. Not rebalancing a portfolio is likely to result in it becoming concentrated in the higher returning – and thus more risky – asset classes over time. If you are lucky you might gather a rebalancing bonus, from selling high and buying low, but definitely don't bank on it.

Make sure that you take advantage of all of the legal tax breaks that you are provided by your tax regime, such as making contributions to a pension plan, using up your capital gains allowance annually and funding tax-sheltered savings pots (e.g. ISAs in the UK). Every little helps, as tax can become a significant cost if not planned for and managed well.

Remind yourself, from time to time, of the power of a diversified portfolio, implemented using funds that let the markets do the heavy return-lifting over time. Be confident that it is likely to deliver you with the greatest chance of a successful outcome. Be patient; investing is a long-term, two-steps-forward and one-step-backward process, where the tortoise beats the hare. Only look at your portfolio once a year, and keep an eye on the bigger picture. An inevitable consequence of owning a diversified portfolio is that some parts of it will be doing worse than others. Keep the faith and stick with your programme. Investment activity is almost always in surplus, as the legendary Charlie Ellis would say.

Parsimony pays

Occam's razor, as we have seen, shaves away the layers of complexity and cost burden that surround the efforts of a highly talented pool of ambitious and dedicated professional fund managers to whom the maths of the zero-sum game, market efficiency and the empirical data are so utterly cruel. There are many ways to invest, but to many, the simplicity and efficacy of 'smarter investing' might well be appealing. I wish them well.

Endnotes

Blake, David P. and Caulfield, Tristan and Ioannidis, Christos and Tonks, Ian (2015), 'New Evidence on Mutual Fund Performance: A Comparison of Alternative Bootstrap Methods' (October 1, 2015), Pensions Institute.

Fama, Eugene F. and French, Kenneth R., 'Luck versus Skill in the Cross Section of Mutual Fund Returns' (December 14, 2009). Tuck School of Business Working Paper No. 2009-56.

FCA (2016), 'Asset Management Market Study – Interim Report MS15/2.2', November 2016, Financial Conduct Authority.

ICI (2016), *2016 Investment Company Fact Book*, Investment Company Institute p. 238.

Ignites (2013), as quoted in 'The emperor's new clothes', *The Financial Times*, 30 June, 2013.

Kinnel, R., (2015), 'Mind the Gap', 2015, *Morningstar.*

Sharpe, W., (1991). 'The Arithmetic of Active Management', *Financial Analysts' Journal* Vol. 47, No. 1, January/February 1991. pp.7–9.

Sharpe, W., (2013), 'The Arithmetic of Investment Expenses', *Financial Analysts' Journal*, Volume 69, Number 2.

SPIVA® (2017) U.S. Scorecard (year-end 2016), Standard & Poor's.

Vanguard (2017), 'The case for low-cost index-fund investing', Vanguard Research, April 2017.

Ian Heslop

IAN HESLOP *joined Old Mutual in 2000 and is head of global equities at Old Mutual Global Investors. He manages a range of hedge and retail funds and segregated mandates, including market neutral and long-only funds. Ian boasts more than 20 years of investment experience and the team has won numerous awards for its funds. Prior to joining Old Mutual, Ian was a UK quantitative fund manager at Barclays Global Investors. He holds an MA in chemistry from the University of Oxford and a PhD in medicinal chemistry, University of Edinburgh. He is an associate of the Society of Investment Professionals.*

"THE RUSH TO PASSIVES HAS BEEN SO GREAT THAT THERE HAS BEEN A DISTORTING EFFECT ON THE MARKET."

Five Bright Ideas for Taking the Bias out of Investment

1. DISTRUST MACRO BETS.

INVESTMENT IS NOT easy. There are plenty who would like to convince you that they have cracked it. The truth is that investing well, consistently, is hard.

Overconfidence about our ability to predict macro events can be a pitfall for investors. It is very difficult to forecast major macroeconomic events and even harder to divine their effect on the stock market. Even if you get the macroeconomic forecast correct, the market reaction may be unexpected.

For example, many observers failed to forecast that the UK would vote for Brexit in the referendum on membership of the European Union on 23 June 2016. Similarly, many failed to forecast that Donald Trump would win the US presidential election on 8 November 2016. Both political forecasts were hard. But predicting the reactions of the market to these political events was even harder. Many believed that a vote for Brexit, which was expected to damage the UK economy and to throw Europe into turmoil, would lead to a stock market fall. In fact, during the two months after 23 June 2016, the FTSE 100 rose by 9%. So even if you had forecasted the result of the vote correctly, you could easily have incorrectly predicted the market reaction. Similarly, many believed before the US election on 8 November 2016 that a Trump victory would be bad for the stock market, because he was an unknown quantity, and political risk would rise. In fact, during the two months after the Trump victory, the S&P 500 rose by 6%.

I believe that the equity market is, like the weather, or ecosystems, or societies, an example of a complex system. Such systems are often difficult to forecast, because they may respond to the same stimulus in two different ways on two separate occasions.

So be cautious about trying to predict the market based on macro events.

2. BE STYLE-CONSCIOUS.

Investment style is highly important yet often overlooked. Some investors may not realise they have a style, or may underestimate its contribution to their performance.

There are two main styles: a value style and a growth style.

- **Value investors** look for bargains. They like to buy shares cheaply, believing they will recover from their low prices. What does 'cheap' mean? For the more technically minded, one way of measuring it is by a share's price-to-book ratio. The book value is the company's equity according to its balance sheet. The price-to-book ratio is the share price divided by the book value per share. If the ratio is low (compared with other shares, or to historical averages) that is an indication that the share is cheap. Another method of measuring value is to use the price-earnings ratio, which is share price divided by the company's earnings per share (which is to be found in the company's income statement). Both measures are ways of comparing the market's view of a company to figures found in its reports and accounts. Whatever method is used, the value investor's aim is to find a basket of shares whose price is relatively low. General Motors, Macy's and Goodyear are examples of companies with relatively low price-earnings ratios.

- **Growth investors** look for companies growing faster than average. They like to buy stocks in companies with innovative or superior products that are in high demand. Growth investors tend not to mind so much that the shares may be expensive when measured by value metrics. Growth investors look for companies that have higher-than-average growth in revenues, for example. Technology companies like Amazon, Netflix and Nvidia are examples of growth companies.

What style of investor should you be, value or growth? The correct answer, I believe, is: either, depending on the market conditions. You need to understand investment styles and their impact on performance. The ability to shapeshift between different investment styles is an advantage.

3. DON'T FALL INTO THE STYLE-BIAS TRAP.

Some investors think loyalty to their style is a virtue, but often it is merely inflexibility. The market does not reward all styles, all of the time. While there is some evidence that cheap stocks may outperform expensive ones over the very long term, there are periods – and they can last for many years – when cheap stocks just go on getting cheaper. So pursuing a value style in all conditions can be a recipe for very bumpy returns.

To compete effectively in the investment eco-system, style flexibility is vital. To be flexible you need to determine the style most likely to perform well under the current market environment. I believe that a value style tends to do better in risk-on environments, but less well in risk-off. (A risk-on environment is one in which investors are prepared to take greater risk.)

Be flexible enough about your style to adapt to the market environment.

4. DON'T ASSUME THE MARKET IS AN INDEX.

What is the equity market? Many assume it is an index, such as the FTSE 100 or the S&P 500. In fact, those two indices, though useful, both represent a single method of measuring the market.

The FTSE 100 and the S&P 500 are examples of **market-capitalisation-weighted** indices. The allocation to each share is a fraction of the index in proportion to the share's market capitalisation (which is the price of the share multiplied by the company's number of shares). The FTSE 100 and the S&P 500 therefore weight more towards stocks with a larger market capitalisation (large caps). One way to understand this is as follows: if a share with a large market capitalisation (like Apple) rises in price, and another share with a small market capitalisation falls in price by the same amount (and all the other shares in the index are unchanged), then the index rises.

If you feel this is somewhat unfair to shares with small market capitalisations (small caps) you may prefer a different kind of index, called an **equal-weighted** index: in this case, the allocation to each share is an equal fraction of the index. In other words, all the shares in the index are weighted the same.

There are other kinds of index. For example, there are **price-weighted** indices. The allocation to each share is a fraction of the index in proportion to its price: so a share priced at US$100 has ten times the proportion in the index as a share priced at US$10. You may feel this is a somewhat arbitrary way of weighting shares in an index, but the famous Dow Jones Industrials Average, which dates back to 1896, is a price-weighted index, and so is the Japanese Nikkei 225.

Don't just look at market indices: dig deeper.

5. BE AWARE OF OBESITY RISK.

Many are attracted to passive investments, such as equity index trackers and ETFs, because they are cheaper, or because they have lost faith in active managers' ability consistently to outperform indices. In fact, investors have flocked to passives over recent years. The rush to passives has been so great that there has been a distorting effect on the market, in my opinion.

Most trackers, such as ETFs and passive funds, track market-capitalisation-weighted indices like the FTSE 100 or the S&P 500, which as I have explained are weighted more toward large cap stocks. Since trackers have become very popular, and have enjoyed large inflows of funds, proportionately more money has flowed into large cap stocks. This makes their prices rise, and so their market cap grows even more, and so they attract even more inflows, in a feedback effect.

During the first half of 2017, advances in the S&P 500 relied disproportionately on the performance of a small percentage of its constituents. The largest ten stocks in the S&P 500 index by market capitalisation, which include Apple, Google, Microsoft, Amazon and Facebook, sit predominantly within the technology sector. That sector has outpaced others. As at 24 July 2017 those top ten stocks in the S&P 500 accounted for 20% of its market capitalisation. If the S&P 500 were an equal-weighted index their proportion in it would only be 2%. So the index is top-heavy.

Bubbles are a perennial problem in financial markets, and they may be partly caused by feedback effects. The economist John Galbraith, in his book *The Great Crash 1929* (Houghton Mifflin, 1954), describes how in the run up to the crash there was a rapid growth in investment trusts, some of which invested directly in stocks, but others of which invested merely in other investment trusts. In the frantic bull market that preceded the crash of 1929, this was arguably a feedback effect.

I am not predicting that a crash will inevitably happen due to passive trackers. Crashes are at least as difficult to forecast as earthquakes, and their causes are still a matter of dispute. But I do believe that the size of the inflows into passive trackers over recent years may have elevated the potential risks.

Beware of blindly investing in market cap indices: you may be behind the crowd.

Andrew Hunt

ANDREW HUNT *graduated from Cambridge with a Law degree in 2003. He worked in TV production before moving to Edinburgh in 2006 to join Baillie Gifford, where he worked as an Investment Manager until 2016. He is now an Investment Director with Standard Life Investments. Andrew is the author of* Better Value Investing *(Harriman House, 2015).*

"POSITIVE CASH GENERATION IS THE MOST IMPORTANT MEASURE OF FINANCIAL STRENGTH."

Two Mice Fell in a Bucket of Cream – The Art of Contrarian Value Investing

You've probably heard the old tale of the two mice who fell into a bucket of cream. The first mouse, seeing no way out, quickly gives up and drowns. The second one paddles on so hard that eventually he churns the cream to butter and climbs out.

If you identify with the second mouse, contrarian investing might just be for you. This type of investing demands enormous reserves of patience, resilience, perseverance and a willingness to go it alone.

What everyone omits from the mouse story is that the second mouse also gets away with a lifetime's supply of delicious butter! Contrarian investing too, while demanding, can be incredibly rewarding.

1. ALWAYS REMEMBER THAT INVESTING IS HARD.

Too many investors think intelligence or vast amounts of information are enough to achieve success. Nowadays, every investor has these in spades. You need something more.

Investing is like any other business. Long-run excess returns go only to those who can do something different that others cannot do. In investing, there are almost no physical barriers to entry – look how easily capital flows. The only long-term barriers are psychological or institutional. You have to know where your edge lies.

Contrarian investing works because it is difficult in practice. You are effectively preying on the fears, instincts and prejudices of other investors. Further, things often take a long time to work out. That makes it incredibly uncomfortable. For most institutional structures, the level of discomfort makes true contrarian investing impossible. It works because it is hard.

John Templeton had a saying: "Always change your winning game." No matter what style of investor you are, when investing feels easy – as if you are swimming with the tide and can do no wrong – that invariably portends trouble ahead. This is the time to rein things in or change your approach.

2. MAKE THE COMMITMENT.

Stephen King wrote continuously for nine years before he sold his first book. John Coltrane practised the saxophone every day for 17 years before he had his first hit. Becoming really good at anything takes a long time. Investing is no different, especially because it takes so long to get meaningful feedback. Expect to put in at least a decade of hard work before you really begin to invest in an insightful way. There are no shortcuts; you have to learn by doing. You have to see how you perform in different environments and markets, learn from mistakes and experiment widely.

If you study the records of the most successful investors, you'll find that the majority started off poorly. It is a willingness to keep learning and to persevere for years that eventually brings success.

3. KNOW YOUR WEAKNESSES AND OWN YOUR MISTAKES.

There is no such thing as a perfect strategy. All strategies open up the investor to certain risks. Great strategies define what they need to avoid doing as well as what they do. This is second-level thinking and this is where you can gain a real edge. Most investors intuitively focus on their past successes rather than their failures. Thus they repeat the same mistakes over and over again.

You should view your mistakes as your most valuable asset. The likelihood is that you already know what you're good at, and don't need any encouragement to repeat it. Finding your flaws is what will help you improve.

Firstly, make sure you record all your investment decisions and define what you would consider to be a mistake. When you make a mistake, acknowledge it and write it down. Go over your investment work, and if you can, get someone else to look over your analysis with you. Try to understand why you went wrong and what you can learn from it. Then make deliberate changes to your process so you don't make the same mistake again.

Another valuable thing is to actively seek out dissenters. These should be friends or colleagues whom you admire, but who think quite differently.

Meet up regularly, explain your process and show them your portfolio. Ask specifically for tough feedback: Where are my weaknesses? What should I be most worried about? Really listen to what they say.

4. USE CHECKLISTS.

As far as I'm concerned, the simple checklist is the most valuable and underused tool available to investors.

Checklists are lists of objective criteria you go through before making an investment decision. You can make various checklists for different situations; such as investment analysis, dealing decisions, or for specific types of investment.

Above all, keep them short, simple and objective. That way you are more likely to follow them when it matters most. Be willing to evolve your checklists. Over time they should develop as you better understand your mistakes. Checklists are most useful for taking out common errors.

Finally, be strict with yourself. You've built the checklist, so now apply it. If an investment does not meet your checklist criteria, don't buy it. If you find yourself skipping checks or not following your checklists, then stop, take a break and start again.

5. BE PATIENT.

When it comes to contrarian value investing, patience is an absolute must. Because it takes a long time for troubled businesses to turn around and for markets to regain confidence, average holding periods can be five or six years. Further, the best returns often come only after two or three years. This is totally different to most strategies.

Also, be patient with your buying. Sometimes you come across a share and think, 'This is a fantastic company, I've got to have it!' Only to discover that it is a bit expensive. What you need to do then is to hold off, set your target price, and just watch and wait. Ninety per cent of the time you'll get what you want in the end.

6. MAKE VOLATILITY YOUR FRIEND.

Markets are overemotional, with shares swinging between wildly overvalued to wildly undervalued and back. It's important not to underestimate volatility. Look at long-term price graphs or lists of 52-week highs and lows and you'll understand how extreme volatility is.

For successful investors, volatility is the source of opportunity rather than something to worry about. Volatility is what makes buy-low sell-high possible. Always remember that market prices are there for your convenience, you do not have to react to them. Stay focused on the underlying value of the shares you buy – your independent assessment of their true worth. Only buy shares at massive discounts to that value and sell at around full value.

It is best to be systematic about this. If you buy a share and it falls, re-check the investment case and if it is still intact and the financials are sound, gradually keep buying more. When a share goes up, sell when the discount disappears or is close to disappearing. It's that simple.

7. EXECUTION IS EVERYTHING.

We have all these studies of markets showing how contrarian value investing delivers phenomenal long-run returns. Yet there are hardly any cases of real investors achieving anything like those results, even after taxes and costs. Many try: the trouble is most give up, get distracted or plump for something that feels more comfortable.

However, the only way to get those returns is to develop the basic framework and to stick to it. Some investments will not work, volatility is often high, the headlines may be ugly, but you have to keep executing – buying and holding extremely cheap, unpopular and obscure shares.

When it comes to contrarian value investing, it is the system that is the star, not the investor. The investor's job is to focus on following the process consistently. It is sticking to that sound framework, day in day out, year after year, that matters.

8. INVEST INSIDE THE GOLDEN TRIANGLE.

This is a simple three-factor assessment of shares I use as my primary tool for stock-picking. I call it the golden triangle because the investment process rests on three tenets. While it is simple, it has proved incredibly effective and delivered excellent results.

The first criteria is **valuation**. The highest returns from value investing tend to come from the very cheapest shares. By way of example, the average share I bought in 2015 traded on a 35% free cash flow yield, less than half of book and had a Ben Graham P/E (price ÷ seven-year average earnings) of 4. Further, all the shares were more than 50% below my conservative assessment of their true worth. But be warned: these are uncomfortable shares to own. The higher returns are a premium for taking the discomfort.

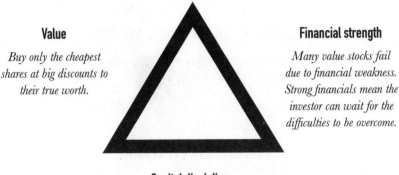

Value

Buy only the cheapest shares at big discounts to their true worth.

Financial strength

Many value stocks fail due to financial weakness. Strong financials mean the investor can wait for the difficulties to be overcome.

Capital discipline

Looking for a record of pay-outs avoids fraudulent or mismanaged situations. It also avoids companies near the peak of their capital or hubris cycles.

The second leg is **financial strength**. Most value stocks fail to recover strongly because their financials are too weak. Thus, a full assessment of financial strength is vital. Make sure the companies you chose are making money, even during the most difficult times. Look for consistent free cash generation and operating profitability. Positive cash generation is the most important measure of financial strength. You also need to check the company can meet all of its liabilities comfortably. These include debt and other obligations such as pensions and leases. Only select companies that can pay off their total net liabilities with no more than two or three years of modest cash flows.

The third and final leg is **capital discipline**. In recent years, an enormous body of evidence has emerged finding capital discipline to be a very powerful alpha factor. Simply put, companies that are consistently paying out cash to shareholders (buybacks or dividends) and/or debt holders (falling debt) tend to make great investments. Also, look for frugality: such as cost cutting, low capital spending and little or no M&A. Avoid companies spending heavily. Buying disciplined companies with generous payouts has many advantages. Firstly, these are businesses making real money for their owners. Thus, it is a great way to avoid fraudulent or mismanaged businesses. A focus on capital discipline will also help you avoid companies near the peak of their business cycle, when corporate spending tends to rocket. Instead, it will identify companies near the bottom of their down-cycles that are ripe for recovery.

Look for those opportunities when all three factors are aligned.

9. LOOK AFTER THOSE AROUND YOU.

This may sound trite but it is essential. Most investors have a reasonable understanding of what to do. However, without the right temperament and emotional balance, that is not enough. At the top, investors tend to become hubristic, arrogant and reckless. At the bottom they can become excessively depressed or lash out. All this emotional chaos is at the heart of why markets go crazy now and again.

Instead, you need to remain cheerful and grounded, and to keep perspective. Take investing seriously, but don't make it the most important thing in your life. Always put the people close to you first – family, friends and colleagues. Give them your time and energy, not just your money. It is amazing how meaningful even small gestures can be – taking the time to write that card, give a few encouraging words or visit a relative. After a few successful investments, the buzz of making money wears off. However, the rewards of kindness keep coming. More than anything else this will help you learn, retain perspective and achieve a sense of fulfilment.

If you're a professional investor, try to make time every day to help out colleagues, especially those who are junior to you or who are struggling – they will really appreciate it the most. This is the most rewarding part of my job.

Contrarian value investing is fascinating, demanding and rewarding, but the best investments you will ever make are in your relationships.

James Inglis-Jones

JAMES INGLIS-JONES *graduated in 1990 with a First Class Honours Degree in Modern History from York University. He went on to gain a D.Phil in Modern History from Christ Church, Oxford. James joined Fleming Investment Management in 1997, assuming responsibility for the management of UK equity portfolios in 1999. Between 1999 and 2002 he worked on JP Morgan Fleming's institutional investment process and managed a wide range of retail and institutional funds as a senior portfolio manager within their European equity group. James joined Liontrust in 2006 to develop and manage the Cashflow Solution investment process. Alongside Samantha Gleave, James currently applies this process to the management of the Liontrust European Growth Fund, Liontrust Global Income Fund, Liontrust GF European Smaller Companies Fund and Liontrust GF European Strategic Equity Fund. James is a CFA Charterholder and a Chartered Management Accountant.*

"CHOOSING AN INDIVIDUAL STOCK WITHOUT HAVING MUCH IDEA WHAT YOU'RE LOOKING FOR IS AKIN TO RUNNING THROUGH A DYNAMITE FACTORY WITH A BURNING MATCH – YOU MIGHT LIVE TO TELL THE TALE BUT YOU'RE STILL AN IDIOT."

How Practising Your Process Makes Perfect

1. DEFINE AN INVESTMENT PROCESS BEFORE YOU START INVESTING.

A GREAT US money manager once described choosing an individual stock without having much idea what you're looking for as akin to running through a dynamite factory with a burning match – you might live to tell the tale but you're still an idiot. Having a clear idea what you're looking for is all about having a well-defined investment process.

In order to capture the full long-term potential of an investment philosophy, it is important to have a distinct investment process that can be rigorously and consistently applied in the short term. The discipline of formally documenting a process is also very constructive; if you can't clearly explain your investment philosophy and process to someone else, it's probably a strong sign that you don't fully understand it yourself.

At the heart of the investment process we developed at Liontrust is the idea that cash flow is the single most important determinant of shareholder return. The basic idea is that companies run by conservative managers who are focused on cash flow delivery should perform significantly better than companies run by aggressive company managers making large cash investments today to secure forecast growth in the future.

When first formulating the process, we spent time thinking about how best to capture these qualities and ended up with two simple core ratios – one focused on how the market values a company's cash flow, the other focused on how cash-generative a company is. All the stocks that we invest in today are underpinned by our basic belief in the importance of cash flow.

2. MAKE FULL USE OF HISTORIC DATA TO TEST THE EFFICACY OF YOUR PROCESS.

An investment process can't simply be theoretical, it also needs to be backed up by historical analysis to show that it works.

Good processes work because they tap into the behavioural biases of investors. For example, investors are often reticent to crystallise losses even when an investment case has deteriorated, but this emotional bias only results in poorly performing investments being held for too long.

I want to see plenty of evidence of strong returns to a strategy. If this is lacking, then I'm inclined to believe it's unlikely that the process is based on an enduring feature of investor behaviour that will repeat itself in the future.

However, analysing the history of a proposed strategy should be approached cautiously. Used incorrectly, a historic data set can be susceptible to 'data mining', where a model is moulded to the data, meaning it looks great in the past but is little use going forward. So to minimise the risk of data mining, it's important to formulate and develop a theory why it should work before you begin testing against the data.

An investment process backed up by a sound theory and validated by historic data is the basis for future success.

3. IT'S IMPORTANT THAT YOUR PROCESS DOES NOT WORK IN EVERY MARKET ENVIRONMENT.

It may be surprising, but an important feature of an investment process is that it does not work all the time. If a process works all the time, everyone would soon adopt it and it would lose its potency. A good investment process is sustained by the fact that from time to time it does not perform that well. This causes some people to abandon the approach, which serves to sustain the anomaly. Academics like to call this effect the 'limits of arbitrage' and in my view it's a critically important part of any good investment process.

4. AVOID CHANGING YOUR PROCESS WHEN TIMES ARE TOUGH.

There's no point in carefully thinking through how you are going to run money and testing the approach on long-term historic data only to abandon it when short-term results are not good. This lack of resilience only leads in the longer term to poor investment returns and loss of investors. As I've already stated, a pre-condition of a good investment process is that it does not work all the time. Indeed the best times to allocate money to a good investment process will always be at a time it's not performing well – using volatility to enhance your expected return rather than detract from it.

It's interesting to note that much of the investment management industry is obsessed by good returns over three to five years. Our studies have shown that whilst good processes generate very impressive long term returns, these returns are frequently characterised by waves of three-to-five-year periods of weak performance that then give way to a spectacular period of outperformance, but it can also work the other way around: strong three-to-five-year returns are frequently followed by a period when a strategy will do less well. This short time frame is therefore a questionable basis for the evaluation of an investment strategy.

5. DON'T LET DIPS IN PERFORMANCE AND EMOTIONS REDUCE YOUR CONVICTION.

I underestimated the emotional pressure that can be brought to bear during the inevitable difficult periods of poor investment performance. People will question whether or not the process is still valid. It can be tempting in these circumstances to question your approach. But I found it was invaluable at these times to be able to fall back on the empirical support for my strategy which showed that these periods were just part and parcel of applying the investment process. This gave me the resilience and fortitude to stick with the process through difficult times.

6. ENHANCE RATHER THAN CHANGE YOUR INVESTMENT PROCESS.

The emphasis should be on evolution rather than revolution. As you gain experience and familiarity with a process, it's possible to identify ways in which it can be enhanced or refined. We have done a lot of work looking at the types of good cash flow stocks we select and introducing a more systemic approach that ensures better diversity and a higher proportion of high conviction stocks make the cut. However, this work has only been possible as a result of practically applying the process over a long period of time.

7. FINALLY – DON'T BASE INVESTMENT DECISIONS ON FORECASTS!

We pick investments based on forensic analysis of cash flow as presented in companies' reports and accounts. Some critics will say this is driving using the rear-view mirror, but our analysis shows that this is by far the superior approach precisely because of the difficulty in forecasting the road ahead.

In fact, I believe that investors often place too much emphasis on their ability to make forecasts despite a wide body of academic literature that affirms none of us is very good at it. In my view, opportunities arise as a result of investors not paying enough attention to the cash flow they can observe today in a company's report and accounts, and too much attention on what they think is going to happen tomorrow. My experience tells me that eschewing the temptation to second-guess the market and make forecasts and sticking to a successful well-defined investment process pays off in the long run.

Niels Jensen

NIELS JENSEN *has over 30 years of investment banking and investment management experience. He began his career in Copenhagen in 1984 before moving to London in 1986. He founded Absolute Return Partners in 2002 and today is the Chief Investment Officer of the firm. In 2006 he was appointed Director of a leading UK corporate pension fund, advising it on its investment strategy – a position he continues to hold. He is a graduate of the University of Copenhagen with a Master's Degree in economics.*

He is the author of The End of Indexing *(Harriman House, 2018).*

"WHEN SECULAR BEAR MARKETS TAKE CHARGE, EQUITY MARKETS RARELY JUST GO BACK TO THE TREND LINE. MOST OF THEM GO ALL THE WAY BACK TO THE BOTTOM OF THE CHANNEL."

Absolute Returns and the End of Indexing

INVESTMENT RULES SHOULDN'T be static. Investors should adapt their rules per the environment they are in. From experience, I can confirm that those who don't adapt usually get into trouble sooner or later. My first and most important rule when investing is therefore a rule that defines the rules I should adhere to.

What exactly do I mean by that? How can I possibly have a rule about rules? Allow me to explain. As I see things, there are rules, and then there are principles. The most important ones always apply; those are my first frontier rules. There are not many of them, but they are all critically important. The second layer of rules – the second frontier – are strictly speaking not rules but principles. I treat them as rules, though, because I follow them almost whatever happens.

Warren Buffett once uttered the now famous words: "If you aren't willing to own a stock for ten years, don't even think about owning it for ten minutes." From my 30-plus years of investment experience, I can confidently say that those who lose their shirt on investments are almost always those who don't stick to their rules and principles; those who get carried away when an opportunity presents itself.

I have a less than outstanding short-term track record (as most investors do) but, over the years, I have found that my track record over the long term is better than just good, so I stick to the long term – just like Warren Buffett does. The three rules that I will present in this chapter have all worked very well for me over the years, but don't expect them to work particularly well if your time horizon is only until next week.

1. ADAPT YOUR INVESTMENT PRINCIPLES TO THE ENVIRONMENT YOU ARE IN.

Let me give you a very simple example why my investment principles change subject to the environment we are in. Many investors are in love with growth stocks, and it is not difficult to understand why. Growth stocks have outperformed value stocks for many years – but if you do your homework properly you find a close link between bond yields and the relative performance between growth and value stocks.

When bond yields decline, growth stocks outperform value stocks, and vice versa when bond yields rise. With declining bond yields for most of the last 35 years, it is easy to understand why many investors are infatuated with growth stocks. An entire generation of investors has never seen value stocks outperform growth stocks for long periods of time, and those who have can hardly remember because it is more than 35 years ago.

Now, assuming we stand in front of a multi-year rise in interest rates, even if it is of modest proportions (as I think it will be), all that could be about to change. Investors who are wedded to their growth stock rule may be disappointed, while those who are prepared to adapt to the changing regime are more likely to outperform.

Another example is the wider performance of equity markets. At the very highest level, I divide equity markets into secular bull and secular bear markets. Over the last 150 years or so, the US has enjoyed six secular bull markets and only five secular bear markets (exhibit 1).

Exhibit 1: Secular US equity bull and bear markets since 1877

YEAR	MARKET MILESTONE	PERCENT CHANGE	NUMBER OF YEARS	ANNUALIZED RETURN, NO DIVIDENDS	ANNUALIZED RETURN WITH DIVIDENDS
1877	Low	-	-	-	-
1906	High	396%	29.3	5.1%	10.10%
1921	Low	-69%	14.9	-7.50%	-2.00%
1929	High	396%	8.1	21.90%	28.40%
1932	Low	-81%	2.7	-44.90%	-41.20%
1937	High	266%	4.7	32.10%	38.70%
1949	Low	-54%	12.3	-6.20%	-0.80%
1968	High	413%	19.5	8.80%	13.30%
1982	Low	-63%	13.6	-7.00%	-3%
2000	High	666%	18.1	11.90%	15.30%
2009	Low	-59%	8.5	-9.80%	-8.10%
Now	-	172%	8	N/A	N/A

Source: Jill Mislinski, Advisor Perspectives

A secular bull market is characterised by rising earnings multiples, whereas in secular bear markets earnings multiples decline. Falling earnings multiples lead to the sharply lower returns that characterise secular bear markets. As you can see, the difference in total returns between secular bull and bear markets is quite dramatic.

There are no rules as to how long a secular bull or bear market should last for, but history provides some guidelines. Only one has run for more than 20 years, and both bull and bear markets tend to stay in a relatively predictable channel – at least they have done so for the past 150 years (exhibit 2).

Exhibit 2: S&P Composite – 1877 to present (inflation-adjusted regression channel)

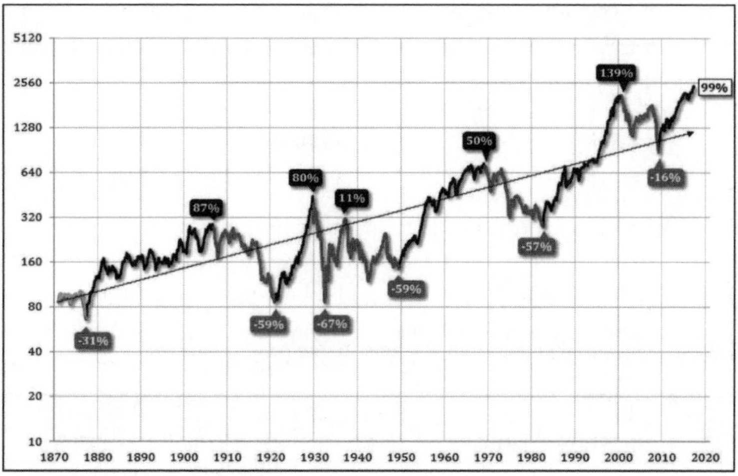

Note: As at March 2017 | Source: Jill Mislinski, Advisor Perspectives

As is also apparent from exhibit 2, the secular bull market we have been in since 2009 is (at the time of writing) almost 100% above the long-term trend line but, when secular bear markets take charge, equity markets rarely just go back to the trend line. Most of them go all the way back to the bottom of the channel.

This leads me to conclude that equities in general, and US equities in particular, are priced for problems in the years to come; hence I would allocate only a limited amount to this asset class at present.

Having done my very best to dampen your expectations, let's kill another sacred cow. There is a firmly entrenched view amongst investors – probably driven by the so-called Fed Put (aka the Greenspan Put) – that, whenever the going gets tough, the Fed will bail you out, and it won't take long before equities get back on track.

For that very reason, many investors have chosen to sit out most storms in recent years. If you subscribe to that philosophy, let me remind you that equities sometimes spend decades under water before they finally come back with a vengeance (exhibit 3).

Exhibit 3: Longest runs of negative real equity returns since 1900

	REAL RETURN	PERIOD	NUMBER OF YEARS
US	-7%	1905-20	16
UK	-4%	1900-21	22
FRANCE	-8%	1900-52	53
GERMNAY	-8%	1900-54	55
JAPAN	-1%	1900-50	51
WORLD	-9%	1901-20	20
WORLD EX US	-11%	1928-50	23

Source: Dimson, Marsh and Staunton, London Business School

I could mention many more principles that investors should adhere to, but time doesn't allow me to go into too much detail. One deserves at least a mention, though. With interest rates hovering not far from all-time lows, and with a growing number of people retiring every year, the demand for alternative sources of income is on the rise.

Investment-grade government bonds simply don't yield enough to meet the growing demand for income from the elderly, so the search for income is becoming ever more creative. The simplest way to find that extra bit of income would probably drive you towards higher-yielding equities (European more so than US equities) and non-investment grade bonds, but many investors think those asset classes are already too expensive.

Before you write them off, though, bear in mind that circumstances have changed. As the number of elderly with a need for regular income has already risen substantially, and will only grow further in the years to come, it is not entirely impossible that assets offering a decent yield will become even more expensively priced.

In other words, one needs to incorporate changing demographics, and the effect such changes are likely to have on various asset classes, into one's investment principles. One cannot assume that just because 15 times has been the average earnings multiple in the past (which it has – at least in the US), 15 is also a fair earnings multiple going forward.

In that context – one word of caution. I have assumed that earnings multiples on higher-yielding equities can be expected to remain relatively high for many years to come, but I have established a principle that a company should not only pay an attractive dividend. It should also generate enough cash from operating earnings to finance that dividend internally. Too many high-dividend companies resort to borrowing when paying dividends, and that will come back and bite them at some point.

2. NEVER LET SHORT-TERM TRENDS DRIVE YOUR PORTFOLIO CONSTRUCTION.

Different sorts of trends and themes set the tone in financial markets, and I divide those trends into tactical trends and structural trends. Tactical trends are either cyclical in nature or they are behavioural, and most of them are short- to medium-term in length. Structural trends are very long term (as in many years), and they are mostly unaffected by investor behaviour; they unfold regardless.

Cyclical trends refer to the economic cycle, and how they are likely to affect financial markets. Behavioural trends are a tad more complex. Investor behaviour changes over time, and financial markets are affected accordingly.

One simple example – following the financial crisis, investors have typically been in either risk-on or risk-off mode. When risk is on, virtually all risk assets rise, and when risk is off only risk-off assets do so. US Treasuries and gold have been the primary risk-off assets since the financial crisis, but JPY has also stood out as a solid performer in risk-off times. This has had rather dramatic implications for investors, as reducing risk through portfolio diversification has become a great deal more complicated post-2008.

Now to the structural trends – by far the most important in my approach to portfolio construction. I have identified a total of eight of those, but I would not recommend letting any of those trends dictate your investment strategy if you are a day trader.

However, if you invest like me, I can virtually guarantee you that these eight trends will shape the world we live in, and the markets we invest in, for many years to come. The eight trends – which I call structural mega-trends – are as follows:

1. The end of the debt super-cycle.
2. The retirement of the baby boomers.
3. The declining spending power of the middle classes.
4. The rise of the East.
5. The death of fossil fuels.
6. Mean reversion of wealth-to-GDP.
7. Disruption.
8. Running out of fresh water.

In addition to those eight mega-trends, I have identified several structural sub-trends, all of which are driven by one or more of the eight mega-trends, and those sub-trends again drive my portfolio construction.

A good example would be the first of 'my' structural mega-trends – **the end of the debt super-cycle**. Debt super-cycles run for 50+ years on average, and the one we are in at present was established in the late 1940s. Following six years of devastating warfare, Europe needed major reconstruction, and much of it was financed with debt.

Debt-to-GDP has risen ever since, but only since the early 1980s has the pace of debt growth gained substantial momentum – so much that financial regulators are now seriously concerned and want to curb bank lending. The European banking regulator is particularly hostile, and banks all over the EU are being forced to reduce their loan books. I call that structural sub-trend *regulatory arbitrage*, as it has opened the door for a myriad of investment opportunities in the alternative space.

It never ceases to amaze me how little time investors typically allocate to structural trends when constructing their portfolios. It is probably a function of impatience; many investors find it hard to look beyond next Monday.

That said, constructing your portfolio based on longer-term structural trends makes long-term success much more likely, but there are no safety valves you can rely on in the short to medium term. Because of that, I never use financial leverage. Back in 2008, I learned that leverage can do substantial damage, even if your strategy is perfectly suitable for the long term.

When I say *never let short-term trends drive your investment strategy*, I need to explain exactly what I mean. I construct portfolios so that there is a structural core – which is the key driver of returns – and a tactical overlay. In other words, the core of the portfolio is constructed on the back of the eight structural mega-trends I have just mentioned, and the tactical overlay is designed to take advantage of shorter-term opportunities. The tactical overlay's contribution to long-term returns is usually quite modest, though.

Let me give you an example as to how it all works. As I just explained, the end of the debt super-cycle leads to plenty of regulatory arbitrage opportunities, and many of those are denominated in US dollars, as the Americans are a step (or two) ahead of us Europeans in terms of providing finance to corporates away from commercial banks.

Because the US economic cycle is further advanced than the European cycle, it is only fair to expect a more dramatic rise in US interest rates in the short to medium term, and for that reason a simple cyclical analysis would lead one to expect USD/EUR to appreciate further in value. European investors should therefore leave any US dollar investments unhedged, and US investors should hedge any investments they have in euros.

An approach where the structural analysis is combined with a tactical/ cyclical overlay would undoubtedly lead to that conclusion, but things are not always that simple. Some of the most powerful short-term trends are behavioural in nature, and various studies suggest that being long USD is already a *very* crowded trade.

Although behavioural trends can, and do, change at short notice, they are extremely powerful, and ignoring them when constructing portfolios can be very expensive indeed. Consequently, they form a critical part of my tactical overlay, but they never drive the portfolio construction process. Only the eight structural mega-trends do.

3. PICK YOUR MOMENTS TO BE CONTRARIAN.

My third rule is the one that has made me the most money over the years, but it is admittedly also the trickiest one. *Be contrarian, but pick your moments carefully*. Don't be a contrarian just for the sake of being contrarian.

Many moons ago, my then-boss taught me the art of making the right noise at the right time. Go long and get loud, was his simple advice, and that advice has followed me ever since. His philosophy was simple. Smart investors *never* express what they truly believe in, until they have positioned themselves accordingly. When somebody goes on TV and claims to be bullish (bearish), he is simply talking his own book. He is already *very* long (short), he told me. And he was, and still is, spot on.

If long USD is already a very crowded trade, where is the buying power going to come from? Experience has taught me that these sorts of issues *must* be taken into consideration when engaged in portfolio construction.

Here is the tricky part. Being a contrarian doesn't always work. I have learned over the years that it is not enough to have a majority of investors subscribing to a certain view. You need a *substantial* majority to be behind that consensus for the contrarian strategy to work.

Secondly, it also makes a difference where you are in the cycle. I have found that, the earlier in the cycle you are, the less likely it is that the contrarian view will work. Going back to the USD example from before, the USD index started to form a bull trend in mid-2014. Following a very powerful bull run that lasted about nine months, the USD index began to consolidate, and has moved (largely) sideways ever since.

The combination of large gains, more recent consolidation and a marketplace that is very crowded turns my contrarian instincts on. The only reason I haven't made any moves yet is the overwhelming likelihood of a more hostile Federal Reserve Bank, as the US output gap continues to shrink.

Going back to my trend model, my current reading on USD is as follows:

- Structurally: NEUTRAL to BULLISH.
- Cyclically: BULLISH.
- Behaviourally: BEARISH.

Most of my structural trends are not particularly bullish or bearish as far as USD is concerned with one noticeable exception. The US workforce will continue to grow between now and 2050, whereas the European workforce will shrink. All that is because of ageing – or because of the retirement of the baby boomers, as I call that structural trend.

This will lead to trend GDP growth in the US that is about 1% higher than that of Europe, assuming productivity gains are broadly the same on the two continents (which is a fair assumption). All other things being equal, that will lead to higher interest rates in the US and a stronger USD.

That said, in a perfect world, and for me to go head-on into a contrarian trade, I need at least two, and if possible all three, trend models to send the same signal – but they don't in this case, which is why I continue to sit on my hands.

John Kingham

JOHN KINGHAM *is the founder and editor of* www.ukvalueinvestor.com, *a website and investment newsletter for defensive value investors. Defensive value investing is a systematic approach to building a high-yield, low-risk portfolio of shares.*

Mr Kingham also writes the regular Dividend Hunter column for Master Investor *magazine, and is the author of* The Defensive Value Investor *(Harriman House, 2016).*

"DIVIDEND INVESTORS SHOULD DEMAND A TEN-YEAR UNBROKEN RECORD OF DIVIDENDS PAYMENTS."

Dictums of a Defensive Value Investor

1. ONLY INVEST IN COMPANIES THAT HAVE CONSISTENTLY PAID A DIVIDEND.

FIRST AND FOREMOST, dividends provide an income which can be spent today or reinvested to create additional growth tomorrow. However, dividends can also be used as an indicator of a company's stability and underlying growth rate.

Dividend investors should demand a ten-year unbroken record of dividends payments as that immediately rules out young untested companies and companies that have suspended their dividends in the recent past. This leaves companies that have been willing and able to pay a dividend over many years, although of course that is no guarantee of future dividend payouts. However, it is a very good place to start.

2. ONLY INVEST IN COMPANIES WITH STEADY INFLATION-BEATING GROWTH.

In addition, you should also look for companies where the dividend has grown steadily and is supported by growing revenues and earnings.

One way to measure the steadiness or quality of growth is to count how often the dividend increased in the last decade. If the dividend went up every year then that's very high-quality dividend growth. If the dividend grew overall but was cut twice in the last decade, then that is lower-quality growth. This idea can be applied to revenues and earnings as well to get a picture of the company's overall growth quality. At the very least, you should be looking for companies where revenues, earnings and dividends went up at least 50% of the time, and preferably 75% of the time or more.

In terms of growth rate, total growth can be measured across revenues, earnings and dividends over the last ten years and then compared to total inflation over the same period. If a company is not growing as fast as inflation then it is effectively shrinking in real terms.

3. ONLY INVEST IN COMPANIES WHERE PROFITABILITY IS ABOVE AVERAGE.

Another sign of a good company is above-average profitability. For most companies, profitability is driven towards average because of competition from other companies. However, some companies are able to generate above-average profits for extended periods of time, and these are often companies that will continue to be successful long into the future. You can find these companies using return on capital employed (ROCE), by measuring their average ROCE over ten years.

As a rule of thumb, the market average ROCE is about 10%, so sticking to companies that consistently generate returns above that level is a good idea.

4. ONLY INVEST IN COMPANIES THAT HAVE MANAGEABLE FINANCIAL OBLIGATIONS.

A major risk to future dividend growth comes from excessive debts and pensions. Debts are not necessarily a bad thing because they can be used to amplify profits. But debts also amplify losses, so while a little debt can be useful, too much is definitely a bad thing.

A good way to measure debt is against profits, since profits relate to a company's ability to pay back its debts and cover interest payments. Defensive sector companies should not have borrowings of more than five times the company's recent average profits, while cyclical companies should be more cautious with a ratio of less than four.

Defined benefit (DB) pension schemes and any related pension deficits can be a serious problem, too, so DB pension liabilities should be less than ten-times the company's recent profits.

5. ONLY INVEST WHEN THE SHARE PRICE OFFERS BETTER VALUE THAN THE MARKET AVERAGE.

Low PE ratios and high dividend yields are often used as indicators of an attractively valued stock. However, rather than comparing today's share price to today's earnings or dividends, a better approach is to compare today's price to a company's ten-year average earnings and dividends. This cyclically adjusts the earnings and dividends, reducing the potentially misleading impact of unusually high or low earnings or dividends in a single year.

What you should be looking for is companies with above-average growth rates, growth quality and profitability, combined with below-average debts and valuation multiples. Average in this case means relative to a major index such as the FTSE All-Share, since the goal of most investors is to beat the market index.

If you can't find companies that beat the market on all of those counts then compromise; look for companies that have the best combination of growth, quality, profitability and value.

6. ONLY INVEST IN COMPANIES THAT AREN'T OBVIOUS VALUE TRAPS.

Attractively valued companies usually have low share prices because other investors are worried for one reason or another. To some extent, then, you'll have to be willing to bet against the crowd and invest in companies where the current situation is often quite negative.

But being brave and investing in a company that nobody likes is not a good strategy if that company subsequently goes down the tubes. To avoid that fate you'll need to differentiate between companies with problems that are short-term and cheap to fix and those with problems that are long-term and expensive (or impossible) to fix. Here are some features to look out for:

1. A clear and consistent goal and strategy.
2. A dominant core business which has operated for many years.
3. A market leader.
4. Freedom from major projects which could permanently damage the company if they failed.

5. Total capital expenses that are less than total profits over the last decade.

6. Sales generated from a large number of small-ticket items rather than a few large projects or contracts.

7. Total acquisition costs that are less than total profits over the last decade.

8. A stable pattern of market demand.

9. Markets that are expected to grow.

10. Key products or services which are likely to remain largely unchanged over the next decade.

11. Immunity from volatile commodity prices.

12. Freedom from current problems which could cause the company serious long-term damage.

If the company is missing more than half of these features then it is probably a value trap and should be avoided.

7. ONLY INVEST IN COMPANIES THAT HAVE DURABLE COMPETITIVE ADVANTAGES.

If a company doesn't have a competitive advantage then the chances of it growing consistently can be alarmingly thin. Some of the main sources of competitive advantage are:

1. Strong brand names or patents – these can give an almost monopoly-like dominance of a particular product.

2. High switching costs – where it is expensive in terms of effort, time or money for customers to switch to a competitor, e.g. bank accounts.

3. Strong network effect – this makes a product or service better as more customers use it, which makes it very hard for smaller competitors to get a foothold, e.g. eBay or Facebook.

4. Durable cost advantages – from greater size, unique assets (e.g. better retail locations or the world's lowest cost oil field) or unique processes or technology.

These competitive advantages cannot guarantee future success, but consistently successful companies usually have at least one of them.

8. ONLY INVEST IF YOU ARE WILLING TO HOLD THE SHARES FOR AT LEAST FIVE YEARS.

Even if a company is destined to grow its earnings and dividends at 20% per year, you are just as likely to lose money as you are to make money if you hold its shares for one day. That's because in the short term the market's random volatility will outweigh any positive aspects of the underlying company. You have to hold shares for several years before you can be confident that the company's earnings and dividend growth will outweigh the random fluctuations of the market.

Given this fact, it's a good idea to make sure you're comfortable owning a company for at least five years before you buy its shares. If you're not comfortable then perhaps there's a doubt at the back of your mind that you hadn't previously noticed. This is a good chance to uncover such doubts and analyse them in order to decide if they should be listened to or ignored.

9. DIVERSIFY ACROSS MANY COMPANIES, SECTORS AND COUNTRIES.

Diversification is often described as the only free lunch in investing, because it can reduce risk and increase returns at the same time. There are three dimensions to diversification which can give you the biggest risk reduction bang for your diversification buck:

- Company diversity – most investors should hold around 30 companies, with position sizes starting at 3% to 4% of the overall portfolio. This reduces the impact of any one holding performing badly.

- Sector diversity – holding 30 copper mining companies would not create a very diverse portfolio. To avoid this problem you should never have more than 10% of your holdings in any one sector.

- Country diversity – if all of the holdings in a portfolio generate all of their revenues from the UK then the portfolio will be highly dependent on the UK economy. To reduce this risk, make sure that no one country is responsible for more than 50% of the portfolio's overall revenues.

10. ONLY MAKE BUY OR SELL DECISIONS ONCE PER MONTH.

Most active investors like to be active, buying and selling whenever they fell like it. This is a problem because: a) more trading means shorter holding periods, and in the short-term the odds of making or losing money are about 50/50; b) trading incurs fees, so your 50/50 odds of making money are made even worse because of the negative impact of tax and broker fees.

To reduce the number of trades whilst always giving the active investor some activity to look forward to, one option is to have a rule of trading only once in any given month. If buy and sell trades are alternated each month, that's six buys and six sells in a year. At that rate the average holding period in a 30-stock portfolio would be five years, which ties in with the earlier rule about being willing and able to hold for at least five years.

11. DON'T PANIC SELL WHEN A PROFIT WARNING OR DIVIDEND CUT IS ANNOUNCED.

Panic selling on bad news is usually a bad idea. Not only do stocks typically outperform after a bad news crash, this sort of knee-jerk reaction also disempowers the investor by making them reactive rather than proactive.

If a company announces a profit warning or dividend cut, do nothing. Read the announcement and then wait for the effect to show up in the next annual results statement, which may be many months away. At least then you can analyse the situation in a calm and measured way, rather than reacting with little thought and much emotion.

12. TAKE PROFITS ON WINNERS BUT DON'T DOUBLE-DOWN ON LOSERS.

If a company's share price increases rapidly, it will also increase the stock's position size in your portfolio. At some point the portfolio will be excessively dependent on that one company, which is an unacceptable risk. With 30 holdings and an average position size of 3.3%, you might want to cut in half any positions that grow to more than 6% or so of the portfolio and reinvest the proceeds into other holdings.

On the other hand, I would be reluctant to aggressively double-down on losers. If a company goes from 3% of the portfolio to 1% it is not necessarily a good idea to top it back up to 3%. It could easily go back down to 1% again, at which point you might top it back up to 3% again. Keep doing this and you could end up with an excessive amount invested in a failing company.

13. REGULARLY SELL YOUR LEAST ATTRACTIVE HOLDING.

The quality of a company and the attractiveness of its valuation will change over time. At some point either the price will become unattractively high or the quality of the company will become unattractively low. This will always be true and any reasonably diverse portfolio will always have some holdings that are far more attractive than others. As part of your alternating monthly buy/sell process (Rule 10), sell the company with the least attractive combination of quality and value characteristics. That company should then be replaced the following month with a significantly more attractive stock.

14. CONTINUOUSLY IMPROVE YOUR INVESTMENT PROCESS.

Perform a post-sale autopsy on each investment that you sell. This will help you learn from both successful and unsuccessful investments, and often the unsuccessful investments provide the most powerful and valuable lessons. Change your approach based on these lessons, but for the most part make small incremental changes rather than large radical changes.

Lars Kroijer

LARS KROIJER *(born 1972) is the founder and managing director of* **Alliedcrowds.com**
*– the leading directory and aggregator of alternative capital into the world's 132 lower
and middle income countries. He is the author of* Money Mavericks *(FT Pearson,
2010 and 2012) and* Investing Demystified *(FT Pearson, 2013 and 2017).*

*Mr Kroijer currently serves on the advisory board of alternative investment funds in
London, New York, and Hong Kong. He has frequently appeared as a finance expert
on a broad range of media, including BBC, CNN, CNBC, the* Financial Times,
Bloomberg, Reuters, the New York Times *and* Forbes.

*Previously Mr Kroijer was the CIO of Holte Capital Ltd, a London-based market-
neutral special situations hedge fund which he founded in 2002 before returning external
capital in the spring of 2008. Prior to establishing Holte Capital, Mr Kroijer served
in the London office of HBK Investments focusing on special situations investing. In
addition, he previously worked at SC Fundamental, a value-focused hedge fund, and the
investment banking division of Lazard Frères, both in New York. While in graduate
school Mr Kroijer held internships with the private equity firm Permira Advisors (then
Schroder Ventures) and management consulting firm McKinsey & Co.*

*Mr Kroijer graduated magna cum laude from Harvard University with a degree in
economics and received a MBA from Harvard Business School. A Danish national,
Mr Kroijer lives in London and is married with twin daughters.*

"EVEN IF SOME PEOPLE ARE ABLE TO OUTPERFORM THE MARKETS, MOST PEOPLE ARE NOT AMONG THEM."

How to Invest Without Speculation or Sleepless Nights

1. MOST INVESTORS ARE UNLIKELY TO HAVE AN EDGE.

M OST LITERATURE OR media on finance today tells us how to make money. We are bombarded with stock tips about the next Apple or Google, read articles on how India or biotech investing are the next hot thing, or are told how some star investment manager's outstanding performance is set to continue. The implicit message is that only the uninformed few fail to heed this advice and those that do end up poorer as a result. We wouldn't want that to be us!

What if we started with a very different premise? The premise that markets are actually quite efficient. Even if some people are able to outperform the markets, most people are not among them. In financial jargon, most people do not have edge over the financial markets, which is to say that they can't perform better than the financial market through active selection of investments different from that made by the market. Embracing and understanding this absence of edge as an investor is a key premise of the investment methods suggested in my recent book *Investing Demystified* (FT Pearson, 2013 and 2017), and something I believe is critical for all investors to understand.

Consider these two investment portfolios:

A.   S&P 500 Index Tracker Portfolio like an ETF or index fund.

B.   A portfolio consisting of a number of stocks from the S&P 500 – any number of stocks from that index that you think will outperform the index. It could be one stock or 499 stocks, or anything in between, or even the 500 stocks weighted differently from the index (which is based on market value weighting).

If you can ensure the consistent outperformance of portfolio B over portfolio A, even after the higher fees and expenses associated with creating portfolio B, you have edge investing in the S&P 500. If you can't, you don't have edge.

At first glance it may seem easy to have edge in the S&P 500. All you have to do is pick a subset of 500 stocks that will do better than the rest, and surely there are a number of predictable duds in there. In fact, all you would have to do is to find one dud, omit that from the rest and you would already be ahead. How hard can that be? Similarly, all you would have to do is to pick one winner and you would also be ahead.

Although the examples in this piece are from the stock market, investors can have edge in virtually any kind of investment all over the world. In fact there are so many different ways to have edge that it may seem like an admission of ignorance to some to renounce all of them. Their gut instinct may tell them that not only do they want to have edge, but the idea of not even trying to gain it is a cheap surrender. They want to take on the markets and outperform as a vindication that they 'get it' or are somehow of a superior intellect or street-smart. Whatever works!

But when considering your edge, *who* is it exactly that you have edge over? The other market participants obviously, but instead of a faceless mass, think about who they actually are and what knowledge they have and analysis they undertake.

Imagine the portfolio manager of the technology-focused fund for a highly rated mutual fund/unit trust who, like us, is looking at investing in, say, Microsoft. Let's call them Ability Tech and the fund manager Susan.

Susan and Ability have easy access to all the research that is written about Microsoft including the 80-page in-depth reports from research analysts from all the major banks including places like Morgan Stanley or Goldman Sachs that have followed Microsoft and all its competitors since Bill Gates started the business. The analysts know all of the business lines of Microsoft, down to the programmers who write the code to the marketing groups that come up with the ads. They may have worked at Microsoft or its competitors, and perhaps went to Harvard or Stanford with senior members of the management team. On top of that, the analysts speak frequently with the trading groups of their banks who are among the market leaders in the trading of Microsoft shares and can see market moves faster and more accurately than almost any trader.

All research analysts will talk to Susan regularly and at great length because of the commissions Ability's trading generates. Microsoft is a big position for Ability and Susan reads all the reports thoroughly – it's important to know what the market thinks. Susan enjoys the technical product development aspects of Microsoft and she feels she talks the same language as techies, partly because she knew some of them from when she studied computer science at MIT. But Susan's somewhat nerdy demeanour is balanced out by her 'gut-feel' colleagues, who see bigger picture trends in the technology sector and specifically see how Microsoft is perceived in the market and ability to respond to a changing business environment.

Susan and her colleagues frequently go to IT conferences and have meetings with senior people from Microsoft and peer companies, and are on first-name basis with most of them. Microsoft also arranged for Ability to visit the senior management at offices around the world, both in sales roles and developers, and for Susan to talk to some of its leading clients.

Like the research analysts from the banks, Ability has an army of expert PhDs who study sales trends and spot new potential challenges (they were among the first to spot Facebook and Google). Further, Ability has economists who study the US and global financial system in detail (after all, the world economy will impact the performance of Microsoft). Ability also has mathematicians with trading pattern recognition technology to help with the analysis.

Susan loves reading books about technology and every finance/investing book she can get her hands on, including all the Buffett and value investor books.

Susan and her team know everything there is to know about the stocks she follows (including a few things she probably shouldn't know, but she keeps that close to her chest), some of which are much smaller and less well-researched than Microsoft. She has among the best ratings among fund managers in a couple of the comparison sites, but doesn't pay too much attention to that. After doing this for over 20 years she knows how quickly things can change and instead focuses on remaining at the top of her game.

Does Susan have edge?

Do you think you have edge over Susan and the thousands of people like her? If you do, you might be brilliant, arrogant, the next Warren Buffett or George Soros, be lucky, or all of the above. If you don't, you don't have edge. Most people don't. Most people are better off admitting to themselves that once a company is listed on an exchange and has a market price, then we are better off assuming that this is a price that reflects the stock's true value, incorporating a future positive return for the stock, but also a risk that things don't go to plan. So it's not that all publicly listed companies are good – far from it – but rather that we don't know better than to assume that their stock prices incorporate an expectation of a fair future return to the shareholders given the risks. We don't have edge.

When I ran my hedge fund I would always think about the fictitious Susan and Ability. I would think of someone super clever, well-connected, product savvy yet street-smart who had been around the block and seen the inside stories of success and failure. And then I would convince myself that we should not be involved in trades unless we clearly thought we had edge over them. It is hard to convince yourself that this is possible, and unfortunately even harder sometimes for it to actually be true.

2. EVEN IF YOU HAVE EDGE, IT'S USUALLY NOT ENOUGH TO JUSTIFY THE TIME COST.

The cost of time spent managing a portfolio is individual (we all value our time differently) and while some consider it a fun hobby or a game akin to betting, others consider it a chore they would rather avoid.

Someone may spend ten hours of work time per week on their portfolio, which at an opportunity cost of time of £50 per hour for 40 weeks a year is £20,000 per year on top of all the other costs discussed. This clearly makes no sense for a £100,000 portfolio, and is too costly even for a £1m portfolio, and on top of all everything else they would benefit from less time spent.

Also consider that it is only the outperformance you get paid for. Since owning an index tracker takes no time, the cost of time – £20,000 above – actively managing your portfolio is only for the amount you beat the index by. If the index is up 10% and you are up 11% then it is only the 1% excess return that you spent all that time to make. So even in the very unlikely case that you can consistently beat the index you either have to be able to beat it by a lot, or manage a large amount of capital for the time spent to be worth it.

3. INVESTING IN ACTIVELY MANAGED FUNDS STILL REQUIRES AN EDGE.

If you conclude that Susan is as plugged in and informed as anyone could be, why not just give her our money and let her make us rich?

Many investors do give their money to the many Ability Tech type products and Fidelity and its peers continuously develop mutual funds for everything you can imagine. There are funds for industrials, defensive stocks (and defence sector stocks for that matter), gold stocks, oil stocks, telecoms, financials, technology, plus many geographic variations. In my view many investors have become 'fund pickers' instead of 'stock pickers'. Even today, years after the benefits of index tracking have become clear to many investors, there is perhaps £85 invested with managers that try to outperform the index (active managers) for every £15 invested in index trackers.

When investors pick from the smorgasbord of tempting looking funds, how do they know which ones are going to outperform going forward?

Is it because they have a feeling that IT stocks will outperform the wider markets?

If so, you are effectively claiming edge by suggesting that you can pick sub-sets of the market that will outperform the wider markets. Consistently picking outperforming sectors would be an amazing skill.

Is it because of Susan's impressive resume (you think that someone with her background will find a way to outperform the market)?

If so, your edge is essentially saying that you know someone who has edge (Susan), which is really another form of edge. This is the kind of edge many investors in hedge funds claim. They'll say stuff like "through our painstaking research process we select the few outstanding managers who consistently outperform". Maybe so, but that is also a case of edge.

Is it because they feel Ability Tech has come up with some magic formula that will ensure their continued outperformance in their funds generally?

There is little data to suggest that you can objectively pick which mutual funds are going to outperform going forward.

Is it because their financial advisors consider it a sound choice?

First figure out if the advisor has a financial incentive to give you the advice, like a cut of the fees. The world is moving towards greater clarity on how advisors get paid, making it easier to understand if there is a financial incentive to recommend some products – keep in mind that comparison sites also get a cut of the often hefty active manager fees. Now consider if your advisor really has the edge required to make this active choice. Unless she has a long history of getting these calls right I would question if she has the special edge that eludes most (and would she really share this incredibly unique insight if she had it?).

They have done so well in the past?

Countless studies confirm that past performance is a poor predictor of future performance. If life was only so easy – you just pick the winners and away you go…

We are also often driven by the urge to do something proactive to better our investment returns instead of passively standing by. And what better than investing with a strong-performing manager from a reputable firm in a hot sector we have researched?

Unfortunately, as seen above, the logic just doesn't stack up.

4. AGAIN, EVEN IF YOU CAN PICK GOOD FUNDS, THE COSTS MEAN YOU NEED EXCEPTIONAL EDGE.

Mutual fund/unit trust charges vary greatly. Some charge upfront fees (though less frequently than in the past), but all charge an annual management fee and expenses (for things like audit, legal, etc.), in addition to the cost of making the investments. The all-in-costs span a wide range, but if you assume a total of 2.5% per year that is probably not too far off. So if someone manages £100 for you, the all-in costs of doing this will amount to approximately £2.50 per year come rain or shine.

If markets are steaming ahead and are up 20% or more every year, paying one tenth to the well-known steward of your money may seem a fair deal. The trouble is that markets are *not* up 20% per year every year. We can perhaps expect equity markets to be up 4–5% on average per year above inflation, so you need to pick a mutual fund that will outperform the markets by 2% *before* your costs to be no worse off than if you had picked the index-tracking ETF, assuming ETF fees and expenses of 0.5% per year.

In fact, you need to be able to pick the best mutual fund out of ten for it to make sense!

To give an idea of how much the fees impact over time consider the example of investing £100 for 30 years. Suppose the markets return 7% per year (5% real return plus 2% inflation, a fairly standard expectation) and the difference becomes all too obvious over time (2% fee disadvantage in this case compared to a tracker fund).

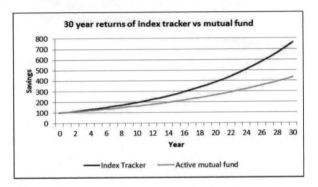

Ability Tech and its many competitors go to great lengths to show their data in the brightest light, but a convincing number of studies show that the average professional investor does not beat the market over time, but in fact underperform by approximately the fees.

There is of course the possibility that you are somehow able to pick only the best performing funds. Take the example that you had £100 to invest in either an index tracker, or a mutual fund that had a cost disadvantage of 2% per year compared to the tracker. Suppose further that the market made a return of 7% per year for the next ten years, and that the standard deviation (standard measure of risk that gives an idea of the range of returns you can expect and with what frequency) of each mutual fund performance relative to the average mutual fund performance was 5% (the mutual funds predominantly own the same stocks as the index and their performance will be fairly similar as a result). Below is a chart of returns of an index tracker compared to 250 mutual funds with those inputs:

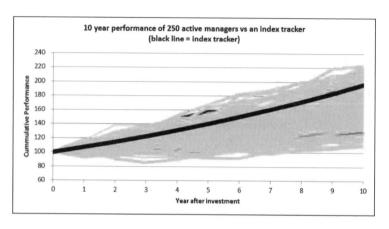

Comparing an actively managed portfolio to an index tracker is unfortunately not as simple as subtracting 2% from the index tracker to get to the actively managed return. The returns will vary from year to year, and in some years the actively managed fund will outperform the index it is tracking. Some funds will even outperform the index over the ten-year period; if you can pick the outperforming fund consistently, you have edge. If you can't, you should buy the index.

In approximately 90% of the cases in the ten-year example above the index tracker would outperform the actively managed mutual fund, which is roughly in line with what historical studies suggest. So in order for it to make sense to pick a mutual fund over the index tracker you have to be able to pick the 10% best performing mutual funds. That would be pretty impressive.

If you did not have edge and blindly picked a mutual fund instead of the index tracker you would on average be about £30 worse off on your £100 investment after ten years because of the higher costs.

To put in perspective the cumulative impact over a saver's life, consider someone earning £50,000 a year on average between ages 25–67 who puts aside 10% of savings in the equity markets (ignoring tax). If equity markets perform similarly to how they have in the past (so about 5% per year above inflation) the average difference in money for the saver at retirement for someone who invested with an active fund manager compared to a product that simply tracks the market will be the equivalent of the value of about seven Porsche cars (or approximately £280,000 in today's money). Think about this – a fairly typical saver left poorer by a staggering total amount of money over a lifetime with the money going to the financial sector.

The finance sector won't like you doing it, but unless you have an amazing ability to pick only the best active fund managers, buy the product that replicates the market and you'll be much better off in the long run.

While you can bet your bottom dollar that the 10% of mutual funds that outperformed the index would market their special skills in advertisements, historical performance is not only poor predictors of future returns, but it can be very hard to distinguish between what has been chance (luck) and skill (edge). Just like one out of 1,024 coin flippers could get heads ten flips in a row, some managers do better simply out of luck. In reality the odds are much worse in the financial markets, as fees and costs eat into the returns. However, ask the manager who has outperformed five years in a row (every fiftieth coin flipper…) and she will disagree with the argument that she was just lucky, even as some invariably are. Likewise some managers underperform the market several years in a row simply due to bad luck, but those disappear from the scene and thus introduce a selection bias where only the winners remain, and sometimes thus make the industry appear more successful than it has been.

5. FOR EQUITY EXPOSURE, GO BROAD, CHEAP AND TAX EFFICIENT.

The only equity exposure you should buy is the broadest, cheapest, and most tax efficient world equity index tracker.

Let's look at why. Many readers are hopefully already willing to accept a couple of facts that in my view over time will massively improve the financial performance of their portfolios:

1. They accept that most investors don't have an ability to outperform the financial markets (often called having an edge) and that as a result where possible they should invest in index tracking products.

2. They accept that by keeping trading to a minimum and investing tax-efficiently with the lowest fees their investment portfolio will perform far better in the long run.

3. They accept that to have some hope of long-term financial returns they should probably have some equity exposure, to avoid the dull returns provided by safe bonds or cash in the bank.

But which equities should they own?

The only equity exposure anyone who can agree to the points above should invest in is the broadest, cheapest and most tax-efficient equity index tracker they can find. And this product should track the overall global equity markets as closely as possible.

From the perspective of an investor who can't outperform the markets, each amount invested in stock markets around the world is presumed equally smart. What this means is that if the markets say that a share in Apple is worth $100 and a share in Microsoft is worth $50 then we as investors don't have a preference of owning one of those shares over the other at those prices. If we did have a preference we would effectively say that we know more about the future movements in share prices than the existing investors in those shares, which we don't unless we believe we can beat the markets. The person buying Apple is no more or less clever or informed than someone buying Microsoft. Extrapolating this logic to the whole market means that we should own the shares in all the stocks in the market according to their fraction of the overall value of the market. If for a second we assume that the market refers only to the US stock market and that Apple shares represented 3% of the overall value, 3% of our equity holdings should be Apple shares. If we do anything other than this, we are somehow saying that the money that allocated 3% of the market value to Apple shares was less informed or clever than we are.

Of course, buying hundreds of shares in a stock market in the proportions of their overall market capitalisations is today much simpler than it was a generation ago. It is close to what many index-tracking products offer.

But why stop at the US market? If there is $25 trillion invested in the US stock market and $5 trillion in the UK market, there is no reason to think that the UK market is any less-informed or efficient than the US one. And similarly with any other market in the world investors can get access to. We should invest with them all, in the proportions of their share of the world equity markets and within the bounds of practicality.

If you were able to over- or underweight one country compared to its fraction of the world equity markets you would effectively be saying that a dollar invested in an underweight country is less clever/informed than a dollar invested in the country that you allocate more to. You would essentially claim to see an advantage from allocating differently from how the multi-trillion dollar international financial markets have allocated, which you are not in a position to do unless you have edge. So besides it being much simpler and cheaper, since investors have already moved capital between various international markets efficiently, the international equity portfolio is the best one.

Many investors overweigh 'home' equities. The UK represents less than 3% of the world equity markets, but the proportion of UK equities in a UK portfolio is often 35–40%. Investors feel they know and understand their home market, and perhaps think they should be able to spot opportunities before the wider market (in fairness the concentration is also often because of investment restrictions or perhaps because investors wrongly are matching their investment with liabilities connected to the local market). Various studies suggest that this 'home-field advantage' is not real, but we continue to have our portfolios dominated by our home market.

The world equity portfolio is the most diversified equity portfolio we can find. The benefits of diversification are great. To give an idea of the benefits of diversification in the home market consider the following chart:

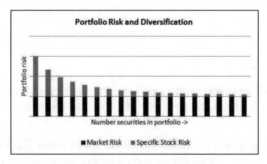

As the chart suggests, the benefits from diversification decline as we add securities in the home market. This makes sense. Stocks trading in the same market will tend to correlate greatly (they are exposed to the same economy, legal system, etc.), and after picking a relatively small number of them you have diversified away a great deal of the market risk of any individual stock. You could actually gain a lot of the advantages from US index funds by picking 15–20 large capitalisation stocks and sticking with them, assuming they did not all act like one (if you only added stocks from one sector that all moved in the same way the diversification benefits would be far lower). It is not the broadest or most effective US portfolio (if it was, why did you deselect those other stocks?), but from a diversification perspective you have accomplished a lot.

By expanding the portfolio beyond our home markets, we achieve much greater diversification in our investments. This is both because we spread our investments out over a larger number of stocks, but more importantly because those stocks are based in different geographies and local economies. Only decades ago we did not really have the opportunity to invest easily across the world, and while it is still not seamless for investors in many places, investing abroad in a geographically diversified way is a lot easier than it used to be.

In summary, in my view the key benefits of a broad market-weighted portfolio are as follows:

- The portfolio is as diversified as possible and each dollar invested in the market is presumed equally clever; consistent with how an investor who can't beat the markets should invest. I bet a lot of Japanese investors wished they had diversified geographically after their domestic market declined 75% from its peak over the past 20 years.

- Since we are simply buying the market as broadly as we can it is a very simple portfolio to construct and thus very cheap. We don't have to pay anyone to be smart about beating the market. Over time the cost benefit can make a huge difference. Don't ignore that.

- This kind of broad-based portfolio is now available to most investors whereas only a couple of decades ago it was not, as most people thought 'the market' meant only their domestic market, or at best regional. Take advantage of this development to buy broader-based products.

6. CURRENCY FLUCTUATIONS DON'T MATTER SO MUCH WHEN YOU INVEST THIS WAY.

When you buy a world equity product you will naturally incur foreign exchange exposure as the majority of the underlying securities will be listed in a currency other than your own. For example when you as a UK-based investor buy the GBP-denominated world equity index tracker you will indirectly be buying shares in the Brazilian oil company Petrobras. Petrobras is quoted in the Brazilian currency Real so in order to buy the Petrobras share the product provider has to take the GBP, exchange them into Real, and then buy the stock. Likewise with all the other currencies and securities represented in the index.[*]

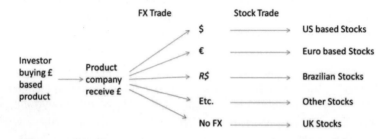

In the example above you are now exposed both to the fluctuation in the share price of Petrobras and also movements in the GBP/Real exchange rate. As an example:

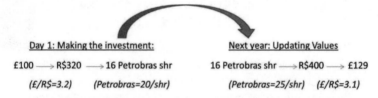

In this example I assumed that the Petrobras share price went from R$20 to R$25 while the £/R$ went from 3.2 to 3.1. The aggregate impact on this on the portfolio was that the £100 investment went up in value to £129 because of the mix of share price appreciation and £/R$ currency movement.

The many different stocks and currency exposures in the world equity portfolio add further to the diversification benefits of the broad-based portfolio exposure. If your base/home currency devalued or performed poorly, the diversification of your currency exposure would serve to protect your downside.

Some investment advisors argue that you should invest in assets in the same currency that you eventually need the money in. By that logic a UK investor should buy UK stocks, a Danish investor should buy Danish

---

* The trading setup may sound cumbersome and expensive, but major product providers naturally have off-setting flows that reduce trading, but are also set up to trade FX and stocks very cheaply, or have derivative exposures or sampling that can also reduce costs and keep things simple.

stocks, someone who eventually need monies in different currencies should do a mix (if you have different costs in different currencies), etc. While I think there is some merit in currency-matching specific and perhaps shorter-term liabilities I think the matching is better done through the purchase of government bonds in your home currency – if you worry that major currencies fluctuate too much for you I would question if you should be taking equity market risk in the first place.

The broader investment and currency exposure is in my view favourable not only from a diversifying perspective, but also a protection against bad things happening in your home country. Typically, whenever a currency has been a poorly performing one it is because of problems in that country (there are exceptions to this rule of thumb), and it is exactly in those cases that the protection of diversified geographic exposure is of greatest benefit to you.

7. NO PROMISES, BUT EXPECT 4–5% RETURNS AFTER INFLATION.

The return expectation from equity markets are driven by our view of the *equity risk premium*. The equity risk premium is a measure of how much extra the market expects to get paid for the additional risk associated with investing in equity markets over the minimal risk asset. This does not mean that we are suggesting stock markets will be particularly poor or attractive right now; it means that investors historically have demanded a premium for investing in risky equities, as opposed to less riskier assets. And that we assume that investors expect to be paid a similar premium for investing in equities over safe government bonds going forward, as they have historically.

The size of the equity risk premium is subject to much debate, but numbers in the order of 4–5% are often quoted. If you study the returns of the world equity markets over the past 100 years, the annual compounding rate of return for this period is close to this range. Of course, it is impossible to know if the markets over that period have been particularly attractive or poor for equity holders compared to what the future has in store.

RETURNS 1900–2015 (%)		
	REAL RETURN*	RISK
World equities	5.00	High
Short-term US government bonds	0.80	Low
Equity risk premium	4.20	

* Nominal: before inflation. Real: after inflation.

Source: Credit Suisse Global Returns Handbook 2016

The equity risk premium is not a law of nature, but simply an expectation of future returns, in this case based on what those markets achieved in the past, including the significant drawdowns that occurred. Economists and finance experts disagree strongly on what you should expect from equity returns going forward and some consider this kind of 'projecting by looking in the rear-view mirror' wrong. I disagree: in my view the long history and volatility of equity market returns gives a good idea of the kind of returns we can expect going forward. Equity market investors have in the past demanded a 4–5% return premium for the kinds of risks that equity markets entail, and I think there is a good probability that investors going forward are going to demand a similar kind of return premium for a similar kind of risk in the equity markets.

A criticism of using historical returns to predict future returns is that it will predict higher returns at peak markets, and lower returns at market lows. Historical returns looked a lot better on 1 July 2008 than on 1 July 2009 after the crash, and perhaps because you were attracted by the high historical returns in mid-2008 this was exactly the time that you invested in equities. Combining high historical returns with low expected risk at the time made equity markets look very attractive at precisely the wrong moment.

I understand this criticism of the expected return, but think the length of data mitigates it. With hundreds of years of data across many geographies (some have used only US data in the past, but that introduces selection bias by excluding markets that have performed poorly), incorporating great spectacular declines, great rises, and everything in between, I think historical data is the best guide to the kind of risk and return we can expect from equity markets going forward.

Practically speaking, investors have not been able to buy the whole world of equities for many years. One of the leading index providers, MSCI, only started tracking a world index in late 1960s, but finding liquid products that actually followed this or similar indices did not follow in earnest until decades after that. Below are the historical returns for the MSCI World Index since inception. In this case I think it is fair to say that the time horizon is too short (40+ years) to use the data to make predictions about future world equity returns, when we have longer historical data sets (albeit not as an index done at the time).

So in simple terms, on average I expect to make a 4–5% return per year above the minimal risk rate in a broad-based world equity portfolio. This does not suggest that I expect this return to materialise every year, but rather that if I had to make a guess on the compounding annual rate going forward it would be 4–5%.

EXPECTED FUTURE RETURNS*		
	REAL**	RISK
World equities	4.5-5.5%	High
Minimal risk asset	0.5%	Low
Equity risk premium	4-5%	

* Including dividends.

** After inflation.

Note that while the equity premium here is compared to short-term US bonds, I would expect the same premium to other minimal risk currency government bonds – this is because the real return expectation of short-term US government bonds is roughly similar to that of other AAA/AA countries like the UK, Germany, Japan, etc.

For those who consider these expected returns disappointing, I'm sorry. Writing higher numbers in a book or spreadsheet won't make it true. Some would even suggest that expecting equity markets to be as favourable in the future as in the past is wishful thinking. Besides, a 4–5% annual return premium to the minimal risk asset will quickly add up to a lot; you would expect to double your money in real terms roughly every 15 years!

It probably sits wrong with many people to have something as important as what you can expect to make in the stock markets be based on something as unscientific as the historical returns or my 'guesstimate' of that data. Perhaps so, but until someone comes up with a reliably better method of predicting stock market returns it is the best we have and in my view a very decent guide. Also, we know that the equity premium should be something – if there were no expected rewards from investing in the riskier equities we would simply keep our money in low-risk bonds.

Another problem with simplistically predicting a stable risk premium is that we don't change it with the world around us. It probably sits wrong with most investors that the expected returns going forward should be the same in the relatively stable period preceding the 2008 stock crash as it was during the peak of panic and despair in October 2008. Did someone who contemplated investing in the market in the calm markets of 2006 really expect to be rewarded with the same return as someone who stepped into the mayhem of October 2008?

Someone willing to step into the market at a moment of high panic would expect to be compensated for taking that extra risk, suggesting that the risk premium is not a constant number, but in some way dependent on the risk of the market. At a time of higher expected long-term risk, equity investors will be expecting higher long-term returns. The equity premium outlined above is an expected average based on an average level of risk.

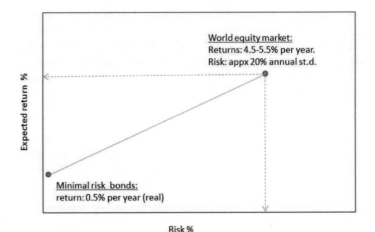

As an investor who seeks returns in excess of the minimal risk return, you can add a broad portfolio of world equities. You can reasonably expect to make a return of 4–5% per year above the rate of minimal risk government bonds that we expect to be about 0.5% per year, although expect that return to vary significantly for a standard deviation of about 20% per year.

If the world equity markets are too risky for you, combine an investment in that with an investment in minimal risk bonds to find your preferred level of risk. Briefly told:

MINIMAL RISK	LOW RISK	MEDIUM RISK	HIGH RISK
100% Minimal risk 0% Equities	75% Minimal risk 25% Equities	50% Minimal risk 50% Equities	0% Minimal risk 100% Equities

Or you can do any combination that suits your individual circumstances.

Follow this approach and in my view you will over the long term do better than the vast majority of investors who pay large fees needlessly, with consequent poorer investment returns. And keep in mind that this portfolio can be created by combining just two index-tracking securities; one tracking your minimal risk asset, and one tracking the world equity markets. An excellent portfolio with just two securities – who said investing is difficult?

If this seems too simple, perhaps remember that the world equity exposure represents an underlying exposure to a large number of often well-known companies in many currencies all over the world. Your two securities thus get you a mix of amazing diversification along with a minimal risk security that gives you the greatest amount of security you can get. How much you want of each depends on you and the risk/ return profile you want.

John Lee

JOHN LEE *(Lord Lee of Trafford) was born in Manchester in 1942, the son of a family doctor father and child psychologist mother. After qualifying as a chartered accountant and spending a period in stockbroking, he established a company specialising in amalgamations and mergers, which developed into a small public investment banking group. He was elected as a Conservative Member of Parliament in 1979, spending 13 years in the House of Commons, including six years as a Minister in Defence, Employment and Tourism. Following his defeat in the 1992 election he chaired the Christie Hospital NHS Trust and the Museum of Science and Industry in Manchester, becoming High Sheriff of Greater Manchester in 1998–9. In 2006 he was created a Life Peer – Lord Lee of Trafford – and currently sits in the House of Lords as a Liberal Democrat.*

For more than 50 years John has been a serious private investor, having bought his first shares at the age of 15. For more than a decade he wrote his 'My Portfolio' column for FT Money, *resulting in over 200 articles for the* Financial Times. *In December 2003 he disclosed that his PEP/ISA portfolio was worth £1 million, from £126,000 invested. It has since grown significantly. Over the years John has been on the boards of a number of public and private companies.*

He is the author of How to Make a Million – Slowly *(FT Pearson, 2013).*

"I OFTEN WISH THAT MORE COMPANIES HAD REMAINED INDEPENDENT FOR LONGER, CONTINUING THEIR GROWTH STORY RATHER THAN SUCCUMBING TO PREDATORS."

Twelve Golden Rules for Making a Million – Slowly

IT WAS THROUGH my father that I first became conscious of the stock market. He was a medical practitioner who enjoyed investing his modest savings, and one of my lasting memories is of him sitting on the floor of his study/library – pipe in mouth – surrounded by two large piles, one of issues of the *Stock Exchange Gazette* (now defunct) and the other of copies of *Investors Chronicle*, still going strong (with me a weekly reader and occasional contributor). Initially I would jest at the time he spent on what seemed to me to be a remarkably boring leisure activity, but curiosity eventually got the better of me and I started to delve into the magazines' mysterious world of investment techniques and company analysis. At the age of 16 I bought my first share – £45 of shipping company Aviation & Shipping – heaven knows why! It was the proud owner of one ship which sadly sunk within months of my coming aboard, taking my own shareholding with it. Hardly the most auspicious start to a long investment life!

Now, nearly 60 years later, I look back on a hobby which has given me enormous pleasure and interest, has developed into my core activity, and thankfully has delivered over the years a considerable degree of financial independence for me. I have bought and sold literally hundreds of shares, made many mistakes, but thankfully I have had rather more successes. It has been an absorbing, never-ending journey of accumulating and retaining a large amount of knowledge on particular companies and personalities, hopefully learning from where I had gone wrong, and brick-by-brick building my portfolios – ISA and non-ISA. I have been on the receiving end of around 50 takeovers; many familiar names like Forte, Pifco and Wyevale, but many also less familiar to the reader like Breedon, Delcam, Friedland Doggart and Wintrust, all predominantly small cap stocks, which is the sector I have mainly focused upon. Invariably bids have come in at a much appreciated premium to prevailing market prices, but I often wish that more companies had remained independent for longer, continuing their growth story rather than succumbing to predators.

So what conclusions have I reached after years of stock market activity? Three above all:

1. There are only two absolute essentials for investment success; common sense and patience, of which the latter is the most important.

2. It is vital to avoid losses. I draw a parallel here between golf and the stock market: just as it is the shot into the river or woods on the 17th hole which ruins one's round, so it is the losses which drag down overall stock market performance. So avoid taking unnecessary risks. I, for example, do not invest in start-up situations or buy mining, exploration or biotech stocks. These are best left to specialists who focus and become expert on such sectors. The amateur investor can be severely burnt.

3. If one has invested in a good and growing company which one likes and has confidence in and which increases its profits and dividends most years – for heaven's sake stay with it! Don't sell too soon and chop and change. The stock market is not a casino – the aim has to be to buy into a growing business, hopefully letting your holding become more and more valuable; don't hesitate to buy more of it if you really believe; and above all put time into the equation. My largest holding is flavours/fragrances Treatt Plc, based in Bury St Edmunds and in Florida. I have bought Treatt shares on 24 separate occasions, building up as my confidence, belief and knowledge increased. Sadly, from my experience, very few investors apply any real strategy or structure to their investing, buying randomly following a hunch, a tip, or gossip from the 19th hole!

My portfolios are increasingly concentrated on a small number of holdings – perhaps 20 or so – and I rarely sell. When PEPs were introduced in the 1980s I invested the yearly maximum, reinvesting all dividends. They were superseded by ISAs – to all intents and purposes the same thing – and in 2003 I was judged to be the first ISA millionaire (i.e. to have made sufficient profits that the ISA had grown to over £1 million, despite caps on how much cash be added to your ISA from outside each year). Today I would argue that ISAs are probably the most attractive wrapper/savings product in the Western world! Free of income tax, capital gains tax and inheritance tax (the latter only for 'approved' shares quoted on the Alternative Investment Market), with taxation benefits additionally being transferable to a surviving spouse on death – every serious investor should have an ISA. Today my annual ISA dividends exceed the total capital I have put into it, and I am still reinvesting those dividends!

The following are my 12 golden rules for investors – you will see they are focused on ISAs, but the same principles also apply to non-ISA portfolios.

1. TRY TO INVEST WHAT YOU CAN AFFORD EACH YEAR.

Re-invest all dividends and avoid withdrawing money from your ISA if possible. The aim is to build up a significant portfolio over the longer term. Do not worry if in one tax year you cannot afford to put any more money in.

2. AIM TO HOLD SHARES FOR A MINIMUM OF FIVE YEARS.

Too many investors chop and change frequently and take profits far too soon. Real money is made by staying with a share and hopefully letting it grow – and grow.

3. CHOOSE ESTABLISHED, CONSISTENTLY PROFITABLE COMPANIES PAYING INCREASING ANNUAL DIVIDENDS.

Investors are more likely to be consistently successful if they choose companies that are already doing well rather than going for recovery or loss-making companies.

4. AVOID THE BIG GAMBLES.

So avoid start-ups, exploration and mining stocks, and biotech firms. These are inherently higher risk. No doubt some will do well but others could lose you a substantial amount of money.

5. ONLY CHOOSE SHARES WHERE DIRECTORS OR A CONTROLLING FAMILY HAVE SIGNIFICANT SHAREHOLDINGS.

Directors with substantial amounts invested themselves are less likely to take excessive risks with their companies. Ideally I go for businesses where you feel those running them are focusing on stewarding a company carefully and concentrating on developing it over the long term.

6. ONLY INVEST IN SHARES IF YOU FULLY UNDERSTAND THE UNDERLYING BUSINESS.

Generally I avoid hi-tech companies or those with a range of unrelated activities.

7. IDEALLY CHOOSE COMPANIES WHICH TRADE INTERNATIONALLY, RATHER THAN JUST WITHIN THE UK.

Here my preference is for a company registered in the UK, operating under our more stringent corporate governance rules. But I also prefer a company which recognises that developing countries are growing at a faster rate than perhaps a mature economy such as ours.

8. AVOID COMPANIES WITH HIGH DEBT OR FREQUENT BOARDROOM CHANGES.

I have done particularly well by investing in conservatively managed companies which generate high levels of cash and keep plenty in reserve. This stands them in good stead, particularly if they experience a more difficult trading year, and enables them to continue paying dividends.

9. LET PROFITS RUN, EVEN IF HOLDINGS BECOME DISPROPORTIONATELY LARGE.

Investment advisors frequently suggest that if a holding becomes particularly large it should be topsliced – with some profits taken. Personally I believe that successful holdings should be kept intact, even if they do become large relative to other holdings. It is why Treatt dominates my ISA in value – it is treble the size of my next biggest holding.

10. FACE-UP TO MISTAKES QUICKLY.

I apply a 20% stop-loss rule, unless markets overall fall. It avoids experiencing irritation, or near depression, if you see a loss-making holding within your portfolio. Every time you look at it with a loss-maker still being there it will prick and sap your confidence. So for financial and emotional reasons get rid fast.

11. DO NOT BE PUT OFF BUYING BECAUSE A SHARE YOU FANCY HAS RISEN BY A FEW PENCE.

Too frequently investors shy away from paying a little bit more. Looking back five years later, whether you paid 55p or 50p will hopefully be irrelevant. Either you will have got it right or wrong. Have confidence in your judgement and remember you are investing for the long term.

12. FOR ISA INVESTORS TRY TO GET YOUR PLAN MANAGER TO INVOICE THEIR CHARGES OUTSIDE THE TAX WRAPPER ITSELF, RATHER THAN JUST DEBITING THEM FROM THE TAX-FREE FUND.

It is too easy for the plan manager just to debit your ISA pot half-yearly or yearly with their charges. If they do, they are reducing your valuable tax-free pot.

Nick Louth

NICK LOUTH *is a bestselling thriller writer, award-winning financial journalist and investment commentator. He is a former Reuters correspondent, and was a regulator contributor to the* Financial Times, Investors Chronicle *and* Money Observer. *Nick Louth is married and lives in Lincolnshire.*

He is the author of: Bite *(UK No1 bestseller on Amazon Kindle)*, Heartbreaker, Mirror Mirror, Funny Money: The Investment Diary of Bernard Jones, Bernard Jones and the Temple of Mammon, Dunces with Wolves, Multiply Your Money *and* Double Your Wealth Every Ten Years (Without Really Trying).

His most recent book is the novel The Body in the Marsh *(Canelo, 2017), and his website is at* nicklouth.com.

"ACCEPT THE RISES AND FALLS OF THE MARKET LIKE THE SEASONS OF THE YEAR, AND CLEAVE TO THE MODEST AVERAGE WHICH WILL ACHIEVE YOUR LONG-TERM OBJECTIVE."

Make Meaningful Returns with the Help of a Marvellous Mathematical Principle

D ESPITE EVERYTHING YOU might be told, successful investing is not rocket science. Anyone who has a small slice of savings to put away for the long term can make it work without any knowledge of companies, balance sheets or markets. It involves one rather marvellous mathematical principle: compound interest. The rest is merely patience and consistency.

1. SAVE EARLY AND CONSISTENTLY, SEEK MODEST GAINS AND REINVEST THEM.

The path to making the best from compound interest is to start saving early, to do so consistently without withdrawal, to seek modest and predictable gains from dividend or other forms of income rather than capital gain, and then to plough those gains back into capital.

2. REPEAT.

Then repeat, every year for at least one decade, but preferably three or more.

More than 100 years of market history shows that pursuing this quiet course of action through very low cost market tracker funds or investment trusts will result in a typical annual gain of seven per cent. That may not sound much, but is enough to double your money each decade. You cannot reliably do better!

3. AVOID THE TEMPTATION TO JUMP IN AND OUT OF THE MARKET.

In doing so there are just a few pitfalls and temptations to avoid: Don't try to get rich quickly by trading or jumping in and out of the market. The average trader by definition cannot beat the market average, because every sell is someone else's buy and vice versa. Indeed, most traders underperform when costs and time are accounted for, and some lose all their cash. Instead, accept the rises and falls of the market like the seasons of the year, and cleave to the modest average which will achieve your long-term objective.

4. KEEP COSTS AS LOW AS POSSIBLE.

Minimise all costs so that your gains fall to your capital, not to some intermediary. Costs compound too. Use tax breaks in pensions and ISAs, but don't try to be too clever. Investment is what makes money, not some tax scheme which is too good to last. The beauty of the slow approach is that you make your gains reliably, night or day, without having to concentrate on it. You then have the freedom to get on with the rest of your life.

Yoram Lustig

YORAM LUSTIG *is the Head of Multi-Asset Solutions EMEA at T. Rowe Price. Yoram and his team engage clients and prospects in Europe, the Middle East and Africa in consultative discussions to identify how T. Rowe Price can best meet their investment needs and objectives through the firm's broad equity, fixed income and asset allocation investment capabilities.*

Yoram has 15 years of investment experience. Prior to joining T. Rowe Price in 2017, he was Head of Multi-Asset Investments UK at AXA Investment Managers, Head of Multi-Asset Funds at Aviva Investors and Head of Portfolio Construction EMEA at Merrill Lynch. He began his career in 1998 as a lawyer.

He is the author of Multi-Asset Investing *(Harriman House, 2012) and the award-winning* The Investment Assets Handbook *(Harriman House, 2014), both translated to Chinese. His latest book is the bestselling* The Financial Times Guide to Saving and Investing for Retirement *(FT Pearson, 2016).*

"FIRST UNDERSTAND WHY YOU INVEST, AND THEN INVEST."

Eight Questions You Should Ask Yourself Before Investing

1. WHY DO I INVEST?

How you invest, in what you invest, the risk you can and should assume all depend on your goals. First, determine your investment objectives, and then design an investment solution to try to achieve them. Just beating some generic index like the S&P 500 is nice, but it does not address your financial needs.

What investment outcomes are you seeking? What is your risk tolerance? What is your time horizon until needing the money? How much of your investments should be liquid so you can sell them quickly if you must? Where should you put your money to shield it from taxes? How do you mitigate costs? These are some questions to answer before investing. First understand why you invest, and then invest.

One aspect to consider in particular is time. Time is your best friend when plentiful. The more you have it, the more you can contribute to your portfolio, letting compounding work longer, as well as correct mistakes and recoup losses. But time is your worst enemy when scarce. Try to invest for the long term with abundant patience.

2. DIY OR PROFESSIONAL?

Most choices are trade-offs, a balancing act between a decision's pros and cons. The DIY investing approach requires commitment: doing your homework, learning, experiencing and understanding investing, while risking making regretful mistakes. But it saves fees you must pay for a professional's services.

A financial advisor can help and do things you might not do yourself properly, unless you are confident in your skills. However, advisors might also make mistakes and some incompetent ones might not take care of your financial wellbeing as you would.

It comes down to trust. Do you trust your ability to manage your wealth? Are you willing to commit? If so, DIY is an option. Do you trust a professional to manage your wealth for you? Are you willing to pay? Do you have sufficient wealth to justify the fees? The professional must be your paid trusted advisor, not a friend doing you a favour – pay for accountability. And do not fall for fancy talk and slick presentations. Choose someone who looks proficient with a proven track record.

Whether DIY or not, learn enough to challenge your advisor. Blindly trust no one.

3. HOW TO PLAN TO ACHIEVE MY GOALS?

A good professional ought to start by defining your return and risk investment objectives, as well as your investment constraints (time horizon, liquidity needs and so on). Then the professional should formulate an investment plan with the highest likelihood of achieving your financial goals. We are talking *likelihood* as investing is a probabilistic, not a deterministic exercise – a risk of missing your goals always exists. But even when uncertain, you must have a plan.

Investment strategy specifies:

- in what you invest – stocks, bonds, other classes of investments
- the proportions you allocate to each class – stock/bond/others
- how you invest in each class – active funds, index trackers, individual securities
- how dynamically you manage your portfolio – changing it because of varying personal circumstances and external market conditions.

The decision with the biggest impact on investment results is your asset allocation – how much you invest in stocks, bonds and other types of investments.

If you do it yourself, your plan should be simple – do not overcomplicate it. Armed with a plan, stick with it while at the same time retaining flexibility to adapt it for ever-changing circumstances. Successful investing requires discipline and discipline comes from following a structured plan, not letting noise and distractions derail you. It is like blinkers preventing a horse seeing the rear and sides, focusing the animal on the road ahead. Our world is full of scary events and concerning news. If you let them influence your investment decisions, you might panic, selling at the bottom of the market and buying with euphoria at its top. Adhering to a long-term plan, keeping your sights on your final destination and your head clear is a way to avoid capricious, bad investor behaviour.

Nevertheless, plans must adjust. A crash in the stock market may be a buying opportunity. Even if buying stocks now is not part of your plan, consider it. If you invest for retirement, break down your journey into stages, formulating a different plan fitting each stage. When young and accumulating assets, your strategy may focus on inflation-beating growth by investing mainly in stocks. About a decade before retirement, consider gradually reducing risk, gliding from an aggressive growth strategy to a capital preservation strategy. In retirement, you may switch to a strategy focusing on generating income and keeping pace with inflation.

Things are unlikely to go as planned, but lacking a plan you cannot know where to go.

4. WHY RISK IT?

The elephant in the room of investing is risk. How does saving differ from investing? Saving in a bank comes with little risk (bar the chance of the bank failing) and therefore awards a modest return. You do not risk much, so you deserve low compensation. When investing you must assume risk – your investments may go up and down. So why invest? Because the potential returns are higher than those of risk-free* saving.

If risk-free and risky investments offered the same returns, everyone would buy the risk-free one. This would push its price upward, and its future returns downward, until the risk-free expected return would be low enough to incite investors to turn to the risky investment, now offering an expected return compensating for its risk. The market tends to correctly price risk, as it is reflected in the price of investments and hence their future potential returns (risk premium). A fundamental law of investing is that potential return is aligned with risk.

---

* While nothing is completely risk-free – inflation might turn interest on savings negative in real (inflation-adjusted) terms – everything is relative and relative to investing, saving is nearly riskless.

If you pursue returns then embrace risk, as it is the flipside of return. If you do not want to risk it, investing is not for you. Your return objective should match your risk tolerance: your ability and willingness to take risk. Higher returns come with higher risk. If you can afford losing money because you have enough of it and sufficient time to recoup losses, you have higher ability to take risk. If you cannot sleep well at night while risking your money, your willingness to take risk is low. Risk tolerance is personal.

What is risk? Simply put, it is the chance of missing your financial goals. If you aim not to lose, losing is your risk. If you aim to beat inflation, lagging inflation is your risk. While volatility or standard deviation is a common measure of risk, it is not risk per se. The true risk of investing is a permanent loss of wealth (downside risk). Understand your risk, take it, but control it and do not take more risk than is comfortable for you.

5. DO I KNOW WITH CERTAINTY WHAT IS GOING TO HAPPEN?

No, you do not. Nobody does.

Do not put all your eggs in one basket. If you drop a single basket with all your eggs, you are left with nothing. If you diversify your eggs among a number of baskets, even if one drops, you still have eggs. This is the gist of diversification. Since the future is unknown and you cannot know which investments are likely to go up or down, spread your portfolio among different investments that are likely to behave differently, increasing the chances of holding some investments that will perform well. By diversifying across investments with differing behaviours (lowly correlated) you reduce your overall portfolio's risk. It is said that this is the only free lunch in investing, since you reduce risk without paying a fee or forsaking all potential returns.

When should you not diversify? When you know what is going to happen – which investments are going to do well. When is this going to happen? Very rarely indeed, or when you have an edge. The shortcoming of diversification is that it gives you an average return, not a spectacular one. But it also means that if you lose, your loss is an average one, not a spectacular one. The future is unknown, so diversify.

6. ACTIVE OR PASSIVE?

One of the never-ending arguments in investing is whether to actively or passively manage your money. Active management means selecting securities you think are likely to do better than the market's average and shifting your asset allocation depending on how each type of investment or market is likely to do in the future. Passive management means using trackers to follow the broad market's performance and keeping your allocation static – buy and hold.

If done right, active can add value. However, it requires time, money and talent – being selective sustainably works only with skill. Passive delivers average market returns less transaction costs, but it is simpler and its fees are lower than those of active. The answer to the question which method to choose is an annoying: 'it depends'.

Active management can generate better performance than that of the market. If you select securities that outperform others or sell investments before they drop and buy ones before they rise, you can profit. The trick is that active management requires forecasting the future. If your crystal ball works, you win – but if it is cloudy, you lose. Predicting the future is notoriously difficult, even for the most talented professionals. Since you cannot rely on luck, you should opt for active management only if you truly commit to it or use the services of a trusted professional. Otherwise, passive management is for you.

Bad active is value-destroying. But even if it can add a bit of value every year, the benefits of active management can accumulate over a long horizon, making a big difference. Nevertheless, trying to get into the market and out of it (market timing) usually ends up in underperforming a strategy of just investing and remaining invested for the long term.

7. SHOULD I BE STINGY?

Generally speaking, being stingy is not a positive trait. You should try within your means to spend on yourself and your loved ones – there is no point taking your wealth with you to the grave, unless your aim is caring for your heirs. But being stingy with your investments is actually a good trait. Every penny you save on costs and taxes is another penny added to your performance. One of the only things under our control in investing is charges and taxes – controlling everything else is limited. So control what you can control.

Try to negotiate down your advisor's fees (financial advice is a competitive market), aim to buy funds and securities at a low fee and put as much of your investments as possible in tax-efficient vehicles – it is not only asset allocation but asset *location* that matters. However, the caveat is that you should save on fees and costs without compromising quality – you pay peanuts, you get monkeys. Do not choose your advisor or investments just because they are cheap. If your advisor or investments are lousy it might cost you much more dearly than any savings on fees and costs.

Another aspect of price is that the price you pay for your investments determines their future performance. Higher price means lower future returns and lower price means higher future return, everything else being equal. Buying investments is like buying anything else – you do not want to overpay. The challenge with investments is that it is difficult to know what the right price is. History is the best guide. After the stock market has risen a lot, it is likely to be expensive. But it does not mean it will not rise some more before perhaps reverting back to some mean valuation. That is unless a structural change warrants a new price level.

The price you pay today sets the return you receive tomorrow. Do not overspend on your investments, but do not underspend.

8. SHOULD I JUST INVEST AND FORGET ABOUT MY PORTFOLIO?

Fiddling around with your investments usually hurts you because of generating unnecessary transaction costs and making emotional investment decisions grounded in fear and greed. But neglecting your investments might hurt you as well. Take care of your portfolio like a plant so it grows nicely. Be dynamic but not overly active.

Invest cash quickly and regularly so it participates in the market and you average the price you purchase your investment over time, avoiding buying high and selling low. Rebalance your portfolio not too often but not too infrequently (annually or semi-annually) to align it with your investment strategy. Review performance to check it does not surprise you and you are on track to achieve your desired outcomes. And ensure you remain happy with your investment choices and strategy and they are relevant to your needs and market conditions. Investing is a never-ending story, requiring patience and maintenance. And perhaps above all requiring luck. Good luck.

Chris Mayer

CHRIS MAYER *is the Investment Director of the Bonner family office. He is the author of several books, including* 100-Baggers: Stocks That Return 100-to-1 and How to Find Them. *His forthcoming book is titled* How Do You Know? A Guide to Clear Thinking About Wall Street, Investing and Life *to be published in early 2018.*

"EQUITY OWNERSHIP IS THE BEST FORM OF SKIN IN THE GAME. AS THE OLD SAYING GOES, 'NO ONE WASHES A RENTAL'."

Four Simple Things You Should Do to Succeed in the Stock Market

1. INVEST WITH PEOPLE WHO HAVE SKIN IN THE GAME.

"My experience as a money manager suggests that entrepreneurial instinct equates with sizable equity ownership."

— MARTIN SOSNOFF, *SILENT INVESTOR, SILENT LOSER*
(RICHARDSON & STEIRMAN & BLACK, 1986)

I HAVE TO agree with Mr Sosnoff, a tough-minded, sharp-tongued money manager who only recently hung up his spurs after 50 years in the saddle. (He also penned a few delightfully quotable books about his experiences. My favorite is *Humble on Wall Street* from 1975.)

I lead off with Sosnoff's quote because I've absorbed its deep lesson in my own career. And if I could share just one investing strategy with you it would be this: Invest with people who have skin in the game.

There is a lot of research to support the idea that stocks with significant insider ownership outperform their peers. It also makes intuitive sense.

Owners do things hired guns don't do. Sometimes these things can be small, but they add up over time. For example, I remember reading a IHS Markit study that looked at over 3,000 public companies and found that just 225 paid special dividends in the fourth quarter of 2012 – ahead of looming tax increases. The average insider ownership of those 225 companies was 25%. Owners think about things like taxes.

Equity ownership is the best form of skin in the game. As the old saying goes, 'No one washes a rental.' But it is not the only one. Pay attention to the incentives of the management team before you invest alongside them. Look at compensation schemes. Do they reward *per share* value creation? Do they use meaningful metrics such as return on invested capital, or do they just focus on a less relevant number such as earnings?

Read the proxy. It is the most important disclosure companies make and the one I start with. (In the US, the proxy, known as Form DEF 14A, details stock ownership, management compensation and more.)

The key idea is that you want to invest with management teams that think like owners. That's easier to do when they are owners to start with.

2. BE PATIENT.

Phil Carret was a long-time investor, right up until his death in 1998 at the age of 101. Warren Buffett called him "one of my heroes."

In 1996, Louis Rukeyser interviewed him on TV and asked: "What is the single most important thing that you have learned about investing over the past three quarters of a century?"

Carret's reply: "Patience."

I've never forgotten this exchange. Harvesting the power of compounding lies at the heart of investing successfully. And the power of compounding needs time to work. And you won't reap its rewards if you keep yanking out your money, like pulling your tomato plants before they bear fruit.

Here's an example I like: If you take a penny and double it every day for 30 days, you'll have $10.7 million on the last day. That shows you two things. First, it shows you the power of compounding. But it also shows you the returns are back-end loaded. After all, if you have $10.7 million on the 30th day, how much do you have on the 29th day? The answer is $5.35 million. And on the 28th day? Just $2.6 million. Think about that.

Another important reason why patience is important: Even the best investments go through periods where they go nowhere. Or worse.

My favorite story here comes from Chris Mittleman at Mittleman Investment Management. He says imagine if a friend had introduced you to Warren Buffett in 1972 and told you how much money he made with him. You check it out and find that Berkshire Hathaway had gone from about $8 in 1962 to $80 at the end of 1972. So, you buy the stock for $80 on 31 December 1972.

Three years later, you'd be down 53%. And to make you feel worse, the S&P 500 was only down 14%. So you sell in disgust. What a mistake. By 31 December 1982 the stock would rise to $775... on its way to $272,000 today.

Investing is a game that rewards sitting on your hands.

3. DON'T EXPECT TO WIN ALL THE TIME.

I like to study the track records of great investors. One thing I've learned is that no investor is great all the time.

A 2011 study by investment firm Davis Advisors looked at a universe of 190 mutual fund managers whose ten-year performances put them in the top 25 for the decade ending 31 December 2011.

Davis Advisors then posed an interesting question: What percentage of these top performers had at least one rolling three-year period during which they put up lousy numbers? More specifically, what percentage of these top managers put up numbers in a three-year period where they were at the bottom 25%?

The answer may shock you: 96%.

In other words, almost all of them. Moreover, a third of them spent at least one three-year period where they were in the bottom 10%. Meaning 90% of their peers beat these top dogs for at least a three-year period.

Another good example is Sir John Templeton. He started the Templeton Growth Fund in 1954. This would be his flagship fund. The average return was about 16% per year for 38 years under his watch. This was almost four points better than the market over that time, an astonishing record. If you had put $10,000 with Templeton in 1954 and left it there, you had $1.7 million when he stepped down in 1992. That's a 170-fold return. He did this without using debt and often had excess cash.

And yet, his fund lost money in ten of those 38 years – almost 25% of the time.

Investment returns in any given year mean very little. They ebb and flow in unpredictable and uneven ways. If you chase performance, you're apt to sell out of ideas just as they are about to turn up and buy into ideas just as they are peaking. Don't chase performance.

4. DON'T DIVERSIFY TOO MUCH.

Most people own way too many stocks. I've seen personal portfolios with 30 or 40 stocks. That's ridiculous. There is no way a single person can follow all those names or know much worth knowing about any of them.

Further, I'd ask you this: Is your 30th best idea really worth owning? How about your 29th best idea? I always tell people to concentrate their investing. I think 10–15 names is a good number. Maybe even fewer.

I always remember what Joel Greenblatt said. Greenblatt compiled an enviable track record running Gotham Capital and later wrote books about his methods. Greenblatt pointed out that owning just eight stocks in different industries eliminates about 80% of the non-market risk (or the risk not related to the overall market's movements). And 16 stocks will eliminate 93% of that risk.

In other words, after a point, adding more stocks doesn't do you any good as far as reducing risk.

Besides this, there is all kinds of research out there that shows the best returns often come from concentrated portfolios. I'd point you to the book *Concentrated Investing* by Allen Benello, Michael van Biema, and Tobias Carlisle for more. The book includes profiles of investors who ran such concentrated portfolios.

Lou Simpson was one of these. He ran GEICO's investment portfolio from 1979 to retirement in 2010. His record is extraordinary: 20% annually, compared to 13.5% for the market.

Simpson's reason for concentrating his portfolio was a simple one: "Good investment ideas, that is, companies that meet our criteria, are difficult to find. When we think we have found one, we make a large commitment."

Simpson's focus increased over time. In 1982, he had 33 stocks in a $280 million portfolio. He kept cutting back the number of stocks he owned, even as the size of his portfolio grew. By 1995, his last year, he had just ten stocks in a $1.1 billion portfolio.

Now, this runs counter to almost everything you'll hear from financial advisors. And it could be dangerous advice if you don't know what you're doing. But my contention is you are likely to do much better if you focus only on your best ideas, the ones you really know something about, than if you spread your bets under the mistaken belief that you're safer.

Tim
Morgan

Described in the press as 'Dr Gloom' and 'Terrifying Tim', **TIM MORGAN** *has never avoided controversy, whether he is pointing out the crippling weaknesses of the British economy, calling for greater justice for a younger generation robbed by its elders, or explaining the link between inner-city riots and thwarted materialism. He developed the Essentials Index, which provides invaluable insights into the real cost of living.*

Educated at Cambridge, Tim has always been fascinated by economic, political and military issues. His fascination with maritime warfare has taken him from commando exercises to the flight-deck of an aircraft carrier.

As head of research at leading finance house Tullett Prebon from 2009 to 2013, Dr Tim Morgan gained a reputation for supplying radical answers to pressing economic and political issues, and garnered significant media coverage for leading-edge reports including his Project Armageddon *study of the British economy.*

He is the author of Life After Growth *(Harriman House, 2013), the product of extensive research into how the economy really works, which presents radical explanations for the economic problems of today and tomorrow.*

"PERCENTAGES ARE USEFUL, BUT NO ONE EVER BOUGHT LUNCH WITH ONE."

Risk and Return in an Age of Abnormality

T HERE ARE MANY ways of setting rules or parameters for investment. Let me say at once that there is no single set of golden rules that suits everyone, not least because the circumstances and the aims of individual investors differ considerably. The rules or guidelines that you adopt have to be those best tailored to your own requirements.

But these rules must also take into account the broader context, meaning the economic, political and fiscal times in which we live. These times are highly abnormal. Most obviously, asset markets, including equities, bonds and property, are at or near record highs. Debt, meanwhile, is also at record levels, whilst interest rates have been at or near zero ever since the global financial crisis (GFC) brought the financial system to the brink of catastrophe in 2008.

The new abnormal

All of these circumstances are abnormal. Interest rates, close to zero in nominal terms, are negative after adjustment for inflation, meaning that, in real terms, savers are losing money. This is most visible in pension funding, where low rates have dragged anticipated future returns down to levels far below expected future payments, creating huge deficits and putting funds at risk. Low rates also bail out businesses which, in more normal circumstances, would fail, creating space for new and better enterprises as part of an essential process known as 'creative destruction'. Asset values, including property, are at levels which reflect ultra-cheap credit, not robust economic growth or rising incomes.

These abnormal circumstances pose significant challenges for the investor. For a start, highly priced asset markets impose a squeeze on income, making attractive returns hard to find. At various times in recent years, huge swathes of government bonds have traded at negative yields, meaning that investors are paying governments for the privilege of lending to them.

However you look at it, this is unusual, both theoretically and historically. The investor can no longer simply hold low-risk instruments, earning a small (but positive) return on capital. In other words, the amount of risk associated with any given level of return is far higher than has traditionally been the case. As well as the emergence of big pension fund deficits, the downside of low rates includes a severe loss of income to savers.

'Abnormal' need not mean 'soon to change'. As the economist Keynes remarked, "the market can remain irrational longer than you can remain solvent". But we do have to ask ourselves whether some form of equilibrium will in due course be restored – might we return to an environment of higher interest rates, which are positive in real terms? If so, would the stimulus of cheap credit swing into reverse, forcing asset values down, and incomes up?

Before turning to my own investment rules, the aim here is to explore some of the risks implicit in 'the new abnormal' of cheap money.

Addicted to debt?

Here is a statistic that should make any investor ask questions about what is really going on. Over the ten years between 2006 and 2016, and whilst world economic output (GDP) increased by $29 trillion (32%), global debt rose by $98 trillion (61%). *What this means is that $3.39 was borrowed for each $1 of additional GDP.*

We also added $43 trillion to inter-bank debts over that period, and worldwide pension saving may have fallen as much as $94 trillion short of what it needed to be.

There are two, starkly different ways in which we can see this relationship. One view is that there is nothing much to worry about in this situation, particularly since the cost of servicing debt is extraordinarily low. The other view, to put it bluntly, is that this is 'Ponzi economics' – that we are mortgaging the future by racking up debt and other 'hostages to futurity' in order to maintain a semblance of 'business as usual'.

The general consensus favours the relaxed interpretation, but anyone tempted to side with this view might remember that this same majority also saw nothing to lose sleep about as debt (and risk) escalated in the years before 2008. They were wrong then, and are likely to be equally wrong now.

Let me say at once that the absolute quantum of debt is not the biggest problem posed by this dynamic. Repayment can always be pushed into the future and, should there at any point be an acceleration in inflation, the real value of historic debt will be eroded.

Rather, what is disturbing about the relationship between growth and borrowing is that the former seems to have become a hostage to the latter. In other words, our current rate of growth *depends upon ever-expanding indebtedness.*

Britain as exemplar

Figures for the United Kingdom illustrate this process. Between 2006 and 2016, and stated after adjustment for inflation, British GDP increased by £203bn (12%), whereas debt expanded by £1,181bn (32%). Clearly, some, at least, of that borrowing was used to fuel consumption, which in turn is by far the largest component of GDP. Each £1 of growth was accompanied by £5.80 of new debt – obviously, this is not a sustainable situation.

So, had borrowing *not* grown in this way, what would have happened to GDP? Put another way, how much of the 'growth' recorded during this period really amounted to nothing more than the spending of borrowed money? This matters, because if, for any reason, the ability to borrow were to become constrained, how much growth would then remain?

Britain is a telling example of why perpetual borrowing might be a dangerous assumption. The increase of £1.18 trillion in the decade after 2006 lifted aggregate debt to £4.88 trillion at the end of 2016, equivalent to 252% of GDP. In 2016 alone, borrowing totalled £152bn, compared with growth of only £34bn.

But this debt number tells less than half of the story. It excludes debt in the inter-bank or 'financial' sector. Official figures put this at £1.77 trillion, or 91% of GDP, but some respectable estimates are twice this much. Unfunded public sector pensions stand at about £1.5 trillion (the difference between expected future employee contributions and anticipated future outflows). Immediately after the most recent cut in interest rates, the *Financial Times* reported that deficits in private pension funding had risen to £975bn.

Even this combined total for pension shortfalls (about £2.6 trillion) may be an understatement. A recent report from a respected international organisation estimated Britain's overall underinvestment in pensions at $8 trillion (about £5.54 trillion) as at the end of 2015. Worldwide, these pension shortfalls are a direct consequence of monetary policies which have all but destroyed rates of return on investment.

For every £1 that you put aside towards a pension in 2007, you probably need to save £2.70 just now to achieve the same result.

There is no doubt that, taken together, British debt and 'quasi-debt' has become enormous. The total of 'economic' and inter-bank debt is somewhere between £6.6 trillion (343% of GDP) and £8.4 trillion (435%). On top of this, pension shortfalls may be somewhere between £2.6 trillion (138% of GDP) and £5.8 trillion (300%). Even this does not include commitments for nuclear decommissioning, and liabilities under PFI (private finance initiative) schemes.

Of course, quasi-debt is not the same as formal debt, which is subject to contractual force. At the same time, it is difficult in the extreme to imagine any government reneging on promises to its employees, or standing by whilst private pension provision disintegrates. At this point, we should admit at least the possibility that making large and continuous additions to debt (and quasi-debt) may not be an indefinitely sustainable process.

So what might happen to growth were the ability to borrow to become cramped? My estimate – based on a formula but, nevertheless, ultimately an estimate – is that, of the £1.37 trillion added to British debt between 2005 and 2015, 13% was used to subsidise inflation. Though a modest proportion of total borrowing, this still amounts to £182bn, or the vast majority (85%) of all growth recorded over that period. Furthermore, using borrowing to boost consumption (and hence GDP) started well before 2005. My calculation is that, without borrowed consumption, GDP in 2016 might not have been £1.94 trillion, but only about £1.55 trillion.

This, of course, leads to two further, very disturbing implications. The first is that, stripped of 'borrowed consumption', underlying growth might be nowhere near the generally accepted level of close to 2%, but might be as low as 0.4% *in the event that activity could no longer be boosted by borrowing*. Second, the ratio of debt to GDP might be far higher than the reported 252%, standing at somewhere nearer 320% *if measured against a GDP figure stripped of borrowed consumption*. And that, of course, is even before you start looking at inter-bank debt and shortfalls in pension provision.

The systemic problem

Though rather extreme, the British situation is not otherwise dramatically different from that of other Western developed economies. Stated in inflation-adjusted terms, the United States added $11.1 trillion to debt between 2006 and 2016, when growth in GDP totalled $2.3 trillion. Over those same years, France added debt of €1.9 trillion for growth of just €0.16 trillion, and Spain borrowed €460bn whilst growing by only €35bn. Italy's economic output actually decreased (by €100bn) over that decade, but debt still expanded by almost €500bn.

Moreover, the Western habit of using debt to boost GDP has been spreading into the emerging market economies (EMEs). Between 2006 and 2016, reported growth of RMB43 trillion in China was accompanied by net new borrowing of RMB146 trillion, plus a big increase (of RMB82 trillion) in inter-bank debt.

The 'why' of this process can be explained in several ways. First, globalisation, by outsourcing skilled jobs to the EMEs, seems to have pushed Western consumers into borrowing in order to sustain their levels of consumption. The wage-depressing effect of globalisation pushed Western governments, too, deeper into debt, as tax revenues fell short of expectations. Attitudes to indebtedness became more relaxed under an economic ideology known as 'neoliberalism'. 'Deregulation' of financial services made borrowing easier and cheaper than ever before.

The causes, though, matter less than the consequences, the resulting risk, and the implications that all of this has for investors. After the GFC, the authorities slashed their official or 'policy' interest rates, and used QE (quantitative easing) to push bond prices up, and thus yields down. The aim was to circumvent the problem caused by the difficulty of paying interest on the world's huge debt mountain. ZIRP, or 'zero interest rate policy', was meant to be a short-term fix in a period of emergency.

But this 'emergency' has now lasted a lot longer than the second world war! Low interest rates, of course, encourage people to borrow, and debt has increased even more rapidly in the years since 2008 than it did in the pre-crisis years.

Two rules for risky times

1. THE WISE INVESTOR STARTS BY KNOWING HIS OWN AIMS.

The central point for investors to note is the issue of risk. Asset values, since they have been driven sharply upwards by cheap credit, could fall back sharply were borrowing to become more expensive. If the practice of boosting economic activity using borrowing ceases to be sustainable, growth could slump, or indeed reverse, with adverse consequences for investment. We could face a re-run of the banking crisis, starting from a point at which debt is much higher, and governments' ability to intervene has been weakened by the escalation in their own levels of debt. Conceivably, inflation could take off, acting to destroy the real value of historic debt as part of a process of a return to equilibrium.

A climate of subdued returns and elevated risk can only increase the importance of acting on solid investment principles. Whatever the circumstances, the wise investor starts by knowing his own aims. Am I looking for income, or capital appreciation? Am I a trader, or a longer-term investor? And what is my attitude to risk?

The risk question is always critical, because risk and return are linked. A low-risk investment is likely to offer modest returns as well. If you want high returns, you generally have to accept greater risk.

Of course, it is perfectly possible for investments to be mispriced, offering both high returns and low risk, though, to find these, you have to be able to spot something that the market generally has missed. Since market prices are supposed to represent the aggregate knowledge of all participants, spotting an anomaly may seem difficult. Logically, however, market prices also sum up the aggregate misconceptions of all participants, so anomalies do happen.

The tricky bit is spotting them, but here's one to be going on with. Have you noticed how many highly valued companies depend, for almost all of their revenues, on the same limited pool of income, namely advertising revenue? And have you also noticed the exponential rate at which consumers are not just loading ad-blockers, but also finding out how to write their own?

As an analyst, my stance is avowedly low-risk, for the simple reason that, as all forms of investment are implicitly risky, there seems little to be said for taking on more risk than you have to.

2. COUNT THE CASH.

My attitude to investment in equities is a fundamental one – this means that I want to buy facts, not hype. Accordingly, my lodestar has always been 'count the cash'. Call me suspicious, but I take a big pinch of salt when someone tells me how super-profitable a company will become. I need to be convinced, which means I need to see the cash flow, or at least know where it's going to come from. Percentages are useful, but no one ever bought lunch with one, and we should never forget that the aim of investment is to put some cash in now, in order to get more cash back later.

This means paying more attention to cash flow than profits – after all, it's cash that pays dividends, and cash which lets businesses invest enough to move ahead of competitors, or at least keep up with them. Cash measurement can help you understand how strong a company really is. What is the cash flow coverage of dividends? How does debt compare with annual cash generation? How does the share price stand as a multiple of cash flow per share? And, above all, how much visibility do we have on future trends in cash inflows?

Obviously, we need a 'clean' cash flow number if our measurement is to be effective. This means leaving out one-off gains or losses when measuring cash flow, and excluding movements in working capital (inventories, debtors and creditors). Despite my remark about percentages not buying lunch, it's a good idea to measure cash returns, meaning cash flow as a percentage of gross (undepreciated) invested capital.

The aim at all times should be to secure the most advantageous combination of risk and return. What is claimed for investments, and what they can actually deliver, may be very different, and a cash-based approach can help us measure how wide any such 'perception gap' actually is.

Even in normal times, measuring cash can be a reliable guide. In these highly abnormal times, a grounding in cash is more important than ever.

Charlie Morris

CHARLIE MORRIS *is Chief Investment Officer at Newscape, having joined in May 2016 to restructure and oversee the direct Funds business. He is the Lead Manager of the Newscape Diversified Growth Fund, the Co-Manager to the Newscape Emerging Markets Equity Fund and is a senior member of the investment committee.*

Prior to Newscape, Charlie spent 17 years at HSBC Global Asset Management as the Head of Absolute Return managing a multi-asset fund range with assets in excess of $3 billion. He is a familiar face in the financial media and writes frequently as the editor of Atlas Pulse *and the* Fleet Street Letter, *Britain's oldest financial newsletter. Prior to fund management, Charlie was an officer in the Grenadier Guards, British Army.*

"WHEN THE TIDE RISES IN ONE AREA OF THE STOCK MARKET, IT INEVITABLY EBBS IN ANOTHER. YOU CAN TAKE ADVANTAGE OF THAT."

Everything is Connected: An Investor's Guide

HAVING FOLLOWED FINANCIAL markets since the early 1990s – firstly as a private investor, and then as a fund manager – one thing has become clearer: everything is connected. Back then, I ignored bonds, glazed over currencies and dismissed commodities altogether. I only looked at the stock market. Yet when you look closely, and see the tide rise in one area of the stock market, it inevitably ebbs in another. Moreover, I eventually learnt that the driver of change comes from the other asset classes that I once ignored. Especially bonds.

Over the years, I saw how consumer companies, which make the likes of toothpaste and dog food, never seemed to boom at the same time as cement or auto companies. And if there's a boom in gold, then watch out for tech stocks. In this brief chapter, I'll explain why – and how investors can take advantage of it.

Active managers have failed to build 'portfolios'

Many active managers style themselves as quality, growth or value, making the case that their approach is best positioned for long-term success. Growth stocks rise far and fast, value stocks offer a bargain while quality is resilient. All of these are attractive qualities, yet the world is forever changing and it pays to be diversified. Being wedded to a single style is an inefficient investment strategy, as at some point your approach will find itself in the doghouse. Preserving capital is the investor's highest priority, as a 50% loss requires a 100% gain to get you back to the start line.

You'll see that it's all about bonds, those dull things I ignored until the age of 30. The global bond market is vast and estimated to exceed

$100 trillion, roughly twice the size of the equity market. Bonds fund governments, municipals, companies and consumers. A range of factors including credit risk, expected inflation, issuance, economic outlook, demographic trends and government policy determines their prices. That drives the cost of money, which in turn dictates which parts of the stock market will thrive or slump.

Oil sets prices

Energy is the most important input cost into the economy and that has macroeconomic implications. Oil is the most dense and transportable form of energy and it is therefore little surprise that it drives inflation. If inflation is the rate at which the value of money declines, money is most valuable when oil is cheap and least when it isn't.

If oil rises, then costs rise as consumers have less to spend on discretionary items. A rising oil price, which is normally caused by economic strength, also tends to be bullish for other commodities, as the production of wheat and copper (for example) are heavily dependent on oil. Increases in long-term inflation expectations also cause the price of bonds to fall as money is expected to be less valuable in the future. That means today's bond buyers require a higher return in compensation for future losses.

Assuming the economy is strong, higher consumer prices will feed through into higher interest rates as the government attempts to reign in the rate of inflation. During this period both inflation and bond yields rise and so the 'curve is rising'. A rising curve (bond yields plus inflation) also tends to favour insurance companies and banks as their profit margins improve. That strength will also tend to be seen in emerging markets and across the industrial spectrum.

China reawakes

A recent example of this came during the 'China years', which kicked off in 2002. Chinese GDP per capita had just passed $1,000 having come from $156 in 1978, the year of Deng Xiaoping's reforms. As of 2016, that number subsequently ballooned to $8,123.

$1,000 marked the tipping point. As China raised its head, it became an economic force to be reckoned with. Passing tipping point saw the country consume commodities on a scale never previously seen. Copper rose more than tenfold while oil rose from $10 in 1998 to $148 by 2008. 'Peak oil' became a popular theme.

Value traps

The era of breathtaking Chinese demand saw inflation rise along with bond yields. Unsurprisingly, there was a bubble in commodities, emerging markets, financials and industrial companies, and especially those that had built up leverage. The economy had enjoyed a phase of pricing power.

Yet when the credit crisis came about in 2008, it was precisely these stocks that performed the worst which had been driven higher by a rising curve. Many were owned by value managers, which aim to own cheap assets that can't fall as far. They deem themselves to be conservative, yet they were the worst performing group of managers during the crisis. Why did they sink? Because the curve, having risen since 2002, suddenly dropped like a stone during the crisis.

The irony is that value managers are the most arrogant crowd within fund management. They believe that they are intellectually superior to others. They're not.

Quality, the saviour

Not only did the crisis see the curve collapse, it also saw real interest rates collapse from 3%, at the darkest hours of 2008, to -1% by 2012. That is, the bond yield less the rate of inflation. Investors switched into defensive stocks such as consumer staples. These companies are makers of the products we need rather than want. Their profits are relatively predictable, and their balance sheets are strong. While those are fine qualities, they tend to be slow growers. And as a result, they have bond-like qualities.

Gentlemen prefer bonds

Bonds perform best when interest rates and inflation are falling; when the curve is falling, which is an opposite condition to the China years. Post-2008, quality stocks surged, and by 2016 they traded at markedly higher price-to-sales ratios than in the past. That should come as no surprise as bond yields fell to historically low levels. These companies have seen their free cash flow yields follow. They have become expensive, and it stands to reason that they will cheapen as bond yields rise.

Given quality prefers a falling curve and value stocks prefer a rising curve, they could be described as opposites, and indeed they are. A portfolio that combines quality and value is more robust than one that holds just one. Warren Buffett could reasonably be described as a quality and value manager. There's no harm in following him.

Growth stocks are also cyclical

During the late 1990s, oil was cheap and the economy was strong. That saw rates rise at a materially slower pace than inflation. Hence, real interest rates (the difference between interest rates and inflation) soared. Despite a crisis in commodities and emerging markets, that era saw the greatest stock market bubble since 1929. And throughout that bubble, more stocks slumped than spiked. That's because only one part of the market surged: growth stocks.

Of course, there was the birth of the internet, the Y2K thing whereby all toasters would explode on New Year's Eve and so on, but the behaviour of the bond market set the trend in motion. Although the peak stock prices reached in March 2000 were irrational, the move over the preceding years was entirely rational. And regardless of whether the dotcoms rose or fell, the internet never stopped growing thereafter.

Companies that are expected to grow faster than the market, will be deservedly more valuable when there is less competition from other investments. At the time, the non-tech market was lazily grouped together as the 'old economy'. As real yields rose in the late 1990s, the present value of low-growth or zero-growth assets, such as bonds and consumer staples, declined. The revulsion towards the old economy was rational, but as always in markets, it went a giant step too far.

The bubble busts

Eventually, every bubble must burst. When tech peaked in March 2000, that neatly coincided with a peak in real interest rates. As those real rates started to fall from dizzy heights, investors clambered to buy bonds, and bond-like stocks, in the subsequent bear market.

Over the course of the technology boom, the growth managers did extremely well and thought they were gods, while the dull old quality and value managers became the laughing stock. Yet the real winner that followed the technology bubble was neither quality nor value: it was gold.

Don't ignore gold

Some say that gold gauges central banks, as if it's rising in their currency, they're doing a bad job. That's because if inflation is rising when the economy is cool (when bond yields fall), then real interest rates are falling too (real rates are bond yields less the rate of inflation). Inflation describes the rate of devaluation of money. In this environment, the best performing asset is gold (or creditworthy inflation-linked bonds), because it is the most reliable store of value under such adverse economic conditions.

In 1999, the price of gold started to rise from the doldrums at $250 per ounce. By my calculations, gold was 43% undervalued at that time, and a fairer price would have been closer to $400. But markets have a mind of their own, and that low price presented an opportunity.

Decomposing the gold bull

The gold bull market saw a 611% surge that took it 48% above fair value by the peak. On that basis, 480% of the 611% rise was justified. I say justified, because it started too cheap, there was 35% compound inflation over the period and the collapse in real interest rates from 4% in 1999 to -1% in 2012 justified a further rise of 103%.

Over that period, the stock market offered little. The S&P 500 returned just 1.5% pa including dividends, while the FTSE All-Share returned 3.8%. The big loser was the Nasdaq that returned just 0.5% over the 11-year period, while gold annualised at a staggering 15.7%. It seems that growth and gold are opposites.

Holders of gold between 1980 and 1999 saw terrible returns, yet great times followed. Sadly for the gold bugs, gold only seems to perform about 40% of the time. It's best to hold gold and growth together.

A simple portfolio that combined both gold and the Nasdaq did very well, despite bubbles and crashes in both assets, for the simple reason they were negatively correlated. Over the past two decades, gold has appreciated by 4.3 times, whereas the Nasdaq has risen six-fold. If you went 50:50, and rebalanced your portfolio each year-end, then your returns would have been seven-fold. Not bad for such a simple idea.

Opposites detract

If you are in a growth environment, when real interest rates are rising, the worst performing asset will be gold. That's logical as rising real rates make bank deposits more attractive. That, in turn, puts downward pressure on the gold price. I have also shown that quality and value strategies are natural opposites. Over the long term, holding both beats either or.

In summary, value enjoys a rising curve, and quality, a falling curve. Growth enjoys rising real interest rates, whereas gold prefers them to be falling. Yet if growth surges, quality and value don't have to slump, as they aren't opposites. Just avoid gold, or at least own less. Similarly, in a value environment, gold and growth can be held. At that time you should avoid quality, as bonds and their stock market comparables slump.

An efficient portfolio

Taking this argument a stage further, we should combine all four styles, and periodically rebalance our portfolio. That means whatever the mighty bond market throws at you, there's a surging winner in your portfolio. There's also a loser, but rebalancing will mean buying more on the cheap. Which is fine, because the regime will eventually turn and you'll be prepared for it. The other two styles are likely to bumble along, and their turn will come at some point down the line. This is how to keep on climbing up those escalators.

The point is not to explain the past, but to prepare for the future. Bond market regimes dictate what will happen in different areas of the stock market. Don't be confused by growth, value, quality or gold; own all of them and there'll be no such thing as a shock. Naturally, you'll still have rough patches, but you'll be better off than a focused investor with a preference for one individual style.

Index funds

Oh, just track the index, I hear you cry. That's fine, but which index? The S&P 500 is highly diversified, yet since 1998 when I started working as a professional fund manager, it has managed to decline by 50% twice. Other indices have seen far worse. That's because they all have a composition bias.

For example, the Nasdaq is dominated by growth companies, as is Taiwan's TWSE. The FTSE 100 has a heavy weight in natural resources. The Swiss Index is overloaded with quality. Emerging markets tend to do best in a value environment, yet have their own quirks. Countries' indices merely capture what is there, and any portfolio efficiency that exists is coincidental. I'm not saying indices are poorly constructed, just that you can do much better over time without much effort. That means higher returns while being more diversified. And remember that diversification doesn't mean owning everything, just things that are fundamentally different.

Summary

Don't forget that growth companies, in aggregate, didn't stop growing when they were out of favour. They still drove forward the economic frontiers such as the internet, biotechnology or software. Their premiums eroded as other, and cheaper, assets offered a better opportunity for investors. Similarly, the cement plants or oil companies never went away, they just fell out of fashion.

The evidence for the linkage between the behaviour of asset classes is not only circumstantial, but also logical. You could attempt to forecast the bond market, and then pounce on the correct sectors, but that's harder than it sounds.

What is possible is to use feedback loops. Ask yourself what's cheap and what's dear in the stock market? Then consider the prevailing trends in the bond market. Are rates and inflation rising or falling? Once you've made your decisions, have a little more of the most favourable regime, and a little less of the least. But don't go mad, as it pays to be diversified. You'll soon see this working in action. Your portfolio will do better and your volatility will be lower. This is what I do at Newscape each and every day.

Ned Naylor-Leyland

NED NAYLOR-LEYLAND *joined Old Mutual Global Investors in 2015 and manages the Old Mutual Gold & Silver Fund. He is a well-known figure in the world of gold and silver investing, having over 17 years' investment experience. He joined from Quilter Cheviot, having founded a dedicated precious metals fund for Cheviot Asset Management in January 2009, investing in gold, silver and the underlying equities. He previously worked for Smith & Williamson. Ned holds a BA (Hons) in Spanish from the University of Bristol.*

"THE ECHOES
OF HISTORY ARE
GETTING LOUDER.
CHANGE IS AFOOT."

The Wheel of History
– and a Golden Future

---

1. HISTORY MATTERS.

T HE PAGES OF economic and financial market history books are time-worn and tired. Market commentators spend their days rooting through history to draw parallels, to flag lessons seemingly unlearnt. And while history rarely provides the perfect answer, commentators are right to try to do so; there is a cyclicality and flow to financial events and trends that justifies such an approach.

Going back almost 600 years, global reserve currencies have tended to enjoy a prolonged but finite lifetime, spanning between 80 and 110 years. And as today's market carries clear echoes of the 1970s – when the US dollar's reserve currency status came into question following the shock closing of the gold window – so we near the end of the greenback's likely lifespan as reserve currency. The echoes of history are getting louder. Change is afoot.

2. GOLD IS RETAKING ITS RIGHTFUL PLACE.

To have a clearer picture, it is important to go back to 1944, when the Bretton Woods Agreement formalised the dollar's position as the world's reserve currency, making US Treasuries convertible to gold at US$35/oz. Bretton Woods formalised a system which established huge synthetic demand for US debt.

At that point, we still had a form of the long-standing gold-for-oil standard – for example, Saudi Arabia was receiving gold equivalence (in the form of US Treasuries) in return for its oil; the historic gold/oil equilibrium was still intact. The 1970s, though, brought change and lots of it. In 1971, US President Richard Nixon announced a 'temporary suspension' of the dollar's convertibility to gold, in an effort to address the spectre of a run on this so-called 'gold window'.

On the back of this, a new way of ensuring continued demand for dollars was required, and the Saudis were quick to lend a helping hand. Indeed, in 1973 Saudi Arabia agreed to accept only dollars for its oil in exchange for military support and resources. It also agreed to buy US Treasuries with these dollars. Once the rest of OPEC was on board by 1975 – agreeing to no bilateral currency deals for oil – the circle was complete for King Dollar. With a formal petrodollar agreement in place, gold had been temporarily suspended from the heart of the monetary system. And in one fell swoop, the unfettered 'exorbitant privilege' of global reserve status was bestowed upon the dollar.

Fast forward 42 years. This agreement is crumbling and gold is retaking its rightful place as apolitical money par excellence. But is the global monetary system undergoing a tectonic re-shaping, or are the tectonic plates merely returning to their natural position?

3. EAST AND WEST ARE DIVERGING: AND GOLD IS AT THE HEART OF IT.

Countries that have not benefited from the dollar's reserve currency status are now creating direct bilateral swap agreements, adding to their gold reserves, and reducing US debt holdings. China and Russia have done long-term oil and gas deals, in renminbi, to the value of almost US$700bn. China is paying in renminbi for oil from Iran, while India has paid for oil from Iran in gold. These are but a few examples of dollar disintermediation.

In what seems a game-changer, the new Shanghai International Gold Exchange permits the direct exchange of renminbi for physical gold. So we now have the renminbi as an oil-gold intermediary, much as the dollar once was: sell oil for renminbi and convert to gold.

China has reduced its Treasury exposure by more than 7% since May 2016 – providing further evidence of this global shift. Russia and Saudi Arabia, too, are sellers. We are in a moment of flux; the East is bypassing the long-agreed way of doing things, as prescribed by the West. Projects and organisations such as the Silk Road Economic Belt and the Asia Infrastructure Investment Bank are taking the place of the likes of the International Monetary Fund (IMF) and the World Bank as the go-to providers of financial support for the emerging world.

The East and the West look to be diverging, with dollars, renminbi, oil and gold at the heart of this shift.

4. BLOCKCHAIN IS HERE TO STAY – AND GOLD WILL MOVE ON IT.

Also central to the re-shaping of the global monetary system sits the distributed ledger technology of Blockchain, the electronic system that does away with the need for third-party intermediaries – such as banks or governments – in a financial transaction. We already know from the transfer of renminbi into gold that the precious metal is used as a conduit for intermediation, but the presence of Blockchain further moves the global monetary goalposts and potentially accelerates the re-emergence of gold as a global currency. Gold's issue of portability and divisibility is resolved by Blockchain.

One of the challenges of the existing system is the friction caused by third-party intermediaries. Such friction – whether through banks or currency exchanges – doesn't need to exist. The disintermediation of the monetary and banking sectors is happening whether you like it or not. Those dismissing the arrival of Blockchain and new crypto-currencies are as short-sighted as the mounted American farmer, ear of corn in his mouth, scoffing at the mechanic monstrosity he saw in the form of a passing Model T Ford. Much like the motorised vehicle in the early 20th century, Blockchain is here to stay.

Of course, the need for a new global monetary system isn't news to those within the IMF and World Bank. Back in 2010, the then-president of the World Bank, Robert Zoellick, predicted this scenario. He spoke of how the world needs a new, cooperative monetary system that reflects today's economic and monetary landscape. He predicted that any such new system would likely involve "a renminbi that moves towards internationalisation and then an open capital account."

"The system should also consider employing gold as an international reference point," he added.

And once gold is formerly reintegrated into the global monetary system – which seems just a matter of time – it too will inevitably start moving on the Blockchain.

5. THE LAST DAYS OF THE DOLLAR.

With the world's powers jostling at the edges of the global monetary system, the prospect of conflict is not a far-fetched one. The dollar's days as the world's reserve currency are in their autumn and the vultures are circling. But the stage may be set for the IMF, World Bank and G20 to come together to formulate a mutually beneficial currency agreement with gold at the centre – rather than the might of West or East. In other words, an agreement that services all.

Such a creation would likely involve the IMF's special drawing rights – an international reserve currency created by the IMF in 1969 to operate as a supplement to existing reserves of member countries – the dollar, the renminbi and, you guessed it, gold. And with the combination of the speed and frictionless nature of Blockchain and the natural discipline of real money, we should have the global monetary system that for so long we have lacked.

The people get sound money back, immediate and frictionless payments globally, and the state potentially gets total surveillance of the financial system – the cashless society it has long lusted after.

The wheel of history keeps turning.

Matthew Partridge

MATTHEW PARTRIDGE *is an experienced financial journalist. He writes for* MoneyWeek *magazine, Britain's biggest-selling personal finance weekly. A trained historian, Matthew did a degree in economics and history at the University of Durham, before doing a master's and a doctorate in economic history at the London School of Economics. He has taught at Goldsmiths, University of London, as well as spending time at various investment banks and a well-known economics consultancy.*

He is the author of Superinvestors *(Harriman House, 2017).*

"THE IMPORTANT THING IS TO MAKE SURE THAT YOU'RE EXPOSED TO OTHER VIEWS AND INFORMATION THAT ISN'T JUST THE DAILY CHATTER OF THE MARKET."

What I Learned From Studying the Greatest Investors in History

T HE AMOUNT OF information and advice available to ordinary investors has never been greater. The problem is distinguishing between genuinely useful information and advice which is useless or counterproductive. One approach is to look at those professional investors who have managed to beat the market by a significant amount over an extended period. In my book *Superinvestors: Lessons from the greatest investors in history*, I examine 20 such successful investors, including traders, venture capitalists, growth investors, value investors and some who are impossible to categorise. Here are the top ten lessons I learned from studying them.

1. IT IS POSSIBLE TO BEAT THE MARKET.

A few decades ago many academics believed in the efficient market hypothesis. This stated that it was impossible for someone to consistently outperform the stock market, unless they had some form of (illegal) inside information. It's hard to reconcile this hypothesis, at least in its strict form, with people like George Soros who made billions from the market, or with newer stars like Neil Woodford and Nick Train. A growing amount of research has also revealed a large number of market anomalies as well as evidence that behavioural quirks have a surprisingly large influence on market behaviour, creating opportunities.

Of course, it has to be admitted that many of the investors were extremely intelligent people. However, a surprising number came from more modest educational backgrounds, with some of the older generation of investors like the early 20th-century trading legend Jesse Livermore leaving school at a young age. Interestingly, barely more than half the investors in this hall of fame formally studied economics, finance or business. This suggests that a good training in the humanities or hard sciences can be just as useful to the investor. Overall, even in today's liquid, computerised markets, where information moves around the world in the blink of an eye, there are still a lot of opportunities out there for savvy investors.

2. THERE ARE MANY ROADS TO INVESTMENT SUCCESS.

Some investment strategies stand a better chance of success than others. For example, studies have shown that, over extended periods of time, fund managers who focus on buying cheap shares tend to do better on average than those funds and trusts that try to buy into fast-growing companies. Venture capital funds also tend to outperform the market, perhaps due to their illiquidity. However, the variety of approaches successfully employed by the greatest investors demonstrates that there are multiple ways to beat the market. Indeed, even those investors who had the same overall approach, such as growth investing, each had their own individual take on it.

Because there are multiple routes to success, the best idea is to find a strategy that matches your skills and resources, rather than adopting an approach that might be completely inappropriate. For example, short-term trading requires a lot of time to constantly monitor your positions and a high tolerance for risk. Therefore it isn't recommended for people who have a full-time day job, or are investing money to create a long-term pension pot. In that case, a more long-term strategy, such as buying shares in high-quality companies that have enough competitive advantage to deliver decades of growth and then holding them (like Philip Fisher) might be a more logical approach.

3. FLEXIBILITY IS IMPORTANT.

A surprising number of the great investors profiled in the book changed, or at least modified, their approaches as their investing careers developed. The most obvious example of this was John Maynard Keynes, who eventually abandoned both asset allocation and leveraged currency trading in favour of becoming an extremely successful value investor. Even those who maintained their overall approach throughout their careers were willing to make occasional exceptions, such as Benjamin Graham's decision to stick with his investment in GEICO long after it ceased to be a value stock.

Perhaps the best example of someone who didn't let his views restrict his investment behaviour is Paul Samuelson. Even when he started down the research path that would culminate in him (and others) coming up with the efficient market hypothesis, he would still actively invest his money, while his advocacy of passive investing didn't stop him being involved with the very active management of Commodities Corporation. His decision to respond to a letter from one of Buffett's fans by investigating Buffett, which ultimately led him to buy shares in Berkshire Hathaway, shows how being open-minded can help you make money.

4. DON'T CHOP AND CHANGE TOO MUCH.

While flexibility can be useful, too much of it can be dangerous. It's one thing to ditch a strategy that clearly isn't working, but changing it on a whim can lead to sloppy decision-making that can get you into trouble. One big problem is that the skills required for one type of investing don't always work in a different context. For example, successful traders need to be fleet-footed and ruthless about closing losing positions. In contrast, venture capitalists need huge reserves of patience as it may take years of losses for a company to start to be profitable. As a result, whenever traders get involved in long-term investments, or venture capitalists get involved in short-term trading, it usually ends badly.

The same can apply when picking funds to invest in. Investing with Fidelity Special Situations when it was run by Anthony Bolton would have made you a lot of money. However, those who followed his move to China experienced a lot of turbulence, even if they ended up slightly ahead in the end. Indeed, those who piled in after the first few good months saw the value of their investments plunge. Bolton himself admitted that the methods and assumptions that enabled him to prosper with British companies simply didn't work in an emerging market where fraud was rampant and the needs of shareholders came a distant second to the whims of management.

5. DON'T INVEST UNLESS YOU HAVE AN EDGE.

One thing that supporters of the efficient market hypothesis get right is that it is impossible for everybody to outperform the market, because for every winner there has to be a loser. Indeed, once you take transaction costs into account it is really a negative-sum game, where both sides of a trade collectively lose money. This doesn't mean that active investment is necessarily a bad idea, because a shrewd investor is more than able to compensate for the costs of trading, just as a card counter is able to overcome the house's edge in blackjack. However, if you don't have an edge then you would be better minimising the 'croupier's take' by sticking your money in a low-cost index fund.

Whether they found a successful strategy and stuck with it, or experimented until they found one that consistently worked, all the investors profiled in *Superinvestors* had some 'edge' that enabled them to beat the market. This ranged from Edward Thorp's use of statistical analysis to identify those stock options that were cheap (and those that were expensive) to John Templeton's awareness that there were far more undervalued companies in the rest of the world compared to America alone.

6. TAKE ADVANTAGE OF THOSE OPPORTUNITIES THAT ARISE.

Trading without an edge, or where the potential reward is relatively small, is a poor idea. However, when an opportunity to make a lot of money comes up, you should take the opportunity to put a large chunk of your portfolio into it. Most of the investors profiled in my book tended to have portfolios that were much more concentrated than their peers, because they felt that there were only a limited number of great opportunities. Even those traders who made their fortunes by grinding out a steady stream of small profits, like David Ricardo and Jesse Livermore, were willing to be much more aggressive at certain points in their careers.

Warren Buffett famously used the analogy of someone playing baseball. While mediocre baseball players swing at everything, the best will wait until the ideal pitch comes along which they can hit for a home run. Of course, investors are in an even better position than baseball players because there's no possibility of them being struck out, no matter how many pitches they allow to pass them by. Similarly, Edward O. Thorp bet heavily when his blackjack card-counting system indicated that the odds were in his favour and scaled his bets right down to the minimum when they weren't.

7. BEFORE BUYING, THINK ABOUT WHEN YOU'RE GOING TO SELL.

Deciding when to buy, or open a position, is clearly important. However, in some cases picking the correct time to sell, or cover a short position, can also play a huge role in determining how much money you can make from a trade. Sell a winning position too soon and you can pass up the opportunity of large profits, as Warren Buffett did with his initial investment in GEICO in the 1950s. Conversely, holding on to a losing position for too long can result in a minor loss turning into a disaster, as memorably happened in the case of Robert Wilson and Resorts International (discussed in more detail in chapter 16 of my book).

However, while useful, the old adage of 'sell your losers and let your winners run', also has its risks. Those who prematurely bail out of a losing position can end up sitting on the sidelines in frustration as it subsequently soars. Indeed, both Warren Buffett and Robert Wilson seemed to have long-term success by accepting the occasional short-term reversal. The overall lesson seems to be that whatever exit strategy you end up adopting, it's important to have some sort of plan. Such a plan needs to be appropriate to the time frame of your investment, the amount of risk that you're willing to take, and your ability to ride out periods of poor performance.

8. THE PLAYING FIELD IS LESS TILTED THAN YOU THINK.

Most of the investors profiled in *Superinvestors* managed other people's money. This meant they faced the threat of being removed from their positions, or investors withdrawing their money. They also faced various restrictions on how they invested their money, such as the amount of their portfolio they could put in each stock. While all of them managed to prosper, these restrictions negatively impacted their ability to make money. For example, Neil Woodford admits that he came under a lot of pressure to buy into overvalued technology shares during the height of the technology bubble. Keynes was extremely bitter about the extent to which the investment committees that he was on encouraged groupthink and discouraged original thinking.

Of course, professionals do have some advantages, such as teams of analysts at their beck and call and ready access to company executives. They also have the luxury of being able to spend all their time thinking about investments, rather than trying to make decisions during their spare time. It's also very hard for retail investors to invest in unlisted companies. Still, private investors have a lot more freedom to take positions that go against the consensus of the market, make big bets and don't have someone breathing down their necks. These factors help level the playing field somewhat, though only if you take advantage of them.

9. LARGE FUNDS CAN STRUGGLE TO BEAT THE MARKET.

Professionals benefit from having a large amount of money under their control, because fixed costs, like research and admin, can be spread over a greater asset base. Having a large amount of assets can also enable professionals to influence company policy at the board level. However, there are disadvantages as well. Unless the manager wants to spread his investments across a wider range of companies, with possible negative consequences for returns, having a large asset base effectively stops the manager from investing in companies below a certain size, making it hard to make the contrarian investments that will generate outsize returns.

One manager who has become too big to succeed as he used to is Warren Buffett, who has struggled to beat the market after the market cap of Berkshire Hathaway reached hundreds of billions of dollars. Indeed, he has repeatedly stated that if he were back to managing millions of dollars, he would be able to make the sort of deep-value investments in obscure companies that allowed him to generate huge returns during the 1950s and 60s when he was running BPL. It's notable that many investing legends, like George Soros, eventually shutter their funds to outsiders once they get beyond a certain size, and just focus on running their own money.

10. DON'T BECOME TRAPPED BY THE BUBBLE.

The majority of the great investors in *Superinvestors* located their funds or investment offices outside both London and New York, the two major global financial centres. Part of the reason was a desire to keep physical and emotional distance from the Wall Street (or City) consensus. This distance allowed them to see things with fresh eyes and therefore avoid making the same investments that everyone else was making. Naturally, this also applies to the ordinary investor. On the one hand, the rise of 24-hour financial television and financial websites means that you have access to the same information as the professional. However, if you're not careful then you can easily succumb to Wall Street (or City of London) groupthink.

It's therefore a sensible idea to take the occasional step back now and then. This can involve turning off the television, putting away the financial section of the newspaper, and looking at something that takes a different, more long-term view. This can be a general interest magazine (like the *Economist*) or even a financial magazine that has a slightly different take on things (like *MoneyWeek*). The important thing is to make sure that you're exposed to other views and information that isn't just the daily chatter of the market.

Jacob Rees-Mogg

JACOB REES-MOGG *attended Eton College and Trinity College, Oxford, where he graduated from in 1991. He started his career working for J. Rothschild Investment Management in London before joining Lloyd George Management in Hong Kong in 1993.*

Jacob pioneered the Global Emerging Markets equity products at LGM where, as lead portfolio manager, he grew the strategy's assets to over $5bn. In 2007 he co-founded Somerset Capital Management, a specialist Global Emerging Markets investment management firm. Over time the firm has grown to $8.9bn under management based in London and Singapore. Jacob was elected as the Member of Parliament for North East Somerset in May 2010.

"THE WHOLE POINT OF A COMPANY WITH HIDDEN VALUE IS THAT IT IS HIDDEN. IT WOULD BE A MIRACLE IF IT BECAME OBVIOUS JUST AFTER AN INVESTOR'S POSITION HAD BEEN FILLED."

Investing in Emerging Markets with Veins of Ice and Nerves of Steel

---

1. GO WHERE THE OPPORTUNITIES ARE.

"Some races increase, others are reduced, and in a short while the generations of living creatures are changed and like runners relay the torch of life."

— LUCRETIUS

THIS LIES BEHIND the attraction of emerging markets. It is the thought that there is no magic behind the economic success of the West in the past 200 years. It has come from stable political structures, property rights and an atmosphere that welcomes commerce. In recent decades countries which had followed a different path, with tightly controlled and centralised economies, have changed. This has led to economic growth and the flourishing of investment opportunities.

In the early stages, growth can be staggeringly high in percentage terms because of the low base effect. It can run for years and does not require the West to become poorer. However, the baton of economic growth has passed from the developed to the developing nations and it has taken with it the best stock market possibilities. So rule one is go where the opportunities are.

2. HAVE VEINS OF ICE AND NERVES OF STEEL.

"The time to buy is when there is blood in the streets."

— BARON ROTHSCHILD

This rule basically encourages contrarianism. In an area where the main theme is well known, the long-term prospect may well be priced in. However, investor sentiment waxes and wanes. It can be moved by matters that have nothing to do with economic fundamentals. When I first went to Hong Kong, rumours of Deng Xiaoping's death used to hit the market. As he was very old and the Chinese ruling elite were discreet, gossip abounded. However, each time the news provided a buying opportunity until his actual death when the market did not move. The same principle has applied when relations between China and Taiwan, or those between North and South Korea, have been tense.

Rule two, then, is to have veins of ice and nerves of steel.

3. DO NOT FORGET THE GLOBAL CONTEXT.

"If gold ruste, what shal iren do?"

— GEOFFREY CHAUCER, *THE CANTERBURY TALES*

As emerging markets have become a centrepiece of investors' strategies, so the issue of de-coupling has been a constant source of debate. It is a chimera. The world's largest economy remains the United States; and as was shown in 2008, if it is under strain this will hit emerging markets too. Likewise when it is doing well or its monetary policy is loose, this benefits global markets.

Thus the wise investor in emerging markets must keep an eye out for events in the mature ones. This does not contradict rule one but it is a reminder of the risk. The long-term prospects may be terrific but there will be short-term squalls which investors need to be prepared for. Over the years I have known people leave emerging markets at such times of crisis only to miss out on ensuing good years as the primary theme reasserted itself. Therefore rule three is do not forget the global context.

4. DO NOT LET THE BIG PICTURE DISTRACT YOU FROM THE DETAIL.

"The toad beneath the harrow knows / Exactly where each tooth-point goes; / The butterfly upon the road / Preaches contentment to that toad."

— RUDYARD KIPLING, 'PAGETT M.P.'

The investor needs to know his position relative to others in the market and stick to doing what he is good at. The toad by force of circumstance has to be a specialist; all he needs to focus on is the tooth-point of the harrow. The butterfly on the other hand can afford to look at the broad horizon. It could be dangerous for either to confuse their relative positions.

This means it is important to get both the macro and micro decisions right. It is easy to be beguiled by the strength of the emerging market story into investing in weak stocks with poor corporate governance. This will not lead to success. Company visits and a diligent study of reports and accounts are essential. Rule four is be like the toad.

5. KNOW AND ACCEPT THE LIMITATIONS OF ANY ANALYSIS.

"I cannot forecast to you the actions of Russia. It is a riddle wrapped in a mystery inside an enigma."

— WINSTON CHURCHILL

There are aspects of emerging markets which, while interesting, are essentially unfathomable. This applies particularly to political events which sometimes move markets but can on other occasions be ignored. Understanding the Chinese Communist Party is a particularly specialist task and yet its machinations determine economic policy. Even the discussion of politics is undertaken in a beautifully obscure language, so '7 in 8 out' means that the leaders have to retire at 68 unless of course it is Xi Jinping where the rule may not apply.

China is not alone; the power of the late King in Thailand was shrouded in mystery as military coups came and went. Similarly, Kremlinology has been a game for Russian specialists for centuries, working out what the Supreme Leader wants. Nonetheless, no foreign investor can have a truly clear view of the Kremlin. So the fifth rule is to know and accept the limitations of any analysis.

6. BACK YOUR OWN JUDGEMENT.

"If it were done when 'tis done, then 'twere well / It were done quickly."

— WILLIAM SHAKESPEARE, *MACBETH*

When a decision needs to be made or an idea has formed, act swiftly. The fear that there may be a currency devaluation or a coup, if it turns out to be correct, will not leave an opportunity to exit. If, therefore, it seems well-founded, place the sell order.

Equally, if a stock appears over-valued, sell it. Do not wait for everyone else to come to the same conclusion. Likewise, when detailed stock analysis shows a company to be worth buying, go ahead before the market realises the same.

Clever traders may be able to scrape a living on the margins of a multitude of orders but an investor who has come to the right conclusion must benefit from it by placing the order promptly. Delay often indicates uncertainty rather than prudence. Thus, the sixth rule is to back your own judgement.

7. BE DILIGENT AND KNOW MORE THAN THE COMPETITION.

"Knowledge itself is power."

— FRANCIS BACON

Market participants tend to have short memories; the United Kingdom, for example, had property bubbles in the late 80s and again 20 years later. But the knowledgeable investor knows what is happening and remembers what has happened.

Detail is important not only as to what a company does but as to whether the owners and managers are honest. Do they have a good reputation? Is the reputation justified? Detailed analysis can reveal hidden assets or non-consolidated liabilities. As accounting standards have become more uniform, this is less common than it was – but off balance sheet items remain potentially important and are normally listed in the notes to the accounts. When momentum is carrying the market away, debt to equity levels, accounts receivable or inventory days may be ignored. But when momentum turns, the problems come to the fore.

The knowledgeable investor will not be caught out and will live to invest for another day; the amateur could be wiped out. Rule seven is thus to be diligent and know more than the competition.

8. SELL THE BAD IDEAS.

"A man should never be ashamed to own he has been in the wrong, which is but saying, in other words, that he is wiser today than he was yesterday."

– ALEXANDER POPE

All the risks have been evaluated, the company visited and the fateful decision to buy the stock is made. Then the stock falls – so it is even better value. Surely it is right to buy more?

This will all depend on the circumstances. If some failing of the company has become apparent or the corporate governance is shown to be weak, then sell the stock. Sometimes, it may be that the country risk has changed and given a reason to sell. There is no shame in an investor changing his mind about a stock. His clients will forgive the trading cost much more readily than they will forgive an unnecessary loss.

The eighth rule requires a degree of modesty and humility rarely found in financiers. It is to sell the bad ideas.

9. RECOGNISE WHERE POWER LIES AND DO NOT TRY TO INVEST AGAINST IT.

"Political power grows out of the barrel of a gun."

– MAO TSE-TUNG

Emerging markets often have autocratic governments or have only recently become democracies. They rarely like being told what to do by foreign investors. It is, therefore, advisable to recognise where power lies and not to invest against it.

Yukos is the great Russian example, where Mr Putin decided that the owner, Mr Khodorkovsky, was an enemy, and so attacked the whole company. It is better and safer to invest in companies backed by the government and to avoid those run by opponents. Assuming politicians are rational, they will not attack companies they own with excess tax or regulation but will seek to protect them and help them grow. Sometimes this leads to inefficiency, as with Petrobras, but often it is a good route for investors. Hence rule nine is a version of 'do not fight the Fed', applied to emerging markets.

10. BE PATIENT – FORTUNE SOMETIMES TAKES A WHILE TO FAVOUR THE BOLD.

"How poor are they that have not patience!"

— SHAKESPEARE, *OTHELLO*

Investment managers profit by discovering stocks that other people have overlooked. Unfortunately, other people or the market do not necessarily realise this immediately.

The whole point of a company with hidden value is that it is hidden. It would be a miracle if it became obvious just after an investor's position had been filled. It can instead sometimes take a year or more for others to see the same virtue in a stock.

As long as this remains the case it is essential to wait. The easiest mistake to make is to lose heart and sell. Thus the final rule is to be patient. Fortune sometimes takes a while to favour the bold.

David Schneider

DAVID SCHNEIDER *is an analyst and writer who specialises in the inconsistencies and psychological basis of the modern financial landscape. He acquired his insights through experiences in the field of investment research and asset management.*

David bought his first stock in 1994 at age 18. He subsequently trained as a commercial banker in Germany and studied finance in London and Tokyo. David's time in the world of finance includes stints as Equity Research Associate at WestLB Panmure in Tokyo, covering Japanese consumer electronics stocks, and as financial consultant at Thomson Financial and Lloyds of London. In 2005, he co-founded two hedge funds with a Long/Short Equities strategy, working in Tokyo and Singapore.

*David is the founder of Nomadic Investor (**www.schneiderai.com**), a provider of international investment research, and co-host of the 80/20 Investing Show – a financial podcast which covers topics including wealth management, global financial markets, and finding investment opportunities around the world. In his free time, David likes to hit (and get hit at) his local boxing gym, or chase the F1 circuit around the world.*

He written works include the bestselling The 80/20 Investor *(2016).*

"THE PREREQUISITE OF FINANCIAL SUCCESS IS HAVING HIGH STANDARDS."

Before You Invest in
Businesses, Start a
Business

I F YOU STUDY the wealthiest people in your country, you will notice that they are either the largest land and property owners, or own businesses, or have a combination of both. In other words, they own and control income-producing assets. Hence, the best way to get extremely wealthy – or at least financially secure – is to own these types of assets. (I also count high-paying jobs, or unique and properly exploited talents, as income-producing assets.)

Despite this, the conventional wisdom when it comes to investing is to put your money into mutual funds (or other financial products) and wait. You are then encouraged to pass more of your money to various financial service providers, preferably on a monthly basis. They assure you they will take good care of it. Then all you need to do is hope like crazy that it all works out in the long term.

If it doesn't – tough luck.

More engaged folk might take it into their own hands. They study modern financial literature for the drop on the way the industry actually works. Oh boy, are they in for a treat! Besides Nobel Prize winners battling it out for intellectual supremacy, you'll notice buzzwords and phrases like 'P/E and Sharpe ratios', 'modern portfolio theory', 'asset allocation models', and so on. For the average retail investor, these terms have no meaning, and no value, if they don't help you avoid losing money. But the sad fact is, the average buyer of stocks or mutual funds and neophyte day traders in general suffer losses, or dramatic underperformance, no matter how well they've convinced themselves they know the game. Study after study shows that most retail investors stink at selecting investment products or timing the markets by trading them.

What passes for most 'investing' is really betting on price differentials. Many approaches involve techniques such as stock screenings, data or chart analysis – and nothing to do with long-term investment, generating monetary value, or contributing to society as a whole.

If you want to become a trader and full-time speculator, fine. But if you are interested in the subject of investing – that is, laying out money now in order to get more back in the future – you need to follow a different set of rules. The first might surprise you:

1. BEFORE YOU INVEST IN BUSINESSES, OPEN A BUSINESS.

Warren Buffett, with his usual sagacity, once said "I am a better investor because I am a businessman, and a better businessman because I am an investor."

If you study Warren Buffett's early life you can read up on how he started out by delivering newspapers, and then invested his savings in a pinball machine and a beaten-down Rolls-Royce car he rented out. He created his own business platform based on income-producing assets that could finance his future endeavors. He admitted that his early experiences going into businesses of his own taught him valuable lessons for his future career in money management and investing.

So before you even consider buying other people's assets, create your own assets first like Buffett did. That could be investing in yourself, or creating a business from scratch.

If you start your own business you need to monetize your passions, strengths or personal affinities. Today, with the diversity of digital platforms and the reach of the digital world, anyone can bootstrap simple income-producing assets.

Your first platform might not turn a profit quickly – but managed well, it will never bankrupt you. It will also teach you every valuable lesson about true business investing. You will learn the basic concepts of economics first hand – such as input and output, as well as price determination depending on demand and supply. You will learn the impact of economic cycles, and how to make your business less prone to them. You will truly understand the magic of compounding returns, which so many financial gurus rave about. You'll also experience a crash course in basic accounting and budgeting; you will see your money going out, but little (initially) coming in. You will learn to control your spending – a vital skill for any financial success. You will also come to understand the difference between real cash flows – i.e. cash hitting your bank account vs accounting earnings.

Finally, you will learn everything about modern marketing and promotional techniques needed to generate sales – how to encourage potential customers to open their wallets for you, from limited-time offers, to buy-one-get-one-free or those dreaded pressure-sales techniques Expedia.com is famous for (*"50 customers have booked this hotel in the last hour!"*). At the very least, you will become aware of these elaborate techniques when they're used on you.

2. ALWAYS ASSESS THE ODDS OF SUCCESS – AND GET USED TO KEEPING YOUR WALLET ZIPPED.

Having gone through your personal MBA course, you will know how difficult it is to establish and maintain profitable businesses. You will be aware that whenever you open your wallet to pass your money to someone else, you take substantial risks. Having your own assets will have taught you the skill of assessing the odds of success of each financial transaction. This alone will prevent you from gambling and taking stupid bets in financial markets. You will most likely end up keeping your wallet zipped most of the time.

3. COMPARE POSSIBLE RETURNS IN THE STOCK MARKETS WITH YOUR PERSONAL COST OF CAPITAL.

If you established your own cash engine first, and you have your own income-producing assets, you will soon realize that it would be foolish to put the money into the stock markets or any type of mutual fund *all the time*. The reason is you usually get much higher and better returns from the assets you control. Always compare potential returns with the returns you can achieve yourself at much less risk. Buying index funds – which might make you 5%, but could cost you 50% – will be far less attractive a prospect than investing in your own business, where you could make double-digit returns.

Ever wondered why top traders and investment managers are so eager to share their tips in expensive research and educational courses, or why they are so eager to manage your money? Well, they know that doing this is a very profitable business that generates far better returns *than actually following the investment advice and tips they give.*

4. AVOID OVERPAYING FOR OTHER PEOPLE'S ASSETS.

The biggest risk in investing in financial markets is not price volatility, but overpayment risk. Overpayment risk is simply to pay too much for the value you receive in return, i.e. you get much less than previously anticipated. It's common sense to ask for at least equal value for the price you paid. Having your own income-generating assets will train you for this; overpaying happens in public markets day in and day out. You always pay the price for popularity, and the result is mediocre returns, or even losses.

5. LET DIVERSIFICATION COME NATURALLY.

With assessing the odds of success with each financial transaction comes the topic of risk management. Today, there is an emphasis on over-diversification – people arguing that we need to hold 500 stocks or even thousands of stocks, with hundreds of bonds and several funds spread over all major asset classes at all times. This is what I like to call 'dumb diversification', and it has its limitations. What you end up with excessive diversification is meager returns at a high fee structure. Elaborate risk management always costs money, even if you use cheap index funds.

Investing by definition means taking chances on the future. We cannot completely eliminate this through diversification. Alternatively, with establishing your primary cash engine comes the understanding of natural diversification. All future cash flows must come from your primary income stream. Hence, efficient diversification means building several income streams over time and having sufficient cash reserves that will allow you to withstand any financial shock, like the one we experienced in 2008. With that you will never be forced to sell any of your assets at subpar prices or worse.

6. FOLLOW THE 80/20 WAY TO INVESTING.

Financial success relies on only a few decisions. For most, we ourselves are the best cash generators. So we should take care of ourselves first or own business endeavors. Realizing that, you should aim to simplify and streamline your investment strategy and portfolios.

By focusing only on the tasks and decisions that count in your life, you naturally become more selective with your investments and how you spend time on them. A consequence of this attitude is only to occasionally invest in financial markets – in other words when you are getting offered unbelievable odds of winning, and true value that will make all your efforts worthwhile.

7. NEVER FORGET RULE 1.

All the rules mentioned here lead back to the mother of all investment rules: Never lose money. By establishing your own income-producing assets first, you will appreciate this rule right from the start, instead of betting on price differentials and rising markets. With establishing your own assets comes awareness of the risks you are taking – and the demand for proper compensation. The prerequisite of financial success is having high standards.

For those already in business and with plenty of cash around, I would like to remind them why and how they got into the position they now find themselves in. It was certainly not through speculating wildly in stock markets and buying those esoteric financial products only bankers truly understand. I always refer them back to my first rule above, by elaborating what Benjamin Graham already observed almost 70 years back:

> "Investment is most intelligent when it is most businesslike. It is amazing to see how many capable businessmen try to operate in Wall Street with complete disregard of all the sound principles through which they have gained success in their own undertakings."

Edmund Shing

EDMUND SHING *is Global Head of Equity & Derivative Strategy at BNP Paribas, based in London.*

Edmund has previously worked at BCS Asset Management (as Global Equity portfolio manager), Barclays Capital (as Head of European Equity Strategy), BNP Paribas (as a Prop Trader), Julius Baer, Schroders and Goldman Sachs over a 21-year career in financial markets based in Paris and London.

He also holds a PhD in Artificial Intelligence from the University of Birmingham.

You can follow him on Twitter @TheIdleInvestor and his website – featuring regular market commentary and investing thoughts – can be found at **www.idleinvestor.com**.

"A FIRM DISCOVERED THAT THE CLIENTS THAT HAD SEEN THE BEST PERFORMANCE IN THEIR INVESTMENT PORTFOLIOS OVER THE LONG HAUL WERE THOSE WHO HAD (A) DIED, OR (B) FORGOTTEN THAT THEY HAD AN INVESTMENT ACCOUNT."

Know Thyself! And Pick a System to Suit You

A FTER OVER 20 years of working in finance for investment banks and fund managers, I have managed to make a lot of investing mistakes.

However, I had the misfortune of doing well with my early investments, made when I was still at school, and later on, when I was working in my first permanent job after university.

Why was this bad news? Simply because it gave me the impression that I could be a successful investor without much knowledge, experience or a system. Subsequently, I made a number of expensive investing mistakes, which underlined just how much I had to learn…

So the first investing rule I have learned over time is:

1. DON'T MISTAKE BEGINNER'S LUCK FOR INVESTING SKILL!

You will always make mistakes as an investor, the key is to make sure that you learn from them and do not repeat them in future. One of the biggest mistakes any investor can make is overconfidence in their own investing ability – in investing, as in many areas of life, pride often comes before a fall.

2. FIND AN INVESTING SYSTEM THAT SUITS YOUR AVAILABLE RESOURCES, AND YOUR CHARACTER.

Lots of very successful investors share a number of common characteristics. One of the most important of these is that they have an investing system that suits their temperament and character.

Investing is much easier once you have decided on a specific investing system or process that suits you. The first step is to ask yourself: *where are you going to concentrate your resources, i.e. your time and effort?*

I am relatively lucky, in that I work in finance on a full-time basis, so I have access to a lot of resources via my work, and I can also legitimately spend time on researching good investment themes and ideas.

I can therefore afford to use an investing system that is relatively time- and resource-intensive, as I have both at my disposal. In contrast, others may not, so will have to choose a different investing system that is not so time- or resource-hungry.

Personally, I have decided to devote my time and effort to two areas where academic research suggests that investors can create the most value in their investment portfolios over time:

- asset allocation, and
- small-cap value stocks.

3. PAY CLOSE ATTENTION TO YOUR ASSET ALLOCATION, AS YOU HAVE A GOOD CHANCE OF MAKING A BIG DIFFERENCE TO YOUR INVESTMENT RETURNS IN THIS AREA.

A mountain of academic research suggests that investors spend too much time researching the relative merits of buying the shares of one company rather than another, while over the long term the biggest difference we can make to our investment portfolios (both in terms of absolute performance and also in terms of reducing portfolio investment risk) is in **what asset classes and geographic regions** we invest in.

So I have dedicated a large slice of my personal investment portfolio to asset allocation, comparing the relative benefits of investing in equities, government bonds, corporate bonds, real estate and commodities. I use ETFs for the most part, as they can be easily bought and sold at any point during the trading day with certain knowledge of the price at which this is done (unlike unit trusts, which are priced just once per day).

However, I do also use investment trusts for certain asset allocations such as the European stock market, as:

1. certain regions and segments of asset classes like emerging markets stocks and small-cap stocks remain relatively inefficient, allowing plenty of scope for good fund managers to consistently outperform their benchmarks, and

2. I can also take advantage of any temporary widening of the share price discount to net asset value that investment trusts can sometimes trade at, i.e. a value strategy within asset allocation.

I force myself to diversify my asset allocation away from the UK to have investments in Continental Europe, the US and in emerging markets, and also try to make sure I don't just invest in stocks but in bonds and other asset classes such as commodities in order to reduce the risk of the overall portfolio. This also has the benefit of diversification in terms of currencies, making sure that I am not too tied to the vagaries of fluctuations in the pound sterling, for instance.

The overriding system I use for the asset allocation portion of my investment portfolio is trend following, which according to academic research has been demonstrated to generate strong absolute performance while limiting downside risk.

4. TRY TO FIGURE OUT WHERE YOUR INVESTING EDGE IS: WHERE CAN YOU HAVE AN ADVANTAGE OVER THE MARKET?

Another area that academic research has identified as inefficient are small-cap and micro-cap stocks. Professional fund managers tend not to look so much at this segment of the stock market, given the limited liquidity of these stocks. And this is what provides an excellent opportunity to the discerning private investor.

Value investing has also shown to work well over the long term, albeit with sometimes prolonged periods of underperformance. But for investors with a long time horizon like myself (I am investing in small-cap stocks in my personal pension), this can be an excellent investment strategy.

The system I employ is two-fold:

1. Firstly I screen the universe of small- and micro-cap stocks in the UK and Europe using a company database like Stockopedia for companies that fit my initial statistical criteria of appearing to offer value (on measures like enterprise value/earnings before interest

and tax) and also quality (such as return on invested capital and the Piotroski F-Score).

2. Once I have narrowed down this initial broad universe of stocks to a shortlist of candidates, I research each company to see whether I believe the company is well-run, has potentially hidden or under-valued assets, and has potential to grow well in the future.

I also look for potential catalysts to realise this value, including the attractions of the company as an acquisition for a bigger competitor, or the potential sale of an asset or division at a high price. As an obvious starting point, I check out the company's website and any recent investor presentations I find there.

This fits my character, as I do like to get value for money when I am out shopping, and I find difficulty in buying highly valued go-go growth stocks. Additionally, academic research has shown that buying expensive growth stocks over time does not deliver superior investing performance, but instead exposes the investor to greater risk of big losses.

5. RESIST THE TEMPTATION TO OVERTRADE YOUR PORTFOLIO.

While I am sitting in front of several computer screens full of financial information for much of my typical working day, this is not as helpful for my personal investment portfolio as you might think.

Devoting a lot of time on a frequent basis to investing is generally not a good thing for most people, as it can encourage screen-watching and thus overtrading of one's investment portfolio.

Remember that in a recent survey of their investment clients conducted by the US investment management firm Fidelity, they discovered that the group of clients that had seen the best performance in their investment portfolios over the long haul, were those who had either (a) died, or who had (b) forgotten that they had an investment account with Fidelity.

That is to say, the portfolios were left undisturbed for long periods of time, and thus had very low trading and administration costs detracting from their investment performance. So remember: often the best investment decision is to sit on your hands and do nothing.

6. ANY INVESTING SYSTEM WILL ONLY WORK IF YOU APPLY CONSISTENCY AND PATIENCE.

You may have worked through all the steps outlined above to come up with the investing system that you feel suits you and your investment goals best.

But this system will only work for you over time if you can summon the personal discipline to be both consistent in applying the system, and patient in giving the system a long time (I am talking years, not days or months here) to work for you.

Again, returning to the greatest investors of our time, these two qualities come up time and again as key characteristics of the best investors – much more than raw intelligence, for example. So be patient, and resist the temptation to change course!

7. LET PROFITS RUN, AND TAKE LOSSES BEFORE THEY BECOME TOO BIG AND PAINFUL.

I have to be honest: when I look back at my history as a private investor, I end up feeling quite disappointed. I can see that I have often taken investment risks that were too large, and as a result taken losses that were all too avoidable had I really learned from my previous mistakes.

Equally well, too often I have done my research on a particular company, bought a decent stake but then sold out for a quick profit, only subsequently to see the stock rise much, much higher on the back of the factors that I had identified in my research. In many cases, this is an even worse error. After all, you can only lose 100% in any given stock, but you can gain theoretically many multiples of that from continuing to hold a strong performer over the long term.

A fun fact for you to illustrate this point: did you know that just 4% of the companies in the US stock market have been responsible for the outperformance of the stock market in aggregate over cash since 1929?

So that means that the majority of companies didn't do very much, while a handful of stellar performers like Apple and Microsoft have generated the real excess performance of stocks over bonds and cash over the last few decades.

All the more reason to hold on to your winners.

There are several ways I am trying to avoid repeating these errors in future. Most importantly, I document each investment decision to buy or sell, writing down each time the reason for buying and selling.

When it comes to selling an existing position, I always ask myself the question: "Is there a good reason for me to sell today, at this level?" Behavioural finance research establishes that investors tend to take profits too quickly (thus missing out on large additional future profits), and hold on to losses for too long (i.e. not admitting their mistakes and managing investment risks appropriately). I have been just as guilty as the next man of making these mistakes, but I am trying to retrain myself.

I would never claim to be a great investor today: all I can do is to aim to practise these investment rules in my quest to become one.

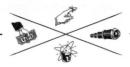

Peter Spiller

PETER SPILLER *founded CG Asset Management in 2000 and has been the lead manager of Capital Gearing Trust since 1982. He held previous roles as a partner and Strategy Director at Cazenove & Co Capital Management and as US equity investor at Capel Cure Myers.*

"MARKETS CAN
BE TIMED IF THE
HORIZON IS FAR
ENOUGH AWAY. IT
IS ONLY THE SHORT
TERM THAT IS
RANDOM."

In Investing, Only the Short Term is Random

1. FUNDS ARE A TAX HAVEN.

A LONG-TERM PORTFOLIO in a tax-paying account should invest in a fund if possible. The reason is that any capital gains tax is deferred until the investment is realised, or extinguished if held to death, rather than charged each year on realised gains. The difference over long periods can be startling.

I have been running Capital Gearing Trust for 35 years. Assuming an average 25% capital gains tax rate, an annual turnover of 20% (probably conservative) and an annual return of 15% (the actual rate achieved by the trust over the period), an investment of £1,000 in a discrete portfolio would have produced, after tax, cash proceeds of £51,298. Inside the fund, the actual return, even after paying a terminal capital gains tax of 25% to make the comparison fair, would be just over £100,000, and that is after all fees, which were ignored for the direct portfolio. That leads to the final advantage of a fund over a direct portfolio: namely that the fees are deducted before distributions, so that they are in effect tax-deductible.

Of course, these advantages are less the lower the tax rate, the fees and the return, but they are always positive.

2. ASSET ALLOCATION SHOULD RESPOND TO VALUES.

It is well established that asset allocation should reflect the time frame of the investor. Those close to retirement cannot afford the risk of having to sell assets at the bottom of a bear market, whereas a young worker can tolerate much greater volatility and illiquidity in her pension fund.

Academic institutions have an even longer, essentially unlimited time frame.

But that does not mean that those with a long horizon would always hold only equities, the asset class that has the best record of long-term returns and the highest volatility. That is because the balance of risk against returns is determined by the price of the asset. Far better for long-term investors is to shift the duration of their portfolio to reflect the prospective returns of each asset class. Fundamentally, the valuation of most assets reflects the long-term real risk-free interest rate. When real interest rates are high, valuations will be low and prospective returns good. The key point is that attractive prospective returns should be locked in for as long as possible; since equities are broadly speaking the longest duration asset, the asset allocation should heavily overweight them. Similarly, bond portfolios should have long duration. By contrast, when risk-free returns are low, duration on the portfolio should be as short as possible. That means short-dated bonds and low allocation to equities and probably property. Of course, relative values play a large role in all asset allocation. But the main point is that markets can be timed if the horizon is far enough away. It is only the short term that is random.

3. BEWARE OF ETFS.

ETFs are growing in popularity and often with very good reason. Few looking at the track record of active fund management in the S&P 500 in the US would conclude that the extra costs of an active fund are money well spent. Unfortunately, the great insight of index-tracking – that in well-researched liquid markets, prices are sufficiently efficient that the winners will be those with the lowest cost rather than the brightest mind – is not applicable to all markets. The less efficient and the less liquid a market, the less appropriate it is to invest through ETFs. That is true even of quite large asset classes like corporate bonds and smaller company equities. In both cases, ETFs purport to offer daily liquidity in an asset class that is of limited liquidity. In ordinary times, sales of underlying stock either by the ETF or the Authorised Participant (AP) with whom investors actually trade are easily absorbed. But in the event of sustained redemptions, those APs will not be willing to finance large inventories, not least because regulatory change has raised their cost of capital. They will simply lower their bid for the shares in the ETF, perhaps to a significant discount to the NAV or enough at least to show a profit after accepting discounted prices themselves to place the above-normal market size of the individual assets.

Effectively, investors will be unable to realise their assets at close to their 'real value'. If investors hold on until markets have stabilised, they should not suffer too much harm – but it is easy to see how downward momentum could gather in difficult markets. Given the size of ETFs, their problems could powerfully effect the valuation of the asset class. Put another way, the change in nature of the ownership of illiquid assets could make the dynamics of the next bear market in various assets quite different from those of the past. And the consequences for the real world are important. If the primary market for junk bonds, for instance, dries up, then companies may have difficulty in refinancing maturing debt.

4. CORPORATE GOVERNANCE MATTERS.

In the world of investment trusts, the board of directors is critical to the long-term success of an investment. The two critical variables are the total investment return, which is down to the manager, and the relationship of the share price to the net assets. Where those assets are liquid, there is no real excuse for a large discount; all discounts are voluntary. Unfortunately, not all directors understand that. Often they are appointed with little experience of investment trusts, though usually a record of success in something else. So that if, for instance, a trust is controlled by a manager who is indifferent to the interests of shareholders, it should be the job of the directors to make sure that the other shareholders, who may be called an oppressed minority, do not have to accept a large discount if they wish to sell their shares. Sadly, on occasion, directors fail to exercise that responsibility, whether through inertia, ignorance or lack of gumption.

Less extremely, powerful management houses sometimes give the impression of putting the size of their own funds under management ahead of the interests of shareholders. Once again, it is the role of directors to assert the interest of the latter, particularly where commitments made by the board are broken, e.g. the discount will never exceed x%. The lesson for investors is to avoid such trusts. The apparent attraction of a significant discount now can turn into the nightmare of a much wider discount in a bear market. Far better to buy on little or no discount where corporate governance is good and particularly where a zero discount mechanism is in place.

5. DON'T TRUST VOTES IN INVESTMENT TRUSTS.

Wind-up votes were introduced by imaginative investment bankers so that they could launch new trusts in a world where discounts were widespread. The concept was that new investors could relax about discounts in the short term because the vote, typically five or seven years later, would ensure a tight discount, or none at the point of the vote: a wide discount would always lead to a vote to liquidate the trust. Turkeys don't vote for Christmas and shareholders would always vote in their own interest.

In practice, that did not turn out to be true. Trusts on large discounts and sometimes dreadful performance have sailed through wind-up votes. The reasons are too numerous and on occasion ignoble to go into here, but the lesson is clear. Investors should buy such trusts only with deep knowledge both of the board and their fellow shareholders.

6. TURNOVER IS THE ENEMY OF PERFORMANCE.

It has become fashionable to note the importance of fees as a determinant of future returns. But fees are merely a subset of total costs and the impact of turnover can be substantial; think of commissions, dealing spreads and, for UK equities, stamp duty. Furthermore, since the short-term direction of markets is more or less random, with a slight bias to momentum, there is usually little advantage to high turnover. Much better to buy good value for the long term and simply ride out short-term fluctuations. That helps to avoid the final trap: trying to be too clever.

Greg
Steinmetz

GREG STEINMETZ *is a securities analyst for a New York investment firm. He is the author of* The Richest Man Who Ever Lived: The Life and Times of Jacob Fugger *(Simon & Schuster, 2015).*

"JACOB FUGGER (1459–1525) MADE A FORTUNE THAT, WHEN COMPARED TO THE GDP OF HIS DAY AND PUT IN CONTEMPORARY DOLLARS, CAME TO ABOUT $400 BILLION."

Value Investing in the Age of Leonardo

JACOB FUGGER DIED a century before the launch of the first stock exchange. But he nevertheless knew as much about value investing as anyone. Fugger was a banker in Renaissance Germany who was born in 1459. His customers included kings and several popes. He persuaded one of the popes to legalize the charging of interest on loans. He tangled with Martin Luther. He handpicked an emperor who presided over the largest realm in history until the arrival of Napoleon and Hitler. Along the way, Fugger made a fortune that, when compared to the GDP of his day and put in contemporary dollars, came to about $400 billion.

Fugger made his money by following some simple rules that will surprise no one:

1. Buy when others fear.
2. Focus resources on the best ideas.
3. Listen to one's own counsel.
4. Know the numbers before plunging.
5. Compare the reward with the risk.
6. Stay abreast of new information.
7. If the facts are on your side, stay the course.

None of these are blinding insights. The list is nothing more than the value investor's playbook.

So what's the point of studying Fugger? I think the value comes from the inspiration his story provides to stick to the rules. Fugger's example shows that value investing has stood the test of time. Modern markets are generally efficient. The same could be said of markets in Fugger's era. The Frankfurt Trade Fair, by allowing goods from all over Europe to be compared side by side, saw to that. But inefficiencies still occurred. For centuries, it has been the inefficiencies that have created opportunity for the value crowd.

Fugger's first big trade came when he was in his 30s. After the Venetians threatened to topple Sigmund of Tyrol, the duke's bankers abandoned him. Fugger borrowed everything he could from friends and family. He loaned money to the duke to pay the Venetians and make them go away. The duke paid Fugger back at 20% interest. He used Fugger as his primary banker for the rest of his life. Fugger would have been ruined and in debtor's prison had the duke not repaid. But Fugger calculated the odds of failure as small. He knew the Venetians from his time as an apprentice on the Grand Canal. He knew their price. He also knew Sigmund was good for the money because his collateral consisted of the largest silver mines in Europe. Everything the duke needed to repay Fugger was in the ground just waiting to be mined. An inefficient market would not have allowed Fugger to charge 20%. But fear – the incalculable emotional component of investing – kept others away.

Fugger showed his cool under fire a few years later when one of his largest lenders, an Austrian bishop, abruptly died and the church sought to withdraw the money immediately. Fugger's money was tied up in loans. He was insufficiently liquid to meet the request. If word got out that Fugger lacked ready cash, there would be a bank run and Fugger would be finished. Fugger quietly negotiated the withdrawal while at the same time, in a bit of play acting, loaned money at a furious pace in a bid to quash rumors of financial distress.

Fugger knew his numbers. To say he was an early adopter of double-entry bookkeeping is an understatement. He learned accounting from Venetian merchants a few years before the appearance of the first accounting textbook. He was the first to send auditors to the field to verify numbers sent by his managers. He was the first to keep a consolidated balance sheet. It combined numbers for all his operations in a single statement. This is all routine now. It has survived since Fugger's time because of its brilliance.

Fugger had supreme confidence in his ability to analyze a situation. Towards the end of his life, the king of Hungary seized Fugger's copper mines in the Carpathian mountains. The Turks were plotting to take Hungary and had gotten as far as Belgrade. Fugger knew the king needed Fugger and his cash more than he needed the king. He refused to give an inch and demanded full restoration of his property plus penalties. The king refused and, lacking Fugger's financial support to mount a proper defense, was killed by the Turks in combat. With the king dead, Fugger put up money to fund the defense of Hungary. The Turks were repelled and the dead king's successor gave up the claim to Fugger's mines.

The most common mistake of mutual fund investors is to buy when stocks are high and sell when they are weak. That's not a mistake Fugger would have made. Again and again over his long career, he allocated capital at times when asset prices were down. His reliance on the facts made him one of the richest people who ever lived. What more evidence does one need to follow the principles of value investing?

Tom
Stevenson

TOM STEVENSON *is an investment director at Fidelity Personal Investing, the division of Fidelity International serving self-directed investors. He is responsible for formulating and articulating investment strategy and representing the business as a spokesperson, broadcaster and columnist.*

Before joining Fidelity, Tom was a financial journalist, working for a range of publications in the UK including The Independent *and* The Daily Telegraph, *for which he continues to write a weekly column. He appears regularly on Sky News and the BBC.*

"LOSING MONEY IS VERY BAD PREPARATION FOR RATIONAL DECISION-MAKING."

Don't Lose Money – It's Hard to Replace

1. DON'T CONFUSE RISK AND VOLATILITY.

O NE OF THE myths about the stock market is that it is volatile and therefore risky. Equity markets are often volatile but the long-term evidence is that it is far more risky to be out of the market than in it. Our research shows that £1,000 invested 20 years ago in the UK stock market would be worth £3,700 today with income re-invested. Missing just the best ten days in the market over that period, however, would reduce the total return to £2,000 and missing the best 40 days would take the final amount down to just £670. The only risk that matters to an investor is permanent loss of real, inflation-adjusted capital. The short-term ups and downs of the market are not a risk but an opportunity to buy the best-performing asset class at a temporarily attractive price.

2. DON'T DITHER – BE A HUNTER OR AN ASSASSIN, NOT A RABBIT.

One of the best books I have ever read on investment is Lee Freeman-Shor's *The Art of Execution* (Harriman House, 2015). One of its central ideas is that different investors react differently to significant moves in the price of an investment. For example, a 20% fall in a share price might lead one investor to cut his loss immediately. Freeman-Shor calls this investor an assassin. Another might take the opportunity to buy more of the stock. This investor is a hunter. The type of investor that comes in for the biggest criticism is the one who ends up frozen in the headlights, doing nothing but desperately hoping that the price will rise again. This is the rabbit, the ditherer who can't decide what to do. That's most of us, unfortunately!

3. WRITE DOWN WHY YOU ARE MAKING AN INVESTMENT.

This is a tip I picked up from Anthony Bolton, the Fidelity legend who ran the Special Situations fund so successfully for 28 years. Anthony always recommended making a note of the investment thesis underpinning every investment. By doing this, you will have something objective and unemotional to hang on to when a share has fallen below your entry price and you are starting to panic. Losing money is very bad preparation for rational decision-making. Knowing why you liked the stock in the first place will help you decide whether you still like it when things are moving against you.

4. JUST DO IT – START NOW.

One of my favourite investment allegories tells the story of Prudence and Extravaganza, two sisters with very different approaches to investing. The first starts young and saves hard for 20 years. Her sister enjoys herself for those two decades and delays saving, although when she does start she saves the same amount, just as regularly. Both benefit from the most powerful force in investment – the magic of compounding. The only difference is that only one of them also benefits from the second most powerful force – time. The outcomes of their respective investment strategies could not be more different. Prudence saves £1,000 a year between the ages of 18 and 38 and then stops saving but continues to watch her investments grow. By the time she is 60 she has invested £20,000 and has a retirement pot worth £500,000. Her sister also saves £20,000 between the ages of 38 and 58. By the time she is 60, her pot is worth just £80,000.

5. BE DIVERSIFIED – NO ONE HAS A CRYSTAL BALL.

Trying to predict the best-performing asset class year in year out is a fool's errand. Indeed, over the last 20 years no asset class has managed to hold on to its title of being the best performer over consecutive years. A balanced portfolio, split between equities, bonds, real estate, commodities and cash, can help smooth investment returns and lead to better long-term outcomes. What's interesting is that the relationship between risky assets such as equities and commodities and defensive assets like bonds and cash is not symmetrical. Over the past 20 years there have been a number of years when risky and defensive assets have balanced each other out, leading to a neutral overall return. There have been some years when everything has risen together. But what the past 20 years has not delivered is a single year in which everything has fallen together. This is good news for a hands-off, long-term investor because it means that they can sensibly invest in a well-balanced portfolio and just forget about it.

6. DON'T DISMISS THE OBVIOUS – SOMETIMES THE TRUTH IS UNDER YOUR NOSE.

One of the biggest surprises of 2016 was the result of the UK referendum. Right up until the votes were counted, no one expected Britain to vote to leave the EU. What took many investors even more by surprise was the market's reaction to Brexit. By the end of the year, the UK stock market had soared. This should not have been so surprising. Everyone assumed that the uncertainty of Brexit would be bad news for UK-listed shares. But what everyone forgot to factor in was the impact of sterling. The pound also dislikes uncertainty and it fell sharply after the referendum. That turned out to be very good news for the FTSE 100, which is one of the world's most international stock indices, full of exporters and overseas earners and so a major beneficiary of a weaker currency. It's amazing how few people understood that in the panicky aftermath of the Brexit vote.

7. WHEN SOMETHING LOOKS CRAZY, IT PROBABLY IS.

I have lived through a few market cycles during my investing career. None has been more spectacular than the dotcom bubble and subsequent crash. With the benefit of hindsight, it is now obvious that investors took leave of their senses in 1999, inflating valuations to ridiculous levels that bore no relation to reality. I remember taking part in the launch of a so-called incubator fund – essentially a pile of cash looking for a home in then red-hot internet stocks. At launch the fund had a net asset value of 5p per share. On the first day of dealings, the share price rose to around 50p. When someone offers you £10 for a £1 coin, you know that something has gone badly awry.

8. ASK YOURSELF: 'WOULD I BUY THIS IF I DIDN'T OWN IT?'

Of all the behavioural biases that lead us to poor investment outcomes, few are as powerful as the *endowment effect*. It's a fancy term for putting a higher value on something we own than the same asset that we do not. It's why houses can sit on the market for such a long time – all those happy memories make the same bricks and mortar worth a lot more to the owner than the potential buyer. Another way of expressing this is falling in love with what you own, a common fault among investors. We think that because we chose an investment it must be a good one. Admitting we got it wrong is just too hard. Step back from all the emotion invested in the house or share and you are more likely to form an objective view. If you wouldn't buy it now, maybe you shouldn't hold on to it.

9. DON'T LOSE MONEY – IT'S HARD TO REPLACE.

This one is stolen from Warren Buffett. Who hasn't done that? Buffett puts it nicely: *Rule number one, don't lose money; rule number two, don't forget rule one.* The arithmetic behind this adage is simple. If you lose 50% on a share you need to gain 100% just to get back to square one. It's quite easy to lack the self-discipline to cut your losses and so to lose half your money. Doubling your money on an investment is altogether more challenging.

10. REINVEST YOUR DIVIDENDS – LET COMPOUNDING WEAVE ITS FULL MAGIC.

Deferred gratification is one of the hardest rules to apply but learning to wait is the key to successful investment. The Rule of 72 says that dividing your annual rate of return into the number 72 tells you how many years it takes to double your money. It should be obvious that achieving a higher rate of return will deliver your financial goals more quickly. And there is no easier way of increasing your annual return than adding the dividend yield to the capital gain. According to the Barclays Equity Gilt Study, £100 invested in 1899 in the UK stock market would have turned into £16,000 by the end of 2016 if you had spent the dividends on your shares each year. If you had reinvested them, however, that same £100 would have turned into a staggering £2.6m.

Van K. Tharp

VAN K. THARP *is a leading international professional trading coach. Dr Tharp has written 11 books about what creates trading success. His research and modeling work with outstanding traders over the past 30 years has made his training programs among the most well-respected in the world. His programs offer unique learning strategies and effective techniques for producing Super Traders.*

Dr Tharp is the only trading coach featured in Jack Schwager's bestselling book, Market Wizards: Interviews with Top Traders *(Wiley, 2012).*

He is the author of Trading Beyond the Matrix: The Red Pill For Traders *(Wiley, 2013),* Super Trader *(McGraw-Hill, 2009),* Trade Your Way to Financial Freedom *(McGraw-Hill, 2006) and* Safe Strategies for Financial Freedom *(McGraw-Hill, 2004).*

His self-published Definitive Guide to Position Sizing Strategies *is the textbook serious traders keep by their side, and the five books in his acclaimed* Peak Performance Home Study Course *offer powerful exercises to accelerate market success.*

"WHAT YOU CREATE INSIDE YOUR HEAD IS AN ILLUSION THAT JUST REPRESENTS THE WORLD OUT THERE, BUT IS NEVER THE SAME AS THAT WORLD."

You Don't Trade the Markets: You Trade Your Beliefs About Them

M Y PRIMARY ROLES in life are coaching traders and modeling neuro-linguistic programming (NLP) processes. As a modeler, I determine how the best in the world do what they do, and then teach those skills to others. As a result of modeling many great traders, I have developed one fundamental belief about trading – you don't trade the markets: you trade your beliefs about the markets. This chapter explores important premises about what that means.

My NLP work has been strongly influenced by the work of Alfred Korzybski. Korzybski is known for founding a field of study called General Semantics,[*] an interdisciplinary methodology that encompasses not only semantics, but also linguistics, grammar, behavioral sciences, physiology, etc.

In his development of General Semantics, a fundamental presupposition of Alfred Korzybski was that the map is not the territory. To boil this down to its essence, your sensory experience of the world is simply a map of the world; it is not the world itself.

Think about this: what is 'out there' in the world is energy and particles. Our senses, instead, detect these waves and particles, and convert them into specific types of neural representations. Let's take a specific example from the world: color. Color does not exist out there in the world. From the wide range of wavelengths we sense as light, cone cells in our retinas transform the vibration of a narrow wave length into a specific color. Humans are trichromatic (the retina contains three types of color receptor cells, or cones). Each of these types of receptors work together to translate the vibrations into the spectrum we know as visible light.

---

[*]   Alfred Korzybski. *Science and Sanity*, 5th Edition. Fort Worth, Texas: Institute for General Semantics, 1994. Third printing 2005.

CONE	COLOR	WAVELENGTH
Short Wavelength S-Cones	Blue/Blue Violet	450 nm
Middle Wavelength M-Cones	Green	540 nm
Long Wavelength L-Cones	Red	570 nm

We see colors – but that is a map of the world and not the world directly. This is important to understand, because even at the sense level, our experience is not the same as what's out there in the world. The world gives us 570 nm waves and through our L-Cones, we experience that energy as red. While we see red, green, blue, or some combination of those, we don't experience the energy that is actually out there. That's just our experience and we tend to think of that as real or reality. The world has many more wavelengths of energy that we can never see at all. Still, those wavelengths are everywhere out there nonetheless.

Once we have had a sensory experience, we extend our map to something more beyond just our sensory experience itself. We look at our internal representation and name it using language. This process is really a meta commentary about our sense representations. "Yes, I see that. It's a color and it's red." After labeling, wavelengths at 570 nm become at least two steps removed from the word 'red'.

Furthermore, we all give words different meanings. For example, what does the color red look like? How about rose, chestnut, cherry, magenta, fuchsia, burgundy, crimson, scarlet, cerise, or claret? Would your meaning for each word match someone else's meaning? In this example, we are just talking about colors.

Now, what if I say the word 'dog'? Close your eyes, think of 'dog' and notice what you picture? Was it any of the types of dogs shown in the following pictures, or was it something else? Even if you pictured a German Shepherd, did it look exactly like the one in the picture? Probably not.

Let's look at examples of what else people do with language. I would describe my dog Tigger (he's a Papillon, not represented in the pictures) as an athletic dog. Why? Because he can do things that my other Papillon cannot do – like jump over the living-room couch. But how athletic is he really? He doesn't spend the entire day jumping over couches or running around. Tigger's athletic feats might happen two to three times a day and each one might take him about ten seconds. So out of a whole day, he does athletic things for maybe 30 seconds and I have labeled him athletic, simply because that's how I think about him. Thirty seconds each day is approximately 0.0003472% of the day that he spends being athletic. What does he do for the rest of the day? Mostly, he naps. In fact, it's safe to say that he spends probably more than 50% of his day lying prone on the floor in the house, with his eyes closed. But… I call him athletic.

That's how misleading our words can be – I use the description *athletic* based upon Tigger's potential, not what he spends his time doing. And even the judgment of his potential is based upon comparing him with my other Papillon, Ari, who I would say is not athletic. I labeled something I think I know and then I treat that as real without spending any more time thinking about it. As illustrated with this very simple example, thinking about the label for a bit reveals how my map does not match the territory.

We do even more with language than we do with the senses. We turn verbs or processes into nouns and then assume that the noun is real. For example, 'the map is not the territory' might be restated as: internal reality is not the same as external reality. While this may be true, I wouldn't make that statement because reality is just a process. Reality – whether internal or external – is always changing, but we've turned something dynamic into a noun, and we think we know what it is. Even deciding what reality is is a process. So, what do you think is the process of deciding what reality is?

The market is an example of turning a process (numerous buy and sell transactions that occur throughout the day) into a noun. What is the market to you? Write down your answer before you continue.

Is it watching a tape of stock prices on CNBC? Is it a bar chart showing daily prices for a major index over the last year? Is it Jim Cramer dramatizing about certain stocks? It is a bunch of traders at a bank giving bid/ask prices for the Swiss franc?

If I asked someone to show me the market, they'd probably show me some kind of price chart. But, is that the market? Look at the daily bar chart of Google below that covers about six months. Is that the market? There are also three simple moving averages (MAs) on the chart, the 10-day, the 21-day, and the 50-day. Do those MAs in any way represent the market?

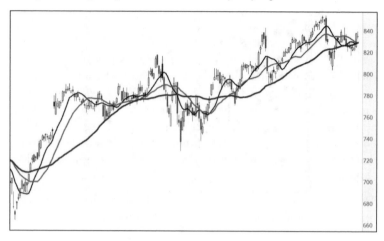

Remember that *you* create your maps of the market. You give meaning to those maps. So, you can decide that the market is anything you want it to be. When you do so, however, it's important to be aware of what you are doing in the process of deciding what it is. If you have that awareness, then you can ask a simple question that can change everything about your experience: Is my representation useful? Or better yet, can I form any beliefs about this representation that are useful (for example, useful to make money)?

If the market really is buyers and sellers getting together to agree upon a particular price at a particular time, then perhaps a tick chart would be the best representation. Each tick would be a dot, representing a buyer and a seller agreeing on a price at a point in time.

Also, remember that you decide (invent) the size of the window you use. One window could have a million ticks or a thousand ticks. In addition, when you have a tick data feed, there is no way that you can get all the ticks from the market when you attempt to collect them. You will have to ask, "What's missing? Why are they missing?"

If we take a tick chart, we could organize it arbitrarily by grouping the ticks into windows of ten minutes or a certain number of ticks, say 100. Such a tick chart might look like the following, where the vertical lines could separate time periods or numbers of ticks. For our purposes, we'll say that each vertical line represents ten minutes' worth of ticks.

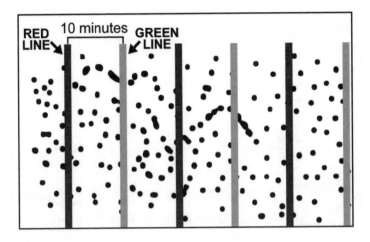

Most people would look at such a chart and say it's meaningless or I can't make heads or tails of it or it's just a bunch of dots. Because human beings are meaning makers, it's our nature to make meaning out of what we are dealing with and if we find something that doesn't seem to have much meaning for us we'll convert it to something that does. Thus, you might look at the hundreds of tick dots and decide that graph is meaningless. It might be the best visual representation of the market but you don't like it because it seems meaningless. As a result, you decide to convert the tick chart into a bar chart or a candlestick chart.* Many traders use bar charts or candlestick charts believing they are good representations of the market (even though, statistically speaking, they are not).

So, look at the tick chart and imagine that between the vertical lines, the first tick means something, the last tick means something, the high tick and the low tick also mean something. You could then plot those points. By doing so, remember that you have decided that certain points on the tick chart mean something while the others might have a different meaning – or are meaningless. When you assign a meaning to the first, last, high and low ticks, you get a price bar or a candlestick which you can see below. But does that price bar or candlestick have more meaning than the tick chart? Or does it have different meanings than the tick chart? Does it mean anything?

---

*   A bar chart is a line that emphasizes the high and low (the two ends) and the open and the close. A candlestick chart is a bar chart that shades the area between the open and the close green if the close is higher and red if the close is lower. Both show the same information, but we tend to think that the candlestick gives us more meaning.

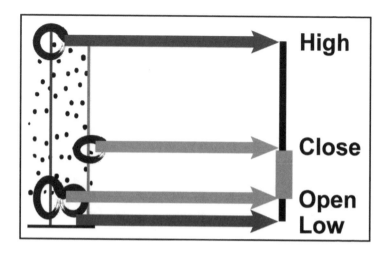

Notice that in converting ticks for a five-minute period into a candlestick, we have produced something that might help us interpret price action. Someone might say, "Price went way up and slightly down compared to the open. Also, the closing price was way down from the high but it was above the open." Those are meanings you could easily give that particular candlestick. But if you examine the open tick:

1. it could have been the selected one or another one near the top instead

2. the high of the period was probably the second or third tick

3. there were two ticks on the ending time line and either one might have been selected for the close.

If you had selected the lower one, the close would have been lower than the open instead of above the open. Most importantly, however, any conclusion you might draw from the candlestick would probably never be drawn from the chart showing all the ticks during the five minutes. Yet some people might argue that the five-minute candlestick is one of the purest forms of information that most traders use to represent the market. Candlesticks are how many traders make sense out of the market or give it meaning.

Let's think some more about what might happen just using ticks. What if the low of the bar represented just one tick and all of the rest of the ticks centered closely around the mean of the prior period of ticks? In addition, another tick might be way out of the cluster but it is the high of the day. In a bar chart, you cannot see that a single outlying tick made the high price or low price for the period. You just see that the bar reached the low or the high and suddenly those two prices have particular meanings for you. You might even label those prices as *support* or *resistance*… more names and more meanings.

In fact, when you ignore the chart showing raw ticks, you are saying that the first chunk does not have any meaning with respect to the second chunk because we arbitrarily drew lines to separate the ticks. No statistician would do something like this. Neither would an engineer. A statistician would probably find the mean of each time period and then use the standard deviation as a reasonable measure around the mean.

Also, remember that you decide (invent) the size of the window you use. One window could have a million ticks or a thousand ticks. In addition, when you have a tick data feed, there is no way that you get all the ticks from the market when you attempt to collect them. What's missing? Why?

It goes further. Someone trying to make sense of the market might then average the closing price on a certain number of bars, create a moving average, and decide that the moving average means something. They might say, "prices just crossed above the moving average, the market is going up."

Let's think some more about what might happen with just ticks. What if there were a few extreme ticks? What if the low of the bar just represents one tick (which is way down) and everything else is just within one standard deviation of the mean of the prior bar? You could have one tick that is way out but is the high of the day. Moreover, you do not see that in the bar chart. You just see that one tick represented as the high of the day and suddenly it has meaning for you. You might even call it a support/resistance point… another name that you give some meaning.

Let's say that you see that the market is going up but that is not enough of a reason for you to buy. You can't make enough meaning from a bar chart with an upward trend. You need some more indicators. You add some moving averages based on each bar's close (i.e. why did you decide to use the close rather than something else like (hi+lo+close)/3 ?). Then you might decide that when one moving average crosses the other, that is significant. You want a 'solid signal' like the ten-day moving average crosses above the 21-day MA. In the Google chart shown earlier, that signal shows up the first time on the far left and it's a pretty good buying signal, but when it crosses below it's often near a market low. Notice how much meaning you have now given to these particular signals – they are causes for action. But can you decide about buy and sell signals from just a few examples in a single chart? Probably not.

If you cannot get enough meaning from moving averages on candlestick charts, then you might want to distort the price data a little more to give you something else to which you can give meaning. You look at stochastic signals. You look at ADX and DMI signals. You look at relative strength signals. You even invent your own indicators. Eventually you find something that manages to give you enough information (according to the meaning you give it) to convince you that an idea might work.

How do you convince yourself, for example, that a set of rules in a trading system works? Did you know that you have a mental strategy for convincing yourself? You use it all of the time. What's your strategy? Do you have to see something for you to be convinced? If so, how many times? Do you have to hear someone else tell you that something works? If so, how many times or from how many people? Do you have to do something like go through 50 different trades, bar by bar, to see that a system works? Maybe the experience of going through it convinces you. Do you have to understand intellectually why it will work? Perhaps your convincer strategy is a complex combination of two or more of the simpler strategies.

The bottom line is that you do have some mental strategy that will convince you a trading system works. It might or might not be a great strategy. After seeing about ten successful trades of buying when the green arrow appears on the screen and selling when the red arrow appears, some people will spend thousands of dollars on software that shows arrows on charts. That kind of convincer strategy and other similar ones might get you in a lot of trouble, but nevertheless, you'll try anything that meets your convincer strategy criteria.

Can you begin to understand what people do?

1. We take the process of buying or selling equities or futures or forex or options and turn it into a noun called the market.

2. We then have to make some meaning out of the market, so we re-present it to ourselves in some way. Tick dots are probably the closest to what actually happens. Structurally, a tick dot is the most similar to the sell-buy process between two individuals but even still, representing the pricing process with a dot is a big distortion.

3. Nobody looks at tick dots, so perhaps the closest thing to what's actually happening in the market is a tick candlestick. But that can be very misleading as shown by the figures in this chapter.

4. Because you need to make meaning out of how you represent the market, you continually transform information about the market

into something to which you can give enough meaning to allow you to make a decision. By the time you give the information meaning, it may have become quite distorted. For example, you go from dots representing ticks to a stochastic.

5. You need to decide when to buy and sell, so you make up some rules. And if you can convince yourself using some arbitrary convincer strategy that fits you, you might actually use those rules and trade the system.

Can you begin to understand how you are trading your beliefs about the market rather than the market itself? How it's all an illusion, the map that you have created? If you pay attention to the various internal maps that people have created you will find that many of them, if not most, are useless and only a few are useful. Finding the useful maps is what modeling excellence is all about.

Warren Buffett has said "you should know every detail about every listed stock". When someone responded by saying there are 7,000 listed stocks, his retort was "Start with the As." Some people think that because Warren Buffett said it, it might be the secret to making money in the market. To me, however, that advice is a completely useless belief that will waste a lot of your time if not also waste a lot of your money if you were to try and follow it. You have to be able to sort garbage beliefs from useful beliefs.

Useful beliefs help you make money in the appropriate contexts, but how do you find useful ones? In my book, *Trading Beyond the Matrix: The Red Pill For Traders and Investors*, I present a series of 55 beliefs about the market that are really useful for trading which I named 'Tharp Think'. They are not necessarily true or real, but if you adopt these beliefs personally, then your chances of making money in the market will go up dramatically.

Here are six Tharp Think beliefs that could make you a trading genius:

1. Before you enter into a trade, always know your initial risk point which tells you when you are wrong. Have a stop order on that initial risk (which I call R for short).

2. Make sure you only enter trades that have a potential reward of at least three times the size of your initial risk.

3. That way if you have four trades with +3R gains and six trades with -1R losses, you will have made +12R in your four winners and lost -6R in your six losses. You earned a net +6R or an average of +0.6R per trade in spite of being wrong 60% of the time.

4. If you can make ten trades per month like that using a position sizing strategy that risks 1% of your portfolio on each trade, you will be up about 6% at the end of the month. Trading this way over a year would put up 72% – which could make you one of the best traders in the world.

If it's really that easy, then why aren't most people trading geniuses? Let's look at two more Tharp Think beliefs for an explanation.

5. A trading mistake is when you don't follow your rules. Let's say you make two mistakes out of ten trades each month, which means that you are only 80% efficient as a trader. Let's say that each mistake costs you 2R. Using the results in #3 above, instead of making +6R each month you make +2R after you subtract your 4R in mistakes. Your annual return has plummeted from about 72% per year to about 24%. Some people repeat the same mistake over and over; I call that self-sabotage.

6. Finally, there are at least six market types that each have a direction component and a volatility component. The market directions are: up, sideways, and down while the volatility conditions are either quiet or volatile. If you apply beliefs 1–4 to any one particular market type, it becomes quite easy to design a great trading system. Expecting one trading system to work well in all market types, however, is insane. You need a different way to apply the beliefs in different market types.

Summary

What you create inside your head is an illusion that just represents the world out there, but is never the same as that world. This means that your internal map is not the territory. We make up the entire world through the meanings we give things.

The difference between the average investor/trader and a top performer is that the top performer (even if he doesn't understand that it's all made up) will at least have useful beliefs that help him make money in the markets. Four beliefs were given that could help you make very high returns a year – however, most people cannot do this. First, because they probably trade at 70–80% efficiency, making mistakes on lots of trades and often generating negative results from good trading systems. Second, because they don't realize that the useful beliefs for making money change as market conditions change. The rules for entering and exiting profitable trades in a quiet bull market will not make money in a volatile sideways market. Applying the four beliefs differently in each market type would allow for profitable trading in each one.

Nick Train

NICK TRAIN *co-founded Lindsell Train Limited in 2000. He is the portfolio manager for UK equity portfolios and jointly manages Global portfolios. Nick has over 30 years' experience in investment management. Before founding Lindsell Train he was head of Global Equities at M&G Investment Management, having joined there in 1998 as a director. Previously he spent 17 years (1981–1998) at GT Management which he left soon after its acquisition by Invesco. At his resignation he was a director of GT Management (London), Investment Director of GT Unit Managers and Chief Investment Officer for Pan-Europe. Nick has a BA honours degree in Modern History from Queen's College, Oxford.*

"ANGLO-SAXON EQUITIES HAVE DELIVERED 6–7% PA TOTAL RETURNS OVER AND ABOVE INFLATION OVER DECADES, IF NOT CENTURIES. BUT THEY HAVE NEVER DONE SO WITH A METRONOMIC, REGULAR 6–7% PA PACE."

The Seven Pillars of
Investing Wisdom

A NUMBER OF years ago a friend asked my advice about his financial affairs, having recently come into a pot of capital. My first thought – which indeed I acted on – was to direct him toward the capable hands of any of Lindsell Train's valued counterparties in the Private Wealth Management industry.

However he was insistent that I express some opinions – if only to provide context for his future discussions. "OK", I said, "so long as you acknowledge that I'm not professionally qualified to advise you – indeed, LT's regulation means that I'm specifically barred from giving you any advice – so long as you recognise all that: here are my seven pillars of investment wisdom."

These are seven propositions – appropriate for private, individual investors – which I try and remember before considering what to do with my own cash (before I give up and just buy more shares in Finsbury Growth & Income Trust). I long ago gave up seeking the 'answer' to the investment challenge and my seven propositions certainly don't add up to even an attempted answer. I just find that if I ruminate on them my eventual decisions feel less impulsive, better founded.

I wrote the below in 2011 but I think it is still valid today.

1. THE PURPOSE OF INVESTMENT IS TO PRESERVE THE REAL, POST-TAX PURCHASING POWER OF CAPITAL, IN THE LEAST RISKY WAY.

This may seem a truism, but it's always important to set out on any endeavour with a clear objective. What's more, it may seem an unambitious target – though protecting capital over time from the twin ravages of inflation and the taxman has not proven a trivial challenge. But what this first proposition really achieves is to inoculate me against over-reach. One of the most sobering, but refreshingly realistic, financial headlines I ever saw read as follows – "It is unlikely that God's plan for the universe involves making you rich." Sad, but true. So, let's now get on with achieving a realistic investment objective.

2. INVEST YOUR AGE IN FIXED INTEREST. OR DON'T.

I apologise for the fudge here – but this one is really crucial and really tricky. It used to be said, admittedly decades ago, that you should invest your age in gilts. For instance, a ten-year-old child, whose grandparents are saving for her, should have no more than 10% of those savings in fixed interest. She has a lifetime ahead of her to make back any setbacks in her equity holdings. Whereas a 75-year-old, more or less dependent on investment income, might as well have 75% of his wealth in government bonds. Carpe diem. You can't take it with you. Spend and enjoy.

With increasing life expectancy, however, it is clear that this rule of thumb no longer holds. Inflation can pauperise you quicker and when you're more vulnerable (i.e. when reliant on a fixed income) than our wisest forebears could conceive. We need to hold more equity for longer – particularly when one can invest in some very decent companies offering starting dividend yields above gilt yields, as now.

3. NEVER CONSUME MORE THAN 4% OF YOUR CAPITAL EVERY YEAR – WHETHER YOU TAKE IT AS CAPITAL GAIN OR INCOME – IF YOU WANT TO MAINTAIN THE REAL VALUE OF YOUR WEALTH.

No worries if you don't care about preserving real value of capital, but don't kid yourself. Long-term real returns on shares are circa 5% pa and that includes reinvested dividends, taxed at the standard rate (an element of index return unavailable to most of us). In the real world, peeling off more than 4% of capital a year, or trying to earn much more than 4% annual income from higher-risk instruments, will erode your stash over time (and perhaps quicker, if the junk bond market crashes and burns).

4. DON'T LET ANYONE TELL YOU THAT CAPITAL PRESERVATION AND 'GROWTH' ARE POSSIBLE AT THE SAME TIME.

They're not.

5. IF YOU NEED TO MAKE MONEY – CONCENTRATE YOUR INVESTMENTS. IF YOU WANT TO PRESERVE CAPITAL – DIVERSIFY.

Big returns require successful big bets. Diversification may not make you rich, but it lessens the potential for unpleasant surprises.

By the way, Mrs Train insists that the Train family fortune is not yet even remotely sufficient. For this reason LT's UK and Global strategies, where I invest, are run in a concentrated fashion. We willingly take this risk, because we know it offers the best chance for the exceptional returns Mrs Train insists on. But I'd be mortified if any of our clients invested in these vehicles without eyes wide open and without adequate diversification relative to their own objectives.

6. MOST PROFESSIONAL INVESTORS WILL DO WORSE THAN THE BENCHMARKS OVER TIME, LARGELY BECAUSE OF FEES AND TRANSACTION COSTS.

As Anthony Hilton of the *Evening Standard* wrote in 2010, "Remember, the only difference between investment professionals and investment amateurs is that the professionals make their mistakes with your money, not their own."

I don't table proposition 6 just to advertise index funds or ETFs, though it's hard to argue with the cumulative effects of their inexorable mediocrity – long periods of average performance, relative to benchmark, push you up the long-term performance tables – rather to demystify the investment profession. Smart suits and smooth patter will almost certainly not compensate you for 150bps of annual management fee.

7. TIME, NOT TIMING, IS THE KEY TO INVESTMENT SUCCESS. THE BEST TIME TO INVEST, THEREFORE, IS NOW.

You've got to be in it to win it. Don't believe anyone who claims they know where prices will be next week, month or year. If you need to earn a return, then invest for that return today – and let Capitalism do its steady work.

Be optimistic.

How I run equity capital

The Seven Pillars, as said, are aimed at private, individual investors deciding what to do with their money (including me). There are additional issues to consider in running equity capital as a portfolio manager. In this second half of the chapter, I review in more depth the ideas that shape the UK Equity portfolios that I manage at Lindsell Train. This time I will turn for the most part to another piece that I wrote for investors, in January 2014, that I believe (with a few updates) is equally relevant today.

Dr Samuel Johnson is a great hero of mine. In one of his many memorable flashes of wisdom, he wrote:

> "Men more frequently require to be reminded than taught."

After 35 years as a professional investor, I find myself acknowledging the truth of Johnson's statement. Everyone who faces the intellectual and emotional challenges of the capital markets needs to keep learning. I know that I benefit from a periodic revisiting of the longstanding principles that Lindsell Train uses to run clients' equity capital. Reminding ourselves of those principles keeps us on the straight and narrow.

1. "IF YOU WANT DIFFERENT INVESTMENT PERFORMANCE YOU MUST INVEST DIFFERENTLY." – SIR JOHN TEMPLETON

This is an unpalatable but incontrovertible truth. If you want different performance – for which I suppose read 'better performance' – then you have to do something that others don't. Our UK Equity portfolios have at times performed very differently from the FTSE All-Share benchmark and will do so again, for good or for ill, in the future.

Perhaps the most obvious difference about our approach is the unusually long time horizon we work with, as measured by levels of portfolio turnover. The long-term average turnover of our UK Equity portfolios is below 5% pa whereas we expect that the typical UK Equity OEIC will experience annual turnover of closer to 100%.

We think it's helpful – though not strictly scientific – to say if a given portfolio turnover is 100% in a year that implies the investment manager is taking on average a one-year time horizon for each holding. By contrast, at less than 5% pa the implication is that each position will be held for over 20 years or longer. And consistent with that, many of our holdings are 16 years old and counting. The one certain benefit of our relative inactivity – although there are uncertain disadvantages too – is that total running costs will tend to be lower, potentially much lower.

2. "STOCKS ARE SIMPLE. ALL YOU DO IS BUY SHARES IN A GREAT BUSINESS FOR LESS THAN THE BUSINESS IS INTRINSICALLY WORTH, WITH MANAGERS OF THE HIGHEST INTEGRITY AND ABILITY. THEN YOU OWN THOSE SHARES FOREVER." – WARREN BUFFETT

The explanation for our low turnover (and our choice of the type of company we invest in) is found in the above advice from Buffett. Now, I always feel a bit guilty tabling this quote as an account of what we do. How can such a simple suggestion – even from the world's greatest investor – be the basis of a credible and competitive investment philosophy? But it is what it is and by and large it has worked – for Buffett obviously. In passing, let me assure you that it's not so easy to identify, then stick with investments, even in great companies. The pressure to 'do something', particularly when a great company is going through an inevitable dull patch, is intense. The dull share performance of Unilever in 2013 is an example (although of course more recent events have helped to remind investors of the value of obviously special companies like Unilever). We fortify ourselves during such episodes by remembering the comment below of another outstanding investor – Peter Lynch – who, just like Buffett, is famous for running his winners.

3. "OTHER INVESTORS INVENT ARBITRARY RULES FOR WHEN TO SELL." – PETER LYNCH.

Lynch ran his winners, arguing that if a share has done well – at least for reasons that are explicable and not wholly speculative – then there is every reason to expect it to continue to do well (although always remembering that nothing goes up in a straight line). He (and we) dispute the conventional wisdom that says: "It's never wrong to take a profit". It can be very wrong, if by doing so you permanently reduce your interest in a great long-term investment. Share prices of the best companies double, then double again and again over time. Locking into that observed propensity for wonderful businesses to compound wealth for their owners is at the heart of our approach.

4. "IF A COMPANY'S PRODUCTS TASTE GOOD BUY THE SHARES." – VIVIAN BAZALGETTE

We continue to find inspiration in our stock selection from this recommendation made by my former, much admired boss – Vivian Bazalgette.

We are drawn to companies whose products or services are regarded as irreplaceable by their customers. So, for instance, scientists and lawyers around the world have little option but to subscribe to Reed Elsevier's (now re-named RELX) services – they can't do their work without them; the same is true for investment bank customers of Fidessa's software. But, as Vivian recognised, consumer loyalty to a tasty product is just as reliable and highly profitable. Our portfolios' investments are supported by peoples' insatiable love of, for instance – Guinness, Johnnie Walker, IRN-BRU, Rubicon, Fullers' London Pride, Old Speckled Hen, Dr Pepper, Cadbury Dairy Milk, Oreos, Toblerone, Magnum ice cream, Hellman's, Knorr and my own 'that without which I cannot do', Marmite. These products will be enjoyed 30 years from now and, in an uncertain world, that is enough to mean the companies that own these brands are likely to be terrific investments over time.

We run concentrated portfolios, with rarely more than 25 holdings. In part the inspiration and example for this policy comes from the man who gave me my break into the investment industry. This was Richard Thornton, the 'T' of GT Management, who hired me in 1981. Sadly Richard died in 2013, mourned and respected by colleagues as a rainmaker of the first rank, as well as a formidable stock market operator. I've never forgotten Richard's account – to a group of then-feckless graduate trainees – of his secret to investment success:

5. "FIRST, IDENTIFY YOUR GREAT IDEA. NEXT, INVEST INTO IT AS MUCH AS YOU CAN POSSIBLY AFFORD. THIRD, DOUBLE THE SIZE OF YOUR HOLDING, SO YOU CAN NO LONGER SLEEP AT NIGHT. FINALLY – TELL EVERYONE ELSE ABOUT IT!" – RICHARD THORNTON

Richard knew that great investment opportunities are rare and must be backed with conviction, when you happen across one. He also knew how easy it is to suffer 'diworseification', from a lazy proliferation of 'it seemed like a good idea at the time' holdings cluttered across a portfolio. So we stick to his advice and all the rest from our elders and betters.

Turning to the outlook for equity markets – we remain bullish for both global and UK equities. It seems to us that the background conditions are as encouraging for equity investing as at any time since, say, 1801, when the London Stock Exchange was founded. For sure, three current macro factors are unequivocally positive. First, technology change is creating new industries, new companies and new opportunities for existing companies – at a faster pace than ever. Next, the world's population not only continues to grow; in addition more and more people on the planet are being lifted out of poverty. Finally, the risks to the real value of the competing asset classes to equity – namely government bonds and cash – look as scary as ever. To us that adds up to a compelling case to commit long-term capital to stocks.

We know it would be comforting for cautious shareholders to be offered more certainty as to the likely shape and timing of those promised equity returns. The fact is Anglo-Saxon equities have delivered 6–7% pa total returns over and above inflation over decades, if not centuries. But they have never done so with a metronomic, regular 6–7% pa pace. No, the truth of the likely shape of equity returns is best expressed in this wonderful observation from light versifier, Ogden Nash:

6. "SHAKE AND SHAKE THE KETCHUP BOTTLE, FIRST NONE WILL COME AND THEN A LOT'LL" – OGDEN NASH

It is indeed hard, we might say impossible, to time the equity markets. And yet it is imperative investors maintain adequate exposure to equity. This is the reason that our portfolio remains fully invested.

Eoin Treacy

EOIN TREACY *has spent a decade as a global strategist and partner at* Fullermoney.com, *where he has represented the service on sell-out speaking tours to the USA, Australia and Singapore. He is an expert in the firm's unique macro behavioural approach to financial market interpretation and has appeared on Bloomberg TV, CNBC, CNN, CNBC India, NDTV Profit and the BBC World Service as a commentator on equities, bonds, commodities and currencies.*

As well as frequent appearances on Indian financial media, Eoin travels regularly to China to gain first-hand experience of the evolution of its market. He is a world-renowned speaker and has been invited to deliver talks to financially minded associations in a host of countries, not least for the CFA Institute, the Market Technicians Association, Society of Technical Analysts in the UK and the Australian Technical Analysts Association. He is also a regular presenter at The World Money Show in London and at the Contrary Opinion Forum in Vermont.

Following a degree in Philosophy from Trinity College, Dublin, Eoin went on to spend more than three years at Bloomberg, teaching seminars across Europe on the interpretation of price action. He joined David Fuller at Fullermoney in 2003 to specialise in the service's approach to research – combining technical, fundamental and behavioural factors. He shares his views on markets in Fullermoney's Comment of the Day *on a daily basis and regularly records the service's daily audio updates.*

As an active trader, Eoin also details all of his personal trades and investments in the service. Finally, Eoin developed the Fullermoney Chart Library, which is fully customisable and includes more than 17,000 instruments, ratios, spreads and multiples.

In 2013 David Fuller and Eoin Treacy formed FT-Money.com to take their service to the next level and to enhance the product experience for their many subscribers. The same year, Eoin published his first book, Crowd Money (Harriman House, 2013).

Eoin is married and has two daughters. In his spare time he is a keen scuba diver.

"CAPITAL IS BOTH GLOBAL AND MOBILE SO IT STANDS TO REASON THAT WE SHOULD HAVE AN EQUALLY WIDE VISION WHEN WE CHOOSE WHERE TO INVEST."

Investing in Explosions Waiting to Happen

1. SCAN THE GLOBE.

I KNOW WHAT I'm looking for, but how do I find it?

There is a particular set of circumstances that lead to outsized gains. The results are impressive and the reliability is high. The problem is they don't happen all the time so I have to keep my eyes peeled for when they do occur.

That is why I scan the globe for markets of interest. Capital is both global and mobile so it stands to reason that we should have an equally wide vision when we choose where to invest. More importantly, because of the competitive nature of our capitalist global economic system, money will naturally flow to the assets with the most attractive characteristics such as yield or potential for capital growth.

The law of averages also works in your favour when you cast your net as wide as possible. After all, the more markets you monitor, the greater the possibility that just the right set of circumstances will evolve so that you can move in and profit with relatively low risk. That is why I consider myself a global strategist. I don't simply focus on the UK market, despite it being one of the world's largest pools of liquid capital. I keep a close eye on many markets because when the right set of circumstances comes together, the low risk and high reward of buying when sentiment changes makes the wait worth it.

2. LOOK FOR BASE FORMATIONS.

I'm talking about buying when no one else cares anymore because they have been so conditioned by disappointment to never expect it to end. It's all well and good being a value investor and suffering through years of underperformance because you are waiting for everyone else to realise your analysis has been spot on all along. However, it can take time for the crowd to come around and prices can move substantially lower before turning around.

My preference is to look for at least *some* evidence that other investors might also hold my view. That at least tells me I'm not the only one buying and at least partially limits the potential I'm wrong in my analysis. That means I look for base formations.

They are about the easiest thing in the world to identify on a chart because you will see a lengthy period of often volatile ranging. This coincides with the first of three psychological perception stages of a bull market which I discuss in my book *Crowd Money*. Here is a key section explaining what I mean:

> On a chart the disbelief/dismissal stage is consistent with base formation development. As with the foundation of a building, a base formation is what the subsequent uptrend is built upon and appears to emerge from. How long the disbelief/dismissal phase takes will depend on two separate factors. The first is that the excesses of the prior bull market will have to be worked through. This can take years but will proceed for as long as it takes people who failed to sell on the way down to liquidate their inventory and accept the loss. Expectations will be low because everyone will have seen that as soon as prices get back up towards the higher side of the base they are quickly stamped back down. However, sooner or later, everyone who wanted to sell will have sold so that the overhang of potential supply above the market will have dissipated, which is a necessary condition for the next bull market to begin.

> A corollary is that once everyone has sold and is sitting with cash, this represents a potential pool of liquidity that will eventually help to fuel a new bull market in something.

> The second prerequisite is that there will have to be a compelling fundamental reason to shake the demand side of the equation out of its torpor. Major bull markets in equities generally start from historically attractive P/E ratios and relatively high yields. Whatever the reason is will have to be powerful enough to act as a catalyst for how supply and demand have been relating to each other within the base. If it is a stock market sector, the company will have discovered a new way to drive efficiency or a new source of demand for its products emerges. If it is a bond price or a currency, the country concerned will need to have finally begun to get its economic act together. If it is a commodity, then some new technology or source of demand will be helping to sponge up available supply. The biggest bull markets have

genuinely inspiring stories. In order to generate the faith in an idea necessary to propel an asset class into a secular bull market, the story has to be big. As participants, investors want to feel that they are at the forefront of a new movement which will literally change the world.

At this stage of the new cycle, the most important factor about the new fundamental story is that the majority of people will be ignorant of it. If they have heard of it they will dismiss it and even those who have heard of it and believe are likely to underestimate the powerful effect new sources of demand can have on thin supply.

The people who survive in an industry during a lengthy period of highly volatile trading – where there is no certainty in profitability and rationalisation is clearing out legions of workers – are not risk takers. In fact, because they have survived in their sector, they are among the most conservative people as a result of their experience. They don't have any interest in taking risks because to do so would result in potentially even worse trading conditions so they hunker down and try to ensure the company's survival.

When conditions begin to improve, the media will naturally migrate towards those with the most experience of this particular market. Who else are they going to talk to? However, because they have been so conditioned by the bear market they will be among the least optimistic about future potential because their experience is that rallies don't hold and that optimism will be crushed. Donald Coxe has an elegant way of describing this phenomenon "those who know it best, love it least because they have been disappointed most".

3. TWO CONDITIONS NEED TO BE MET BEFORE A BREAK TO NEW HIGHS CAN BE SUSTAINED.

The first is a natural outcome from the formation of a range. The second is a condition of human psychology.

When prices have been going sideways for a long time, investors who want to sell at new highs don't have much success. They have three choices and the longer the price takes to rise to the level at which they wish to sell, the greater the chances are that impatience will take a tool on persistence and they will make a choice about what to do.

The easiest way to get out of the position would be wait for a rally to the upper side of the range and lower their offer into the market, which contributes to the inability of the price to sustain new highs.

They could conclude that a lot of the bad news is already in the price of the security, so they could become 'born-again bulls' and decide to withdraw their offer in the hope of a new bull market starting. That decision withdraws supply from the market above the range.

The third is that they could simply continue to wait – but the numbers of people willing to wait indefinitely will dwindle as days stretch to weeks, months and even years.

Therefore the range itself is a decision-making process and contributes to a vacuum of supply forming above the range.

The next condition is that there has to be a new bullish fundamental story. A long-ranging base formation might be a decision-making process but in order for the asset to be able to attract new investors – and enough of them to drive a bull market – there needs to be a story. Human beings are social animals and we thrive in a community-based society because we yearn for communication. Stories are about the most effective way we have come up with to condense often complicated data into bitesized chunks that are easily relatable. The more compelling the narrative, the easier it is for people to get behind the idea.

Tesla Motors is a great example. Between the middle of 2011 and early 2013, the share ranged with a mild upward bias but was prone to 40% pullbacks when it pulled back from the $35 area. That kind of volatility, for a company that was losing money on every car, was probably enough to scare most people away. Then in early 2013 something happened. Elon Musk's force of personality and ambitions to make SpaceX the first privately owned space explorer made investors feel like anything was possible. Then Fisker Automotive, Tesla's main competitor for luxury electric vehicles, went bust. That left Tesla with almost the entirety of the market for subsidies for green vehicles – and what is more, it was making cars people aspired to own, a virtual first in electric vehicles. The share cleared $35 and didn't look back until it tested $200 before the end of the year.

That's why I define ranges as explosions waiting to happen. You see a market is only ever trending or ranging – and when it moves from one condition to the other there is enormous potential for profit. The conditioning effect of the range means the breakout will always be surprising for market participants, because they have survived by limiting their expectations and giving up on wishing for better prices.

The breakout unleashes waves of new buying. Sticking with the Tesla example above, think about the poor chap who was shorting the stock at $35 in the expectation that price would fall in the order of 40%, just like it had on a number of occasions in the preceding couple of years. He is under enormous pressure and quickly has to cover as the price explodes higher.

Then there are the bargain hunters who wished they could have bought at the last test of the $22 area. They now tend to panic in because their wait-for-better-prices strategy is clearly failing.

Then there are all the buy-the-breakout, momentum, black box and algorithmic traders that will buy new highs as a matter of course in the expectation of future upside. Then because the breakout is so powerful the media will have to write a story about it and that lends further fuel to the rise because more people hear about it. The price rallies for as long as it takes for these sources of new demand to be satiated by an excess of investors willing to sell at elevated prices.

That's why I scour the investible universe of shares for signs of base formation with a progression of higher reaction lows inside the formation. That progression of higher reaction lows tells me two things. First, it tells me that the people who want to own it are not willing to wait until the price makes a new low before buying it. In other words, they do not want to miss out on a bounce and would rather be early than miss it. That is indicative of investors building positions rather than traders who are only in for a quick turnaround.

I wrote a book in 2013 because there were so many shares that met those criteria and many have doubled and more since. Long base formations occur in ever asset class and they are all without exception explosions waiting to happen. We know what the potential is, so it makes sense to simply scan the market for the profit formation we can rely on rather than punting in otherwise uncertain terrain.

Pertti
Vanhanen

PERTTI VANHANEN *is Global Head of Property at Aberdeen Standard Investments. He was appointed to this position in November 2013 following his involvement in the strategic development of Aberdeen's global property products and processes as Head of Fund Management – Property from 2000. Prior to this, Pertti served as Head of Direct Property and Head of Nordic and Eastern Europe Property.*

Pertti joined Aberdeen in 2000 following the company's major expansion into the Finnish market. Prior to this, he held senior positions in several companies including Varma Mutual Pension Insurance Company subsidiary and Ilmarinen Mutual Pension Insurance Company subsidiary. Pertti began working in the industry in 1988 and has been a key driver in the launch of several non-listed property funds. Pertti holds an Executive MBA and he is a Certified Real Estate Manager. He is also a fellow of the Royal Institution of Chartered Surveyors (FRICS) and a member of the British Property Federation Policy Committee.

"BY IGNORING THE LURE OF UNREALISTIC RETURNS, AND FOCUSING INSTEAD ON WHAT RISKS YOU CAN HANDLE, YOU MAY JUST BE PLEASANTLY SURPRISED AT THE RETURNS YOU CAN ACHIEVE."

Nine Home Truths of Property Investing

1. IT'S NOT ALL ABOUT GROWTH.

ALTHOUGH THIS MAY come as a shock to many property investors, values don't always rise. And a lot of money can be lost by restless investors seeking short-term capital gain.

Long-term returns from property are really about generating a consistent, attractive income. To achieve a good income, though, you need a property that people want to rent. And you need tenants who make enough money to pay you rent.

If you focus on nurturing properties that can give you a strong and prospectively growing income, then good capital performance is more likely to follow.

2. NEGLECT LEADS TO DECAY.

Property owners have to be active. They cannot ignore the importance of maintenance and housekeeping.

Even if a tenant signs a long contract, the building's physical characteristics and environment will evolve over time. Whether it be legal or regulatory issues, or external factors like changes to the surrounding location, it pays to stay on top of what's going on.

Taking active responsibility for environmental, social and governance factors should be second nature, and embedded into the ongoing management of properties. It follows that successful property investing requires a long-term view.

A property owner must not neglect the work required for necessary upkeep. And if you aren't prepared to maintain a property, then it's advisable to invest via specialist managers.

3. 'WHAT' MATTERS MORE THAN 'WHERE'.

You can spend a lot of time pondering which country, sector or market to invest in. But, in reality, the characteristics of a specific property have a far greater influence on returns. It doesn't really matter whether you're buying in the UK, Germany or France. Or, indeed, whether France's economic growth rate is plus or minus a percentage point or two compared to Germany. The important thing is the actual asset you're buying – whether that be an office block, a rental flat or a warehouse. Is the property fit for purpose? Is it in demand? And can it generate good income over the long term?

Your potential return will only be as good as the asset you invest in – so it is an imperative to focus on the property itself, not just the location.

4. ACCEPTING REALITY CAN BE HARD.

Property is often called an illiquid asset class, meaning that it can take a long time to buy or sell. But that's partly because – more than any other asset class – investors tend to have a fixed idea of what the price of a property should be. And once they have an idea of this, it's very hard for them to be persuaded otherwise. Unwillingness to sell an asset for less, or buy for more, than you think it's worth is what makes property a more illiquid asset.

Make sure the price you envisage for a property is grounded in reality – including market demand, projected rental yields and what comparable properties are trading for. If you don't, illiquidity is likely to be a persistent feature of your property investment career.

5. QUALITY PROPERTIES ARE RARELY EMPTY.

Most people misunderstand what 'high quality' means when it comes to property. Investors often describe quality in terms of a property's physical features. But in fact it's much simpler: is the property in demand or not? Put simply, if your tenants can easily substitute one property for another, your property is of low quality. You really want the opposite: a property that tenants would have a hard time replacing.

A property that enjoys strong tenant demand and a minimal risk of vacancies offers the greatest likelihood of a durable and rising income and, in turn, potential for capital growth.

6. KNOWING THE RISKS GIVES YOU CONTROL.

It's easy to spend an inordinate amount of time forecasting property returns – usually with little success. We flip convention on its head and focus on risk instead. Because, after all, returns are ultimately the result of risks we take. Property risks include debt levels, disrupting structural changes, vacancy periods, lease lengths, rent levels and a tenant's financial resilience. Understanding these risks, and being comfortable with them, gives you more control. At any given point in the cycle, you'll know how the property is likely to behave and can prepare accordingly.

By ignoring the lure of unrealistic returns, and focusing instead on what risks you can handle, you may just be pleasantly surprised at the returns you can achieve.

7. NOT ALL PROPERTY PROTECTS AGAINST INFLATION.

A widely accepted wisdom is that property is an 'inflation hedge', meaning that over time investment returns will keep pace with the cost of living. This isn't always true. Like any investment, property returns are driven by supply and demand – meaning that not all property rents or values will rise in tandem with the cost of other goods and services. Understanding this is key.

The corrosive power of inflation needs to be thoughtfully navigated. By ensuring that you have a high-quality property, and a decent understanding of what's driving supply and demand in your market, you're less likely to see inflation erode your returns.

8. DON'T RELY ON THE ADVICE OF OTHERS.

It's easy to rely on other people to tell you whether an investment is a good idea. Property is no different. But you need to do your own research to work out if a particular property is suitable for your investment needs. You also need to work out what you think it is worth, and not rely unquestioningly on third-party opinion.

In short, do your own research if you want to be a successful property investor.

9. DEBT CAN BE YOUR WORST ENEMY.

In a rising property market, taking on debt to fund an expanding property portfolio can seem very alluring. But more debt always means more risk. When you take on debt, you hand over some control to the bank, and even more to the market. Should interest rates rise and/or property values fall, the impact on your portfolio can be swift and severe.

Unless you're flexible enough to cope with swings in the property market, it's probably wise not to get involved with debt at all.

Edgar
Wachenheim

EDGAR WACHENHEIM III *is the founder and CEO of Greenhaven Associates, a Purchase, New York-based investment management company with $7.2 billion under management. He is Vice Chairman of Central National Gottesman Inc. (a worldwide paper and pulp distribution company with revenues of about $6 billion), a trustee and member of the executive committee of the Museum of Modern Art, a trustee of the New York Public Library, and Chairman of the Board of WNET (National Education Television).*

Mr Wachenheim is a graduate of Williams College and the Harvard Business School, where he was elected a Baker Scholar after his first year of studies.

Mr Wachenheim is married and the most happy father of three grown children and six growing grandchildren. His interests include tennis, golf, hiking, art, and photography.

"SHARP DECLINES
IN THE STOCK
MARKET ARE
NOT A RISK TO
THE LONG-TERM
INVESTOR."

Learn to Love
Common Stocks

I LOVE MY wife, I love my children, and I love common stocks. Why do I love common stocks? Because they are highly marketable and transparent and because they provide high returns.

1. COMMON STOCKS COME WITH A SPECIAL 3% GIFT.

Over the past 50 years, the total return on the S&P 500 has averaged about 9.5% per year.

I believe that it is both interesting and informative to analyze the attractiveness of the roughly 9.5% average annual return provided by common stocks. Theoretically, after adjusting for risk, all types of investments should provide identical returns. Over the past 50 years, the average yield on ten-year US Treasury notes has been about 6.5%. US Treasuries are considered risk-free. Thus, one can conclude that the risk premium on common stocks has been about 3% vs intermediate-term risk-free bonds.

Investors face two risks when investing in common stocks. The first risk is the threat of permanent losses on particular holdings. The Enrons. The Kodaks. The second risk is the threat of sharp declines in the stock market. With respect to the first risk, the historic 9.5% average annual return of the S&P 500 already is, of course, net of all permanent losses on the stocks that were in the index. If Enron, Kodak, and the other permanent losses are excluded, the S&P 500 returned something higher than the 9.5% – maybe 10.5% or 11%. Thus, none of the 3% risk premium can be attributed to permanent losses in individual stocks.

And, with respect to the risks of sharp declines in the stock market, importantly, every time the stock market has declined sharply, it subsequently has fully recovered and then has appreciated to new heights. On the single day of 19 October 1987, the S&P 500 declined by 20.5% from 282.70 to 224.84. A scary disaster! The largest one-day percentage loss in the index ever – by a wide margin. On the evening of 19 October, a portfolio manager told me that the decline of the stock market that day was the "worst collapse since the Great Depression", that many investors would lose complete confidence in common stocks, and therefore that it would take many years for the stock market to recover. The portfolio manager was wrong. The stock market fully recovered by mid-January 1989 – and then rose sharply for the next several years, reaching 468.45 on 18 October 1993. An investor who purchased the S&P 500 just before the 20.5% decline would have suffered the "worst collapse since the Great Depression" and yet, during the next six years, would have enjoyed an 8.8% average annual return on his investment before dividends – and above a 12% average annual return including the dividends he would have received during the six-year period. Thus, I conclude that sharp declines in the stock market are not a risk to the long-term investor.

I am so fixated on the concept that the stock market is not risky for the long-term investor that I will give another example of a sharp decline in the market. An even more striking example. The financial crisis. On the last trading day in August 2008 (the 29th), the S&P 500 closed at 1282.83. Over the next several weeks, all hell broke loose after the bankruptcy of Lehman, and, by early March 2009, the S&P 500 was selling at below 700, or more than 45% below its August 29 close. An apparent disaster! In the fall of 2014, I made a presentation to a board of directors. During the presentation, I mentioned that, if an investor in an S&P 500 index fund had departed the earth on 29 August 2008 for a holiday on the moon and then had returned to earth exactly six years later, bearing no knowledge of events on the earth during the six-year interim, he would have returned to earth to find that his investment in the fund happily had appreciated by 70% (including dividends) during the time he was away. Thus, the financial crisis was not relevant to the man who had vacationed on the moon.

Therefore, I strongly believe that there is no pragmatic reason why common stocks deserve to earn a 3% premium to the risk-free Treasuries. The 3% is a gift from investors at large to those longer-term investors who are analytical and rational – and who can correctly assess risk. The 3% gift makes US common stocks a particularly attractive investment vehicle.

2. DON'T DIVERSIFY AWAY FROM SOMETHING GOOD.

I note that I am largely attracted to common stocks of companies that are mainly dependent on the US economy, but am much less enthusiastic about stocks of companies that conduct most of their business in Europe, in Japan, or in most developing countries. I believe (and most businessmen and economists agree) that Europe and Japan face many systemic problems, including stagnant populations, high social costs, relative lack of raw materials (especially low-cost energy), over-regulation, educational systems that still overemphasize rote memorization and underemphasize creativity, and, in the case of most of Europe, a common currency among nations with uncommon cultures and varying cost structures.

And, with respect to most developing countries, corruption, political risks, and currency risks are major hurdles that can lead to permanent losses.

The US, in comparison, enjoys some population growth, efficient agriculture, large reserves of oil and gas that can be extracted using new technologies, an education system that breeds creativity, a business system that fosters technological progress and efficiencies, and a relatively honest and steady government. Given this analysis, I am surprised that so many investors and investment committees have decided to diversify their portfolios by investing in international stocks. Why diversify away from something that is good to something that is less good (or not good at all)? I believe that Warren Buffett had it correct when he said, "diversification is protection against ignorance. It makes little sense if you know what you are doing."

3. STOCKS OR AN INDEX FUND? SPEND TIME ANALYZING YOURSELF FIRST. AN ABOVE-AVERAGE INVESTOR REQUIRES A FEW KEY CHARACTERISTICS.

I have now made a strong case for US common stocks. The next question is, should an investor actively select a portfolio of common stocks or should he passively select index funds or passive ETFs?

Mathematically, roughly half of all investors will outperform the stock market over time – and roughly half will underperform. In my opinion, investors should spend considerable time analyzing which half they are likely to fall into. I am surprised that most investors spend large amounts of time trying to analyze companies and industries – and relatively little time trying to analyze themselves and their own innate abilities to outperform the market. I am reminded of a quote by Woody Allen: "I am astounded by people who want to know the universe when it is hard enough to know your way around Chinatown."

I have given considerable thought to the qualities needed by an investor to outperform the market. Certainly, a successful investor should have an analytical mind and should have access to good information. But, in my strong opinion, an above-average investor also must possess several behavioral qualities – in particular, the ability to be a contrarian, the ability to ignore short-term negative noise, and the ability to control his emotions during periods of stress.

Almost by definition, a successful investor must be a contrarian. At any one time, the price of a security reflects the opinion of the majority of all investors in the security. Therefore, if an investor believes that a particular security is materially undervalued given the fundamentals of the underlying company, he is taking a position that differs from the prevailing sentiment. He is being a contrarian.

Most investors claim that they are contrarians, but my experience is that relatively few investors actually have the confidence and daring to break from the crowd – and to adopt differing positions that are lonely, unpopular, and often uncomfortable. Because most investors who attempt to be contrarians and leaders actually end up being trend followers, I have come to the conclusion that the proclivity for an investor to be a follower or to be a contrarian largely is hard-wired into his DNA.

I have a friend who is a hard-wired trend follower. I call him Danny Dinner Date because I frequently dine with him to discuss stocks. Often, I will describe a stock to Danny that has a high probability of appreciating sharply due to a positive change that is not being anticipated by other investors. Danny usually will listen intently when I describe the stock, will ask intelligent questions, and will appear interested in purchasing the stock. However, in follow-up conversations, Danny most often will say that he will purchase the stock only once there is actual news that the positive change is taking place. Of course, by the time he hears such news, the positive change already has become apparent to many other investors – and the price of the shares already has discounted part or all of the anticipated positive change. Thus, Danny usually misses exciting opportunities and is prone to purchasing stocks that already have appreciated sharply. Because Danny is experienced, knowledgeable, highly intelligent, and fully aware that he usually is late to the party, I have concluded that Danny's inability to be a contrarian is hard-wired – part of his DNA.

I also believe that the abilities of an investor to properly weigh short-term adverse news and to adequately control his emotions are hard-wired. My belief is based on conversations with many investors who continually make emotional and irrational decisions during periods of stress, even though they fully acknowledge that their decisions are heavily being influenced by temporary short-term adverse circumstances – and not by any erosion in the inherent values of their holdings. A specific example is the portfolio manager who believed it would take many years for the stock market to recover after its 20.5% decline on 19 October 1987. He sold stocks on 20 October. The prices he received on 20 October were far below his estimates of what the stocks were worth at 9am on the previous day. Did the 3M Company become materially less valuable because the stock market declined by 20.5% in one day? Did Microsoft become any less valuable? At a later date, I asked the portfolio manager about his decision to sell stocks on 20 October 20. His answer was that "I lost my cool." I believe that Seth Klarman had it right when he said: "people don't consciously choose to invest with emotion – they simply can't help it."

Therefore, investors should spend considerable time analyzing their own DNA – their own innate abilities to outperform the stock market. And, those who objectively conclude that they are blessed with above-average investment abilities should invest actively – selecting individual stocks to own. And, those who objectively conclude that they possess less-than-average abilities should invest passively – selecting index funds or passive ETFs.

By investing passively, an investor is guaranteed that his results will be average, even if his investing abilities are far below average. This is an amazing concept. Can you think of any other business, any sport, or any other human endeavor where a person of inferior abilities is absolutely guaranteed of achieving average results? Absolutely amazing! And another reason why I am in love with common stocks.

Todd
Wenning

TODD WENNING, *CFA is an equity analyst at Johnson Investment Counsel. Before joining Johnson in 2015, Todd was an equity analyst at Morningstar and ran a dividend-focused newsletter for* The Motley Fool *UK. He is an adjunct professor of finance at Xavier University and his articles have been published by Morningstar,* Investors Chronicle, *CFA Institute, and* The Motley Fool.

He is the author of Keeping Your Dividend Edge: Strategies for Growing & Protecting Your Dividends *(2016).*

Todd's opinions are his own and not necessarily those of his employer.

"A COMPANY THAT'S CONSISTENTLY INCREASED ITS DIVIDEND AT THE SAME PACE AS EARNINGS GROWTH IS ONE SIGN THAT MANAGEMENT IS LOOKING OUT FOR LONG-TERM SHAREHOLDERS."

How to Keep Your Dividend Edge

1. PATIENCE IS A PREREQUISITE TO DIVIDEND SUCCESS.

WHEN YOU FIRST invest in a dividend stock, the income return is meager. In the short term, the expansion and contraction of the price/earnings ratio drives the bulk of your returns. With time, however, the underlying strength of the business, reflected in dividend growth, accounts for the lion's share of your investment's success (or failure). Don't become a dividend investor if you aren't willing to give the shares enough time – at least five years – to see the balance shift from speculative returns to investment returns.

2. FOCUS ON FREE CASH FLOW FIRST.

There is far too much attention paid to a company's earnings-based dividend cover. As the saying goes, profit is an opinion, but cash is a fact. Ultimately, dividends are funded by free cash flow – that is, cash flow left after the company has reinvested in its business – and not accrual-based profit estimates. Companies can temporarily support dividends by issuing debt, but this is not sustainable.

3. USE DIVIDENDS AS AN ALTERNATIVE BENCHMARK.

Most investors gauge their performance relative to a broad market index like the FTSE All-Share or S&P 500. There's nothing wrong with this approach in itself, but annual performance can be misleading. Your style may not have been in favor that particular year, for instance. Instead, set a target dividend growth rate for your portfolio – e.g. 6% annual growth – and see if you beat that figure on a yearly basis. Analyzing dividend growth keeps your attention on long-term business fundamentals – exactly where it should be if you want to be a successful dividend investor.

4. UNDERSTAND THE COMPANY'S COMPETITIVE POSITION.

How successful a company is at reinvesting cash flows in high-return projects will determine how quickly it can grow the dividend. If competitors enter the market and eat away at your company's profit margins, the management team and directors will be less-inclined to open up the dividend spigot. Before investing, then, always ask yourself, "If I had enough capital, how could I disrupt this business? And what would stop me?" If you don't have suitable answers to these questions, walk away.

5. SPEND TIME RESEARCHING MANAGEMENT.

If you were going to buy a small stake in your local butcher shop, you would first want to know if the butcher was a person of integrity and skill. The same should be true when you're researching a larger publicly-traded company. Scour the internet for interviews with a company's CEO or CFO, read their biographies in the annual reports, consider their bonus metrics (found in the remuneration report), and see how much stock they own themselves. A company that's consistently increased its dividend at the same pace as earnings growth is one sign that management is looking out for long-term shareholders.

6. OVER-LEVERAGE OFTEN LEADS TO DIVIDEND CUTS.

Just as a debt-free company can't go bankrupt, I have yet to hear of a debt-free company cutting its dividend. This isn't to say that you should only invest in debt-free companies, but pay close attention to how much leverage a company has relative to its peers. All else being equal, more cyclical companies (miners, oil and gas, commodity producers) should have low leverage whilst more defensive companies (consumer products, healthcare, utilities) can handle more debt given the relative stability of their cash flows.

7. BE MINDFUL OF COMPETITORS' DIVIDEND POLICIES.

A company's board of directors doesn't decide on dividend policy in a vacuum. When deciding how much to pay out in the next year, most boards compare their yields to those of their peers. If the company has a 5% yield when its peers are yielding 2%, management and the board may begin to wonder why they shouldn't retain more cash to reinvest in the business. In such cases, they may look to reset their dividend policy following a sizeable acquisition or in a recessionary environment.

8. DON'T FORGET SMALL-CAP DIVIDEND PAYERS.

Dividend portfolios are often stocked with blue chips, many of which are strongly correlated with broader market returns. Smaller dividend payers can fly under investors' radars and present attractive long-term opportunities. Focus your attention on small caps with low (or preferably no) debt, a consistent track record of raising their dividend, and an invested management team that owns at least 5% of the outstanding shares.

9. AVOID ULTRA-HIGH DIVIDEND YIELDS.

Those 8%-yielders can certainly be tempting. In times of market panic, they might even be worth buying. Most of the time, however, a yield that's more than twice or 2.5 times the market average is likely an indication something's wrong with the company. The market doesn't routinely give away such juicy yields. If other investors weren't concerned about the company's ability to fund that dividend in the coming years, they would have already bid the stock price higher, thus lowering the yield.

10. VALUATION MATTERS.

Some dividend-minded investors focus too much on the yield and not enough on valuation. Whilst a higher yield in itself can be a value signal, prudent investors should weigh yield alongside other factors such as free cash flow yield (FCF per share ÷ price), price/earnings, and perhaps a discounted cash flow model. A 3% dividend yield is cold comfort if the stock price falls 20% in the next year or two.

Gervais
Williams

GERVAIS WILLIAMS *is an award-winning equity fund manager and Senior Executive Director of Miton Group. He received Grant Thornton's Quoted Companies' Award Investor of the Year in both 2009 and 2010; then in 2012 his Diverse Income Trust was recognised as the Best New Investment Trust by the Association of Investment Companies. He was also* What Investment's *Fund Manager of the Year 2014.*

Gervais is a respected commentator on prospective market trends. He outlined his controversial views in his book Slow Finance *(Bloomsbury, 2011) and developed those ideas in* The Future is Small *(Harriman House, 2014). In 2016 he published* The Retreat of Globalisation *(Harriman House).*

Gervais has worked in the City since 1985, where he is particularly well known for the management of clients' investments in small- to medium-sized UK companies.

"MARKETS HAVE BEEN SO GOOD, FOR SO LONG, THAT MANY INVESTORS ARE TRIVIALISING THE ADVANTAGES OF ACTIVELY MANAGING PORTFOLIO RISK."

Make the Most of the Market Environment

1. COMPLACENCY IS DANGEROUS – AND DOUBLY SO FOR PASSIVE INVESTORS.

OVER THE LONG term, markets tend to appreciate. And a quick glance in the rear-view mirror highlights the long-term pattern. Stock market indices have risen more or less continuously for the last three decades, along with the dividends they pay. Overall, the total return on the FTSE All-Share Index has been coming in at around 9.6% pa since the early 1980s. Returns like this are excellent, most especially when they compound over time. On average the value of our collective equity holdings have been doubling every eight years.

As markets have appreciated after the global financial crisis in 2008, and gone on to new absolute highs, the active consideration of downside risk has seemed relatively unimportant. So most investors now link active value-add solely with picking out stocks with the most attractive risk/reward ratios. And since few active funds outperform a rising market, the follow-on assumption is that the easiest way to participate in the full appreciation of markets is via an equity index fund. These capture all of the market rise, and have the added advantage of minimal costs as well.

However index funds do have two specific disadvantages.

- The first is that many are dominated by a limited number of very large individual stocks. This puts the investor at risk of losing out badly if one or more of these stocks gets caught out. The severe setback of the BP share price following the accident in the Gulf of Mexico is a good example.

- Secondly, index funds are often narrowly based in terms of industry sector weightings as well. Worst still, the largest sector weightings often have a bias toward those industries that have been successful in the past, rather than those best placed for the future. So passive funds tend to perform particularly badly when market trends change. For example, just prior to the global financial crisis, most mainstream equity indices had large weightings in the financial sector. And it is no coincidence that during the crisis banks were amongst the worst performing stocks.

The longer the market recovery lasts, the greater the danger of investors becoming complacent. Markets have been so good, for so long, that many investors are trivialising the advantages of actively managing portfolio risk. But there are real advantages to keeping an eye on the investment horizon.

2. BEING ABLE TO ACTIVELY MANAGE PORTFOLIO RISK ALSO HAS TREMENDOUS UPSIDE.

Please don't fall into the trap of assuming that managing portfolio risk is just about minimising the downside either. It can add to upside returns as well. For example just after the global financial crisis, when UK interest rates had been reduced from 5.75% to 0.5%, and when quantitative easing was first introduced, I found that the stocks with the best risk/reward stocks were almost exclusively those with the most stretched balance sheets. The point was that stocks with the greatest recovery potential were those that had fallen the most during the crisis.

And in the early part of 2009, there was a radical change in the investment weather. Giant injections of market liquidity transformed the opportunity for the over-borrowed to fund a recovery. Indeed, as markets moved up from the bottom, the share prices of companies announcing fund raisings tended to rise the fastest. Effectively once an over-borrowed company had announced a rights issue, investors could be completely confident that it would survive for the financial recovery, and hence their share prices rose. So being attentive to the investment weather at this time meant I suspended my normal investment rules, and heavily selected for those with the most stretched balance sheets!

The bottom line is that active investing's true value often lies in the scope to actively manage portfolio risk. Therefore it pays handsomely to remain constantly alert to changes in investment market trends. Keep an eye on the investment horizon at all times, so you are early to notice when the investment weather changes, and adjust your preferred method of stock selection as appropriate.

3. LOOK FOR FIRMS WITH UNUSUALLY STRONG FINANCIAL POSITIONS.

If this premise is accepted, then the BIG question is what's on the investment horizon currently? Investment markets have been benign for years. And many companies that were over-geared during the financial crisis have not only survived, but gone on to deliver very attractive returns to investors. For some, the long market recovery has become so unsettling that they have become overly cautious, and sold all their holdings – missing out on a further rise in equity markets.

Where do I stand on all this currently? My scan of the investment horizon suggests that the risk of individual companies going bust will eventually rise back towards the norms more often seen in the 1970s and early 1980s. It conceivable that they might move even above the previous norms in future. When interest rates are so low, and access to debt is so easy, there is a real danger that far too many companies will be over-stretched when the next setback arrives. That could be a big problem.

Remember there is almost no opportunity for interest rates to be reduced from here. And there's little scope for UK bond yields to fall much further either, so additional QE may not reliquify the markets in future as it did last time. Those caught out at the time of the next setback may be out on their own. Don't expect central banks to bail them out as they did during 2008. And don't expect rescue rights issues to be easy to get funded either.

Therefore my view of the investment horizon suggests that quoted companies with unusually strong financial positions could be disproportionately well-placed for the future. Of course, all share prices will be vulnerable to an economic setback, even those of well-financed businesses. The value of a well-financed portfolio of stocks will suffer a market setback when it comes. But if numerous companies do go bust in future, then the strongest will find it easier to scale up their market positions at that time. For example, those with surplus capital will be well-placed to acquire businesses from the receiver at unusually low valuations. And the quoted companies with the very strongest prospects will be able to raise additional capital from their investors as well, even during the market setback. So they could have even greater upside, since they will be able to buy into a whole lot more recovery potential than most others.

So my glance around the investment horizon suggests that this is a time when there are excellent opportunities for adding extra value through actively managing portfolio risk. For now, in the latter stages of a bull market, portfolios of well-financed stocks will participate in any further ongoing market rise. And when there is an economic setback, companies with the best balance sheets may be able to take disproportionate advantage of the weakness of others, and therefore subsequently outperform the market recovery thereafter.

Craig
Yeaman

CRAIG YEAMAN *started his career in the industry in 1999 when he joined Clydesdale Bank's investment department as an analyst. From there he moved to Glasgow Investment Managers in 2001, where he was the Manager of both Shires Income PLC and Shires Smaller Companies PLC Investment Trusts. In addition to this, he was also involved in the management of segregated mandates for many of the firm's pension clients. In August 2007, following their takeover of GIM, Craig joined Aberdeen Asset Management before joining Saracen in 2008.*

Craig was appointed Manager of the TB Saracen UK Alpha Fund in January 2009 and since taking over stewardship of the fund he has delivered top quartile performance, outperforming the benchmark in six years out of eight.

"OFTEN THE BEST
INVESTMENTS
INITIALLY
FEEL THE MOST
UNCOMFORTABLE."

Good Ideas Are Finite

INVESTMENT IS, IN theory, a simple concept. The idea is to buy low and sell high – what could be easier than that? At times, however, this can prove incredibly difficult, even for the most seasoned of investors. It is important to remember that there are only two important points of every investment – namely, the buying and selling prices. Everything else is simply noise. The following rules are those I use on a daily basis.

1. CARRY OUT YOUR OWN RESEARCH, DON'T RELY ON OTHERS.

This may seem an obvious rule but many firms have teams of analysts where the fund manager will rarely get involved in the more mundane aspects of examining a potential investment. Often, more junior members of the team are relied upon to construct a model and fill in historic numbers. It is only once the template is completed that the idea will be presented to senior team members for their final decision on the stock purchase.

Like every member of the investment team at Saracen Fund Managers, I carry out my own research on a company before deciding whether it merits a holding. The job of trying to outperform the peer group is difficult enough without relying on others to carry out the most important job of fundamental research. At Saracen, the roles of fund manager and analyst are entwined as it is crucial to have a working knowledge of a business before considering an investment in it.

External research from sell-side brokers is abundant but one should use this analysis with a high degree of cynicism. These reports can be helpful in terms of background knowledge but firms and analysts often have their own agenda. For example, if an organisation is broker to a stock you can bet your bottom dollar the analyst will rate the shares a buy. Caveat emptor!

2. RUN CONCENTRATED PORTFOLIOS.

The vast majority of my time is spent evaluating stocks; either companies I own already or potential investments for inclusion in the funds. There is a finite number of good ideas at any point in time and, as an investor, you want to benefit fully from them. I invest in 30–45 stocks at any time unlike some of my peer group who will hold 100 companies or more. As I have a meaningful position in each stock held, this means if I am right about a company's prospects, my shareholders should benefit.

Conversely, if I were to invest in, say 100 companies, it is likely the 100th name on that list would be a holding of less than 0.5%. What is the point of doing lots of due diligence to then have such an insignificant position? If it were to double, it would make very little difference to performance – and likewise if it were to halve, no damage would be done. If you want to generate meaningful returns, it is important to back your judgement. It is also nigh on impossible to have an intimate knowledge of so many companies, regardless of what anyone tells you!

3. DON'T INVEST IF YOU DON'T UNDERSTAND WHAT A COMPANY DOES.

Once again, this may seem an obvious statement but there is a temptation to invest in the next big thing even if you can't quite understand the business model or how the company makes a return. The area I tend to shy away from is technology, as I am certainly not the next Bill Gates and I would not profess to have a working knowledge of many of the companies in this sector.

The rule of thumb I stick to is: if I can't explain to an investor in simple terms what a business does, I should not be buying shares in it. Keep it simple!

4. DON'T SET PRICE TARGETS.

I never set price targets on any of my investments as businesses evolve – a company may grow via acquisitions, it might increase its market share, it could sell non-core subsidiaries or find its end markets changing rapidly. Companies at different stages of both the economic cycle and their life cycle, deserve to trade on different valuations and, therefore, it is crucial to determine what this is.

One example is Howden Joinery Group plc. I invested in the business at the beginning of 2011, when the share price was around the 100p level. Fast forward five years and the shares had increased to over 500p. However, I believed the stock to have been better value in 2015 than when I first invested. This may seem a perverse assertion but by then the company had a nationwide depot network, operating margins had increased 500 basis points to over 18%, its balance sheet was in a very strong position and it had reduced its other liabilities. Had I set a price target in 2011 I can assure you it would have been substantially lower than the level it attained, leading to a missed opportunity.

5. DON'T LOOK AT SHARE PRICE GRAPHS, LOOK AT THE UNDERLYING RATING OF A STOCK.

Many investors will look at share price graphs and if they see a stock moving from bottom left to top right will disregard the proposition, thinking they have missed the chance to make money. A company's share price may be moving north for any number of reasons. For example, the fundamentals of a business might be improving, earnings have been upgraded or, indeed, there might have been a change in management.

It is much more important to look at the valuation of the business than simply the share price. Increases in share prices often follow earnings upgrades, meaning a company which has performed well in share price terms hasn't been re-rated. On this basis, the stock may still be worth investing in.

6. DON'T BE AFRAID TO SELL AT A LOSS.

It is impossible to get every investment correct and often it is best to quickly identify a mistake and sell the stock before more damage is done to both performance and your portfolio. Often investors will hold on in the misguided view that if they wait long enough, the price will recover. Sometimes that will be the case but often it is not. Investors also have to reflect about the opportunity cost of continuing to hold a stock where there is little hope, for whatever reason, of the share price improving in the future.

Often the decision to sell a stock and book a loss is the correct one, although painful at the time. The old adage about profit warnings coming in threes is not too far off the mark. An example I often give to shareholders is my own purchase of Fenner, the manufacturer and distributor of conveyor belts. I bought the shares in October 2013 at 390p per share and sold in June 2014 after a profit warning at 336p. Although the decision to recognise the loss was uncomfortable, it was the correct course of action as the price continued to fall, hitting 100p in February 2016.

7. BE GREEDY WHEN OTHERS ARE FEARFUL AND FEARFUL WHEN OTHERS ARE GREEDY.

Prices don't go up forever – it is important to realise this. Human nature dictates it is always easier to book a profit rather than accept a loss. Stocks will be sold for many reasons: a position size might have become too large in the portfolio, a more compelling investment might have been identified or simply the rating of a company has become over extended. If shares are rising, investors often believe they are missing out and are, therefore, happy to pay up for a stock. This is a great opportunity to take profits.

The opposite is most certainly true. An example I often use is somebody who is looking to buy a new car. They have done the research, chosen the model which best suits them and are ready to buy. If the car in question was being sold for £30,000 but the dealer had a one-day only sale with 10% off, everybody would buy in order to save £3,000. If a potential investor has done his homework on a stock but sees the price falling for no specific reason, most tend to hold off, thinking the market knows more than they do. More often than not it is simply the case there are more sellers than buyers at that particular time.

Often the best investments initially feel the most uncomfortable. What do I mean by that? When buying an unloved stock, one which continues to fall, it can be difficult to persuade yourself that you are right and the market is in the wrong. A case in point is my purchase of AGA Rangemaster, which I first acquired in November 2014 at 143p. I subsequently topped up my position on seven occasions as the price continued to move south, last buying at just 88p in April 2015. It is not a pleasant feeling to see investments fall in value but I was convinced the market didn't fully understand the investment case, or more probably didn't care given the small market capitalisation of the business. The company was bought by a US competitor for 185p in September 2015 and we managed to sell a chunk of our investment at over 200p when the market viewed a bidding war as likely.

8. MEET MANAGEMENT BEFORE INVESTING.

There are differing opinions about the value of meeting management. Many think it a worthless use of time, as directors tend to put the best possible spin on events. I disagree, and want to meet the people in charge of the business before entrusting them with my shareholders' money. My natural hunting ground is in the FTSE 250 and small cap arenas and, therefore, I must have complete confidence in those people in charge. These businesses, unlike their larger peers, tend not to be particularly well covered by sell-side firms, and, consequently, I find it very useful to sit down and learn more about the company. When you are meeting with the CEOs of large, multinational companies such as BP or HSBC I agree you are less likely to learn anything new – however, the same cannot be said further down the market spectrum.

The danger in building a relationship with management teams is the potential to believe everything told to you at meetings. Thus, it is essential to have a healthy degree of scepticism when questioning.

My wish list for companies

As well as following my investment rules, I also like companies to have some of the attributes listed below. It is very unlikely a company will possess all of these characteristics but the greater the number they have, the more comfortable I am holding them for the longer term.

Market leading positions

Market leaders tend to be good stocks in which to invest for a plethora of reasons. Firstly, they are most likely to have been around for many years and, more often than not, will have robust balance sheets. Management of financially robust companies will continue to invest in order to maintain their number-one position. In economic downturns, the strong get stronger whereas weaker companies suffer.

High and sustainable margins

Companies which earn robust and sustainable margins tend to be great businesses to invest in for the long term. All businesses will have years when, for whatever reason, the operating landscape is tougher. This could be FX-related, a tougher consumer environment or simply a slowing economy. In these circumstances, I would much rather be invested in a high-margin business where profits are, to a large degree, protected.

An example would be Victrex, a business which has consistently earned an operating margin of 40%. If operating margins fell to 38% it would not be too damaging but if a business was earning a margin of 4% and they fell to 2% then profitability would halve.

Long-term visibility

Nothing upsets investors and frightens markets more than an unexpected profit warning. The greater the visibility a company has, the lower the probability of disappointing. Avoiding the landmines is often as helpful as picking winners when managing money.

Unique assets

Unique assets tend to warrant a premium price and higher margin due to their scarcity value. An example would be Elementis, the specialty chemicals company which owns the only hectorite mine in the world. (If you're wondering, hectorite clay is a premium product which is primarily used in paints and cosmetics.)

Alignment of interest with directors

One of the key characteristics I look for is meaningful director ownership. These companies tend to perform better, quite probably because shareholders' interests are fully aligned with those running the company. At times, the stock market seems to be pre-occupied with the next quarterly or half-year numbers but I prefer investing in companies which have sensible long-term targets. In my experience, those businesses which have high managerial shareholdings tend to look further ahead.

There are numerous examples within my own fund of companies which have substantial director ownership: Victoria, where the chairman owns 33% of the business; Berkeley Group, where its founder has a stake worth in excess of £200m; and Dunelm, the United Kingdom's leading homewares company, where the founding family controls 51% of the business.